WASHINGTON GLADDEN

Prophet of the Social Gospel

Jacob Henry Dorn

WASHINGTON GLADDEN

Prophet of the

Social Gospel

OHIO STATE UNIVERSITY PRESS

71443

For Earl S. Pomeroy and Kenneth W. Porter

Preface

Although historians have long recognized Washington Gladden as an important figure in American religion in the period between the Civil War and World War I, none as yet has written a comprehensive account of his career. For various reasons those who have aspired to fulfil this task have been unable to complete it. Consequently, students of American history have had to rely on brief sketches written by Gladden's contemporaries and on his own *Recollections* (1909). Although *Recollections* outlines Gladden's major interests, it has serious limitations. First, it neglects several of the activities through which he implemented his religious and social ideas and is silent on the last decade of his life. Moreover, Gladden actually intended to write a personal appraisal of the major currents of his lifetime rather than an autobiography. Second, *Recollections* reflects the serene optimism of Gladden's later years; consequently, it often veils his defeats, frustrations, and contradictions. It is, however, a useful summarization of his principal interests and ideas.

In any study of Gladden's life two themes must be foremost, liberal theology and the Social Gospel. They are inseparably related, and the author treats them separately simply to elucidate the evolution of Gladden's thought. Just before accepting a call to the First Congregational Church of Columbus, Ohio, Carl S. Patton, Gladden's associate from 1911 to 1917, told Gladden that he was interested primarily in liberal religious thought and the social application of the teachings of Christ. According to Patton, Gladden looked at him, "let one eyelid droop in a manner that will be remembered by his old friends, and said, 'Well, what else IS there?' "[1] In both areas Gladden was a pioneer if not a profound or original thinker. In the years after the Civil War he was one of the first clergymen to respond to the intellectual and social currents that challenged traditional modes of Protestant thought and social action. By the end

[1] Carl S. Patton in *First Church News*, VI (February, 1936), 6–7.

of the century, when both liberal theology and the Social Gospel had in a sense triumphed in American Protestantism, he had achieved recognition as one of the earliest and most constant exponents of both movements. He was, moreover, one of their chief popularizers, and his writings were unrivaled embodiments of the liberal, socially-conscious Protestantism that distinguished his age.

Gladden's life typified the transition from traditional orthodoxy to a flexible and social faith common to many of his contemporaries. This study, originally a doctoral dissertation submitted to the Department of History of the University of Oregon, is an attempt to trace the currents that affected his thought, his own adjustments to changing conditions, and the practical manifestations of social and theological liberalism in his career. The general structure is chronological. The first three chapters briefly sketch Gladden's life from his boyhood in rural New York to his pastorate from 1875 to 1882 in Springfield, Massachusetts, where liberalism began clearly to dominate his thinking. Subsequent chapters deal topically with the period from 1882 to 1918, his pastorate in Columbus, Ohio, including appropriate discussions of the earlier origins of specific ideas and interests. Though these topical surveys are not strictly chronological, there is a general progression from his theological development, which began earliest, through his formulation of the Social Gospel in response to economic problems, to his application of the Social Gospel to social and international affairs.

For a study of Gladden's theoretical development there are abundant sources. He wrote approximately forty books and hundreds of periodical articles. Many of them, however, are repetitive. Where it seems significant, this study cites the earliest expression of an idea. In other cases, several references to a single idea are given to illustrate the consistency or constancy of Gladden's beliefs. His sermons, over fifteen hundred of which are in the Gladden Papers at the Ohio Historical Society, are most helpful in revealing his specific applications of broad ideas. Occasionally, they include autobiographical comments that are absent from his books and articles. They do not, however, substantially supplement or alter the substance of his published writings. In fact, virtually all of his publications appeared first as sermons or addresses. He often delivered the same sermon on numerous occasions over a long period of years.

The principal sources for this account of Gladden's activities are the Washington Gladden Papers, which include thousands of letters to Gladden; several collections of manuscripts that contain other letters to or from Gladden; the archives of the First Congregational Church of Columbus, which contain correspondence, church records, and mementos of Gladden's career; and contemporary newpapers and periodicals. Newspapers and periodicals that the author has used for appropriate periods of Gladden's life are the *Williams Quarterly* of Williams College, the *Independent*, the *Springfield* (Mass.) *Republican*, the *Congregationalist*, *Sunday Afternoon*, and the *Ohio State Journal*.

The author is indebted to those who have facilitated his research at various libraries, granted interviews, and supplied information or impressions that led to new sources of information and in other ways lightened his task. Those who have aided in the use of collections of manuscripts include: Josephine L. Harper, manuscripts curator of the State Historical Society of Wisconsin, for the Richard T. Ely Papers and the Henry D. Lloyd Papers; Dr. James Pollard, former university archivist of the Ohio State University, for the papers of William Oxley Thompson; (Mrs.) Edith M. Fox, curator and university archivist, Cornell University, for the Jacob G. Schurman Papers and the George Junior Republic Records (1859–1958); Dr. James H. Rodabaugh, professor of history at Kent State University, for the Samuel M. Jones Papers; and Robert W. Hill, keeper of manuscripts, the New York Public Library, for the *Century* Collection and the Edward W. Ordway Papers.

In addition, the First Congregational Church of Columbus has graciously opened its archives without reservation, and Mrs. William Starin, who has charge of the First Church's materials on Gladden, has assisted the author in their use, led him to those with clear memories of Gladden, and herself contributed vivid impressions of her pastor. Gladden's granddaughter, Mrs. Stanton C. Kelton of

Ambler, Pennsylvania, has granted permission to quote liberally from Gladden's unpublished writings and has offered her own recollections of his career. The author's greatest debt, however, is to the staff of the Ohio Historical Society, whose cooperation has been unflagging. (Mrs.) Elizabeth R. Martin, the librarian, Kenneth W. Duckett, the former curator of manuscripts, and Conrad F. Weitzel, the reference librarian, have given untiring assistance through many months of research. Henry J. Caren, former editor of *Ohio History*, has provided helpful advice on literary and technical matters and has shared rich insights into local history.

Professors Earl S. Pomeroy and Kenneth W. Porter of the University of Oregon, Professor Robert G. Torbet, former dean and professor of church history at the Central Baptist Theological Seminary in Kansas City, Kansas, and Professor Robert T. Handy, professor of church history at the Union Theological Seminary in New York City, have read the manuscript and offered invaluable suggestions.

The author is grateful to the library of the Ohio Historical Society for permission to reproduce as the Frontispiece to this biography a portrait of Washington Gladden taken by L. M. Jones, of Columbus, Ohio, in 1905, which is now a part of the library's collection.

Finally, the author is indebted to his wife, Carole Johnson Dorn, for patience and encouragement and for assistance in typing and proofreading the manuscript at various stages of preparation.

For any errors of fact or judgment, however, the author alone is responsible.

J. H. D.

Contents

WASHINGTON GLADDEN

Prophet of the Social Gospel

One

Heritage and Training

The life of Washington Gladden spanned years when the physical environment and way of life of the American people changed more profoundly than in any other time but our own. Born in the Jacksonian "age of the common man," he witnessed the alienation of a large segment of society by the dislocations of the last half of the nineteenth century. In his youth the door of opportunity appeared to be open to every man; but long before his death, it seemed to be all but shut to the average person. In early manhood he experienced both the thrilling ardor of the antislavery movement and the crushing burden of the Civil War. He observed the settlement of vast regions of the West and American entry into the arena of world politics. The problems posed by the rise of the city and by mass immigration assumed their modern dimensions. The swift currents of modern science and philosophy undermined the structure of thought and belief that prevailed in his youth. He grew up in the day of the stagecoach and lived to see the advent of the airplane.

Gladden came of old but undistinguished New England stock. His paternal ancestors descended from John Gladding, who came to Plymouth in 1640; his great-grandfather, Azariah Gladding, served as a bodyguard to Washington in the American Revolution.[1] Gladden

---

[1] William H. Gladden to Washington Gladden, November 15, 1905, Washington Gladden Papers (Ohio Historical Society, Columbus, Ohio). Late in

was named Solomon Washington because of this family tradition, and he used Washington rather than his Christian name. His grandfather, Thomas, changed the surname from Gladding to Gladden. Both of Gladden's grandfathers were shoemakers who found it necessary, because of large families, to supplement their incomes by agricultural labor. Thomas Gladden helped in neighbors' fields around Southampton, Massachusetts, while Grandfather Daniels had a little farm of his own near Owego, in south-central New York.[2]

The Daniels family continued to obtain a meager subsistence by farming the stony soil around Owego or by entering trades or small businesses. Thomas Gladden, however, surmounted the obstacles of a large family and slender resources to send one son, Solomon (1808–41), to an academy in Southampton. Solomon's frail health dictated an academic vocation rather than physical labor. He taught in country schools in western Massachusetts before migrating in about 1830 to Owego. During his one year in Owego he took more than an academic interest in one pupil, for shortly after his departure he returned to marry Amanda Daniels (1813–70). In 1833 Solomon and Amanda Gladden settled in Pottsgrove, a hamlet in northern Pennsylvania, just between the two branches of the Susquehanna. That river also runs through Owego, and travel between the two villages was probably by river craft. Their first son, Solomon Washington Gladden, was born in Pottsgrove on February 11, 1836.[3]

When in 1840 the elder Gladden became headmaster of a village

life, Gladden received from an uncle a button that was ostensibly from one of Washington's military coats. Thomas Gladden to Gladden, January 12, 1903, Gladden Papers. Hereafter, in citations from the Gladden Papers, Gladden is identified by his last name only; relatives bearing the same surname are distinguished by first names.

[2] Much of the information on Gladden's youth is drawn from his *Recollections* (Boston: Houghton Mifflin Co., 1909), chaps. i–v. The later chapters in this admirable volume, primarily observations on public events, contain almost nothing on his private life.

[3] *Ibid.*, pp. 3–4. Birth and death dates of Gladden's parents and brother are from the Gladden family Bible, in the possession of Mrs. Charles C. Shoemaker, Gladden's great-granddaughter. Mrs. Charles C. Shoemaker to author, June 15, 1966.

school in Lewisburg, the family moved to this more thriving center on the opposite shore of the Susquehanna. During his brief career in Lewisburg the new headmaster made a strong impression, and pupils remembered his name many decades later.[4] His premature death in 1841 produced an emotional crisis in his son's life and created chaos in the family that lasted for years. Gladden's memories of his father stemmed from the latter's well-intentioned but pedagogically unsound efforts to develop the precocious child's mind by drilling him in spelling and having him memorize etymological definitions, and from episodes that indicate a genial comradeship. At the age of two and one-half years the youngster was supposedly able to read his verse in the Bible at family prayers.[5]

Amanda Gladden tried valiantly to continue her husband's duties; but late in 1842, she returned with Washington and his younger brother George (1839–65) to her home in Owego. She arranged for Washington to spend a year with his paternal grandparents in their two- or three-room cottage in Southampton. He returned in 1844 to live with his mother's brother, Ebenezer Daniels, on his forty-acre farm about three miles from Owego on Little Nanticoke Creek. Amanda Gladden had remarried, and, perhaps because the later alcoholism and cruelty of her new husband, Asa C. Williams, were already becoming apparent, she thought it best that Washington be in her brother's care. It is not known what arrangements were made for George Gladden.[6]

Owego, founded in the 1780's on the site of an Indian village, had become by the 1840's the bustling seat of Tioga County and the most important settlement on the Susquehanna north of Wilkes-Barre. It was essentially an agricultural center, but it had tanneries, sawmills, a foundry, and, after 1852, a shoe factory. Before the surrounding

---

[4] A. D. Hann to Gladden, January 12, 1910, Gladden Papers.

[5] In 1900 Gladden testified to his deep affection for his father by presenting a memorial window to the First Presbyterian Church of Lewisburg. H. M. McClure to Gladden, February 5, 1900, January 18, 1901, Gladden Papers.

[6] Gladden, *Recollections,* pp. 17–18. That Williams eventually proved irresponsible is substantiated by letters from George Gladden to Washington Gladden.

forests were depleted several decades later, Owego's location on the river made lumbering its most important industry after farming. Rafting was the most common way of sending lumber to markets in Pennsylvania. In addition to farming, Ebenezer Daniels hauled large logs from his woods to the mills along the river and marketed smaller pieces in the village.[7]

Gladden was to work for his uncle until he was twenty-one, at which time he was promised a good suit of clothes and either one hundred dollars or a good horse. The labor expected of him on the rugged farm was strenuous but exhilarating. Only "the most tireless and constant labor, early and late," Gladden recalled, enabled Ebenezer Daniels and his children "to win from the intractable soil the means of livelihood. . . ." Many years later, Gladden spoke of his satisfaction in contemplating the work of his hands:

> We used to have hard work on the farm in my boyhood, following the plow, swinging the axe or the scythe or the grain cradel,—but that work, out of doors, under God's blue sky, with winds in the branches and the birds overhead, with the constant exercise of skill and judgment, and the constant change of scene,—was healthy and happy work compared with most of the machine-tending of these days.[8]

The farm furnished Gladden with a liberal education in folk humor and homespun philosophy; he sometimes repeated stories his uncle first told him in sermons decades later.[9]

During his eight years on the farm Gladden experienced something of an intellectual awakening. To be sure, his formal education in the district school where his father had once taught Amanda and Ebenezer Daniels was primitive enough, but the individual instruction necessitated by lack of uniform textbooks had advantages. The

[7] George Truman, "River Transportation," and William S. Truman, "The Business Growth of Owego," in Leroy W. Kingman, ed., *Owego Sketches by Owego Authors* (Owego, N. Y.: *Gazette* Press, 1904), pp. 18–21, 66–73; Gladden, *Recollections*, p. 26.

[8] Gladden, *Recollections*, p. 26; Gladden, Sermon, September 21, 1890, Gladden Papers.

[9] Gladden, Sermon, May 8, 1910, Gladden Papers.

arrival in the late 1840's of a new teacher, Horace L. Andrews, significantly improved the school, but farm work continued to limit
Gladden's attendance to the winter term of four months each year.
Nevertheless, Andrews transformed Gladden's listlessness into academic zeal. In 1852, Gladden's final year in the school, Andrews
asked him to plead the affirmative in a debate on repeal of the
Fugitive Slave Act of 1850; the youth devoured all the speeches of
Seward, Hale, Wade, Giddings, and Webster that he could find,
and, after several weeks of rising at four o'clock each morning to
study, he won the debate.[10]

Gladden's reading on the Daniels farm was probably as variated
as this limited formal education. A district school library furnished
volumes of history and travel, while two Sunday-school libraries
provided religious literature. Ebenezer Daniels evidently subscribed
to the *New York Observer* and the *New York Weekly Tribune,* and
Gladden remembered Horace Greeley's editorials and the writings
of George William Curtis in the *Weekly Tribune.* Nightly readings
in the farmhouse lasted for two hours, and here Gladden acquired
skill in oral reading. "Sensational fiction" was either banned or simply unavailable, and Gladden was grateful for the "kind providence"
that guarded him from its "mental debaucheries" and led him "into
the delights of more sober literature." Owego prided itself on the
presence from 1837 to 1842 of Nathaniel P. Willis, a poet and journalist then at the height of his fame, and Gladden may have shared
the general interest in his writings.[11]

In an age outstanding for religious fervor, and particularly for a
revivalism whose chief priest was Charles G. Finney, and in an area
later described as the "burned-over district," because of its overcul-
tivation by the evangelical sects, Gladden's religious saturation was
not unusual. His own testimony was that "the one deepest interest

[10] Gladden, *Recollections,* pp. 27–32.

[11] Gladden, "George William Curtis," Sermon, September 11, 1892, Gladden
Papers; Gladden, *Recollections,* pp. 24–25; "N. P. Willis at Glenmary," in
Owego Sketches, pp. 86–87.

of my life through all that period was religion."[12]

Both the Gladden and Daniels families were deeply religious. Solomon Gladden "wore the halo of sainthood" for his son. He had been a Congregationalist in New England, and his wife was a Baptist; but in Pottsgrove the choice was between a Presbyterian and a Methodist church. He found the Calvinist theology of Pennsylvania Presbyterianism less bearable than Methodist emotionalism and chose the latter. He served as class leader and Sunday-school superintendent and preached occasionally. Washington remembered the struggle his father had in the face of indecorous physical demonstrations. On one occasion the younger Gladden was sure that he saw tears streaming down his father's face when, during a service that he was leading, the congregation became particularly violent. Some of those Methodist meetings were "tremendous ones—with men and women shouting, prostrating themselves on the floor, falling in dead faints. . . ."[13] Solomon Gladden's devotion to religion was constant, despite his distaste for the particular forms in which he felt obliged to exercise it.

Religion was no less vital in the household of Ebenezer Daniels, who saw to it that no family in Owego's Presbyterian church had a better record of attendance than his. Family devotional exercises supplemented two Sunday preaching services and Sunday school. For several summers Gladden arose at five o'clock on Sunday mornings to complete his chores in time to walk three miles to a Baptist Sunday school whose singing he preferred to the Presbyterian. The study of the Bible constituted the major part of church life and family religion. Gladden heard it read from cover to cover at breakfast

[12] Gladden, *Recollections*, p. 32; Whitney R. Cross, *The Burned-Over District: The Social and Intellectual History of Enthusiastic Religion in Western New York, 1825–1850* (Ithaca, N. Y.: Cornell University Press, 1950). Finney's lectures on revivals became both chief defense of the movement and archetypal pattern for other revivalists. Bernard A. Weisberger's *They Gathered at the River: The Story of the Great Revivalists and Their Impact upon Religion in America* (Boston: Little, Brown & Co., 1958), chaps. iv–v, provides a lively but somewhat overdrawn discussion of Finney and his followers.

[13] Gladden, *Recollections*, p. 10; Gladden, "The Church and the Social Crisis," Sermon, n.d., Gladden Papers; Gladden, Sermon, [1915,] Gladden Papers.

and dinner about four times before his seventeenth birthday and memorized in Sunday school the four Gospels, long sections of the Epistles, many Psalms and historical parts of the Old Testament, and the early chapters of Genesis. Gladden's fondness for the scriptures remained strong, even after he had discarded the doctrine of biblical infallibility preached in his youth. The Westminster Shorter Catechism, which Gladden memorized in full, and sermons in the village church (that were "often a weariness of the flesh") completed his religious instruction.[14]

The religious atmosphere of his boyhood, though it contributed to his belief in ideals commanding human allegiance and to his sense of fidelity to duty, confused Gladden more than it helped him. His religious problems became "more and more tangled and troublesome." For one thing, sectarian rivalry was intense; "there were other churches in the village," he later wrote, "but they had no more dealings with one another than the Jews had with the Samaritans."[15]

Biblical literalism added further confusion. It was hard for one nurtured in the humanitarianism of the pre–Civil War years to believe that God had specifically enjoined the slaughter of whole tribes, as the Old Testament seemed to teach. William Miller, a New England farmer of Baptist origins who declared that the world would end in 1843 in a cataclysmic holocaust, carried biblical literalism into eschatological predictions that unsettled many in the evangelical churches. His followers were especially strong in western New York. In the Baptist church Gladden saw a blackboard demonstration of Miller's calculations, based on the prophecies of Daniel. He never forgot the "creepy sensation" that came over him and the fear that haunted him, especially when a comet appeared shortly thereafter and his "childish frame quaked with terror!" His mind was put temporarily at ease when 1844 arrived and life went on; a more

---

[14] *Ohio State Journal*, March 27, 1896; Washington Gladden, "Reminiscences of Owego," in *Owego Sketches*, p. 4; Gladden, *Recollections*, pp. 32–33, 36–37; Gladden, "The Worth of the Bible," Sermon, n.d., Gladden Papers.

[15] Gladden, "The Old Time Religion," Sermon, November 27, 1911, Gladden Papers; Gladden, *Recollections*, p. 34.

permanent reprieve resulted from the conclusion of several rural theologians that the dreaded event would probably not occur till 1860.[16]

In "The Story of Humbug," a poem written in 1852 in mockery of
some of New York's new religious groups, Gladden recalled in one
stanza the Millerite excitement:

> When Miller predicted the world was to end
> Infallibly certain one day
> Some fanatics were found who swallowed all down
> And patiently waited their stay.

Whether he had in mind the Millerites or another sect in his last two
stanzas is hard to determine:

> But not yet discouraged o'er mountains & hills
> They spread it from city to town
> Till our own plain Owego looks up in amaze
> For here they can do it up Brown.

> But soon Genius triumphed & rappings expired
> And no ground was left where to croak
> Their meridian sun soon extinguished its fire
> And Humbug was ended in smoke.[17]

A more deep-rooted conflict for Gladden stemmed from the revival
preaching that regularly confronted him. The conflict grew out of
two aspects of that preaching: the emphasis placed on the judgment
of God and the requirements prescribed for religious conversion. He
associated the former primarily with Jacob Knapp, a popular Baptist
evangelist whose forthrightness made him many enemies.[18] According to Gladden, Knapp's forte was a description of "the burning pit,

[16] William Warren Sweet, *The Story of Religion in America* (2d ed.; New
York: Harper & Bros., Publishers, 1950), pp. 277–79; Gladden, Sermon, December, 1889, Gladden Papers; Gladden, *Recollections*, p. 60.

[17] Washington Gladden, "The Story of Humbug," February 2, 1852, Washington Gladden Papers and Church Records, First Congregational Church
archives, Columbus, Ohio.

[18] Weisberger, *They Gathered at the River*, p. 136.

with the sinners trying to crawl up its sides out of the flames, while the devils, with pitchforks, stood by to fling them back again."[19] An incipient sense that the God portrayed in the preaching he heard was one he could respect but not love did not, however, prevent his complete acceptance of the orthodoxy of his youth. On one occasion he marked every passage in the New Testament that seemed to contradict Universalism, and he dreaded William Ellery Channing as an "archapostate."[20]

Gladden also stumbled over current notions of the process of conversion. Led to believe that becoming a Christian involved an emotional crisis accompanied by a consciousness of inner transformation, he tried repeatedly to generate the appropriate effects. Expecting "that a light would break in, or a burden roll off, or that some other emotional or ecstatic experience would supervene," he felt that, when nothing of the kind happened, his efforts had been fruitless.[21] So strong was his desire to be a Christian that he was prepared to sacrifice all his boyish sports to this end.

Ebenezer Daniels became convinced as the boy grew older that he should have opportunities not afforded by farm life. In 1852 he apprenticed him to Hiram Beebe, who from 1843 to 1871 edited the Owego *Gazette*, the local Democratic paper. Several other boys also worked at the *Gazette* office, including George Gladden. Washington was to serve for four years and live in a small room in the attic of Beebe's home. His duties were at first entirely manual—feeding the fires, sweeping, cleaning type, running errands, and working at the case—but Beebe discovered some literary promise in him and allowed him to write local news items.[22]

---

[19] Gladden, *Recollections*, p. 59. Gladden's portrayal of his youth as a time of spiritual terror requires two qualifying considerations: one, that Gladden was a sensitive child and had heightened religious feelings; the other, that he wrote of his youth in a period when, as a defender of liberal theology, he might exaggerate the defects of earlier religion.

[20] Gladden, "William Ellery Channing," Sermon, April, 1880, Gladden Papers.

[21] Gladden, *Recollections*, p. 35.

[22] Gladden, *Recollections*, pp. 41, 43; H. G. Ingersoll to Gladden, February 25, 1907, Gladden Papers.

After Gladden left the Daniels family to live in Owego, he experienced a mild reaction against their religious rigor and frequently absented himself from the Presbyterian church. Reading in the *Gazette*'s office was his usual activity on such occasions, since he still regarded the Sabbath as a day to abstain from ordinary pleasures.

Gladden attributed his spiritual deliverance in 1853 to Jedediah Burchard, an evangelist who conducted special services in the Congregational church:

> [He] . . . made me see that it was perfectly safe to trust the Heavenly Father's love for me and walk straight on in the ways of service, waiting for no raptures, but doing his will as best I knew it, and confiding in his friendship.[23]

Gladden promptly associated himself with the Congregational church. Although a Congregational church, formed in 1810, had been the first religious organization in Owego, it, like many other Congregational churches of that day, had been swallowed by Presbyterianism. Under the Plan of Union in 1801 Congregationalists and Presbyterians had agreed, as a means of meeting the religious needs of the burgeoning frontier, to sanction mixed congregations, which could call a minister from, and affiliate with, either denomination. The Presbyterians proved more aggressive and self-conscious, and churches that began with congregational polity often abandoned it for the greater solidarity of Presbyterianism. After the 1830's, however, Congregationalists began to assert themselves by organizing new churches of their own. This was the pattern in Owego. In 1850 forty-six members withdrew from the Presbyterian church and formed a Congregational society. Their antislavery sentiment had much to do with their secession. According to Gladden, Samuel C. Wilcox, their first pastor, had been forced to leave the Presbyterian church for daring to pray for Negro slaves. It was this

[23] *Ibid.*, p. 38. Weisberger, *They Gathered at the River*, pp. 135–36, ascribes to Burchard a description of hell almost identical to that which Gladden attributed to Jacob Knapp, but Gladden remembered Burchard in quite another light. Such illustrations were probably common to many evangelists of the day; Gladden's memory, however, may have been faulty.

reform-minded congregation that Gladden joined.[24]

Gladden's emancipation from the obstacles to his faith occurred in a context of Christian social activism. This early religious experience, closely related to the antislavery movement and other contemporary reforms, was his first step toward the social Christianity of the post–Civil War era. He asserted later,

> It was not an individualistic pietism that appealed to me; it was a religion that laid hold upon life with both hands, and proposed, first and foremost, to realize the Kingdom of God in this world.[25]

After Gladden left the farm in 1852 to take up his apprenticeship on the *Gazette*, events decisive of his future occurred in rapid succession. His religious awakening was only the most important of these. Thinking seriously about the ministry, quite without any suggestion from his elders,[26] he began early in 1855 to prepare for college. He taught a term in a country school, then entered the Owego Academy with his mind clearly set on the ministry. The academy, chartered in 1827, was a semipublic institution with over three hundred pupils and a faculty of nine or ten.[27] Strenuous academic activity marked the year and a half between his entrance into the Owego Academy and his matriculation at Williams College, an event made possible largely through the financial assistance of the father of Glad-

[24] Williston Walker, *A History of the Congregational Churches in the United States* (New York: Christian Literature Co., 1894), p. 371; Sweet, *The Story of Religion in America*, pp. 210–12; Lois Kimball Mathews, *The Expansion of New England: The Spread of New England Settlement and Institutions to the Mississippi River, 1620–1865* (Boston: Houghton Mifflin Co., 1909), p. 163; Gladden, *Recollections*, p. 63. Gladden is listed as a member in a manual in 1857 but almost certainly joined the church in 1853 or 1854. *Confession of Faith, Form of Covenant, and Catalogue of Members, of the Independent Congregational Church of Owego* (Owego, N. Y.: Printed at the Owego *Times* Office, 1857), pp. 10–11.

[25] Gladden, *Recollections*, p. 63.

[26] Gladden, "Choice of Calling and Chances of Success," Sermon, October 24, 1898, Gladden Papers.

[27] John T. Greenleaf, "Education in Owego," in *Owego Sketches*, pp. 46–47; Allan Nevins, *Study in Power: John D. Rockefeller, Industrialist and Philanthropist* (2 vols.; New York: Charles Scribner's Sons, 1953), I, 5.

den's good friend, Lewis Matson, and a member of the Congregational church. Gladden estimated that he studied fourteen or fifteen hours a day, six days a week, during that year and a half.[28]

Diversions from such a regimen were necessary, however, and Gladden seems to have led an active social life in his spare time. Politics had fascinated him even before he left the farm. As early as 1844, when he was returning to Owego from Southampton, political events impressed him. At Cortland, New York, he observed boys his own age dancing around a hickory pole atop which flew a Polk banner. Listening to men on canalboats and in stagecoaches, he heard that the South wanted Texas for the expansion of slavery. And since politics in the Daniels household were decidedly Whig, Polk's election led Gladden to expect some dreadful turn of events.[29]

Before the issue of slavery became the all-consuming passion in politics, a variety of reform causes, among them prohibition, vied for supremacy in the political arena. Maine enacted the first statewide prohibitory liquor law in 1851; and in the summer of 1852 Gladden and his uncle heard Neal Dow, the champion of the movement in Maine, in Owego's public square. Though Gladden later parted company with the prohibitionists, Dow's initial impression on him was favorable. New York had no united prohibition party, but local prohibition forces were learning the value of co-operation. Gladden's own Tioga County was one of the most pronounced temperance counties in the state. In 1852 he joined the Order of Good Templars, a temperance society organized in New York the previous year, and became secretary of the local lodge. It fell his lot to correspond with other lodges in New York in a general program that resulted in significant victories for candidates supported by the Templars in the elections of 1854. Myron H. Clark was swept into the governorship in a campaign largely devoted to the question of prohibition; and on April 3, 1855, the state legislature enacted a

[28] Gladden, Recollections, pp. 57, 64; N. Matson to Gladden, November 21, 1856, March 6, April 3, 23, 1857, Gladden Papers.

[29] Gladden, Recollections, pp. 21–22; Gladden, Sermon, June 30, 1912, Gladden Papers.

prohibitory law, which, until declared unconstitutional by the state Court of Appeals, remained on the statute books for about a year.[30]

The swelling antislavery movement claimed Gladden's allegiance; but when an irate citizenry met to protest the vote of their representative, John J. Taylor, for the Kansas-Nebraska act, Gladden pointed out the humorous aspects of their proceedings in an "irreverent" report for the *Gazette*. He became a Republican even before he could vote and wrote a song for Frémont's campaign in New York, which a Republican glee club led by Thomas C. Platt popularized.[31]

Other diversions from Gladden's preparation for college were less weighty. He and several close friends participated in the Calliopean Society, evidently a literary club.[32] He corresponded frequently with Lewis Matson, who had gone to Yale. Religion and Gladden's plans for college were their major topics. Preferring Williams College to Yale, Matson urged Gladden to consider going there.[33] They also discussed their various romances. Matson accused Gladden of being the "most 'romantic' man" he knew and attributed it to his reading in Shakespeare and Milton. Rumor reached Matson that three girls shared Gladden's "undivided attention" at the same time. Gladden concentrated on girls at the Owego Academy, like Ophelia Branch and Nettie L. Brister, and his "short but sweet" romances were "coming on every few weeks."[34] A more important name, but one that does not appear in these letters, is that of Jennie O. Cohoon, the daughter of a merchant who lived in Owego from 1852 to 1856. Jennie and Gladden were both students at the academy in 1855–56, and it is likely that Gladden met his future wife either there or at the

---

[30] John A. Krout, *The Origins of Prohibition* (New York: Alfred A. Knopf, 1925), p. 130; Gladden, *Recollections*, pp. 50–51; D. Leigh Colvin, *Prohibition in the United States: A History of the Prohibition Party and of the Prohibition Movement* (New York: George H. Doran Co., 1926), pp. 34, 43–45.

[31] Gladden, *Recollections*, pp. 50, 66; C. N. Shipman to Gladden, September 30, 1906, Gladden Papers. Platt was later senator from New York.

[32] Shipman to Gladden, September 30, 1906, Gladden Papers.

[33] Lewis Matson to Gladden, February 8, June 18, 1855, March, 1856, Gladden Papers.

[34] *Ibid.*, June 2, 17–18, 1855.

Congregational church, where the Cohoons occupied a conspicuous front pew.[35]

At first Gladden had thought of attending Hamilton College, a Presbyterian school at Clinton, New York; but Lewis Matson's advice and the strong urging of the academy's principal, himself a graduate of Williams, decided him in favor of the school in Massachusetts. In September, 1856, with high hopes that his preparation would be adequate, Gladden boarded the Erie train for New York City, where he made connections for North Adams, Massachusetts. From the beginning the quiet grandeur of the Berkshire hills enamored him. Entering Williamstown atop the stage on a clear evening following heavy autumnal rains, he marveled at the shadows and outlines formed by the mountains 'against a setting sun: " . . . To a boy who had seen few mountains that hour was a revelation."[36]

Williams College, founded in 1791, was the cultural and religious center of Williamstown and of a large part of northwestern Massachusetts. The community was prosperous, and its social fabric, "settled, respectable, conventional," was typical of much of New England. Though students came from many states and several foreign countries, most were from northwestern Massachusetts, eastern New York, and Vermont. They frequently became clergymen or missionaries. In fact, the American foreign missionary movement was supposedly born in the first decade of the nineteenth century at a Williams prayer meeting. The college's reputation as a bastion of Congregationalism was unimpeachable.[37]

[35] *Ohio State Journal*, May 9, 1909; S. T. Kidder to Gladden, May 27, 1909, Gladden Papers.

[36] Gladden, *Recollections*, pp. 67–68; Washington Gladden, quoted in Leverett W. Spring, *A History of Williams College* (Boston: Houghton Mifflin Co., 1917), p. 317.

[37] Theodore Clarke Smith, *The Life and Letters of James Abram Garfield* (2 vols.; New Haven: Yale University Press, 1925), I, 69; *Catalogue of the Officers and Students of Williams College for the Academic Year, 1853–1854* (Williamstown, Mass.: Published by the Students, 1853), p. 16; C. Frederick Rudolph, Jr., "Washington Gladden: Essays on Modern Man" (unpublished B.A. honors thesis, Williams College, 1942), p. 8; Walker, *A History of the Congregational Churches*, p. 322.

Gladden's year and a half of preparation in Owego enabled him to pass entrance examinations on the major freshman courses in Greek and Roman literature and to matriculate, the day after his arrival, as a sophomore. The curriculum, inflexible except for a choice between French and German in the junior year, prescribed further study in ancient history and literature, rhetoric, logic, and science for the sophomore year, natural philosophy, political economy, chemistry, astronomy, and botany for the junior year, and advanced studies in philosophy, rhetoric, and theology for the senior year. Since the size of the faculty—nine members—did not permit the division of the four classes for instruction, each class met three times daily in its own recitation room. Teaching at Williams in 1856 stressed memorization and recitation. Infrequent lectures came generally in the last two years, and the heavy weekly assignments consisted of disputations, compositions, and declamations. Saturday morning discussions in the chapel on the Westminster Shorter Catechism, which Gladden considered "a good equivalent for a Seminary course in systematic theology," were an important element in his education, since his subsequent theological training was minimal.[38]

With a curriculum top-heavy in classical studies, science, and religious philosophy, there was little discussion of political, economic, or social questions in the classroom, except perhaps for the issue of free trade. According to the biographer of James A. Garfield, who graduated just before Gladden's matriculation, "not a breath" of the great problems disturbing America in the 1850's "disturbed the secluded calm of Williams teaching. All was abstract, 'elegant,' classical, philosophical."[39]

Mark Hopkins, the heroic figure who led the faculty of nine full professors and dominated the scene at Williams, was the only teacher of philosophy and theology. Hopkins won respect as a great teacher and thinker. Gladden appraised him as "one of the four or five great teachers that America has produced"; and at a Williams alumni ban-

[38] *Catalogue of Officers and Students*, pp. 20–21; Gladden, *Recollections*, pp. 68–70, 73.

[39] Gladden, *Recollections*, p. 74; Smith, *Life and Letters of Garfield*, I, 79.

quet in 1871, Garfield uttered the famous remark, "The ideal
college is Mark Hopkins on one end of a log and a student on the
other." Even S. G. W. Benjamin, a friend of Gladden's and the rebel-
lious son of foreign missionaries, though critical of sermons at Williams, admitted that when Hopkins preached few students desired
to stay away.[40] But Hopkins' conservatism was not likely to unsettle
any of the orthodox foundations.

The one man who might have unsettled these foundations, and
whom Gladden would probably have placed at the other end of the
log, John Bascom, was confined to the chair of rhetoric, a subject he
did not like. Bascom did, however, include in his course as much
literature, aesthetics, and philosophy as he could without giving
offense to Hopkins.[41] Gladden's lifelong friendship with Bascom began inauspiciously when he subjected a theme, which he thought a
commendable performance, to Bascom's searching criticism. Incensed at first by Bascom's merciless treatment of his work, Gladden gradually recognized its justice, and the two men came as close
to being friends as the academic structure would allow. To what
extent Bascom shared his progressive views with his receptive student is uncertain. Evidently, many Williams students were less than
enthusiastic about Bascom, partly because his "rugged and down-
right habit of speech" did not match the polished rhetoric of his
predecessor, and partly because his criticism of their themes humili-
ated them. Bascom preached occasionally in the Congregational
church, until some of his auditors "sniffed heresy in his utterances"
and barred him from that pulpit during Gladden's last two years at

[40] Gladden, *Recollections*, p. 71; Frederick Rudolph, *Mark Hopkins and the
Log: Williams College, 1836–1872* (New Haven: Yale University Press, 1956),
p. vii; S. G. W. Benjamin, *The Life and Adventures of a Free Lance* (Burlington, Vt.: Free Press Co., 1914), p. 149.

[41] Bascom left Williams in 1874 to assume the presidency of the University
of Wisconsin, where he exerted enormous influence on education and political
life. Forced to resign because of opposition from the Wisconsin Board of Regents, he returned to Williams in 1887 to lecture on sociology and, later, political
science. *Dictionary of Wisconsin Biography* (Madison: State Historical Society
of Wisconsin, 1960), p. 73; John Bascom, *Things Learned by Living* (New
York: G. P. Putnam's Sons, 1913), pp. 58, 60.

Williams. Gladden had attended Bascom's sermons, and he regretted their discontinuance. He evaluated Bascom's greatest influence on Williams students as the "bracing of their moral purposes" rather than as a distinctly intellectual influence.[42]

Discipline at Williams in the 1850's was rigorous, and religion was cultivated intensively. In addition to compulsory chapel services twice daily, there were prayer meetings and revivals in the Congregational church, class prayer meetings, spontaneous prayer meetings on Sundays, and voluntary noon prayer meetings four days each week, the latter attended by over half of the students. At one noon meeting Gladden heard a sermon from the text "And the Spirit and the Bride say, Come," and resolved to preach his first sermon on the same text, a resolution he later kept.[43] The administration mailed records of attendance at compulsory services to parents at the end of each term. Punitive action against recalcitrant offenders of regulations was not infrequent.[44] Some students resented the stringent code, the absence of freedom in religious matters, and the "sombre, tremendous, denunciatory character of much of the preaching," but others found satisfaction in the periodic revivals stirred up by Albert Hopkins, the brother of President Hopkins. One major revival, part of a nationwide religious awakening in 1857–58, occurred during Gladden's years in college, but it is not known how it affected him.[45]

Gladden participated in a wide range of the extracurricular activities that graced Williams life. Every student belonged to one of two rival literary societies, the Philologian and the Philotechnian; Gladden chose the Philologian. Each society had a library of three or four thousand volumes and held weekly meetings that featured orations,

[42] Gladden, *Recollections*, p. 74; Gladden, "John Bascom," Sermon, May 11, 1913, Gladden Papers; Gladden, Eulogy of John Bascom at Williams College, [1911,] Gladden Papers.

[43] Rudolph, "Washington Gladden," p. 8; Smith, *Life and Letters of Garfield*, I, 70; Gladden, Sermon, September 13, 1896, Gladden Papers.

[44] *Catalogue of Officers and Students*, p. 23; Rudolph, "Washington Gladden," p. 14.

[45] Benjamin, *Life and Adventures*, pp. 148–49; Rudolph, *Mark Hopkins and the Log*, p. 124; Sweet, *The Story of Religion in America*, pp. 310–11.

poetry, debates, essays, and reports of previous meetings. They were united in the Adelphic Union and through it sponsored three or four debates each year and brought lyceum speakers to give orations at commencement exercises. At these annual exercises Gladden and his fellow students heard such speakers as Edwin P. Whipple, a literary critic, and Wendell Phillips, the abolitionist and reformer.[46]

The Adelphic Union's debates centered on current political and social questions that were neglected in the classroom: in 1858, abrogation of the Clayton-Bulwer Treaty, and in 1859, the justification of large expenditures by the wealthy. In a debate in October, 1857, Gladden led the Philologian team in a negative assault on the proposition, "In the present state of the world, our Army and Navy ought to be abolished"; and in March, 1859, his society elected him secretary. He appeared in June, 1859, as poet for the Philologian in the annual Adelphic Union Exhibition.[47]

Participation in other exhibitions at Williams supplemented Gladden's oratorical experience in the Philologian society. In the Junior Exhibition of 1858 he gave an original poem, "Onward," and he was one of fifteen students to give an honorary oration at the commencement of 1859.[48]

His experience in journalism, begun on a rudimentary level during his years with the Owego *Gazette*, expanded through the *Williams Quarterly*, a forum for undergraduate essayists and poets. The *Quarterly* received the acclaim of the *Springfield Republican:* "Williams College maintains a marked supremacy among the colleges, for good writers; and its students' magazine we believe to be the best issued from any college." Each year five seniors edited the *Quarterly*, and in 1858–59 Gladden was one of the five.[49] The contributions to the

---

[46] Gladden, *Recollections*, p. 75; Rudolph, "Washington Gladden," pp. 16–17.

[47] *Williams Quarterly*, V (1857–58), 191; VI (1858–59), 284, 377.

[48] *Ibid.*, V (1857–58), 286, VI (1858–59), 380; "Program of the Junior Exhibition, Williams College, June 1, 1858," First Church archives.

[49] *Williams Quarterly*, VI (1858–59), 382. Contemporaries of Gladden who also served as editors of the *Quarterly* included Horace E. Scudder and Henry M. Alden, subsequently editors of the *Atlantic Monthly* and *Harper's Monthly*, respectively. Gladden, *Recollections*, pp. 77–79.

Quarterly that can be reasonably attributed to Gladden all appeared in his senior year, his year as editor.

Most of his writings were humorous. In "Our Society" he described a group of philosophers who represented various philosophical approaches as the Plunger, the Clinger, the Clincher, and the Stunner.[50] "My Vacation Experience" told of an embarrassing visit to a friend's home—an experience that may not have been completely fictional.[51] "My Friend's Composition" traced five stages in the student's literary career: the poetic—"very moist, but harmless . . . and if it is completed before the voice changes, so much the better . . ."; the political "when the discovery is first made that Our Glorious Union is in danger . . . from Great Social Evils, which prey like a canker upon the Vitals of our Political System, or from Sectional Animosities and Fanatical Hatreds . . ."; the amatory—"the point nearer Paradise than any other in this long life-march"; the cynical—when he will look at all things "with only one eye . . . an evil one . . ."; and the metaphysical, which "will set in about the beginning of his Senior Year."[52] In the editorial column he mocked the opposition of certain residents of Williamstown to the railroad that came to the village in 1858 and scoffed at long-drawn operations on a new chapel.[53]

He also wrote pungent, serious pieces. A long article, "College Life in America," contained a vigorous defense of student life against the criticisms of "a dozen vinegar-faced Mistresses Grundy, who live in this world for astringent purposes, and die to bequeath their acidity to their daughters." To those who imagined college life to be nothing but frivolity, he answered that it meant "the marshaling of the forces for the conflict of life," and that its fraternal aspects were entirely natural. The positive contributions of college life were the development of the critical faculties, the replacement of an aristoc-

---

[50] *Williams Quarterly*, VI (1858–59), 157–61.

[51] *Ibid.*, VI (1858–59), 362–69.

[52] *Ibid.*, VI (1858–59), 227–29.

[53] *Ibid.*, VI (1858–59), 285–86, 185–86, 281. Since the editorial columns were unsigned, it is only probable that Gladden was responsible for these particular comments.

racy of wealth and birth by one of "talent and social worth," and
the generation of bold enthusiasm.[54]

Two poetic contributions testify to Gladden's continued cultivation
of the muse. "Summer and Autumn," a short, three-stanza poem,
was an idyl on nature.[55] A much longer poem, "Onward," was idealistic in its ringing call for social justice:

> But humanity is calling thee. O, hearken once again
> To the cry that falls upon thy ear from suff'ring fellow-men!
> Every sigh of burdened toiler—every longing for the light—
> Every bloody tear of bondsman—every struggle for the right—
> Every sin and every sorrow calls thee ONWARD, to the van
> Of the army that is working the deliverance of man.

The vision of final triumph pulsated with optimism:

> O, those forms of the departed—how they gather round me now!
> And I see the jewels sparkle upon many a crowned brow;
> And the choral song is ringing now through arches wreathed
>   with palm;
> And the choirs of flaming seraphs join the loud triumphant
>   psalm;
> And golden harps and voices sing the glory that shall be,
> When the martial shout of "ONWARD!" shall be blent with
>   "Victory!"[56]

A related extracurricular interest was music. One winter morning
in 1859 after a walk in the surrounding hills, Gladden wrote "The
Mountains," the first alma mater song in America by an undergradu-
ate. He included it with several other original compositions, such as
"Biennial Serenade," "Philologian Song," "Fifty-nine," "Parting
Song," and "The Summer Dawn Is Breaking," in his compilation in

---

[54] *Ibid.*, VI (1858–59), 193–97.
[55] *Ibid.*, VI (1858–59), 339.
[56] *Ibid.*, VI (1858–59), 15–16.

1859 of *Songs of Williams*.[57] Dedication of the collection to William Cullen Bryant, another Williams man, and Gladden's memory of reading Tennyson while in college indicate that he found considerable delight in poetry.[58] Gladden taught singing while at Williams and founded and conducted the Mendelssohn Society, a singing group composed of college students.[59]

In his journalistic work Gladden made one association of both immediate and future importance. His "newspaper knack" enabled him to become college reporter for the influential *Springfield Republican*. Its astute editors, Samuel Bowles and Josiah G. Holland, sensed Gladden's literary ability and surprised him by printing, with a flattering comment, a poem he had composed for the Philologian society. While his mother prayed that he would not become "puffed up with such things," Gladden rejoiced in this initial recognition.[60] Bowles and Holland took Gladden under wing, entertained him in Springfield, and occasionally printed his stories and poems. One story brought Gladden nineteen dollars, in spite of the editors' policy not to pay for fiction. Another contribution bore evidence of Gladden's devotion to the Republican party.[61]

Gladden looked to the editors for vocational advice. Bowles was confident that journalism offered greater possibilities for public service than any of the professions and tried to discourage Gladden's thoughts about the ministry. Their ties were strengthened in other ways. Holland experimented with Gladden's music in a Congregational church choir in Springfield, and Bowles handled college print-

[57] Gladden, *Recollections*, p. 81; Rudolph, "Washington Gladden," p. 21; S. W. Gladden, ed., *Songs of Williams* (New York: Baker & Godwin, 1859), pp. 17–19.

[58] Gladden, "Alfred Tennyson as Prophet," Sermon, November 28, 1897, Gladden Papers.

[59] Elizabeth R. Cumming to Gladden, July 2, 1859, Gladden Papers; *Williams Quarterly*, VI (1858–59), 40, 95, 379, 381.

[60] Amanda Williams to Gladden, April 2 (no year), Gladden Papers; Gladden, *Recollections*, p. 82.

[61] Nancy A. W. Priest to Gladden, August 6, 1859, First Church archives; Priest to Gladden, April 21, 1859, Gladden Papers.

ing for which Gladden was responsible. Many years later, Gladden preached funeral sermons for both men.[62]

Gladden's personal affairs fluctuated widely during his years at Williams. Family problems invaded the seclusion of the quiet Berkshire village. His mother's second marriage continued to deteriorate. In 1858 George Gladden wrote that Mr. Williams "had been sent up for 25 days for pushing her over the stove & 'raising Ned' generally." This episode apparently reformed Williams somewhat, but George, though able to report two months later that "the old man is still sober," predicted that his good behavior would not last long.[63]

George Gladden had problems of his own. Having stayed in the printing side of journalism after his work on the Owego *Gazette*, he found it increasingly difficult to support himself during the depression of the late 1850's. Gladden's efforts to obtain a position for George with the *Springfield Republican* seem to have failed, but George's work for the LeRoy *Gazette* in Genesee County, New York, afforded him some income against his mounting debts.[64] George's letters to his older brother abounded in frustrated hopes for economic improvement.

Gladden was no recluse from the social whirl of his peers. Because of a complete absence of correspondence between him and the girl he eventually married and because of semantic complications in letters written to him by other young ladies, it is particularly difficult to untangle the strands of his romantic involvement. The major figures in the drama, besides Gladden himself, were Jennie O. Cohoon and Hattie A. Hamilton, both classmates of Gladden's at the Owego Academy. Jennie left Owego with her family in 1856 and after a brief residence in Racine, Wisconsin, finally settled in Columbus, Ohio. Hattie left Owego for the Young Ladies Institute in Auburn,

[62] Samuel Bowles to Gladden, April 2 (no year), April 12 (no year), July 27, 1859, First Church archives; Josiah G. Holland to Gladden, January 12, [1860,] First Church archives; Gladden, *Recollections*, p. 83.

[63] George Gladden to Gladden, December 12, 1858, February 13, 1859, First Church archives.

[64] Bowles to Gladden, n.d.; George Gladden to Gladden, March 27 (no year), May 22, July 17, 1859, First Church archives.

New York. Hattie's letters reveal considerable confusion on her part about the real nature of Gladden's intentions. Her mingling of affectionate jargon with a frank acknowledgment, after Gladden's engagement in 1858 to Jennie Cohoon, of his unavailability indicates that Hattie wanted desperately to preserve a friendship that had once had romantic overtones.

As early as October, 1857, Gladden appears to have leaned toward Jennie. Lamenting his own failure to see the Cohoons while on a visit to Wisconsin, Lewis Matson spoke of Gladden's affections being concentrated only upon Jennie.[65] Somewhat later, Hattie chided Gladden for being so engrossed with Berkshire girls, as well as with the "Buckeyes," that he was neglecting her.[66] After Gladden visited Auburn in May, 1858, less than a month before his engagement to Jennie became a topic of correspondence, Hattie wrote: "It does not seem as though I had actually *seen* you, conversed with you, and even kissed you!" Whether or not Gladden told Hattie on that visit of his engagement to Jennie is unclear, but on June 4, Hattie referred to Jennie as "*Mrs. G.* in perspective."[67] A mutual friend of all three parties, Nettie Brister, scolded Gladden bitterly for his treatment of some "poor girl," perhaps Hattie, who had "bestowed her heart" on him and ruefully added that the girl in question would not regret his engagement when she learned what he was really like.[68]

Gladden and Hattie continued to correspond, albeit spasmodically, at least until September 19, 1859. That Gladden was engaged to Jennie, whom he visited in Columbus sometime in 1858, did not prevent him from visiting Hattie in Auburn and reassuring her of his love.[69] The fragmentary nature of the evidence, however, precludes

[65] Matson to Gladden, October 5, 1857, Gladden Papers.

[66] This is undoubtedly a reference to Jennie, who had moved from Wisconsin to Ohio. Hattie A. Hamilton to Gladden, March 17 (no year), First Church archives.

[67] *Ibid.*, May 12, June 4, 1858, Gladden Papers.

[68] Nettie L. Brister to Gladden, June 28, 1858, Gladden Papers.

[69] Gladden, Sermon on William Dean Howells, [1916,] Gladden Papers; Hamilton to Gladden, September 19, 1859, Gladden Papers.

firm conclusions about an extremely confusing relationship.

Extracurricular pursuits and personal problems may have inter-
fered with Gladden's academic performance, but this speculation
stands only on his later regret for failure to make maximum use of
intellectual opportunities: "All my life I have suffered for certain
defects in my equipment which a better use of my time would have
made good."[70]

Commencement in 1859 brought mixed emotions to Gladden. He
looked back over his college years as "the happiest time" he had ever
known and toward the future with uncertainty. Graduation festivi-
ties, featuring Mark Hopkins' address on "Spirit, Soul, and Body," a
concert by Gilmore's band, and numerous orations, lasted four days.
Gladden suffered an attack of facial neuralgia just before giving an
oration of his own, but a visiting clergyman, Howard Crosby, braced
him for the performance.[71]

In three years at Williams, Gladden had entered a fraternity of
academicians, writers, and clergymen in which he continued to
move for the rest of his life. Many of his acquaintances at Williams
figured largely in later stages of his career. His relationship to the
Hopkins family and to the college was to continue throughout his
life and to become even closer when Mark's son Henry became
president.[72] John Bascom was Gladden's mentor as long as he lived.[73]
Samuel Bowles and Josiah G. Holland encouraged his subsequent
journalistic efforts. Gladden met James A. Garfield at the commencement of 1859, thought highly of him, and supported his political
career.[74] Classmates, such as Charles R. Van Hise, Bascom's successor at the University of Wisconsin, Henry C. Haskell and Henry A.

[70] Gladden, Sermon, February 28, 1897, Gladden Papers.

[71] Gladden, *Recollections*, p. 84; Rudolph, "Washington Gladden," pp. 35–
37; Gladden, Sermon, n.d., Gladden Papers.

[72] Henry Hopkins to Gladden, June 5, 1901, March 26, 1902, November 12,
1904, Gladden Papers.

[73] Emma C. Bascom to Gladden, September 26, 1903, and Leonora Bascom
to Gladden, May 21, 1913, Gladden Papers.

[74] Gladden, *Recollections*, p. 76.

Schauffler, both active in Congregational work in later years, and Eben Burt Parsons, a fellow editor of the *Quarterly* and later secretary of the Williams faculty, were lifelong friends.[75] As the train carried Gladden from Williamstown in August, 1859, the temporary loss of these rich associations aggravated the trepidation with which he faced the future.

[75] *Congregationalist,* XCVI (October 14, 1911), 510; *Williams Quarterly,* V (1857–58), 382; Eben Burt Parsons to Gladden, June 10, 1905, Gladden Papers.

Two

The Years of Uncertainty

After returning to Owego in August, 1859, Gladden contracted to teach in the main school in his native village. Although he had spent the long college vacations from Thanksgiving to January teaching sessions similar to the ones he had attended as a boy during the idle winter periods on the farm, his duties in the one-room school were an emotional strain, as well as a profound disappointment.[1] Giving his situation a humorous touch, he wrote early in 1860:

> . . . It is a glorious work, this work of instructing the youthful mind, especially when you have about 125 of them, one-fourth of whom are Afric's sable sons, another fourth children of the Emerald Isle, another fourth idiots, and the other fourth children of the wicked one![2]

Gladden took the position only because his vocational aspirations were adrift and he needed some temporary means of support. His earlier commitment to the ministry, temporarily overshadowed by literary ambitions, now re-emerged as the dominant influence in his

[1] Gladden, *Recollections*, pp. 75–76, 85; Mrs. L. G. Smith to Gladden, May 9, 1916, Gladden Papers; S. A. Lincoln and John L. T. Phillips, certification of Gladden's teaching experience, August 20, 1859, Gladden Papers.

[2] *First Annual Report of the Class of 'Fifty-Nine*, March 1, 1860, quoted in Rudolph, "Washington Gladden," p. 40.

thinking.[3] With encouragement from Moses Coit Tyler, who became pastor of the Owego Congregational church in August, 1859, Gladden requested a license to preach from the Susquehanna Congregational Association, the oldest ecclesiastical organization in south-central New York.[4] His complete lack of formal theological training made his an irregular procedure, but the Saturday Catechism sessions at Williams, the theological reading through which Tyler guided him, and the leniency of the association's moderator, Thomas K. Beecher, brother of Henry Ward Beecher, saved the day. Gladden had met Beecher when as a student at the Owego Academy he invited the Elmira minister to speak at an exhibition, and he turned to him for advice during his postcollegiate days of indecision.[5]

When a request came to the Susquehanna Association from a church in LeRaysville, Pennsylvania, for someone to assist their minister in a series of special meetings, the association recommended Gladden, who immediately resigned his teaching position and turned toward the struggling church across the state line. These services began in January, 1860, and lasted about two months, with nightly meetings and two or three services on Sundays. The young tyro had little more than one written sermon when he arrived, but he worked

[3] W. A. Bartlett to Gladden, June 7, 1858; W. H. Corning to Gladden, July 9, 1858, First Church archives.

[4] Gladden, *Recollections*, p. 86; Tyler to Gladden, June 3, July 16, 1859, First Church archives; James M. Hastings, "The Congregational Church," in *Owego Sketches*, p. 105. Tyler later pioneered in American history and literature at the University of Michigan and Cornell, and in 1884 helped found the American Historical Association. Howard Mumford Jones, "Moses Coit Tyler," Allen Johnson, Dumas Malone, and Harris E. Starr, eds., *Dictionary of American Biography* (21 vols. and Index; New York: Charles Scribner's Sons, 1928–44), XIX, 92–93. Tyler and Gladden lived in the same boardinghouse and became intimate friends. In an amusing letter to Tyler's brother, written after Tyler's marriage in 1859, Gladden expressed fear that something dreadful had happened to his friend and raised the prospect of selling Tyler's personal effects at public auction. Gladden to Charles Tyler, November 11, 1859, quoted in Jessica Tyler Austen, ed., *Moses Coit Tyler, 1835–1900: Selections from His Letters and Diaries* (New York: Doubleday, Page & Co., 1911).

[5] Gladden, *Recollections*, pp. 86–87; Harris E. Starr, "Thomas Kinnicut Beecher," *Dictionary of American Biography*, II, 136–37; Thomas K. Beecher to Gladden, n.d., First Church archives.

strenuously in the minister's attic study to keep up with his preaching schedule.[6]

His sermons, though supported by the prayers of Owego Congregationalists, were theologically and rhetorically crude.[7] In a sermon inspired by Finney's writings he tried to emphasize human depravity by claiming that the unconverted hated God so much that they would dethrone and send him to hell. But the general tenor of his preaching must have been milder than this, for he afterward recalled one old farmer saying, "He don't threaten an' he don't scold; he jest lets down the bars."[8] His closing words to the congregation in LeRaysville were characteristic of these, his first pulpit orations:

> O what blessed memories will come to me wherever I shall be. . . .
> And this first work of the Lord in which I ever engaged so publicly . . .
> and these first souls I have ever pointed to Jesus—how shall I always
> love them! . . . Oh beloved, forsake him not; deny him not; cleave unto
> him—and your joy shall be a never-failing fountain—your peace shall
> flow as a river,—your evening time shall be light.[9]

The services did, however, enlarge the church's membership by about forty, most of whom were heads of families. Although Gladden hoped to begin his formal theological education in a year or two, this experience convinced him that actual pastoral labor was the best preparation for the ministry. Even before the services ended, he received invitations to preach in other needy churches in the locale.[10]

But the most important result of the work at LeRaysville for Gladden was a call from a metropolitan congregation, the First Congregational Methodist Church of Brooklyn. As its name implies, this

[6] Washington Gladden, *Fifty Years in the Ministry* (Columbus, Ohio: Lawrence Press Co., 1910), pp. 6–8.

[7] Tyler to Gladden, February 25, 1860, First Church archives; Gladden, Sermons, February 12, 1860, "The War that Knows No Discharge," February 22, 1860, "The Combat Deepens," March 1, 1860, Gladden Papers.

[8] Gladden, *Fifty Years in the Ministry*, p. 9.

[9] Gladden, Sermon, [March,] 1860, Gladden Papers.

[10] Gladden, *Recollections*, pp. 88–89; Gladden, *Fifty Years in the Ministry*, p. 8; Earlman Rogers to Gladden, March 3, 1860, First Church archives.

church was in an anomalous position. After a quarrel over a pastor, it had broken its ties with Methodism and adopted congregational polity; but it had not yet affiliated with a Congregational association. Gladden did not enjoy being the pastor of an ecclesiastical orphan. By the autumn of 1860 he had led it to join a local Congregational association and to call itself the State Street Congregational Church.[11]

In Brooklyn, a city of about 275,000 people, Gladden first confronted the overwhelming urban problems with which he wrestled for the rest of his life. His relatives in Owego feared for his spiritual welfare in Brooklyn's "worldly surroundings, but to him the metropolis presented entirely different threats. He had a disturbing "sense of its power to absorb human personalities and to shape human destinies." The "City of Churches" also undermined his self-confidence, which had been nurtured in rural and village communities. Beside Henry Ward Beecher, Richard S. Storrs, and Henry J. Van Dyke, who were only the most conspicuous members of an illustrious clergy, Gladden felt keenly his own insignificance.[12] Storrs, pastor of the Congregational Church of the Pilgrims and one of the most eminent divines of the nineteenth century, presided over the ecclesiastical council that on November 15, 1860, ordained Gladden.[13]

Gladden worked hard in Brooklyn. Since he had no great fund of sermons, preaching itself was a heavy burden.[14] And the church, shackled with a huge building debt and distracted by the excitement of impending war, presented insuperable problems. In addition, after December, 1860, when he married Jennie Cohoon, who had moved

[11] Gladden, *Recollections*, p. 94; *Ohio State Journal*, July 25, 1897.

[12] Ebenezer B. Daniels and S. M. Daniels to Gladden, July 22, 1860, First Church archives; Gladden, *Recollections*, p. 90.

[13] S. Bayliss, Scribe, "Record of Ecclesiastical Council at First Congregational Methodist Church, Brooklyn, November 15, 1860," First Church archives; Harris E. Starr, "Richard Salter Storrs," *Dictionary of American Biography*, XVIII, 101–2.

[14] In common with his contemporaries, he usually designated his sermons in the 1870's by scriptural texts rather than by titles. Gladden, Sermons, June 17, August 19, September 16, 1860, Gladden Papers.

to Brooklyn from Columbus, he encountered unexpected financial difficulties—as he put it, "the wolf was looking in at the door of the parsonage." The combination of overwork and anxiety led to a nervous collapse that crippled him and forced him in June, 1861, to resign.[15]

What might have been a hiatus in Gladden's career became instead a serene transition to future usefulness. A well-established Congregational church in the quiet suburban village of Morrisania—now part of the Bronx—offered opportunity for rest and reflection. The congregation, composed of business and professional people (among them the owner of the *New York Ledger*), was willing to accept minimal service from Gladden until his health improved. The work of the church prospered. Bible classes and prayer meetings received the hearty support of the people. Gladden introduced a plan to involve members more fully in church activities. A large edifice replaced a small, overcrowded chapel. And Gladden initiated a winter lecture course that became an annual affair. The first series, featuring Anna E. Dickinson, a popular speaker on political and social subjects, George William Curtis, editor of *Harper's Weekly*, Bayard Taylor, literary manager of the *New York Tribune*, and Ralph Waldo Emerson, the philosopher of Concord, created "no small stir" in the community. Emerson's lecture, especially, shocked many orthodox church members.[16]

Undoubtedly, the most significant aspect of Gladden's years at Morrisania was his theological study. He had gone to the church in Brooklyn hoping to take courses at New York's Union Theological Seminary, but it was not until he enjoyed the leisure of Morrisania that he could do this. Two of Union Seminary's most advanced thinkers appealed to him: both Roswell D. Hitchcock and Henry B. Smith had studied at Halle and Berlin, and they infused their teach-

[15] Gladden, *Recollections*, pp. 98, 114; John S. Worth, Scribe, "Record of Ecclesiastical Council of State Street Congregational Church, Brooklyn, June 20 and July 1, 1861," First Church archives; *Ohio State Journal*, May 9, 1909.

[16] Gladden, *Recollections*, pp. 115, 121, 123; Gladden, "Plan for Christian Labor," adopted October, 1864, First Church archives; Gladden, "Ralph Waldo Emerson," Sermon, May 17, 1903, Gladden Papers.

ing with the insights of German historical criticism and philosophy. But Gladden was able to devote merely a small part of his time to this, his only seminary work.[17]

Gladden's private study of theology affected him far more than any of his courses in college or seminary. With books furnished by a friend, perhaps a parishioner, and with access to the theological alcove of New York's Astor Library, he pursued this study relentlessly.[18] Growing impatience with systematic theology and a conviction, stemming from his experience in Owego, that religion must touch practical affairs led him to the works of two influential writers, Frederick W. Robertson and Horace Bushnell. Robertson was a Broad Church Anglican, particularly successful in his ministry to the workingmen of Bristol, while Bushnell was a minister in Hartford, Connecticut, noted for his unconventional treatment of theological issues.[19] Their influence on Gladden's theological development was paramount: "I can never tell how much I owe to these two men—to Robertson, first, for opening my eyes; to Bushnell, chiefly, for teaching me how to use them." According to Gladden, they appealed to him because they were men "to whom spiritual things were not traditions but living verities; men who knew how to bring religion into vital touch with reality."[20]

Probably the most influential theologian in New England since Jonathan Edwards, Bushnell was known to Gladden at least by 1859,

[17] Gladden, *Recollections,* pp. 94, 118; William Adams Brown, "Roswell Dwight Hitchcock," *Dictionary of American Biography,* IX, 79–80; Robert H. Nichols, "Henry Boynton Smith," *Dictionary of American Biography,* XVII, 277–78. The biographer of Lyman Abbott has drawn an accurate parallel between Gladden and Abbott in this regard. He holds that, because both men lacked seminary training, they remained untouched by the theological rigidity that such training might have involved. Ira V. Brown, *Lyman Abbott: Christian Evolutionist* (Cambridge: Harvard University Press, 1953), p. 24.

[18] Arthur Gilman to Gladden, June 24, 1862, First Church archives; Gladden, *Recollections,* p. 118.

[19] Lewis O. Brastow, *Representative Modern Preachers* (New York: Macmillan Co., 1904), p. 76. For an analysis of Bushnell's thought see Barbara M. Cross, *Horace Bushnell: Minister to a Changing America* (Chicago: University of Chicago Press, 1958).

[20] Gladden, *Recollections,* p. 119.

when Owego's Congregational minister commended Gladden for reading his *Christian Nurture* (1847) and *Nature and the Supernatural* (1858).[21] Bushnell's primary impact on Gladden in the years at Morrisania came through *God in Christ* (1849), a book that many considered heretical.[22] Its effect was twofold: Bushnell's analysis of language unsettled Gladden's tacit assumption that theological formulations could adequately convey the truths they were designed to express; and Bushnell's exposition of certain cardinal tenets of the orthodox Calvinist faith released Gladden's latent uneasiness with Calvinism and set him in the direction of a new theology.

Bushnell raised the whole question of the value of language. Words, he asserted, "do not literally convey or pass over a thought out of one mind into another. . . . They are only hints, or images, held up before the mind of another, to put him on generating or reproducing the same thought. . . ." He denied that anyone who correctly understood language could "hope any longer to produce in it a real and proper system of dogmatic truth." The legitimate function of language was symbolic and aesthetic: to stir the emotions and will and to sensitize intuition. God had not revealed himself in a body of doctrine but as a historic presence, and he could be apprehended, not through definition and categorical analysis, but through personal communion.[23] Bushnell's reaction against the dialectical methodology of his former mentor, Nathaniel W. Taylor of Yale, and his absorption of the ideas of Coleridge and Schleiermacher led him to a descriptive rather than a definitive theology.

The distrust of metaphysical interpretations inherent in Bushnell's discussions of "The Divinity of Christ" and "The Atonement" had an equally profound effect on Gladden. Bushnell considered Christ an "expression" of God but denied the validity of speculations about

[21] Charles A. Dinsmore, "Horace Bushnell," *Dictionary of American Biography*, III, 350–54; Corning to Gladden, March 7, 1859, First Church archives.

[22] Horace Bushnell, *God in Christ: Three Discourses Delivered at New Haven, Cambridge, and Andover, with a Preliminary Dissertation on Language* (Hartford: Brown & Parsons, 1849); Cross, *Bushnell*, p. 115.

[23] Cross, *Bushnell*, p. 94; Bushnell, *God in Christ*, pp. 12, 45–46, 92; Brastow, *Modern Preachers*, p. 191.

His divine-human nature or about the composition of the Trinity. In a surprisingly modern vein, he affirmed his faith in seeming paradoxes.[24] Gladden, too, in later years, would shy from defense of his faith on rationalistic grounds and take refuge in intuitive or experiential sources of knowledge.

From Bushnell's discussion of the atonement Gladden derived an ethical standard by which theological statements could be judged: attitudes and actions that violated the best human moral consensus could not be attributed to God. When Gladden later claimed that Bushnell had delivered him "once and forever from the bondage of an immoral theology," he had in mind this principle by which he eliminated the elements of Calvinist theology most obnoxious to him. Bushnell held that God had been in Christ "to re-engage the world's love" and thus to effect reconciliation with the world; to view Christ's death as a vicarious or substitutionary sacrifice that vindicated God's justice was to put God in need of the reconciliation rather than man.[25] Furthermore, for God to punish one man for the sins of others would be the grossest injustice. Bushnell's "moral influence" view of the atonement replaced the forensic language that had marked much Protestant thought with the language of familial relationships. And for Gladden the ethical standard became a sharp critique of Protestant theology.

To describe Gladden's theological reflection and tranquil pastoral labor in Morrisania is to tell only a partial story. Throughout his years in Brooklyn and Morrisania he was distracted by events related to the Civil War. He had supported the Republican party since its inception; in 1858 he had followed the Lincoln-Douglas debates in the papers and was struck by "the invincible moral sense of Lincoln." Consequently, when he heard the news of Lincoln's nomination while returning to Brooklyn after a trip to Owego, he threw his cap into the air with a shout of jubilation: "The thing seemed too good to be true." What disturbed him most was the indifference of many

[24] Bushnell, *God in Christ*, pp. 129–36, 156–63.
[25] Gladden, *Recollections*, p. 119; Bushnell, *God in Christ*, pp. 188–89.

of the churches to such momentous national events. At times, he
confronted outright sympathy with the southern cause. A closely-
reasoned argument by Brooklyn's leading Presbyterian minister,
Henry J. Van Dyke, that equated abolitionism and infidelity appalled
him.

A more amusing incident followed a service in Gladden's church
in Brooklyn. Because of the unusual length of a hymn selected by
Gladden, a guest preacher suggested the omission of a stanza that
ran,

> Rebuild thy walls, thy bounds enlarge,
> And send thy heralds forth;
> Say to the South, Give up thy charge,
> And keep not back, O North.

That the hymn paraphrased a passage in Isaiah celebrating the
return of the Hebrew exiles did not matter to an enthusiastic correspondent to a daily paper, who commended the visiting minister for
his ostensible rebuke to Gladden, who supposedly had tried to foist
an abolitionist hymn upon the congregation.[26]

There were more encouraging reactions in the religious world to
current events. Henry Ward Beecher's stout defenses of the northern
cause from his pulpit in Plymouth Church, and particularly his sermon on Thanksgiving Day in 1860, which Gladden went to hear,
were exhilarating. The fateful election of 1860 aroused Gladden's
excitement. He spent the evening of election day in Printing House
Square in New York City, where he could watch the bulletins that
were posted periodically on the Tribune Building, and returned
home only when telegrams brought certainty of Lincoln's victory.
That victory he later called a political revolution that "registered
an ethical advance in the American people. . . . Their ideals had
been, in some good measure, transformed." The change in ten years
from the America of Franklin Pierce to that of Abraham Lincoln he
considered phenomenal. He later recalled the prayer of "thanks and

[26] Gladden, *Recollections*, pp. 91–93.

praise, of penitence and humiliation, of hope and courage" that
Joshua Leavitt, a veteran antislavery man and former editor of the
Emancipator, offered at a meeting of Congregationalists at Syracuse
when news came of Lincoln's Emancipation Proclamation. Perhaps
no northern city experienced the degree of war excitement that
gripped New York City; draft riots, mob scenes, the organization of
a Home Guard to protect Morrisania—all were impressed vividly on
Gladden's memory.[27]

But personal tragedy drove him directly to the scene of battle.
A series of defeats late in 1863 sent northern hopes plummeting.
Shortly after the Union disaster at Cold Harbor, Gladden received
word from his half brother, a private in the Eighth New York Heavy
Artillery, that his brother George, a lieutenant in the same regiment, had fallen at Cold Harbor and had been left on the field of
battle. Deeply shaken by the news, Gladden secured an appointment with the Christian Commission and hurried to Virginia. The
Christian Commission, a voluntary relief organization supported
principally by the Young Men's Christian Association, the American
Tract Society, and various evangelical churches, devoted most of its
energies to meeting the immediate personal needs, especially the
religious needs, of the Union troops. Compared to the United States
Sanitary Commission, the most important northern relief agency during the war and the forerunner of the Red Cross, the Christian
Commission was unscientific in purpose and methodology and limited in scope. But Gladden was not yet sensitive to the complexities
of modern charity; and he was, after all, using his service in the
Christian Commission mainly for personal ends. Needless to say, he
did take seriously his work as chaplain, scribe, and nurse for the
troops around Petersburg and Appomatox. One day he had an uninspiring interview with General Grant in the Christian Commission's
tent.[28]

[27] *Ibid.,* pp. 94–95, 99–102, 128–29, 131–34; Gladden, Sermon commemor-
ating Emancipation Proclamation, n.d., Gladden Papers.

[28] Gladden, *Recollections,* pp. 136–37, 140–42; Robert H. Bremner, *American Philanthropy* (Chicago: University of Chicago Press, 1960), pp. 79–81, 191.

Gladden found his brother's regiment and eventually confirmed his death. According to one report, George had fallen while mounting the Confederate breastworks and, probably because of a Masonic pin that he wore, had been pulled inside the breastworks just before he died. Gladden's work for the Christian Commission was cut short by malaria, and he returned on "fetid transports" and "crowded railway cars" to Morrisania, where he struggled for two months with the fever before he could resume his pastoral duties.[29]

Meanwhile, the last winter of war dragged on in gloom. Gladden learned of the North's final victory when his neighbor, a Wall Street broker, came rushing home, hoisted his flag, and excitedly fired his revolver into the air—all before informing Gladden.[30] The final stanza in a short poem written after Lee's surrender expresses Gladden's jubilation:

> Spirit of earth, now hovering near
>   Stoop thy bright wings as thou fliest;
> Then to the peoples in bondage and fear
>   Speed thee, nor rest, while thou criest
> "Tidings! ye millions in manacles led;
> "Liberty cometh with jubilant tread!
> "Liberty, Freedom! Tyranny's dead!
>   "Glory to God in the highest."

But only five days after Gladden wrote in this hopeful vein, Lincoln succumbed to an assassin's bullet. A dirge that came from Gladden's pen, despite its final ray of hope, stands in stark contrast to his earlier paean:

> Toll!
> Slowly toll, funeral bell!
> Let your solemn pulses tell
> That the white robes of the angel

---

[29] Gladden to Amanda Williams, June 5, 1864, Gladden Papers; Gladden, *Recollections*, p. 144.

[30] Gladden, *Recollections*, p. 146.

Chanting peace are soiled with blood
That Humanity's evangel
Was a curse, misunderstood;
Toll, the staff of strength is broken
That the people leaned upon;
Toll! the grief that hath no token
For our kingliest man is gone.
Toll! Toll!

Weep!
Let the heavens drop tears of woe!
Darkness shroud the land below!
Weep ye millions he hath guided,
Weep, all ye who mourned him here!
Let the land so long divided
Meet in sorrow round his bier!
Weep ye hosts whose chains are falling!
Palsied lies the arm that broke them!
Words of life ye heard him calling,
Silent are the lips that spoke them!
Weep! Weep!

Rest!
He is resting in his grave
Where the prairie grasses wave!
Rest! our father's God ordaineth
That this martyr's blood shall be
Evermore while earth remaineth
Precious seed of liberty!
Rest! our God will watch the sowing;
Wait! the harvest ripens fast!
All the golden fruitage growing
Will be gathered in at last,
And the reapers soon be going
To their rest.[31]

That victor and vanquished should "meet in sorrow round his bier" was Gladden's strongest desire. That the assassination, which might have convinced both the North and the South of the folly of

[31] Gladden, "Recollections of a Lifetime," [1906,] Gladden Papers.

further fratricidal strife, should occasion even more bitterness tore at the fiber of Gladden's idealism. Following Lee's surrender, Gladden, heralding the desire of the North for a "new career of amity and concord that shall be perpetual," had prophesied "new relations of friendship that shall be far closer and far more enduring than the old ones were."[32] Now, in a sermon to a crowded church on the day of Lincoln's funeral, Gladden lamented the tendency to hold the South responsible for the assassination. He maintained that the deed, perpetrated by a small circle of conspirators, had caused "universal sorrow" in the South. Admitting his own instinctive wish for retribution, he called instead for "calm, unprejudiced reason." Peace, union, and freedom would come sooner, he argued, if the North adopted a mild policy toward the South.[33]

It was another poem prompted by the Civil War that led Gladden from suburban Morrisania to a strikingly different community. Like many other American colleges, Williams celebrated the return of peace at its commencement in 1865. Chosen by the alumni society for the honor, Gladden delivered an original composition, "After the War," in the old Congregational church in Williamstown. Reviewing the tragedies and glories of war and lauding its heroes, the poem elicited the praise of the *Springfield Republican*. It also brought Gladden to the attention of a visiting group of Congregationalists from neighboring North Adams. They invited him to preach for them the following Sunday; and by January, 1866, the congregation requested that he become their pastor. Although the evidence bespeaks the mutual contentment of Gladden and his congregation at Morrisania, he apparently welcomed the invitation from North Adams for financial reasons. Initially, Gladden's salary at Morrisania had been ample, but the birth of two children, Alice and Frederick, and the necessity of contributing to his mother's support put him in financial straits. He attempted to resign in 1863 but, perhaps because of an improvement in his salary, was persuaded to

---

[32] Gladden, Sermon, [1865,] Gladden Papers.

[33] Gladden, Sermon, April 19, 1865, Gladden Papers.

stay. When the call came from North Adams, however, he left Morrisania without hesitation.[34]

In North Adams, Gladden's activities took several directions prophetic of the future. He developed a technique of religious work embryonic of later plans of parish organization and expanded his preaching to include literary and social subjects. He deepened his attachment to a nascent theological liberalism and became counselor to at least one distressed heretic. He made the first halting application of his religious thought to postwar social conditions; for the first time he confronted industrial disorder. And he began to write the books and articles that soon swelled into a veritable flood of publications.

North Adams was in 1866 "a smart factory village of eight or nine thousand people." Together with South Adams it comprised the town of Adams, a typical New England community awakened by the aftermath of the Civil War to increasing business profits and social dislocation. In Adams, however, vigorous grass-roots democracy flourished. Its voters conducted public business at regular town meetings, which Gladden likened to the practice of "the primitive New England democracies."[35] Gladden rejoiced that the town, born amid the throes of the Revolution and named for the radical Sam Adams, had "a more thorough fusion of the various social orders than is usually found."[36] Whereas in Morrisania he had influenced only his immediate congregation, he felt that in North Adams, because of the cohesiveness of the community, he was speaking to the entire populace. In addition, the hilly topography of western Massa-

---

[34] Rudolph, "Washington Gladden," p. 46; Gladden, "Recollections of a Lifetime," [1906,] Gladden Papers; Gladden, *Recollections*, pp. 158–59; Gladden to Trustees of First Congregational Church, Morrisania, n.d., and Gladden to First Congregational Church and Society, Morrisania, April 6, 1863, First Church archives; "Preamble and Resolutions adopted by First Congregational Church, Morrisania, February 18, 1866," First Church archives.

[35] Gladden, *Recollections*, p. 159.

[36] Washington Gladden, *From the Hub to the Hudson: With Sketches of Nature, History and Industry in North-Western Massachusetts* (Boston: New England News Co., 1869), p. 108.

chusetts, which he had come to love while at Williams, added to the pleasantness of his residence in North Adams.

Likewise, the Congregational church in North Adams delighted Gladden. Organized in 1827 through the evangelistic efforts of several Williams men, it had by 1866 a membership of 160 and an average Sunday-morning attendance of about 250. Just before Gladden's arrival in 1866 a parishioner reported an attendance of 160 at a recent prayer meeting.[37] The church had no financial problems, and, according to Gladden, the people, like the community at large, were "hospitable to fresh thinking, not afraid of the truth even if it was a new truth."[38] Gladden was able to read extensively and to develop and expound his own views.

His admiration for Horace Bushnell prompted him, when it came time to arrange for his installation over the congregation at North Adams, to invite the Hartford theologian to preach the installation sermon. At first, Bushnell was reluctant to handicap Gladden by allowing him to identify himself with one whose orthodoxy was suspect; but Gladden persisted, and Bushnell finally agreed to come. Bushnell continued to fear theological discord, and in a letter confirming the date of the installation he speculated concerning the probable attitudes of various members of the council. But the council, which included President Hopkins and Albert Hopkins from the church in Williamstown and Dr. John Todd of Pittsfield, was willing to let sleeping theological dogs lie. Dr. Todd, its moderator and, probably, most conservative member, led the questioning so as to

[37] Rudolph, "Washington Gladden," p. 41; J. E. A. Smith (ed.), *History of Berkshire County Massachusetts, with Biographical Sketches of Its Prominent Men* (2 vols.; New York: J. B. Beer & Co., 1885), I, 549–50; Charles R. Keller, "Dr. Washington Gladden," *Our Church Chronicle* (North Adams, Mass.: Published annually in the interest of the North Adams Congregational Church, April, 1953), p. 7; George C. Lawson to Gladden, March 23, 1866, Gladden Papers.

[38] Gladden, *Recollections*, p. 163. A later pastor of liberal views, Theodore T. Munger, corroborated Gladden's testimony to this effect. Benjamin Wisner Bacon, *Theodore Thornton Munger* (New Haven: Yale University Press, 1913), pp. 235–37.

obviate both conflict and compromise.[39]

Bushnell's installation sermon, "The Gospel of the Face," called for less preaching *about* Christ and the gospel and more preaching *of* Christ and the gospel. Restating his views on the function of language, Bushnell contrasted the Incarnation, which gave the world a "concrete personation" of God, with dogmatic abstractions: "There is no proposition, or hundred propositions, that can not be believed . . . having yet no gracious effect whatever." The pastor and his flock must emulate Christ, who "lives on foot, mingles with men in the market-places, touching and touched by everything human," in order to inspire in men the faith that would win salvation.[40]

This first personal contact with Bushnell, who spent a week at the parsonage in North Adams, impressed Gladden even more deeply than had Bushnell's writings. Many years later, he wrote the following tribute for Theodore T. Munger's biography of Bushnell:

> I could not have remained in the ministry, an honest man, if it had not been for him. . . . Dr. Bushnell gave me a moral theology and helped me to believe in the justice of God. If I have had any gospel to preach, during the last thirty five years, it is because he led me into the light and joy of it.[41]

An episode that followed close upon his installation[42] illustrates Gladden's willingness to identify himself with Bushnell's views when

[39] Horace Bushnell to Gladden, March 13, April 7, May 23, 1867, Gladden Papers. The installation, which occurred on June 12, 1867, followed a trial year that Gladden had insisted the church grant before officially hiring him as pastor. After the installation his salary was two thousand dollars a year, and he had a month for vacation each summer. Gladden, *Recollections*, pp. 166–68; Rudolph, "Washington Gladden," p. 46.

[40] Bushnell included "The Gospel of the Face" in his *Sermons on Living Subjects* (New York: Charles Scribner's Sons, 1890 ed.), pp. 73–95. He prepared this collection in 1871 and first published it in 1872. Mary Bushnell Cheney, ed., *Life and Letters of Horace Bushnell* (New York: Harper & Bros., 1880), p. 505.

[41] Gladden, *Recollections*, pp. 166–67; Theodore T. Munger, *Horace Bushnell: Preacher and Theologian* (Boston: Houghton Mifflin Co., 1899), pp. 374–75.

[42] In *Recollections*, pp. 164–65, Gladden reverses this order and places the installation after this episode, but the manuscript evidence substantiates the chronology followed here.

they were still accepted by only a few. Clay McCauley, a young Congregationalist in Illinois, wrote Gladden of the refusal of a Congregational council to ordain him because he rejected the substitutionary view of the atonement and adhered to Bushnell's theory of its "moral influence." Unable to retain his Congregational ties, he sought ordination by the Presbytery of Chicago, but this venture failed because he refused to affirm that any infants might be damned. With this case in mind, Gladden wrote an article for the *Independent*, "Are Dr. Bushnell's Views Heretical?", in which he set forth Bushnell's theory of the atonement. His unsolicited support evoked a letter of gratitude from Bushnell.[43]

Gladden's work lifted the church in North Adams to one of the pinnacles in its history. His sermons introduced the congregation to contemporary theological currents. Portraying the Christian life as a natural development in faith and service, he opposed a popular emphasis on dramatic conversions as detrimental to healthy spiritual growth. He repudiated theological formulations that, to him, not only transcended but also contradicted reason.[44] One parishioner, who had been in her thirties during Gladden's pastorate, later spoke of the intellectual awakening he had brought to her. According to Theodore T. Munger, the church's pastor after 1877, "in Dr. Gladden's ministry a certain sense of freedom and breadth and toleration took possession of this church that has never left it."[45]

Munger attributed much of the church's subsequent success to Gladden's organizational abilities: " . . . As a business man Dr. Gladden would have been a chief among his fellows, and as the administrator of a parish no man could surpass him." He arranged the church's activities under three departments—Sunday school, mis-

[43] Clay McCauley to Gladden, October 21, November 18, 1867; Bushnell to Gladden, November 2, 1867, Gladden Papers.

[44] Gladden, Sermons, "Growth More than Birth," 1869; "The Offense of the Cross," n.d., Gladden Papers.

[45] Elizabeth W. Denison to Gladden, February 9, 1906, Gladden Papers; Theodore T. Munger, in *Address and Papers Presented at the Diamond Jubilee, 1827–1902, of First Congregational Church, North Adams* (North Adams, Mass.: Advance Press, 1902), p. 26.

sionary, and charitable—and urged every member to serve in one of them. He divided the parish into seven neighborhood districts, each supervised by a lay leader and committee that planned social and religious meetings and collected benevolent contributions. Under his leadership the congregation changed its second Sunday service from afternoon to evening, organized a young people's association, assumed partial support of an early ecumenical venture, the Union Church of Blackinton, and removed from its covenant a total-abstinence pledge that had been incorporated in 1833. Both parish and missionary budgets rose rapidly, and the church's membership increased from 160 in 1866 to over 300 in 1871.[46]

The church, for its part, supported his plans. One deacon, against whom Gladden had been warned, became a staunch and loyal worker: "The young man has his ideas," Gladden reported him as saying. "He wants to lead. We want a leader. Let us follow him."[47] On several occasions the congregation tangibly affirmed its appreciation for "the young man"—in 1868, by a testimonial letter bearing 133 signatures, and in 1870 on his tenth wedding anniversary, by filling his house with food and providing money for a piano. Gladden reciprocated their allegiance by rejecting an offer from a church in Cleveland that would have more than doubled his salary.[48] There can be no doubt that such an offer appeared attractive to Gladden, who had not only his own growing family to support but monthly contributions to make to his aging mother.[49]

Although Gladden admired North Adams for its democratic spirit and praised its free mingling of wealthy businessmen and indus-

[46] Bacon, *Munger*, pp. 217–18; Keller, "Dr. Washington Gladden," p. 7; William L. Tenney, "Review of History of First Congregational Church, North Adams," in *Addresses and Papers*, pp. 88–89.

[47] Gladden, *Recollections*, p. 163.

[48] Keller, "Dr. Washington Gladden," p. 7; Rudolph, "Washington Gladden," pp. 48–49. When Moses Coit Tyler learned of Gladden's decision, he jubilantly commended Gladden's preference for a small town to the rush of a big city. Tyler to Gladden, January 22, 1869, Gladden Papers.

[49] Amanda Williams to Gladden, February 8, March 17, 1867, April 30, 1869, Gladden Papers.

trialists with mechanics, clerks, and millworkers, the burgeoning economy of the village threatened to disrupt this idyllic harmony. Economic growth reached unprecedented peaks in the 1860's: by 1869, 3,500 industrial workers earned more than one and a quarter million dollars a year in Adams' textile mills, shoe factories, carriage works, paper mills, machine shops, and other establishments. About one-third of the population was foreign-born, primarily Irish and French-Canadian. Hundreds of children under the age of fifteen worked in the factories throughout the entire year.[50]

That class consciousness was growing, Gladden himself indirectly testified. In a lecture entitled "Our Best Society," which he delivered not only in North Adams but also in numerous towns in Massachusetts and New York, he denounced idleness, extravagance, and display. A newspaper in Pittsfield reported that he handled "the pinchbeck aristocracy without gloves, and exposed mercilessly the shams and frauds of 'our best society' so-called."[51] In assailing these early signs of class polarization, he sounded a note that was to echo through much of his later social criticism. His ideals were simplicity, frugality, and constructive work for all.

Gladden's role in a controversy over what recreational facilities the North Adams Young Men's Christian Association should provide for its members carried overtones of the problems confronting the expanding industrial order. Opposed by the rest of the clergy, he held that the YMCA should provide a room for checkers, chess, and backgammon. It was of vital importance, he felt, that the Christian community provide wholesome and innocent amusements for

[50] Gladden, *Recollections*, p. 161; Gladden, *From the Hub to the Hudson*, pp. 107–8; Frederick Rudolph, "Chinamen in Yankeedom: Anti-Unionism in Massachusetts in 1870," *American Historical Review*, LIII (October, 1947), 6.

[51] Gladden, "Our Best Society," n.d., Gladden Papers; Pittsfield *Eagle*, December 8, 1870, quoted in Rudolph, "Chinamen in Yankeedom," p. 6. Gladden's college classmate, Eben Burt Parsons, whose church sponsored the lecture in Baldwinsville, New York, reported that many of his parishioners considered it the best in that year's series, which included lectures by Henry Ward Beecher, Mark Twain, and President Andrew D. White of Cornell. Rudolph, "Washington Gladden," p. 50.

weary millworkers, who might otherwise find deleterious pastimes.[52] Though he lost the immediate issue, his cause prevailed both in the YMCA and in the churches.

The suspicions aroused by his position constrained him to elaborate his views on the entire question of amusements. A sermon preached in his church on November 26, 1866, and later published at the request of twenty-eight laymen of various denominations, was designed to quash inflammatory rumors about his moral code. Though he avowed that recreation was "indispensable to bodily and mental health" and "as much a part of the divine economy as prayer," Gladden emphasized that work must be pre-eminent in the life of the Christian and carefully differentiated between those amusements that were acceptable and those that were not. Checkers, dominoes, billiards, and bowling were justifiable when used without excess, and even card games would do no harm, provided there was no betting. A school as conservative in its morals as Williams College had a bowling alley, he pointed out. He was not so generous, however, on the subject of waltzes and polkas, which were abominations emanating from the vile dens of Paris. Although he sanctioned square dances in respectable homes at decent hours, he was appalled by the idea of people getting together at bedtime to spend the night in eating, drinking, and dancing less innocent steps.[53] But whatever his specific pronouncements, Gladden's main concern, that the churches recognize the legitimate needs of wage earners for recreation, was progressive.

Reactions to Gladden's sermon varied. Moses Coit Tyler, now a

[52] Rudolph, "Washington Gladden," pp. 55–56.

[53] Washington Gladden, *Amusements: Their Uses and Their Abuses* (North Adams, Mass.: James T. Robinson & Co., 1866), pp. 5 f. A chapter on "Amusement" in his book, *Plain Thoughts on the Art of Living* (Boston: Ticknor & Fields, 1868), pp. 169–86, and an article by him on the same subject in the *Independent* show his preoccupation with the question. He also wrote, though somewhat later, "Christianity and Popular Amusements," *Century*, XXIX (January, 1885), 384–92. Another sermon, probably of this period, pointed out that "worldliness does not consist in loving things which we ought not to love, but in loving things too much which we have a perfect right to love. . . ." Gladden, "Worldliness," n.d., Gladden Papers.

frequent correspondent, commended it and put printed copies in the hands of clergymen in Rockford, Illinois. Horace Bushnell called the sermon "the best and happiest statement" of the question. But "Clericus," an anonymous correspondent, was belligerently hostile; he thought of Gladden as

> . . . lacking good judgment, as having but little humility, but an inordinate desire to be popular with the world, even at the expense of godliness. A minister of the gospel, talking about regulating *dancing* and card-playing and the like! Why not preach that lechery and gambling be regulated!

In a sarcastic and biting letter to the deacons of Gladden's church, "Clericus" belittled the refinement and grace of Gladden's reply to him, then offered this mocking suggestion:

> When you get your church amusements in pious operation please authorize Mr. Gladden to issue a pastoral respecting their happy results. The proper channel of communication with the Christian world . . . is the Independent.

The issue dragged on in its somewhat amusing course, breaking out again in 1868 in an exchange in the North Adams *Transcript* between Gladden and the Reverend George Washington Fitch, a pastor in Williamstown who identified himself simply as "Veritas." Fitch equated moderate card-playing, dancing, and bowling with moderate lying, swearing, Sabbath-breaking, and drinking, and denounced Gladden's efforts at discrimination. His arguments became so irrelevant that the editors of the *Transcript* took Gladden's side against him. The question appears to have subsided shortly thereafter because, according to Gladden, the minister leading the crusade against amusements—whether Fitch or someone else is uncertain—"was discovered a few weeks afterward to have eloped with a young woman of his congregation, and to have feigned suicide by drowning, in order to cover his flight to a distant state."[54]

[54] Tyler to Gladden, March 23, 1867, Bushnell to Gladden, July 7, 1867, "Clericus" to Gladden, April 5 [6], 1867, "Clericus" to "Deacons of the North Adams Congregational Church," June 5, 1867, Gladden Papers; Rudolph, "Washington Gladden," pp. 56–57; Gladden, *Recollections*, p. 171.

The two volumes that Gladden wrote during his years in North Adams reflect his attitudes toward other social problems, especially those related to commerce and industry. In 1868 he published *Plain Thoughts on the Art of Living,* a series of Sunday-evening lectures to young people that had been condensed into weekly articles for the *Springfield Republican.*[55] In them he offered moralistic discussions of work for women, dress, manners, conversation, habits, physical culture, companionship, and marriage.

One chapter, "Stealing as a Fine Art," was an incisive critique of contemporary commercial ethics. Gladden considered his central principle, that each party to a transaction must give a fair equivalent for what he received, to be "only the Golden Rule applied to Traffic." He was alarmed at methods commonly employed to cheat people out of their "fair equivalent": misrepresentation of the quantity and quality of goods, jockeying of prices, and "no small amount of square lying" were among them. Men who "would not lie for fame, for family, or for country," he declared, "will yet lie for sixpence."[56] The better Puritan virtues of integrity, honesty, and modest living reinforced his sensitive awareness of the peculiar temptations generated by postwar conditions in this sombre but pungent volume. Its greatest significance was the infusion of commonplace human concerns with an ethical significance rooted in the Christian gospel.

But Gladden's second volume indicates that he was not yet a perceptive critic of industrial conditions. *From the Hub to the Hudson,* published in 1869, was a travel guide that led the reader westward from Boston to Troy, New York. Gladden had unbounded enthusiasm for the region's natural features and growing industries. He hailed the advantages of machine production and described the intelligent, cultivated faces of the workers. In his survey of workers' earnings and the total income of various towns, he found nothing to criticize; nor was he dissatisfied with working conditions, hours of labor, or

[55] Gladden, *Recollections,* p. 173; Gladden, *Plain Thoughts,* Preface.

[56] This seems to be Gladden's first use of the Golden Rule as a norm for social ethics. Gladden, *Plain Thoughts,* pp. 140–43, 147.

child labor.[57] Though he knew the region well, his information on industrial conditions might have come exclusively from its leading manufacturers.

Gladden seems to have been scarcely aware of labor difficulties in North Adams before 1870, when they broke out openly and he confronted a serious clash between labor and management for the first time. To protect themselves from the effects of machine production, shoemakers in Massachusetts formed in 1867 the Secret Order of the Knights of St. Crispin. They protested the use of unskilled laborers on the new machines. In North Adams the Crispins' chief opponent was Calvin T. Sampson, a shoe manufacturer who imported scabs from other towns in Massachusetts to replace his disaffected workers. Foiled by the Crispins, who converted the scabs to their cause, Sampson began to import Chinese workers through an agent in San Francisco. Protected on their arrival by thirty special policemen, the Chinese fortunately escaped violence; and Gladden, who joined the crowd that curiously watched their entrance, was gratified by the self-restraint of the disgruntled workers of North Adams. The experiment was a great success for Sampson, in terms both of profits and of the final defeat of the Crispins a few years later, but most of the Chinese eventually returned to China with their savings.[58]

Apart from his deliberations over the omens raised by the incident, Gladden limited himself to religious and educational work among the Chinese. Fifty or sixty church members, among them Gladden and some of his parishioners, organized Sunday-afternoon classes in reading and writing for the Orientals, who in turn occasionally entertained their teachers.[59] The rest of the town was never enchanted with the quiet new workers and largely ignored them. Nearly forty years later, a businessman from Columbus, Ohio, discovered one of these Chinese in Florida and asked him if he remem-

[57] Gladden, *From the Hub to the Hudson*, pp. 12–13, 28–30, 38–41.

[58] Gladden, *Recollections*, pp. 171–73; Rudolph, "Chinamen in Yankeedom," pp. 10–13, 15, 20, 27.

[59] Rudolph, "Chinamen in Yankeedom," p. 26.

bered Washington Gladden. "Why! Yes," the Chinese replied. "He was a Congregational Minister."[60]

Besides writing *Plain Thoughts on the Art of Living, From the Hub to the Hudson,* and occasional articles for the *Independent,* Gladden began a highly important relationship with the *Century,* a major American periodical for several decades. After several years of negotiations between its founders, Roswell Smith, Josiah G. Holland, and Charles Scribner, the magazine first appeared in 1870 as *Scribner's Monthly.*[61] Holland arranged for Gladden to write for the initial issue an article about the Hoosac tunnel, then being bored near North Adams.[62] Illness kept Gladden from finishing the article in time for the first number, but it went into the second. Gladden's association with the magazine was close, as a perusal of his frequent articles and poems will show. Roswell Smith, who provided Gladden with suggestions for articles and advice on their composition, was to become a key figure in at least one important juncture in Gladden's career. And Richard W. Gilder, who held major editorial positions throughout most of the magazine's history, was to be one of Gladden's few intimate correspondents.[63]

Gladden's books and articles extended his influence far beyond the boundaries of North Adams. They also laid the foundation for his reputation as a noteworthy writer. Addressing Gladden as "my beloved old Bald-Head," Moses Coit Tyler told of sending a review of one book to the *Independent* and reported that Gladden's fame was spreading so rapidly that students were quoting him as an

[60] Orestes A. B. Senter to Gladden, February 27, 1910, Gladden Papers.

[61] In 1881 Smith acquired sole interest and changed the magazine's name to the *Century.* Herbert S. Robinson, "Roswell Smith," *Dictionary of American Biography,* XVII, 339–40; Frank Luther Mott, *A History of American Magazines, 1741–1905* (4 vols.; Cambridge: Harvard University Press, 1938–1957), III, 457–72; Gladden, *Recollections,* pp. 174–75.

[62] Washington Gladden, "The Hoosac Tunnel," *Scribner's Monthly,* I (December, 1870), 143–59. Gladden had included an account of work on the tunnel in *From the Hub to the Hudson,* pp. 85–95.

[63] Gladden, *Recollections,* pp. 174, 283; Gladden, "Richard Watson Gilder," Sermon, December 5, 1909, Gladden Papers.

authority, together with Shakespeare and Plato.[64] The favorable reception accorded his writings enhanced his own notion of the influence of the pen, and, when in the early months of 1871 a "new field of labor . . . larger and more important" than his church in North Adams beckoned, he put aside his reluctance to leave the ministry for journalism.[65]

[64] Tyler to Gladden, April 18, June 22, 1869, Gladden Papers.
[65] Gladden, *Recollections*, p. 182; Rudolph, "Washington Gladden," p. 67.

Three

The Coming of Maturity

The *Independent*, a weekly paper published in New York, stood among the giants of journalism in the early 1870's; it carried particular weight with the evangelical reading public. Acutely aware of its eminence, the *Independent*'s editors boasted of nearly one million readers, constantly mounting circulation, and advertising patronage exceeding that of any other religious or secular paper in the country.[1] When Gladden received an offer early in 1871 to become the paper's religious editor, he was willing to leave the parish ministry for what he considered a career of greater influence and usefulness. But that he intended to preserve intact his religious orientation is clear from his refusal to accept a prior offer of the literary editorship, just vacated by Justin McCarthy. The new position was also financially attractive. His salary of $3,000, which would increase to $4,000 by the fourth year, was an improvement over his salary of $2,000 at North Adams.[2]

Gladden's primary duty on the *Independent*'s staff was to write news items and editorials on religious topics. But the purposes and spirit of the paper as a whole were religious. Founded in 1848 as an organ for Congregationalists outside New England, the *Independ-*

[1] Mott, *History of American Magazines*, II, 375.

[2] Gladden, *Recollections*, pp. 182–83; Henry C. Bowen to Gladden, January 6, 18, 1871, Gladden Papers.

ent strove originally to strengthen the denominational consciousness of western Congregationalists, many of whom were disappearing through the Plan of Union (1801) into Presbyterianism. But by 1870 the *Independent* had assumed a less denominational tone, although its publisher, Henry C. Bowen, and most of its editors were Congregationalists.[3] Under Theodore Tilton, the editor from 1863 to 1870, the religious emphasis was submerged, but in 1870 Bowen reversed this trend.[4] Gladden's appointment appears to have been part of Bowen's program to strengthen the *Independent's* traditional religious character.

Gladden's association with the *Independent* was bright with promise. Samuel Bowles, who had continually urged Gladden to develop his literary abilities, reiterated his conviction that the press was "a great deal bigger field than the pulpit," and that, since it was Gladden's "proper arena," he "would go to it sooner or later." Moses Coit Tyler hoped his friendship with Gladden would facilitate the frequent appearance of his own writings in the paper. The venerable Dr. Todd, who had supervised Gladden's installation at North Adams, commented laconically that God called men to preach, not to edit. In reply Gladden speculated that, had there been printing presses in the first century, Paul would have published a paper instead of writing letters, "so that we should have had an editor as the chief of the apostles!" The *Independent's* editors regretted taking him from successful pastoral work, except "that he bids fair to be so much better a journalist than he has been a minister."[5]

[3] Its editors before 1870 had been Congregational ministers like Richard S. Storrs, Joseph P. Thompson, Henry Ward Beecher, and Leonard W. Bacon. Mott, *History of American Magazines*, II, 367–69.

[4] In the late 1870's Tilton provoked a *cause célèbre* by accusing Beecher of adultery with his wife. When Bowen became involved in the case against Beecher, both Brooklyn's Plymouth Church, of which Beecher was pastor and Tilton and Bowen members, and the *Independent* were dragged into the controversy. Paxton Hibben, *Henry Ward Beecher: An American Portrait* (New York: George H. Doran Co., 1927), pp. 230–58; William Hayes Ward to Gladden, September 17, [1909,] Gladden Papers.

[5] Bowles to Gladden, January 24, 1871, Tyler to Gladden, January 29, 1871, Gladden Papers; *Independent*, XXIII (April 6, 1871), 6.

William Hayes Ward, who in 1871 replaced Edward Eggleston as managing editor, shared the general editorial management with Gladden, though the latter remained only religious editor in title. On at least one occasion Gladden managed the paper alone for a month during Ward's absence. He felt later that he had been able "to put more of vital interest and enthusiasm" into this experience than into any of the other occupations of his career.[6]

Gladden found the *Independent's* offices a popular resort of notable figures. Vice-President Schuyler Colfax contributed articles to the paper and frequently stopped in to exchange political gossip with the editors, as did Senator, and, after 1873, Vice-President Henry Wilson, whose *History of the Rise and Fall of the Slave Power in America* (1872–75) appeared serially in the *Independent*. Gilbert Haven, later a bishop of the Methodist Episcopal church, and Leonard W. Bacon, a distinguished Congregationalist, were among the religious figures who brought refreshing breezes to the editorial offices. An impressive list of poets and writers, including Bret Harte, Joaquin Miller, and many leading women writers, supplemented their contributions with personal visits. Gladden became acquainted with all of them; consequently, his awareness of contemporary political, religious, and literary currents grew more acute. The pages of the *Independent* carried articles by William Lloyd Garrison, John Greenleaf Whittier, William Cullen Bryant, Horace Bushnell, Charles Dudley Warner, William Dean Howells, and Henry James, Jr.[7]

Affirming its editors' belief in "the three R's—Right, Radical, and Religious,"[8] the *Independent* during Gladden's tenure championed

[6] Gladden, *Recollections*, pp. 183–85. Ward was also a distinguished biblical scholar and Orientalist. George A. Barton, "William Hayes Ward," *Dictionary of American Biography*, XIX, 442–43. Gladden and Ward subsequently worked together in various religious movements. Gladden apparently knew and admired Ward's predecessor on the *Independent*. Washington Gladden, "Edward Eggleston," *Scribner's Monthly*, VI (September, 1873), 561–64.

[7] Gladden, *Recollections*, pp. 189–91; *Independent*, XXIII (May 4, 1871), 6; Rudolph, "Washington Gladden," p. 70.

[8] *Independent*, XXIII (April 6, 1871), 6.

its share of progressive causes. It defended strong central government as essential to the nation's safety and unity,[9] urged a sizable
increase in the President's salary,[10] called for customs reforms,[11] and
advocated coeducation and woman suffrage.[12] With excited admiration for tenements built by wealthy Londoners for the poor, it called
for large-scale public and private housing projects in the United
States.[13] That Gladden shared most of the paper's principles seems
a fair conclusion, on the basis of his close co-operation with Ward.

But Gladden did not share its partisanship. Despite the claim that
it was committed to no party organization, the paper, under the
political editorship of Samuel T. Spear, another minister, advocated
Republican principles "because they represent freedom, equal justice, national unity, fidelity to the public credit, and good government."[14] Gladden may have agreed with all this, but he dissented
in 1872 from the *Independent's* narrowly partisan support of Grant
and its shabby treatment of Horace Greeley. He had preferred a Liberal Republican nomination in which the Democrats might have
concurred and viewed Greeley's candidacy as absurd; but Greeley's
editorials in the *New York Tribune* had been his political bible from
childhood, and he could not sanction the abuse heaped upon the
veteran reformer. The ineffectiveness of his dissent weakened his
sense of editorial influence.[15]

In his own department, however, Gladden had a free hand.[16] He

[9] *Ibid.,* XXIII (December 7, 1871).

[10] *Ibid.,* XXV (January 16, 1873).

[11] *Ibid.,* XXVI (March 12, 1874).

[12] *Ibid.,* XXIII (May 18, 1871), 4; XXV (May 29, 1873), 688–89, (June 5,
1873), 720.

[13] *Ibid.,* XXIII (March 16, 1871).

[14] *Ibid.,* XXIII (April 6, 1871), 6.

[15] Gladden, *Recollections,* pp. 210–14.

[16] Except for two poems and several editorials to which he laid claim in
Recollections, it is imposssible to identify Gladden's contributions with finality.
But he undoubtedly wrote or approved all material on religious topics. His
poems were "The Murderer of the Period," *Independent,* XXV (January 16,
1873), 1, and "My Sabbath," XXV (January 9, 1873), 4.

was able to give sympathetic attention to the progress of Darwinian thought in America;[17] to criticize the temperance and prohibition movements for excessive reliance on legal measures;[18] to deplore the segregation of Roman Catholic children in parochial schools;[19] and to oppose a movement to make the United States a "Christian nation" by constitutional amendment.[20] He leveled strong criticisms at the High Church group in the Protestant Episcopal church and urged Low Churchmen to resist the encroachments of "ritualism."[21]

Gladden's crusade for a more flexible attitude to amusements on the part of the churches, which he had launched in North Adams, continued in the columns of the *Independent*. He focused his attack in one editorial on the inconsistency of those who preached a "Protestant Monasticism": while they turned out of the church a man who "plays a rubber of whist with his wife in the evening," they accorded a seat of honor to "the hoary stock-gambler who has wrung millions of dollars from his fellow-men by knavish overreaching."[22] Contesting evangelist Charles G. Finney's assertion that a converted man would lose his desire for amusements, he held that Christianity "does not deplete and maim, but completes and enlarges the human nature."[23] He gave the question a humorous twist by ridiculing a condemnation of croquet by President Jonathan Blanchard of Wheaton College, whom he labeled "the Pontiff of Wheaton":

> Travel where you will, and you see the signs of its ravages. In every country dooryard you are greeted by the wicked wicket and the satanic stake, the malicious mallet and the baleful ball. . . . As for . . . [Blan-

[17] *Independent*, XXIV (May 16, 1872).

[18] *Ibid.*, XXV (June 12, 1873), 752, (July 3, 1873), 849; XXVI (February 12, 1874), 16, (March 5, 1874), 16, (March 12, 1874), 16, (March 26, 1874), 16, (May 7, 1874), 16, (November 12, 1874), 16.

[19] *Ibid.*, XXVI (July 23, 1874), 16.

[20] *Ibid.*, XXV (February 27, 1873), 272, (June 5, 1873), 720, (October 23, 1873), 1329.

[21] *Ibid.*, XXV (January 9, 1873), 16, (September 11, 1873), 1136, (October 30, 1873), 1360; XXVI (January 8, 1874), 17, (January 22, 1874), 17.

[22] *Ibid.*, XXV (January 2, 1873), 16.

[23] *Ibid.*, XXV (February 20, 1873), 240.

chard], we know that his righteous soul will be satisfied if we assure
him . . . that all the devotees of this diabolical game are sure to come
to the stake at last—if they play well enough.[24]

Enjoying and profiting by his editorial work, Gladden might have
stayed with the *Independent* permanently. But, always sensitive
to ethical questions, he was disenchanted with one practice that
Henry C. Bowen refused to end. In common with other periodicals
of the day, the *Independent* carried advertisements veiled as insurance and financial departments and as "Publisher's Notices." Though
designated as advertisements, they were in editorial type and often,
like editorials, in the first person plural. The uncritical reader might
easily take them as personal endorsements by the publisher. In his
first written protest to Bowen, dated May 22, 1873, Gladden noted
that other papers regularly quoted these advertisements, conjectured
that Bowen got higher rates for them, and questioned the honesty
of the practice. Bowen took no action. As a matter of fact, the practice grew more flagrant, so that by November, 1874, these notices
were encroaching on the editorial page. Gladden's "strong sense of
the sacredness of the newspaper as a public teacher, and of the
grave immorality of perverting its function for hire," led him to
resign. His final protest and resignation, penned on November 5,
1874, called for "a radical change in the management of the paper."
He contended that his editorial work was as much impugned by
these notices as a minister's preaching would be if his trustees kept
a policy shop in the church basement.[25]

Gladden did not want to leave journalism, but he had to admit to
the managing editor of the *Advance,* a Congregational paper published in Chicago, that he had no prospects and was leaving the
Independent "absolutely knowing not whither."[26] As in 1859 when he
left Williams, he was uncertain about what to do. He had preached
regularly while on the *Independent*'s staff and had even served two

[24] *Ibid.,* XXVI (October 8, 1874), 15.

[25] Gladden, *Recollections,* pp. 233–34, 238; Gladden to Bowen, May 22,
1873, November 5, 1874, Gladden Papers.

[26] Gladden to J. B. T. Marsh, November 3, 1874, Gladden Papers.

churches in Brooklyn for about a year each.[27] In addition, he had retained clerical ties by participating in Sigma Chi, a ministerial club in New York City.[28] He was reluctant, however, to return to the parish ministry. Samuel Bowles persistently reminded him that "the harvest [in journalism] is large, and the laborers are few. It is bigger than the pulpit. . . . " But the ministry, as he explained in a dismal letter to Lyman Abbott, seemed to be his only recourse: "Of course I shall go back into the pulpit. Nothing else is left me."[29]

Gladden's return to the parish ministry was permanent. Although he contributed regularly to the periodical press and wrote some two-score books, his primary loyalty after 1875 was to the congregations he served. His subsequent ministry in two important Congregational churches—from 1875 to 1882, the North Church in Springfield, Massachusetts, and from 1882 to 1918, the First Church in Columbus, Ohio—had completeness and diversity unknown to his earlier fields of labor. The interests and ideas that began to crystallize in Springfield in the late 1870's were to distinguish his mature career.

Since 1859, when he came from Williamstown to visit Samuel Bowles and Josiah G. Holland, Gladden had had a strong attraction to Springfield. As a boy he had spent a year at his father's old home, only a few miles distant. He had preached occasionally in Springfield while nearby at North Adams. When friends in the North Church learned of his resignation from the *Independent,* they invited him to fill their vacant pulpit for four Sundays. Before this engagement ended the church offered him its pastorate at a salary of $3,500, and he quickly gave informal assurance that he would accept. Though his contract with the *Independent* expired in February, 1875, he did

[27] Extant sermons for 1872–74 in the Gladden Papers indicate that he also preached frequently in Paterson, New Jersey, and Bedford, New York.

[28] He was introduced to Sigma Chi by Howard Crosby, a Presbyterian minister and chancellor of the University of the City of New York (New York University); it was Crosby who had helped Gladden to overcome his tension and successfully to deliver an oration in 1859 at his commencement. Gladden, Sermon, n.d., Gladden Papers.

[29] Bowles to Gladden, November 6, 1874; Gladden to [Lyman] Abbott, November 3, 1874, Gladden Papers.

not take up residence in Springfield until May, visiting the city a few days each week in the interim.[30]

Springfield, which Gladden had long regarded as "the most attractive of the New England cities," was one of the most important centers in western Massachusetts. Its population—over 31,000 in 1875—exceeded that of any city in the five western counties of the state, with the exception of Worcester, which had nearly 50,000. Almost one-third of Hampden County's inhabitants resided in Springfield. Large towns like Chicopee, Holyoke, and Northampton clustered around it, and Hartford, the capital of Connecticut, was only half an hour away by train.[31]

Much of Springfield's influence was due to the *Springfield Republican,* the oldest daily paper in the state outside of Boston. Samuel Bowles's view of journalism as a sacred trust affected the whole tone of the paper; and the thoroughness with which a staff of part-time correspondents covered regional news created, according to Gladden, "a community of interest and feeling" among its readers. With the *Republican's* columns always open to him, and with its unflagging support of civic and religious progress, Gladden found his normal pastoral influence significantly enhanced. By the time he came to Springfield, Gladden had known Bowles for almost twenty years.[32]

The North Congregational Church presented Gladden with the brightest prospects he had yet encountered in his ministerial career. Organized in 1846 as an offshoot of the First Congregational Church, it was firmly established by 1875. Josiah G. Holland, Gladden's friend and literary adviser, had left the South Congregational

[30] Gladden, *Recollections,* pp. 239–40; Committees for the North Congregational Church and Society to Gladden, January 2, 1875, First Church archives; *Springfield Republican,* January 5, February 20, 1875.

[31] Gladden, *Recollections,* pp. 240–42; *Springfield Republican,* September 27, 1875.

[32] Alfred Minot Copeland, ed., *A History of Hampden County* (3 vols.; Century Memorial Publishing Co., 1902), I, 425–28; Gladden, *Recollections,* pp. 242–43. When Bowles died in 1878, Gladden was chosen to read Scripture and deliver a prayer at the memorial service in the Unitarian church. Gladden, *Recollections,* pp. 248; George S. Merriam, *The Life and Times of Samuel Bowles* (2 vols.; New York: Century Co., 1885), II, 441.

Church to lend his support in the church's early days.[33] Two years before Gladden's arrival, Henry H. Richardson, the famous revivalist of Romanesque architecture, had designed a magnificent edifice that cost over $53,000.[34] The congregation included several leading merchants and was generally composed of people of comfortable means. Gladden's appeal to his congregation during the depression of the 1870's to provide work for the unemployed indicates that his parishioners were not among the needy. Toward the end of his pastorate the church included the mayor, sheriff, president of the city council, and chairman of the Republican city committee.[35]

Congregationalism enjoyed primacy among the denominations The *Springfield Republican* referred simply to "First Church" or "North Church," without adding the sectarian appellation considered necessary for the other churches. The six Congregational churches outnumbered those of any other denomination. The First Church, with 675 members in 1877, was the second largest of all Congregational churches in Massachusetts. Next in eminence came the South Church, whose venerable pastor had by 1877 served it for thirty years. Though not so prestigious as the First or South churches, the North Church was a vigorous institution. Springfield even had a Negro Congregational church, albeit its fortunes fluctuated widely.[36] Except for the Presbyterians, the other principal denominations were well represented. St. Paul's Universalist Church and the Church of the Unity (Unitarian) contained dissenters from Congregational orthodoxy; and Baptist, Methodist, Episcopal, Adventist, Swedenborgian, and Spiritualist churches provided further diversity. There were several Roman Catholic churches, at least two of which had

---

[33] *Springfield Republican*, October 15, 1881. In 1881 Gladden participated in two memorial services for Holland, preaching at one and reading a poem at the other. *Congregationalist*, LXVI (October 19, 1881), 338. The poem, "Hail and Farewell," appeared in the *Century*, XXIII (December, 1881), 307.

[34] Gladden, *Recollections*, p. 240; Copeland, *Hampden County*, II, 287–88; H. Paul Douglass, *The Springfield Church Survey: A Study of Organized Religion with Its Social Background* (New York: George H. Doran Co., 1926), p. 57.

[35] Gladden, *Recollections*, p. 250; *Springfield Republican*, December 10, 1881.

[36] *Springfield Republican*, March 16, April 26, June 22, 1877.

French-Canadian constituencies.[37] One of Gladden's richest contacts
with his brother clergy came through the Connecticut Valley Theological Club, which in 1875 was about ten years old. The club met
one day each month at Springfield's Massasoit House to hear and discuss assigned papers. It practiced complete freedom of expression,
even on controversial questions.[38]

Under Gladden's leadership the North Church quickly solidified
its energies and made substantial gains. He introduced the parish
organization with which he had experimented in North Adams: six
district committees visited church members and newcomers and dis-
tributed aid to needy parish members and, when possible, non-mem-
bers.[39] A women's benevolent society, over which Mrs. Gladden
presided for at least one year, raised funds for philanthropic purposes.[40] Gladden worked strenuously to reduce a building debt of
$37,000, even voluntarily reducing his own salary in 1877 from $3,500
to $3,000.[41] By 1878 the debt was down to $27,000, but Gladden was
never able to erase it completely.[42] Believing that the church must
be accessible to all social classes, he induced the parish to abolish
its pew-rental system and experiment with free seats and weekly
offerings.[43] Membership grew steadily: under 350 at the beginning
of 1876, it reached 454 by the end of 1880.[44] On at least two occasions the church was redecorated and improved during summer
vacations. Gladden enlarged the choir, originally only a quartet, so
it could better lead congregational worship.[45]

[37] *Ibid.*, February 11, 1875. The rector of Christ Church (Episcopal) was a
brother of Boston's Phillips Brooks, and may have introduced him to Gladden.
Ibid., April 6, 1882.

[38] Gladden, *Recollections*, p. 272; *Springfield Republican*, January 27, 1875,
February 11, 1876.

[39] *Springfield Republican*, January 3, June 21, 1878.

[40] *Ibid.*, October 9, 1879.

[41] *Ibid.*, January 18, 1877.

[42] *Ibid.*, July 12, 1875, December 11, 1878.

[43] *Ibid.*, December 19, 1877.

[44] *Ibid.*, December 27, 1876, December 22, 1880.

[45] *Ibid.*, September 4, 1875, September 3, 1879.

Having made lecture series a regular and successful feature of church life in Morrisania, Gladden arranged similar instructional courses for the North Church. The topics were more often literary or historical than religious, although frequently the lecturers were clergymen. The titles of one series included "The Battle of Balaklava," "New England Characteristics," and one by Gladden, "Good Gold." Gladden's college friend, S. G. W. Benjamin, appeared during a later series, and Gladden delivered "Our Best Society," which, since its first presentation in North Adams, had stirred numerous audiences.[46]

Though always in a religious context, Gladden's own sermons often held considerable value as entertainment. On special occasions he read original stories, designed especially for children but usually popular with adults. In "A Christmas Dinner with the Man in the Moon" three children traveled on the Meteor, a space machine propelled by paddles through the earth's atmosphere and then by electric currents to the moon, and enjoyed the hospitality of the lunar people.[47] "Tom Noble's Christmas" and "An Angel Unawares" were entirely fictional,[48] while "The Shepherd's Story" was an embellishment of the biblical record of the Nativity.[49] A "Friendly Talk with the Boys of Springfield," which emphasized discipline and hard work as means of success, was so popular that Gladden repeated it by request to a crowd of twelve hundred at Springfield's Music Hall. A similar talk to girls followed it, and both reached a wider audience through the *St. Nicholas* magazine.[50]

Although theological dispute punctuated Gladden's years in

[46] *Ibid.*, March 7, 1876, January 16, 1877.

[47] Gladden collected this and other stories told repeatedly to groups of children in *Santa Claus on a Lark and Other Christmas Stories* (New York: Century Co., 1890), pp. 27–49; *Springfield Republican*, December 23, 1879.

[48] Washington Gladden, "Tom Noble's Christmas," *Sunday Afternoon*, I (January, 1878), 71–77; *Springfield Republican*, December 24, 1880.

[49] *Springfield Republican*, December 24, 1881; included in Phebe A. Curtiss, compiler, *Christmas Stories and Legends* (Indianapolis: Meigs Publishing Co., 1916, revised and enlarged, 1952), pp. 36–44.

[50] A. P. Stone, Charles R. Ladd, *et al.* to Gladden, October 18, 1879, Gladden Papers; *Springfield Republican*, October 27, 1879, February 9, 1880.

Springfield, his ministry had an auspicious beginning and, at least
in his own church, a peaceful course. The ecclesiastical council
called to instal him accepted the assumption of its moderator that
"one of such experience and success was 'all right'" and conducted
only a cursory theological examination.[51] His sermons dealt with a
variety of religious questions and at times drew the attention of
his congregation to social and political problems. They were attempts to make religion simple but relevant to the experiences of
daily life, and their contents reveal that, in his assessment of contemporary issues, Gladden was clearly in the vanguard of the clergy.

While he was with the *Independent,* editorial duties had completely absorbed Gladden's literary energies. But once back in the
parish ministry, he was able to prepare his best sermons for publication. Of the five volumes that he wrote in Springfield, two dealt with
elementary aspects of the Christian life, one was a meditation on the
Lord's Prayer, one was a theological treatise on the atonement, and
the final work examined the current industrial situation. Discussion
of the last three volumes is reserved for later chapters.

Being a Christian: What It Means and How to Begin, his first
book written in Springfield, grew out of a series of sermons that he
preached early in 1876 during union Congregational revival services.
In it he attempted to sweep common obstacles from the path of those
"contemplating the religious life." His own childhood accounted for
much of the book's distinctive emphasis. And his words must have
reflected the experience of many others, for, with only one exception,
Being a Christian had larger circulation than any of the other books
that he wrote before 1909.[52]

In answering the question framed in the first chapter, "What Is It
To Be A Christian?", Gladden delineated three incorrect approaches
to Christianity: the "ritualist" defined its forms but failed to touch its

[51] *Springfield Republican,* September 22, 1875.

[52] *Ibid.,* January 15, February 5, 1876; Gladden, *Recollections,* pp. 257–58;
Washington Gladden, *Being a Christian: What It Means and How to Begin*
(Boston: Congregational Publishing Society, 1876), p. 1. *Being a Christian* was
one of several books that marked a renaissance in the management of the Congregational Publishing Society. *Springfield Republican,* April 27, 1876.

substance; the "dogmatist" put prime value on correct views of salvation; and the "sentimentalist" trusted "certain delightful feelings of peace and joy and love." None of them touched the vital necessity of personal surrender to Christ's direction and service; none grasped what was for Gladden the heart of religion, its effect on character. Fidelity to trusts, honesty in business, control of the temper, charity —these were among the important concerns of the Christian. To become a Christian, one need not go through any "elaborate and mysterious mental process"; there was "no ordeal to pass through . . . no mysterious process of initiation . . . no oracle to visit . . . no arcanum to discover." "Becoming a Christian is just beginning to be a Christian You become a Christian by choosing the Christian life, and beginning immediately to do the duties which belong to it."[53] Following Bushnell, whose *Christian Nurture* was a watershed in theological discussions of conversion, Gladden attempted to make conversion a natural and rational experience and, indirectly, to minimize the churches' dependence on traditional revivalism.

When Howard Crosby, a prominent Presbyterian minister, read *Being a Christian*, he contrasted its simplicity with more intricate theological analyses of Christian experience and undoubtedly touched the spirit in which Gladden had written the book:

> When I read such a book, I cry "Blessed be God! we are getting out of metaphysics into the Bible!" Christianity is looking up. Men are finding out that God did not need Calvin to piece out his work.[54]

A clergyman in Fall River, Massachusetts, suggested that Gladden write a sequel to *Being a Christian* that would elaborate the ideal development of character subsequent to choice of the Christian life.[55] Whether or not Gladden had intended originally to write a companion volume, he published in 1877 *The Christian Way: Whither It Leads and How to Go On.* Starting with the aspects of the Christian's life that were obviously religious, such as prayer,

[53] Gladden, *Being a Christian*, pp. 9–10, 21, 51, 61–62.
[54] Howard Crosby to Gladden, April 15, 1876, Gladden Papers.
[55] William W. Adams to Gladden, October 13, 1876, Gladden Papers.

Bible study, and church work, Gladden then devoted two highly significant chapters to spheres of activity that many considered wholly secular. A rejection of the distinction between the sacred and the secular was inherent in his application of Christian morality to the whole of life.

In "The Christian in Business" and "The Christian in Society" Gladden called for behavior governed by the ideals of holiness and benevolence, ideals that represented respectively personal religion and its social implications. It was not enough for the Christian in the business world to speak to his customers about religion; he must "shine forth as a light" in truthfulness, be faithful and prompt in his dealings, strive to overcome the "abominable trickeries by which the trade of the world is infested," and prove the genuineness of his religion by "making his business always subordinate and tributary" to it. Recognizing the peculiar ethical challenges of the Gilded Age, Gladden declared, "this realm of mammon, with its selfish maxims and its sordid tendencies and its fierce competitions, is now the stronghold of the world's evil. . . ."[56]

The Christian's obligations to society included safeguarding of the community's health and morals, improvement of popular intelligence through libraries, reading rooms, lectures, and study groups, beautification of homes, streets, and public buildings, and Christianization of recreations and amusements. And into the "fierce and brutal strife" of the political arena the Christian should carry fairness and intelligence.[57] This idea that Christianity must permeate every area of human endeavor was the germ of the Social Gospel. That it should appear in a manual on "how to go on" in the Christian life is indicative of Gladden's early conviction that social problems could be solved by the personal conduct of regenerated individuals.

But Gladden's literary output, despite the responsibilities of administering a large parish, did not stop with the publication of sermons. He wrote occasionally for religious papers, chiefly the *In-*

[56] Washington Gladden, *The Christian Way: Whither It Leads and How to Go On* (New York: Dodd, Mead & Co., 1877), pp. 88, 92–94, 96, 98, 101, 103.
[57] *Ibid.*, pp. 106–12, 119.

dependent. He contributed articles to *Scribner's Monthly*—renamed the *Century* in 1881—on political partisanship, Italian Protestantism, and divorce; and just before leaving Springfield, he began preparation of a serial story on church federation for the same periodical.[58]

Beginning in 1878, he also edited a monthly, published by Edward F. Merriam of Springfield, that was designed to furnish family reading for Sundays. Originally called *Sunday Afternoon: A Magazine for the Household*, it was renamed *Good Company* in 1879. At first, Gladden performed all of the managerial and editorial tasks involved in its publication; but from 1879 until the magazine's demise in September 1881, he wrote only the editorials. In order to perform his editorial work with minimal neglect of his parish, he had to curtail other activities, particularly his occasional lecturing.[59]

Financial weakness seems to have threatened the magazine early in its career, and Merriam may have relieved Gladden of the managerial work to save money. At any rate, Gladden and Merriam did not work well together, and, when in 1880 Merriam heard that Gladden hoped to begin a new publication over which he would have exclusive control, he suggested that Gladden sever his ties with *Good Company* at once. It is unclear when Gladden finally ended his work for the magazine, but, since there were virtually no editorials during 1881, he probably terminated his relationship long before Merriam's failing health resulted in the magazine's total collapse in September, 1881.[60]

[58] *Springfield Republican*, June 23, 1877; Washington Gladden, "To Bolt or Not to Bolt," *Scribner's Monthly*, XX (October, 1880), 906–13, "Protestantism in Italy," XXI (March, 1881), 681–88, "The Increase of Divorce," *Century*, XXIII (January, 1882), 411–20; Richard W. Gilder to Gladden, May 6, 1882, Smith to Gladden, October 25, 27, November 1, 20, 1882, Gladden Papers.

[59] Gladden, *Recollections*, pp. 272–73; *Springfield Republican*, December 28, 1877, May 15, 1878, January 29, 1879. Edward F. Merriam was a son of George Merriam, one of the founders of the G. and C. Merriam Company, the encyclopedia publishers. *Springfield Republican*, June 23, 1880.

[60] Edward F. Merriam to Gladden, January 2, 1879, March 10, 1880, Gladden Papers. Gladden's enigmatic discussion of *Good Company's* fate in *Recollections*, pp. 273–74, offers no explanation of his relations with Merriam or of the circumstances of his own withdrawal.

While it lasted, however, *Sunday Afternoon* offered excellent editorials on current affairs and social questions and brought to its
readers the work of distinguished authors. The first issue carried the
promise that "questions of practical philanthropy" would receive
greatest attention. It would consider such matters as:

> How to mix Christianity with human affairs; how to bring salvation to
> the people that need it most; how to make peace between the employer
> and the workman; how to help the poor without pauperizing them; how
> to remove the curse of drunkenness; how to get the Church into closer
> relations with the people to whom Christ preached the gospel; how to
> keep our religion from degenerating into art, or evaporating into ecstasy,
> or stiffening into dogmatism, and to make it a regenerating force in human
> society. . . . [61]

Among the writers of contemporary renown who contributed stories,
poems, and articles, the names of Lyman Abbott, John Bascom,
Edward Bellamy, Charles Loring Brace, Rebecca Harding Davis,
Edward Eggleston, Edward Everett Hale, Harriet Beecher Stowe,
William Graham Sumner, and Charles Dudley Warner were most
distinguished. Undoubtedly, Gladden's earlier work for the *Independent* served him well in this brave venture, in terms both of
acquaintance with eminent writers and of familiarity with the whole
spectrum of editorial and publishing techniques.

Throughout his years in Springfield Gladden played a large role
in the life of the city, particularly its religious life. He addressed several meetings of the Hampden County Congregational Association,
participated in local ecclesiastical councils, and preached at Congregational festivals and union services. The Young Men's Christian
Association procured his services for one of a series of popular fund-
raising entertainments.[62]

[61] *Sunday Afternoon: A Magazine for the Household,* I (January, 1878), 85.
The historian of the Social Gospel cites *Sunday Afternoon* as one of the signs
of "the birth of Social Christianity." Charles H. Hopkins, *The Rise of the
Social Gospel in American Protestantism, 1865–1915* (New Haven: Yale University Press, 1940), p. 37.

[62] *Springfield Republican,* April 29, May 29, June 18, November 16, December 8, 1875; February 9, 24, April 19, 1876; October 26, 1880; November 2,
1881.

Through his appearances and writings during these years, he achieved the first measure of a fame that was to become increasingly widespread. During two summer vacations he preached in one of the citadels of Congregationalism in Chicago, the Union Park Church. Cornell University's officers twice invited him to preach in their chapel, and Amherst College engaged him to deliver a commencement address. He was a runner-up in balloting by Williams alumni for their member of the college's board of trustees. But perhaps the capstone of his rising fortunes, at least for Gladden, was receipt of the LL.D. degree from the University of Wisconsin in 1881.[63] It is likely that John Bascom, the university's president and Gladden's teacher and friend, promoted Gladden's candidacy.

Gladden's strenuous round of activities brought satisfying recognition, but it also left him "worn and jaded." A hard worker with lofty ambitions, he pushed himself to the limits of mental and physical endurance. Successful in literature, happy in a locale where he was known and respected, and confident of the full support of his congregation, he nonetheless felt by 1882 the need for a change. He even contemplated leaving the ministry.[64]

When "one blue Monday morning" a letter arrived from the First Congregational Church in Columbus, Ohio, inquiring whether he would consider a call to its pastorate, he was more than eager to examine this fresh possibility. Francis C. Sessions, a former resident of Springfield who had moved to Columbus many years earlier and was one of the pillars in the First Church, was evidently responsible for the invitation. While still holding the letter in his hand, Gladden received a telegram announcing the imminent arrival in Springfield of Roswell Smith, the publisher of the *Century*. Smith had lived for several years in the Midwest and urged Gladden to accept. In a later letter Smith repeated his advice: "Every man ought to go to the west & live there a few years of his life. . . . You would tower up there,

---

[63] *Ibid.*, August 2, 1875, July 21, 1877, June 21, 1878, June 30, 1879; William Russel to Gladden, April 14, 1878, Andrew D. White to Gladden, October 18, 1881, John Bascom to Gladden, June 11, 1881, Gladden Papers.

[64] Smith to Gladden, [October 2, 1882,] Gladden Papers.

head and shoulders above other men, in influence." His counsel
weighed heavily with Gladden, who later commented: "He was
then my most trusted friend and counselor . . . and his very positive advice had more to do with my decision than almost any other
influence."[65]

The congregation in Columbus, which was reported to be familiar
with Gladden's writings, voted unanimously to call him; and Gladden, despite the "unfeigned sorrow" of his flock in Springfield, felt
once again the challenge of a "larger opportunity" and turned his
face westward.[66] Columbus was to be his home, not for the few
years of experience that Smith anticipated, but for the remaining
thirty-six years of his life.

[65] Gladden, *Recollections,* pp. 282–83; Smith to Gladden, [October 2, 1882,]
Gladden Papers; Gladden, "Roswell Smith," Sermon, April 24, 1892, Gladden
Papers.

[66] Committee of the Congregational Society, Columbus, Ohio, to Gladden,
November 2, 1882; Committees for the North Congregational Church and
Society to Gladden, November 20, 1882, Gladden Papers.

Four

The Parish Ministry in Columbus

The First Congregational Church of Columbus was not unmindful of its opportunities or of Gladden's potentialities. With its edifice located directly across Broad Street from the state capitol, it had unusual advantages for ministry beyond the limits of its own congregation. The church had already distinguished itself by its courageous posture on social questions. Though flourishing in the Western Reserve of northern Ohio, Congregationalism had not been strong in the central and southern parts of the state, where settlers from the South outnumbered those from New England.[1] As in Gladden's home in western New York, the Plan of Union had operated to the further disadvantage of Congregationalism. Columbus had had Protestant Episcopal, Roman Catholic, Methodist (including native white, German, and Negro bodies), Presbyterian, Lutheran, Universalist, Welsh Congregational, and Baptist churches before it had an English-speaking Congregational society.[2]

It was their antislavery and radical temperance sentiment, coupled with distaste for the Calvinism of the Presbyterian churches with which they had affiliated, that led Central Ohioans of Congregational background to organize their own churches. The Second Presbyte-

[1] Mathews, *Expansion of New England*, pp. 178–82.

[2] Jacob H. Studer, *Columbus, Ohio: Its History, Resources, and Progress* (Columbus: Privately printed, 1873), pp. 175–213.

rian Church of Columbus was formed in 1839 by members of the
First Presbyterian Church with Congregational proclivities. Though
adopting congregational polity, they retained the Presbyterian name
at the urging of Lyman Beecher, who came from Lane Seminary in
Cincinnati to assist in their organization. Finally, in 1852, several
families left to form the Third Presbyterian Church, which in 1856
became the First Congregational Church. The antislavery sentiment
of the Congregational society evoked hostility from a large segment
of the community, but the church grew, particularly during several
long pastorates in the 1860's and 1870's, to a membership by 1882
of almost five hundred.[3]

Without a pastor since May, 1882, the church worked strenuously
to win a favorable decision from Gladden. In an initial telegram to
Springfield it offered a salary of $3,500 and a parsonage near Capitol
Square. A week later, Gladden was in Columbus to meet an over-
flow crowd in the church's lecture room. He impressed people by his
"quiet energy and strength in reserve," but his statements were
guarded. Though his hesitance changed to acceptance within another week, his decision was not precipitate; a committee from the
church had visited Springfield to confer with him at least two months
earlier, and negotiations had been in progress since then. In his resignation to the North Church of Springfield, Gladden noted Columbus' advantages as a political and philanthropic center and the
ample facilities and united spirit of his new congregation.[4]

Columbus welcomed him enthusiastically. The leading paper heralded a new era in the thought of the western city and printed the
full text of his first sermon, delivered on Christmas Sunday. A great
crowd filled the church's social parlors to greet his family. His early
sermons drew audiences too large for the sanctuary, and after chairs
were placed in the aisles even standing space was at a premium.

[3] Alfred E. Lee, *History of the City of Columbus: Capital of Ohio* (2 vols.;
New York: Munsell & Co., 1892), I, 830–36; Records of the First Congregational
Church for 1870–89, March 22, 1882, First Church archives.

[4] *Ohio State Journal*, November 2, 9, 16, 24, 1882; Records of the First
Congregational Church for 1852–83, September 1, 1882, First Church archives.

Accustomed to slow starts, Gladden attributed his immediate outward success to curiosity.[5]

His formal installation in March, 1883, brought some of Ohio's most eminent Congregationalists to Columbus, including pastors from Oberlin, Cleveland, Toledo, and Cincinnati. Josiah Strong, then on the threshold of his pioneer work in the Social Gospel, came from Sandusky, and he and Gladden became warm friends. Evidently at Gladden's request, John Bascom came as a delegate from the First Congregational Church of Madison, Wisconsin, and preached the installation sermon.[6]

The length of Gladden's work in Columbus and the wealth of information on the church's life provide unusual scope for a study of a progressive pastor and congregation in action. Continuity of leadership for over thirty years, a rarity in any local church, prevented the distractions that often attend pastoral changes in churches with congregational polity. By identifying pastor and church to an extraordinary degree, the long pastorate solidified the church's program and message and strengthened its position as a leader of religious and moral forces. Furthermore, as Gladden himself realized, prolonged tenure increased the pastor's ability to understand and serve his flock. He often baptized children whose parents he had baptized a generation earlier. Their problems, needs, and abilities he knew from long experience.[7] But dangers might follow, as well. Solidity could become stolidity. Strong leadership could harden into unwillingness to pass the reins to other, more capable, hands. The congregation might focus its allegiance on the pastor rather than on its independent organic life. Under Gladden's democratic ministry these dangers were minimized, but the tendency for him to become an

[5] *Ohio State Journal,* November 16, December 25, 1882, January 3, 8, 22, 1883; *Congregationalist,* LXVIII (February 1, 1883), 39; Gladden to Mrs. Annie E. Duckworth, January 16, 1883, First Church archives.

[6] Washington Gladden, "Josiah Strong," *Congregationalist,* CI (May 11, 1916), 627; "Installation of Rev. Washington Gladden, D.D.," *Congregationalist,* LXVIII (March 29, 1883), 111; Records of the First Congregational Church for 1852–83, March 22, 1883, First Church archives.

[7] Edward J. Converse Diaries, January 14, 1907, Gladden Papers.

institution was nevertheless strong. On the whole, however, the advantages probably outweighed the disadvantages. Noting the effects of a long pastorate on a community, President William Oxley Thompson of the Ohio State University said, with special reference to Gladden:

> The preacher of the decades is not the occasional orator, the passing evangelist or the man of brilliant though often shallow attainments, but the man of high ideals, of patient industry, of laborious days whose persistent determination will not allow the main issue to be clouded or neglected by passing attractions.[8]

Although Gladden's reputation stems from his participation in national reform movements and from his widely read books, he considered himself first and foremost a pastor. It was in preaching to his congregation that he first propounded the theological, social, and political views that spread ultimately from coast to coast. When, writing his autobiography, he surveyed the vocational alternatives that he had faced periodically, he submerged the memory of past uneasiness in the ministry and emphasized the freedom of speech and the satisfactions of pastoral relationships that had been his. His last published volume, *The Interpreter*, stressed the need for the interpretation of truth and duty to individuals and to social groups, a function performed pre-eminently by the Christian pastor. Contemporary pen portraits accurately assessed his preaching as the central, unifying force in his career.[9]

It is impossible, of course, to penetrate the informal relations between Gladden and his congregation, though they occupied much of his time and put heavy demands on his physical and emotional

---

[8] Remarks by William Oxley Thompson at Gladden's twenty-fifth anniversary in Columbus, December 29, 1907, Record Group 3/e, Office of the President, William Oxley Thompson (1899–1926), Box AA 6-6-16, Item 29 (Ohio State University Archives, Columbus).

[9] Gladden, *Recollections*, pp. 415–16; Washington Gladden, *The Interpreter* (Boston: Pilgrim Press, 1918), pp. 15–17; John Wright Buckham, *Progressive Religious Thought in America: A Survey of the Enlarging Pilgrim Faith* (Boston: Houghton Mifflin Co., 1919), pp. 217, 241; "Washington Gladden," *Outlook*, LXXXII (January 27, 1906), 154.

strength. He preferred the title "pastor," which suggested "a close and sacred friendship between the shepherd and his flock," to more formal address.[10] "Close and sacred" the friendship might be, but the pastor, a servant of Christ as well as of the earthly congregation, could never compromise his message by unseemly intimacy or frivolity. This consideration, buttressed by Gladden's personal reserve and by the demands of his varied responsibilities, seems to have limited his private intercourse to a handful of parishioners. He attempted to visit each family once a year, a considerable project for a large parish; but as he grew old, even this personal contact ended. Some families, particularly several living in his own neighborhood, to coljoal more frequent calls.[11]

He was neither distant nor aloof, but one did not approach him with trivial matters. Genial, warm, a lover of children, he nonetheless appeared shy.[12] His relations with most parishioners were formal; his presence called for good behavior. He lived his vocation so completely that times of abandon or intimate self-revelation were rare. On Sunday-school picnics he would gradually remove his Prince Albert, vest, and cravat and socialize in galluses,[13] but he was not prone to remove the symbolic cloak that covered his inner life.

A sparkling sense of humor, often ironic, endeared him to many and probably saved him from deadening sobriety. In his preaching and writing an ingenious turn of phrase frequently enlivened an otherwise heavy argument; mimicry and caricature were strong weapons in his arsenal, and he aimed them with telling skill at what he considered ignorance and superstition. His humor appears in many of the anecdotes told by those who knew him well. When introduced as "Dr. Gladden" to a gentleman who naïvely asked,

[10] Washington Gladden, *The Christian Pastor and the Working Church* (Edinburgh: T. & T. Clark, 1898), p. 51.

[11] Interview with Kenneth L. Sater, May 21, 1963; interviews with Mrs. William Starin, April 25, May 8, 1963; interview with Mrs. Frederick Shedd, May 14, 1963.

[12] Interview with Mrs. William Lloyd Evans, April 24, 1963; Wilbur A. Siebert, "A Reminiscence," *First Church News*, VI (February, 1936), 10.

[13] Interview with Kenneth L. Sater, May 21, 1963.

"Where do you practice?" Gladden retorted quickly, "Oh, I don't practice. I just preach."[14]

Gladden did preach, as over fifteen hundred extant manuscript sermons testify.[15] He regarded preaching and teaching as one function, and this function as primordial, the justification and glory of the ministry:

> The minister's throne is his pulpit; when he abdicates that, to become an organizer of charities, or a purveyor of amusements, or a gossip in parlors and street-cars, the clerical profession will cease to hold the place which belongs to it in the respect of men.[16]

It was a prophetic function, including both encouragement and reproof.[17] To interpret wisely not only the spiritual life but also the currents of the contemporary world, the pastor must be a student of broad knowledge. Gladden attempted first to assimilate the major writings of his own day, and to a lesser extent those of past ages. His personal library once consisted of about two thousand volumes. The bulk of his reading was in philosophy, religion, history, and the social sciences.[18] According to John Wright Buckham, a writer on religious philosophy and a friend of Gladden's, it was possible to identify the most significant contemporary books by noting those on which Gladden commented.[19]

He tried to avoid both the type of devotional preaching that would make him "a bad kind of sentimentalist" and the teaching without evangelism that would make him merely a "critic or . . . essay-

[14] Interviews with Mrs. William Starin, April 25, May 8, 1963.

[15] Many of these sermons receive attention in subsequent chapters on major phases of Gladden's thought.

[16] Gladden, *Christian Pastor,* p. 107.

[17] *Ibid.,* pp. 69–70.

[18] In the early 1930's, when the First Church moved from its historic edifice, some of the library was given to interested individuals, but a large part went to a junk dealer. A small segment is preserved at the First Church as the Washington Gladden Library. Carl Wittke to Irving Maurer, July 31, 1933, First Church archives; Frederic W. Heimberger to author, December 28, 1964.

[19] Buckham, *Progressive Religious Thought,* p. 229.

ist."[20] He marshaled facts convincingly because of his own scholarly bent and because the intelligence of his audience demanded rational argumentation. One story, though not set in Columbus, illustrates his concern for accuracy. After a zealous anti-Mormon lecturer stirred an audience with the statement that the winding sheets of those murdered by the Mormons would cover New England, if laid side by side, Gladden calculated that exactly 12,692,644,200, more than ten times the earth's current population, would have had to be victims.[21]

Gladden did his scholarly work amid the clatter and confusion of downtown Columbus. His study in the tower of the church lit only by twelve branches and multiple mirrors through dining dog area windows, and filled with heavy fumes from a coal grate, gave the impression of "rugged mental strength." His sermons and book manuscripts in a safe by the door, hymnals, Bibles, and volumes of poetry on the desk and his library scattered around the room, pictures of Bushnell and his other heroes on the walls, a telephone, but no typewriter—it was an appropriate sanctum for the quiet occupant whose freedom from hurry and anxiety impressed visitors.[22]

He carried this serenity into the pulpit, his "throne," which he left only when he heard the call of duty elsewhere. After an hour of meditation in his study, designed to "awaken the mind and quicken the pulses of the heart,"[23] he entered the auditorium to begin the worship service that he normally led without assistance. With calm dignity, enhanced by his rich beard and conservative dress, he laid aside the limp case that held his handwritten manuscript, opened the Bible on the pulpit to the reading for the day, offered an opening prayer, and announced the first hymn. He always collaborated with his organist and choir to assure the presentation of music that would

[20] Gladden, *Christian Pastor*, pp. 83–84.

[21] "Washington Gladden: One Hundred Years," *First Church News*, VI (February, 1936), 13–14.

[22] Irving Maurer, "Glimpses of Washington Gladden," Address delivered in 1930–31, First Church archives.

[23] Gladden, *Christian Pastor*, p. 135.

supplement, not distract from, worship, and for at least one year
trained the choir himself.[24] He told stories or anecdotes rarely, used
few gestures, and generally avoided theatrical effects.[25] His sermons, which he read in unaffected baritone timbre, were so packed
with quotations, literary allusions, and closely-knit discourse that
only rapt attention enabled listeners to follow the ramifications of
his thought. Even when "the banked fires of indignation or noble
affirmation broke through," Gladden retained his composure.[26]

Reactions to his sermons varied. Exceptionally moving sermons
might set the congregation to foot-stamping, which created rever-
berations in the air chamber beneath the ascending floor.[27] Those
who occasionally disagreed did so in silence, recognizing that they
had a great preacher.[28] The First Church attracted all types of visitors to downtown Columbus. Commercial travelers, known then as
"drummers," found Gladden's services, especially those on Sunday
evenings, both accessible to their hotels and stimulating.[29]

Gladden grouped his sermons in two major categories. Sometime
before 1882, he began to preach about private religious experience
on Sunday mornings and about social questions on Sunday evenings.

[24] Some of Columbus' leading musicians, including Oley Speaks, composer
of "The Road to Mandalay" and other popular songs, provided the First Church
with the best in the choral and instrumental repertoires for church. Mrs. Abram
Brown, "The Music of the Church," *The Golden Jubilee of the First Congregational Church, Columbus, Ohio, 1852–1902* (Columbus, Ohio: Privately printed,
1902), pp. 111–15.

[25] Gladden once denounced Dr. James Parker of London's City Temple (Congregational) as a "sensationalist of the worst type and the most colossal egotist
in the world." Parker had used profanity in the pulpit. *Ohio State Journal*,
April 29, 1899.

[26] *Ibid.*, March 6, 1898; interview with Kenneth L. Sater, May 21, 1963;
interviews with Mrs. William Starin, April 25, May 8, 1963; Gaius Glenn
Atkins, *Religion in Our Times* (New York: Round Table Press, 1932), p. 49.

[27] Interview with Dr. and Mrs. Robert Sigafoos, May 6, 1963.

[28] Interview with Kenneth L. Sater, May 21, 1963.

[29] The Gladden Papers contain numerous testimonies from occasional visitors
of all denominations and of no denomination who left the First Church morally
braced and intellectually challenged. For one commercial traveler, Gladden's
sermons were one of the brightest features of trips to Columbus. *Ohio State
Journal*, October 11, 1908.

Since the church existed not to rescue individuals from a sinful world and prepare them for heaven but to herald and assist the transformation of earthly society into the Kingdom of God, its vision must extend beyond the spiritual needs of the individual Christian to the challenges and progress of that Kingdom. The message of the Kingdom was two-pronged: to the individual it gave assurance of God's love and taught truths vital to Christian experience; to society it proclaimed a law of love, righteousness, and justice that would bring corporate redemption.

The problems of the soul with which Gladden dealt in his morning sermons related, fundamentally, to the development of character There could be no spirituality apart from morality, and cultivation of distinctively religious traits was meaningless unless they improved character.[30] Whether on theological issues, the spiritual exercises of prayer, Bible reading, and church attendance, or basic religious commitment, his sermons appealed to his hearers to become better men and women. His message was practical and moralistic, and only rarely abstract or philosophical.

The call to decision rang through Gladden's sermons on the Christian life with a strong evangelical tone. Presuming that conversion was an intelligent act rather than an emotional or psychological upheaval, he appealed to reason, conscience, and affection. The most crucial decision that men must make was whether or not they would accept divine forgiveness and submit to divine influence. To refuse the friendship of Christ was to flaunt reason; the results would be inner discord, disproportion of personality, and, after repeated rejection of Christ, ultimate insensitivity of spirit. The heavy weight of a guilty conscience, distrust, and fear toward God would vanish when sinners accepted the forgiveness and friendship that God had revealed through the Incarnation.[31]

[30] Gladden, "Morality and Spirituality," Sermon, January 24, 1897, Gladden Papers.

[31] Gladden, Sermons, "The Burden of Sin," March 14, 1888; "The Insanity of Impiety," March 19, 1888; "Zaccheus," March 25, 1888; "Forgiveness before Repentance," April 10, 1889; "The Lost Soul," April 15, 1889; "The Lament over Jerusalem," May 27, 1890, Gladden Papers.

To supplement his Sunday-morning appeals for conversion, Gladden began in 1884 an annual Lenten program through which his congregation redoubled its efforts to win the unchurched. Running for two or three weeks before Easter, the series usually included full-scale evening services on Monday, Wednesday, and Friday, vesper services on Tuesday and Thursday, and, at least as early as 1891, daily noon meetings for men. Eventually he instituted Friday Lenten readings from such poets as William Vaughn Moody, Rabindranath Tagore, and John Masefield. While these readings were not strictly evangelistic, they did, however, illustrate the sublimity of the spiritual life from a broad spectrum of experience.[32] Often, he arranged his Lenten evangelistic sermons in series: in one on "Manhood" he dealt on successive days with justice, responsibility, truth, bravery, sympathy, and faithfulness, while in a later series he depicted Jesus visiting the churches, homes, businesses, and social gatherings of Columbus.[33] On one occasion he relinquished his pulpit to Lyman Abbott, the editor of the *Outlook* and a prominent social gospeler, who gave a Lenten series on elementary truths of the Christian religion.[34] Gladden urged church membership upon converts early in their religious experience, and the Lenten services brought large accessions to the church each year.[35]

Gladden's regular devotional sermons were messages of challenge and encouragement. The challenge consisted of an explicitly spiritual interpretation of life that contested the primacy of the materialistic values of an acquisitive society and of a call to sacrificial service. Gladden frequently assumed the attitude of a stern father who had

[32] *Ohio State Journal,* March 22, 1884, April 3, 1886, February 14, 1891, March 18, 1893, February 18, 1899; *Congregationalist,* LXXI (April 8, 1886), 119, LXXVIII (April 20, 1893), 633; Announcement of "Devotional Readings from the Poets," n.d., Gladden Papers.

[33] *Ohio State Journal,* March 23, 1907; Gladden, Sermons, March 17–21, 1913, Gladden Papers.

[34] *Ohio State Journal,* January 30, 1905; Gladden, "Finally, brethren," Sermon, April 30, 1905, Gladden Papers.

[35] Gladden, Sermon, February 26, 1894, Gladden Papers; *Congregationalist,* LXXV (March 6, 1890), 81.

to reprove his children's waywardness. But the encouraging assurance of divine help for the sincere, if frail, Christian mellowed his admonitions.

Gladden was careful to combat complacency. Lest his parishioners rest contentedly in the hope of salvation, he declared that there were no "saved" people but only those who, in pursuit of "a complete, symmetrical, perfect character," were "being saved." Christianity was not a contractual possession but a way of life that they must cultivate assiduously. Although they were being saved by faith, that faith would not be thrust upon them; they must "open the door" to divine influences. They must endure a period of conflict between their higher and lower natures before they would enjoy the freedom of Christ.[36] But though there was inner struggle, they might be sure of salvation if the higher nature prevailed:

> If a man can say with assurance, "I am standing for what is best in myself," then he will welcome and cherish every good wish . . . then he will not be inclined to palliate the mean things that he does, but will hate and disavow them, as unworthy of the man that he knows he means to be.[37]

When Gladden summoned every man "to have a clear understanding with himself as to what the keynote of his life is," he was emphasizing a conscious commitment to Christian ideals that critics of liberal theology have often overlooked.[38]

The moral code to which Christians must adhere was, in Gladden's view, not a legalistic fetish but a practical, broad discipline of mind and spirit. It required intelligence, subordination to the divine will, and consecration, the last a virtue in which Gladden felt his generation of Christians to be deficient.[39] It prohibited such subtle

[36] Gladden, Sermons, "Saving Souls," February 11, 1912; "By Grace Are Ye Saved," February 24, 1889; "Three Stages in the Soul's Progress," October 7, 1888, Gladden Papers.

[37] Gladden, Sermon, February, 1891, Gladden Papers.

[38] Gladden, Sermon, March 26, 1893, Gladden Papers.

[39] Gladden, "The Good Soldier of Jesus Christ," Sermon, June 30, 1889, Gladden Papers.

evils as falsehood, intolerance, avarice, indolence, and excessive pleasure-seeking.[40]

A large proportion of sermons dealt with the singular temptations associated with material acquisition. Godliness, he asserted, precluded pursuit of wealth for its own sake.[41] He gently warned,

> There are some of you, dearly beloved, of whom I cannot help thinking, who are getting far less of solid good out of life than I could wish. You may be prospering in business . . . but your souls are not prospering, I fear.[42]

He criticized lavish expenditures on personal pleasure and urged greater attention to immaterial values. Comparing the immortality of Vergil's poetry with the decay of Augustus' temples, he concluded that "the only enduring realities are those of mind and spirit." The same theme emerged from a discussion of high society, which, he lamented, exalted "that which is outward and material above that which is inward and spiritual."[43]

The fulcrum of Gladden's message was love. God drew men into His Kingdom and into friendship with each other by love.

> Love for the Father God . . . such a love as keeps us submissive and obedient to the divine will whenever we clearly discover it; love for our fellow men . . . such a love as makes us willing to deny ourselves for their welfare and happiness; purity, truthfulness, sincerity of life, these are spiritual things, in contradistinction from that which is selfish and worldly and carnal.[44]

Love for God and love for man could not exist independently in their

---

[40] Gladden, Sermons, "Hidden Faults," January 24, 1886; "Fidelis Minimis," June, 1886; "The Waste of Life," October, 1886; "The Life more than Meat," February, 1888; "The Miser's Creed," January 10, 1897; "The Voluptuary's Creed," January 24, 1897, Gladden Papers.

[41] Washington Gladden, *Myrrh and Cassia: Two Discourses to Young Men and Women* (Columbus, Ohio: A. H. Smythe, 1883), pp. 4, 23; Gladden, "Godliness with Contentment," Sermon, September 14, 1879, Gladden Papers.

[42] Gladden, Sermon, March 22, 1893, Gladden Papers.

[43] Gladden, Sermons, 1890; 1895; November 13, 1898, Gladden Papers.

[44] Gladden, Sermon, November 1, 1891, Gladden Papers.

fullness: love for God—personal faith—must work itself out in service, and love for man—charity—must throb with the "pulse of the heart of the all-Father." Although the ideal Christian life would not be free of suffering, altruism would in the long run be easier than selfishness: "Love is the element in which the soul was made to live; and in any other element it gasps and struggles and suffers."[45]

Gladden's morning sermons were thoughtful, well-written discourses on conventional aspects of religious life. They normally took their direction from a biblical text, and they often narrated stories found in the Bible. Such series as "Scenes in the Life of Paul" and "Bad Men of the Bible and Their Modern Counterparts" were typical.[46] A strong believer in the literary value of sermons, Gladden tried to build his own sermonic literature. He delivered most of his devotional sermons several times; some, first given in the 1860's, were repeated as late as the 1910's, though often with substantial revision. His publication of individual sermons and of collections was another aspect of this attempt to give his work permanence.

Less conventional and certainly more influential in establishing his reputation, his evening sermons ranged over an almost limitless variety of topics. If not limited by topic, they were clearly defined in approach, for Gladden insisted that the minister's concern was with the ethical implications of economics, sociology, politics, and literature—that is, with the application of Christian teaching and the discernment of moral progress. The discernment of progress became a major part of his role as interpreter, as well as an apologetical device. An impartial, thorough study of history and society, based on the presumption of human freedom, would "show that Christianity has never yet been fairly tried anywhere in the world . . . ," but that "partial trials . . . prove it to be the only social rule that will

[45] Gladden, Sermons, April 12, 1891; "The Call of the Cross," April 17, 1908; March 14, 1897, Gladden Papers.

[46] *Ohio State Journal,* September 21, 1889; Gladden, Sermons, "Cain, the Murderer," "Jacob, the Supplanter," "Saul, the Hypochondriac," "Absalom, the Rebel," "Herod, the Monster," and "Judas, the Traitor," January 5–March 2, 1902, Gladden Papers.

bring peace and good-will, with happiness and plenty."[47] Against
frequent criticisms of "secularization of the pulpit," Gladden replied
that manner of treatment, rather than subject matter, profaned the
sacred desk.[48] He advocated revision of seminary curricula to enable
graduates to treat social topics intelligently.

From the first, Gladden announced his evening sermon topics
in the local press. Many of the sermons appeared in the Monday
papers, which from the 1890's on gave considerable space to extensive reports. In 1912 one paper began to print them under the boxed
heading, "Dr. Gladden's Sermon."[49] Gladden provided his audiences
in Columbus with far saner commentary in public affairs than they
often received from other local sources. Sometimes, he surveyed
events in the religious world, such as the work of the Salvation
Army, the proceedings of a recent national Congregational council,
and the growth of Christian Science.[50] He reviewed political developments, economic trends, social conditions in Europe, famine in India,
and the San Francisco earthquake—the list could go on indefinitely.

Because he believed that human progress demonstrated the truth
of Christianity, Gladden preached frequently on historical subjects.
Probably influenced by Carlyle's view of the central role of great
men in history, he concentrated on biographical studies in which he
eulogized the courage or vision of important figures in religion, science, politics, or literature. He generally attributed their shortcomings to the historical circumstances that conditioned them. In an
appreciative sermon on John Milton, for example, Gladden noted his
outmoded cosmology and theology but concluded that, "standing
where he stood, with such light as he had, it was the best he could
see." Gladden braced himself for a similar evaluation of John Calvin,

[47] Gladden, *Christian Pastor*, p. 102.

[48] *Ibid.*, p. 123; *Ohio State Journal*, April 19, 1894.

[49] *Ohio State Journal*, February 12, 1912. A parishioner, Mrs. Abram Brown,
supplied the *Ohio State Journal* with abstracts for about ten years before her
death in 1910. *Ibid.*, November 2, 1910.

[50] Gladden, Sermons, January 4, 1891; October 1, 1899; August 4, 1901,
Gladden Papers.

but the justification seems pale beside his denunciation of the execution of Michael Servetus: " . . . I abhor it, above every other crime of history."[51]

The lives of contemporaries proved more fertile ground for the cultivation of the type of biography that appealed to Gladden, since, in his view, "God's heart is better known to the men of these times than it could have been to the best of those [earlier] times."[52] Henry Ward Beecher, Henry George, John Ruskin, and the English Christian Socialists, Frederick D. Maurice, Charles Kingsley, and Thomas Hughes, were just a few among the dozens whose lives and contributions Gladden sketched for the edification of his listeners.[53] A series that included "The Hero as Statesman—Charles Sumner," "The Hero as Millionaire—George Peabody," and "The Hero as Missionary—David Livingstone" revealed the complimentary character of these studies.[54]

Gladden also believed that literature furnished exemplary models of hope and idealism. The poets, especially, resisting the erosive effects of materialistic philosophy, conserved the soil in which faith could flourish.[55] Gladden was selective, however, in his readings from, and sermons on, poesy. Browning and Tennyson were his favorites, and he more regularly substantiated his statements of faith with quotations from their writings than with philosophical or theological arguments. The intuitive assurances that Browning and Tennyson found for belief in God appealed to Gladden, who dis-

[51] Gladden, Sermons, "John Milton as Poet," December 20, 1908; "John Calvin," June 15, 1890, Gladden Papers.

[52] Gladden, "True Knight of God," Sermon, December 5, 1909, Gladden Papers.

[53] *Ohio State Journal*, March 12, 1887; Gladden, Sermons, "Henry George," November 7, 1897, "John Ruskin," January 28, 1900, "Frederick Denison Maurice," January 15, 1888, "Charles Kingsley," January 22, 1888, "Thomas Hughes," March 28, 1896, Gladden Papers.

[54] *Ohio State Journal*, June 1, 29, July 13, 1889.

[55] [Washington Gladden,] "Materialism in Literature," *Sunday Afternoon*, II (July, 1878), 88–90; Gladden, "The Outlook for Poetry," Sermon, May 27, 1900, Gladden Papers.

trusted logic and found induction a cold and inadequate guide for the human heart.[56]

But literature need not be cheering to claim Gladden's attention. He based sermons on such realistic social studies and novels as Edward Bellamy's *Looking Backward* (1888), William Booth's *Darkest England and the Way Out* (1890), Jacob Riis's *How the Other Half Lives* (1890), David Graham Phillips' *The Reign of Gilt* (1905), Upton Sinclair's *The Jungle* (1906), and Jack London's *The Iron Heel* (1907). But he always rejected pessimistic views of society's future, even when admitting the darkest facts about current conditions. Interestingly enough, another prominent Congregationalist, Newell Dwight Hillis of Brooklyn's Plymouth Church, came under attack in 1899 for basing sermons on novels just as Gladden was concluding a series, "Sermons in Novels."[57]

Gladden's evening sermons had strong appeal to the community at large and particularly to men. Several series of sermons dealt with the relationship of men to the churches.[58] Noting their predominance in his evening congregations during all his years in Columbus, Gladden attributed disinterest in religion among men to the churches' failure to meet their basic needs and wants. This predominance, a reversal of the usual male-female ratio in any morning congregation, provided him with a dramatic answer to those who argued that men wanted the "simple Gospel," not a meddling in practical affairs.[59] It was on Sunday evenings that he offered the latter. Gladden's evening congregations fluctuated more widely than those in the morning, but they averaged a healthy three-quarters of the morning attendance in a day when maintenance of an evening service perplexed many preachers. But, apart from the inversion of the male-

[56] Gladden, Sermons, November 28, 1897; March 24, 1901; "Tennyson's Ancient Sage," January 10, 1904; May 21, 1911, Gladden Papers.

[57] *Ohio State Journal,* June 7, 1899.

[58] *Ibid.,* February 11, 18, 25, March 3, 10, 1888, March 6, 11, 1893; Gladden, "Men and Religion," Sermon, September 24, 1911, Gladden Papers.

[59] *Ohio State Journal,* November 10, 1884, March 1, 1909; Gladden, "Why Do Not Men Attend Church?", Sermon, June 12, 1904, Gladden Papers.

female ratio, there was another difference in the constituency of the evening audience. By Gladden's own estimate, not more than one-third of the morning congregation also attended the evening service.[60] The fact that the majority of his own socially conservative parishioners did not regularly attend the evening service, when Gladden "took wings," has been used to explain the absolute freedom with which he was able to espouse progressive and sometimes unpopular causes.[61] But, in view of the wide circulation that his views had, especially in the local press, this theory does not seem to be totally adequate. More likely, Gladden's ability to speak plainly, but with "no sting of malignity," or ax-grinding, minimized hostility [62]

All of Gladden's preaching presupposed belief in the Kingdom of God as present in the world, encompassing and invading every facet of human life. This did not lead him, however, to minimize the institutional life of the church, though some on the extreme left of the Social Gospel, most notably George D. Herron, the first professor of Applied Christianity at Iowa College (Grinnell), argued that, since religion was to permeate all other institutions, the church need not exist independently.[63] Gladden justified the church as an association to promote the religious ideas and impulses that would transform society and compared its relation to society to that of the brain to the body. "The body is not all brain, but the brain is the seat of thought and feeling and emotion." Gladden carried the physical analogy a step further to elucidate the crux of his view of the church: "The life and health of the brain are found only in ministering to the whole body." When the church became "a snug little ecclesiasticism with interests of its own, and a cultus all its own, and standards and sentiments of its own . . . ," it proved itself "dead and accursed . . . a bane and a blight to all the society in which it stands."[64] In

---

[60] Gladden, "Pastor's Report for 1900," January 16, 1901, Gladden Papers.

[61] Maurer, "Glimpses of Washington Gladden," First Church archives.

[62] *Ohio State Journal,* February 14, 1906.

[63] Clara M. Smertenko, "George Davis Herron," *Dictionary of American Biography,* VIII, 594–95.

[64] Gladden, *Christian Pastor,* pp. 40–45, 103.

his books on pastoral theology, *Parish Problems* (1887) and *The Christian Pastor and the Working Church* (1898), and throughout his leadership of local congregations, Gladden endeavored to adjust religious work to this conception of the church's relationship to the Kingdom of God.

Parish Problems: Hints and Helps for the People of the Churches was, as its title indicates, a handbook on practical means of successful religious work. Based on a well-intentioned but poor manuscript by Margaret Woods Lawrence, and with contributed sections by Austin Abbott and others, all of which Gladden edited, the book was of mixed quality. Gladden undertook the project for Roswell Smith, for whom he did considerable anonymous writing during the early 1880's. In March, 1885, Smith warned Gladden not to divulge the rate of pay he received for his contributions to the *Century,* since he was its most valuable writer and deserved what he got. Gladden began to work on *Parish Problems* in 1883, but it was not ready for publication until 1887.[65] When he wrote Phillips Brooks for his opinion of the book, Brooks replied that such attention to machinery and method would not help any "thoroughly vital man." Unabashed by this rebuff, Gladden acknowledged his indebtedness to Brooks, a man of inspiration who would not need a practical manual that might be helpful to others.[66]

The Christian Pastor and the Working Church, which had wide use as a text in theological seminaries, was specifically written to bring pastoral theology into step with an enlarged conception of

[65] Smith to Gladden, January 13, 19, April 23, 1883, January 5, 18, March 3, June 4, October 30, December 31, 1884, January 9, March 6, 1885, Gladden Papers; Smith to Gladden, October 29, November 14, 1885, March 29, 1886, First Church archives; Gilder to Gladden, December 27, 1883, Gladden Papers; Gladden to Gilder, July 16, 1886, *Century* Collection (Manuscript Division, New York Public Library), on microfilm in Gladden Papers; Washington Gladden, ed., *Parish Problems: Hints and Helps for the People of the Churches* (New York: Century Co., 1887). Letters to or from Gladden in the *Century* Collection are on microfilm in the Gladden Papers and are hereafter designated simply as contents of the *Century* Collection.

[66] Raymond W. Albright, *Focus on Infinity: A Life of Phillips Brooks* (New York: Macmillan Co., 1961), p. 321.

Christian work.[67] Classical works on the subject placed the pastor in the role of spiritual leader of the Christian flock; he would preach, teach, and serve the congregation. But Gladden viewed the church as "an army of occupation" rather than as "an Ark of Safety." It must be a "working church," and the pastor must accept as his "largest and most difficult" task the "enlisting and directing [of] the activities of his people."[68] The church's attention would shift from what the pastor did for it to what it was doing for itself and for others. But the pastor would remain the key figure in the recruitment, supervision, and stimulation of lay workers.

The increasingly close relations that members must have with each other if they were to realize the ideal of the "working church" required, in Gladden's view, a serious reconstruction of parish social structure. For the good of the members themselves, as well as for an effective witness to the community, the local church should be "an epitome of the universal church."[69] Distinctions between "rich and poor, strong and weak, coarse and fine, fast and slow," could not be obliterated, but they must not obstruct harmony and brotherhood. There were weaknesses in Gladden's view of the local church as a microcosm of the universal church. Such diversity in unity would not always be possible if, as he also maintained, the church was to be a neighborhood institution. Even a downtown church, which somewhat transcended the geographic and social limitations of other churches, would find it virtually impossible to achieve catholicity. This was certainly true of Gladden's own congregation, despite his imprecations against class-oriented churches. He was aware of these difficulties. But he felt that the churches were not always to blame. Dismissing them as institutions for the rich and well-bred, working people often created obstacles between themselves and

[67] Seminaries as diverse as Oberlin and Southern Baptist used it. P. E. Lowe to Gladden, October 14, 1901; G. Walter Fiske to Gladden, January 15, 1914, Gladden Papers.

[68] Gladden, *Christian Pastor*, pp. 9–10, 416. For a review of literature on pastoral theology at the time of Gladden's writing, see *ibid.*, pp. 11–22.

[69] *Ibid.*, p. 275.

churches that were willing to accept them as equals.[70]

Although only a thorough classification of the members and friends of the First Church would justify a conclusive generalization, it appears that Gladden's parishioners were for the most part people of education or means.[71] Though perhaps not an exclusive church, it tended to have that reputation. At least, positions of leadership or prominence fell to those of wealth or culture. Faculty and students from the Ohio State University and from the city's medical colleges formed a large contingent. In 1902, for example, 32 of the Ohio State University's 130 faculty members were parishioners or regular attendants. President Thompson found in visiting alumni around the country that they would ask first about leading professors and then about Gladden. It was often Gladden's benign and broad humanity that attracted teachers and students. Such was the case with the distinguished historian, Arthur M. Schlesinger, who, though neither a Congregationalist nor an evangelical Protestant, attended the First Church frequently while a student at the university from 1906 to 1910.[72] Among the many public-school teachers who attended were two successive principals of the Central High School. At one time or another directors of the state's Deaf and Dumb Asylum, Imbecile Asylum, and Blind Asylum were members. Doctors, lawyers, and judges came in large numbers. Eight out of nineteen presidents of the Columbus Board of Trade before 1902 attended or were mem-

[70] *Ibid.*, pp. 29–32, 37.

[71] For a membership that grew from about five hundred to well over a thousand—and these figures do not account for losses by death or dismission—such a study would be a large undertaking. Gladden's own testimony, however, supports this generalization. He wrote in 1905: "Our Congregational churches are not, as a rule, the churches of the common people. My own church is not, and it is a grief and a shame to me that it is not." Washington Gladden, *The New Idolatry* (New York: McClure, Phillips & Co., 1905), p. 140.

[72] Josiah R. Smith, "The Church as a Factor in the Intellectual Life of the City," *Golden Jubilee*, p. 101; remarks by Thompson at Gladden's twenty-fifth anniversary, Record Group 3/e, Office of the President, William Oxley Thompson (1899–1926), Box AA 6-6-16, Item 29 (Ohio State University Archives); Arthur M. Schlesinger, *In Retrospect: The History of a Historian* (New York: Harcourt, Brace & World, Inc., 1963), p. 27.

bers of the church, and eighteen directors of the board were members. Gladden himself was an active member of the board. Several of the most successful capitalists of the city heard Gladden's preaching of the Social Gospel week by week. Some were bankers, others controlled a considerable part of the mines and railroads of southern Ohio, one owned the largest mining equipment company in the country, while not a few were owners or directors of other industries. The notorious Samuel B. Hartman, founder of the Peruna patent-medicine empire of Columbus, was a member of the church.[73] Gladden's relations with so many educational, business, and philanthropic leaders undoubtedly magnified his influence in local affairs.

But it is also clear that, whatever their abilities and resources, such men could give only limited attention to the work of the church. It was not until after the birth of a Congregational Brotherhood in 1907 that Gladden was able to enlist appreciable numbers of men in church activities. He did succeed, nevertheless, in launching the church into new channels of opportunity, as well as in producing an unbroken record of growth. Many church programs reflected the interests and tastes of polite society. The Literary and Social Club, organized by Gladden's predecessor, featured papers on literary and musical subjects and became one of the most prominent clubs in Columbus; Gladden read a paper on Dante at one meeting and sang occasional baritone solos at others. Reorganized in 1887 as the Monday Club, it expanded its scope to include government, political philosophy, and history.[74] The church's program of religious education also had a sophisticated intellectual tone. Professor S. C. Derby of the Ohio State University's Greek department taught a Sunday-school class that used the Greek New Testament for a text. Professors George W. Knight and W. H. Siebert of the same insti-

---

[73] This partial sketch of the First Church's constituency is based on a survey of the *Ohio State Journal* for the years 1883–1918 and on directories of the First Church for 1886, 1891, and 1895.

[74] *Ohio State Journal*, May 15, 1886, May 14, 1887; *Clubana; A Collection of Essays Read before the Literary and Social Club of the First Congregational Church, Columbus* (Columbus, Ohio: A. H. Smythe, 1885).

tution's history department offered Sunday-school courses in church history.[75]

The church extended its intellectual life to the general public through varied educational programs. It offered individual popular entertainments by such diverse lecturers as James Whitcomb Riley and John Fiske. Late in the 1890's, Gladden organized an annual "Citizens' Lecture Course" that emphasized current political and social questions. Speakers of the caliber of Henry Demarest Lloyd, Edward Everett Hale, Lyman Abbott, William Dean Howells, Norman Hapgood, editor of *Collier's Weekly,* and Rabbi Stephen S. Wise of New York's Free Synagogue gave a lustre to the First Church with which no other church in Columbus could compare.[76]

In addition, the church frequently served as a community center because of its spacious auditorium and convenient location. The baccalaureate services of the Ohio State University occurred there regularly during the 1880's,[77] and often civic groups or state and national conventions met in the First Church and invited Gladden to address them.[78] The Ohio State University presented a series of historical lectures by Hermann E. von Holst, Albert Bushnell Hart, and Herbert B. Adams in conjunction with the church.[79] On at least one occasion a civic concert held in the church attracted an assemblage of "ultra society people" in full evening dress, Governor Joseph B Foraker among them.[80]

There were abundant signs of material growth in the church's transition from its modest position in 1882 to its later role as a major urban institution. Gladden's annual reports to the congregation which the secular and religious papers often publicized, indicate regular increases in membership, substantial financial growth, and

[75] *Ohio State Journal,* September 28, 1889, November 4, 1893.

[76] *Ibid.,* February 9, 1886, February 24, 1892, October 19, 1898, November 23, 1899.

[77] *Ibid.,* June 16, 1884, June 21, 1886, June 18, 1887.

[78] *Ibid.,* February 12, 1885, January 7, 1886.

[79] *Ibid.,* January 13, 1895.

[80] *Ibid.,* May 31, 1887.

progressive diversification of parish activities.

The largest net increase in membership occurred during the first ten years of his pastorate. Slightly under five hundred in 1883, it grew by March 3, 1885, to 558, by December 31, 1888, to 727, and by the end of 1892 to nearly 900. Shortly before the completion of his twentieth year in Columbus, Gladden reported that 1,101 members had been received during his pastorate, but that, because of deaths and dismissions, the current membership stood at 920. Frequent revision of the rolls meant that figures for total membership fairly represented the active membership. By 1914, when Gladden became Pastor Emeritus, the membership was 1,014.[81] By carefully pruning "dead" names from membership lists and by colonizing members in other Congregational churches, Gladden kept his expanding congregation from far exceeding the one-thousand mark, which he felt was the natural limit of a "working church."[82] The regularly large percentage who became members by profession of faith, rather than by transfer of membership from other churches, indicates that an effective program of religious education channeled the church's youth into membership, or that, partly through Gladden's Lenten evangelistic preaching, significant numbers of the unchurched were drawn in, or both.[83] The First Church became under Gladden's leadership one of the largest Congregational churches in Ohio. The First Church in Oberlin, the First Church in Akron, and the Euclid Avenue Church in Cleveland normally exceeded it in numbers, but usually by less than one hundred each.[84]

The financial contributions received by the church showed similar but not proportionate growth. The ratio of benevolent offerings

---

[81] Gladden, Pastor's report for 1892, December 18, 1892, Gladden Papers; Washington Gladden, "The Historical Discourse," *Golden Jubilee,* p. 32; William E. Jones, "Dr. Gladden and First Church," *First Church News,* II (February, 1929), 5.

[82] Gladden, *Christian Pastor,* pp. 24–25.

[83] Of 546 new members during Gladden's first nine years, 310 were by profession of faith. Lee, *History of Columbus,* I, 837–38.

[84] *Congregationalist,* LXXXVI (April 20, 1901), 632; LXXXIX (March 19, 1904), 415.

to giving for home expenses presented a nagging problem to Gladden, and he experimented with several schemes to increase the
former. For the fiscal year ending March 31, 1885, benevolences
totaled $3,906.07 and home expenses, $6,669.83. By the end of
1907, benevolences were $5,605.00 and home expenses, $11,152.37.[85]
The proportion varied, but benevolences usually fell below Gladden's expectations. After one year of particularly paltry giving, he
lamented the lack of interest in the denominational agencies for
which a large part of the benevolent offerings was earmarked:

> I hope that nobody, away from home, is going to ask me how much our
> church has given last year for the great causes in which, as a denomina-
> tion, we are interested. I shall diligently stay away from places at which
> such questions are likely to be asked.[86]

That Congregationalists elsewhere, examining their yearbooks, did
wonder about the First Church's generosity to causes beyond its
doors appears certain.[87] But, as Gladden often explained, contributions to Congregational agencies were not the whole of the First
Church's charitable offerings; often far more reached the coffers
of local organizations and other Congregational churches in Columbus than was recorded in denominational reports.

Among the luxuries the First Church allowed itself, a complete
remodeling of its edifice in 1886 was designed to increase its capacity
for service to the community. In projecting his hopes for the reno-
vated structure, Gladden asked for amplitude and comfort, not ele-
gance or ostentation. It must be a church for the people, not one to
make men of modest means uncomfortable. Nevertheless, Gladden
did not think it "seemly that those who themselves dwell in palaces
should offer to the Lord a barn for his sanctuary," and the new
brownstone façade and simple but rich interior eventually cost well

---

[85] *Ibid.*, LXXX (January 24, 1895), 140; Records of the First Congregational
Church for 1870–89, April 21, 1885, First Church archives; Records of the First
Congregational Church for 1898–1913, First Church archives.

[86] Gladden, Pastor's report for 1898, January, 1899, Gladden Papers.

[87] Amos J. Bailey to Gladden, September 25, 1911, Gladden Papers.

over $30,000.[88] Instead of relocating, the church continued to renovate its old structure. Indeed, Gladden made it quite plain that, despite disadvantages inherent in inner-city work, especially as members who had once lived downtown scattered to the suburbs, the church of his dreams would always be on Capitol Square.[89]

The diversification implicit in the idea of the "working church" led the First Church into two significant community projects. Gladden inspired both projects in an effort to increase the church's ties to the community in which he insisted it must minister. They were the church's major conscious efforts to relate itself to the unchurched and largely poor classes clustered near the downtown area. Though not an institutional church in the fullest sense of the word, the First Church adopted many features characteristic of such classic institutional churches as St. George's (Episcopal) in New York and the Baptist Temple in Philadelphia.[90]

The first endeavor, the Sunday-afternoon Bethel school, grew out of a sermon that Gladden preached in March, 1889. Dissatisfied with the church's attempts to reach the neglected, he proposed canvassing the region just north of the church for recruits for a new Sunday school. The sixty parishioners who responded to Gladden's call for workers met a favorable response in the neighborhood. The Sunday school opened on March 17, under the supervision of Walter A. Mahony, a prominent realtor, banker, and businessman, with over two hundred scholars. There were 223 the second Sunday, including many adults. By the fifth week attendance reached 335, while attendance at the morning school declined noticeably. During the

---

[88] Gladden, "Farewell to the Old Church," Sermon, July 25, 1886, Gladden Papers; Gladden, *Christian Pastor*, p. 26; *Congregationalist*, LXXII (December 29, 1887), 461.

[89] *Ohio State Journal*, September 12, 1898; Gladden, Sermons, "Division," May 18, 1902, May 28, 1905, Gladden Papers; Gladden, Pastor's report for 1908, January 13, 1909, First Church archives.

[90] Aaron I. Abell, *The Urban Impact on American Protestantism, 1865–1900* Cambridge: Harvard University Press, 1943), p. 137, points out that many urban churches adopted some institutional features, though never providing the extensive social and recreational facilities that distinguished the more famous experiments.

first year, enrollment rose to 413; the largest attendance was 362, and the school averaged a healthy 239. As an inducement to attendance, Bibles and illustrated storybooks were awarded for certain numbers of attendance tickets.[91]

Attendance was never again as high as during this first year, but the work continued until at least 1913.[92] Average attendance in 1894, for example, was only 165, and between 1898 and 1906 it sank from 109 to 65. During its brave but uneven career, the Bethel school was far more than a typical Sunday school. For two years the First Church employed Miss May Case as a city missionary to work with the Bethel school's families; and when her efforts ended, Gladden organized a corps of friendly visitors from among the women of the church, each of about forty women having responsibility for one family. In addition to Sunday meetings and visitation, the Bethel school provided a Junior Guild and sewing school, both of which met weekly, and, for a while, biweekly popular entertainments with music, lantern pictures, readings, and lectures. Some families were drawn into the church, but their numbers and permanence are unclear.[93]

The demise of the Bethel school is difficult to explain because of scanty records. Though Gladden rejoiced in the opportunity for his parishioners, in the spirit of *noblesse oblige*, to establish not patronage by "lords and ladies bountiful" but friendship with the poor, the church does not appear to have assimilated the school's constituency on a permanent basis. Rumor had it, at least, that the church oper-

[91] Gladden, Sermons, March 3, 1889, "A Prosperous Church," March 10, 1889, Gladden Papers; *Congregationalist,* LXXIV (March 21, 1889), 92, (August 22, 1889), 277, LXXV (January 16, 1890), 21; *Ohio State Journal,* March 23, 30, 1889, March 15, 1890.

[92] In 1913 Gladden's associate, Carl S. Patton, wrote to Gladden concerning the impending end, apparently, of the school's existence. Carl S. Patton to Gladden, July 8, 1913, Gladden Papers.

[93] C. S. Carr, "History of the Bethel," *Golden Jubilee,* p. 61; Records of the First Congregational Church for 1898–1913, First Church archives; Gladden, Sermons, September, 1896, September 25, 1898, Gladden Papers; interview with Dr. and Mrs. Robert Sigafoos, May 6, 1963.

ated two Sunday schools, one for the rich and one for the poor. Whatever his reasons, Gladden himself appears to have opposed merging the church's two Sunday schools.[94] Because of this incongruous relationship, the church undoubtedly found it difficult to maintain heightened interest in the project over a long period of time.

Antagonism between Gladden and Dr. C. S. Carr, the Bethel school's superintendent from 1894 to 1908, as well as between Carr and other members of the congregation, further diminished harmonious support of the school. Carr grew skeptical about the ability of the church, which he felt was excessively concerned with its own self-perpetuation, to reach the unchurched classes in the community. For much of the last eight years of his superintendency the school waned, while questions of policy created misunderstanding and friction. Apparently, Gladden considered Carr's ideas faulty, for in June, 1903, Carr complained of Gladden's lack of confidence in him. When Carr resigned in 1908 he reaffirmed his agreement with Gladden's interpretation of the social teachings of Jesus but rejected Gladden's insistence on subordinating social work to the conventional religious activities of the church.[95]

A new, more daring project that required far greater support than the church had ever given to the Bethel school, and that diverted attention from it, was another factor in the school's decline. This was a full-fledged social settlement, established in 1905 under the auspices of the First Church.

The social settlement movement had occupied Gladden's attention from its inception. During a visit to England, he became acquainted with Warden Samuel Barnett of Toynbee Hall, the oldest of settlements, just three years after its founding. Percy Alden of Mansfield House, a Congregational settlement in London, was a personal

---

[94] Gladden, Sermon, December 5, 1897, Gladden Papers; A. B. Curtiss to Gladden, June 22, 1913, Gladden Papers; *Ohio State Journal,* January 9, 1896.

[95] C. S. Carr to Gladden, January 4, 1900, June 13, 1903, October 15, November 9, 1908, Gladden Papers. Carr continued to appreciate Gladden's exposition of Christian ethics, as he testified in a letter in the *Ohio State Journal,* January 12, 1914.

friend and preached once in the First Church for Gladden.[96] Both of these pioneer settlements were closely related to churches, a fact that gratified Gladden. With American settlements he was equally familiar. Jane Addams of Hull House and Graham Taylor, founder of the Chicago Commons, were his personal friends. He visited both houses and supported the Chicago Commons financially and with contributions to Taylor's publication, the *Commons*.[97] In sermons and published writings he gave frequent and sympathetic attention to the movement.

Gladden called the settlement "one of the most beautiful and noble agencies yet devised for the promotion of the Kingdom of God"; the growth of the movement was "one of the most cheering signs of the coming of that Kingdom." But the dissociation of settlements from the churches did not receive his approval. The work they did belonged properly to the churches, and their very existence was a "bitter and terrible reproach to the churches."[98]

When the first settlement in Columbus was founded in 1898, Gladden, though not prominent in its activities, lent his support in various ways. The First Neighborhood Guild, later named the Godman Guild, took root in "Flytown," a tough, working-class district just northwest of downtown Columbus. The Guild's original name came from a book by Stanton Coit, a native of Columbus and founder of the Neighborhood Guild on New York City's East Side, the first social settlement in America. A large number of its founders were members of the First Church, and the church gave the Guild the use

[96] Gladden, Sermon on Mansfield House, September 30, 1894, Gladden Papers; *Ohio State Journal*, June 1, 1895.

[97] *Congregationalist*, LXXXI (December 17, 1896), 937; Gladden, "The Hero as Citizen: Jane Addams," Sermon, [1901,] Gladden Papers; Jane Addams, *Twenty Years at Hull-House* (New York: Macmillan Co., 1910), p. 109; Graham Taylor to Gladden, January 15, 1901, January 4, November 28, 1905, July 6, 1908, Gladden Papers; Louise C. Wade, *Graham Taylor: Pioneer for Social Justice, 1851–1938* (Chicago: University of Chicago Press, 1964), pp. 127, 155, 161.

[98] Gladden, Sermon, December 5, 1897, Gladden Papers.

of mission facilities it owned in the area.[99]

When it 1905 Mrs. Cordelia Thompson, a member of the First Church who had carried on social work in Columbus for many years, drew Gladden's attention to a depressed neighborhood just west of downtown where she had begun teaching a group of children in a small tenement, he took steps to organize a settlement directly under the auspices of the First Church. With the active participation and financial aid of Mrs. Joseph A. Jeffrey, wife of a leading industrialist, and several other women, the First Church Settlement began in a small rented house on Sandusky Street in "Happy Hollow," a run-down area between the Scioto River and the New York Central tracks. The area was the original site of Franklinton, the forerunner of Columbus, but in 1905, populated largely by native whites from rural areas, it had little historical grandeur.[100]

In 1907 the settlement moved into a "regenerated saloon" a few blocks farther west and took the name West Side Social Center. Though it was excellently located for settlement work, the center's facilities were inadequate: there was no yard for a playground, and almost all activities had to occur in one large room on the first floor, which contained several dreary pictures, a book case partially filled with unattractive volumes, and a few games. This second building was the center's home until after Gladden's death. The center maintained a kindergarten, library and reading room, district nursing service, domestic science classes, music and dramatic clubs, and gymnastic activities. For many years the work was almost entirely in the hands of women of the church, and consequently the center

[99] Jon Alvah Peterson, "The Origins and Development of a Social Settlement: A History of the Godman Guild Association, 1898–1958" (unpublished M.A. thesis, Ohio State University, 1959), pp. 6, 119–20.

[100] *Ohio State Journal,* January 22, 1885, June 21, 1891; Gladden to Mrs. Joseph A. Jeffrey, May 4, 1917, First Church archives; interview with Mrs. William Lloyd Evans, April 24, 1963; Mary Louise Mark and Carl H. Bogart, *Leisure in the Lives of Our Neighbors: Gladden Community House, Columbus, Ohio* (Columbus: Ohio State University School of Social Administration, 1941), p. 3. There are no settlement records for the years here described.

provided very little for the men of the neighborhood.[101]

Despite its humble beginnings, the center, renamed the Gladden Community House in 1920, retained its vitality longer than the Godman Guild and became the most important settlement in Columbus. The Women's Guild of the First Church remained the major contributor of money and workers, but Congregational men took an increasingly active part. Church clubs, the Women's Guild, and interested individuals usually gave more than two thousand dollars annually. The Women's Guild joined other organizations in 1905 to found the Social Settlement Federation of Columbus, an agency in which members of the First Church figured prominently. Mr. and Mrs. J. W. Sleppey, members of the First Church, were residents at the center from 1906 to 1920. They had no special training in settlement work, but they did endeavor to inform themselves in its principles, and they endeared themselves to the people of the neighborhood.[102] When in 1913 the Scioto flooded much of the West Side, the center became a major relief station. At that time Gladden reported that about a thousand people of all ages were "more or less connected with our work." Gifts poured in from all over the country, enabling the center to feed four or five hundred homeless people every day.[103] From 1921 to 1959 Carl H. Bogart, a man with previous experience in social work, served as head resident.

Gladden called the West Side Social Center "the most important enterprise in which this church has ever engaged; it is doing . . . a work in the deepest sense of the word Christian." Founded on the

[101] Gladden to Mrs. Jeffrey, May 4, 1917, First Church archives; *Charities of Columbus: Report of Committee on Charities and Corrections of the Chamber of Commerce* (Columbus, Ohio: Privately printed, 1910), pp. 100–102, 104; Robert A. Woods and Albert J. Kennedy, eds., *Handbook of Settlements* (New York: Charities Publication Committee, 1911), pp. 258–59.

[102] Interview with Carl H. Bogart, Head Resident, 1921–59, Gladden Community House, May 13, 1963; *Charities of Columbus*, p. 101; Gladden, "A New Day for Religion," Sermon, September 18, 1910, Gladden Papers; *Ohio State Journal*, June 17, 1905; Gladden to Taylor, June 6, 1918, First Church archives.

[103] Washington Gladden, "Ohio Flood Experiences," *Congregationalist*, XCVIII (April 10, 1913), 505.

idea that "religion is friendship," it followed closely the lines established by earlier settlements.[104]

Early in his career in Columbus, Gladden discovered the need for assistance in his pastoral labors. The expanding program and rapidly growing membership of the First Church placed heavy demands on him, as did the responsibility for Congregational colonies that the First Church planted elsewhere in the city. Beginning in 1887, the church employed a series of assistants to relieve Gladden of administrative details and to assume the leadership of dependent, daughter churches.[105] Much of the work that Gladden assigned them was merely secretarial. Writing to Gladden in 1888, Roswell Smith expressed the fear that one possible candidate was "too much of a man for what you require." One assistant, Edward J. Converse, spent much of his time in uninspiring routine chores; earlier assistants had been able to preach in the missions, which by Converse's time were all independent. After nine years of tiring service addressing envelopes and filling Christmas candy boxes for the Sunday school, Converse resigned. Although he held Gladden in the highest regard, he was frustrated with "being a little boy and running errands" for $720 per year.[106]

By 1908, a year after Converse's resignation, Gladden was looking for an associate who would assume active leadership of the congregation and undertake a large amount of the preaching.[107] The type of man whom Gladden wanted "to share the oars" with him clearly had to be a man of stature. He never considered elevating Converse or Converse's successor, Charles C. Kelso, but he was sure that any one of the three men who worked with him for the last nine

[104] Gladden, Pastor's report for 1908, January 13, 1909, First Church archives. The Gladden Community House, in 1967 still a thriving institution with extensive modern facilities, ceased to be an organ of the First Church in 1923, but individual members of the congregation have always supported it.

[105] *Congregationalist*, LXXII (November 17, 1887), 398; Records of the First Congregational Church for 1870–89, November 21, 1888, First Church archives.

[106] Smith to Gladden, December 1, 1888, First Church archives; Converse Diaries, December 21–22, 26, 1906, January 14, 1907, Gladden Papers.

[107] *Ohio State Journal*, November 26, 1908.

years of his life would be a worthy successor. Charles E. Burton,
Gladden's associate from 1909 to 1911, came with an established
reputation as a leader of Congregationalists in Minnesota.[108] Carl S.
Patton, whom Gladden had unsuccessfully courted in 1908, came
to Columbus in 1911 from the First Congregational Church of Ann
Arbor, where he had been pastor to James B. Angell, president of
the University of Michigan, and stayed with Gladden until 1917.[109]
In 1914, at his own request, Gladden became Minister Emeritus, at
a reduced salary of $2,500.[110] He did not, however, welcome retire-
ment. His shadow continued to loom over Patton, an impressive
man in his own right. Evidently, not all of Gladden's parishioners
appreciated the change. Writing to Mrs. Jeffrey, Gladden explained
his decision:

> I can't say that I like it either. It costs a pang, of course. But it is best for
> all concerned. The leadership must be Dr. Patton's; and he must have the
> name and the credit of it. It isn't fair to him to put the burden and the
> responsibility on him and leave him in what to many would seem a sub-
> ordinate position.

"I hope to continue to do a great deal of work," Gladden continued;
"I shall preach, probably, about as much as ever. . . . "[111]

Both Burton and Patton possessed remarkable talent, and both
served later as moderators of the national Congregational body.
Irving Maurer, who accepted the pastorate a few months before
Gladden's death, was also a man of stature. Before he came to
Columbus, he had served historic Edwards' Church in Northamp-
ton, Massachusetts, and after his ministry at the First Church he

[108] *Ibid.*, February 13, 1909; Charles E. Burton to Gladden, February 13, 20,
1909, Gladden Papers; *Congregationalist*, XCIV (April 24, 1909), 563.

[109] Patton to Gladden, November 3, 10, December 16, 1908, January 16,
February 5, 28, March 9, 17, October 16, 1911, March 1, July 23, August 16,
1917, Gladden Papers; *Congregationalist*, XCVI (April 29, 1911), supplement.

[110] Gladden, letter of resignation, to First Congregational Church, December
22, 1913, Gladden Papers; *Ohio State Journal*, December 31, 1913; *Congregationalist*, XCIX (January 8, 1914), 50, 67.

[111] Gladden to Mrs. Jeffrey, January 7, 1914, First Church archives.

became president of Beloit College.[112]

Unfortunately, it is impossible to delineate any but the barest details of Gladden's domestic life. In his *Recollections* there are no references to his personal affairs after the Civil War. Apart from an abrupt statement about the date of his marriage, he wrote nothing about his family. Apparently, the Gladdens lived well but simply. Gladden's income was always enough to assure them comfort and security. Gladden was able to afford four trips to Europe, one of them with his wife. In addition, he kept a house in Owego on the banks of the Susquehanna, to which he took his family for part of each summer. Here he wrote many of his sermons for the coming year and, enjoying few things more than driving a good team of horses, reveled in his jaunts to visit old friends in the countryside. Mrs. Gladden found special pleasure in these annual vacations, since her sister, Mrs. Benjamin Loring, the wife of a local judge, lived in Owego. Avoiding unnecessary household chores, the Gladdens regularly took dinner at the town's principal inn. They had household servants in Columbus and were accustomed to freedom from mundane tasks.[113]

Gladden's wife, Jennie, was a cultivated woman, as her letters to her children during a trip to Europe indicate. She strove to complement her "Wash's" career, particularly by serving the church and community unstintingly. As a visitor for the Columbus Female Benevolent Society, the teacher of the mothers' class and leader of the visitors in the Bethel Sunday school, and the president for many years of the Women's Missionary Society of the First Church, she directed her energies primarily to humanitarian causes. At times, the church gave her money to use privately for the poor.[114]

She never neglected her family, however. Though she had a house-

[112] Maurer to Gladden, October 24, November 7, 11, 1917, Gladden Papers; interview with Mrs. William Lloyd Evans, April 24, 1963.

[113] Interview with Mrs. Stanton C. Kelton, May 21, 1966.

[114] *Ohio State Journal,* May 9, 1909; Women's Guild, Emma Brown, president, Mae DeGraff Niven, secretary, to Gladden, May 26, 1909, First Church archives; Records of the First Congregational Church for 1870–89, November 29, 1887, First Church archives.

keeper, Lucy Preston, the wife of Gladden's Negro coachman, John, she supervised many domestic chores herself (one parishioner saw her walking to market the morning before she was to leave for Europe). According to all reports, she was a model pastor's wife. Lauding her "Christlike" sympathy for both rich and poor and her sound judgment, Edward J. Converse testified that he had never known a "more useful one." She was quiet, unpretentious, unassuming.[115] She suffered from arteriosclerosis and was almost totally disabled for four years before her death on May 8, 1909. Gladden wrote to Graham Taylor several years later:

> . . . She lost all power of coherent speech. . . . I could not tell what she was thinking. Happily she seemed to be suffering little pain. But it was good when she was emancipated.[116]

The concurrence of this tragedy with Gladden's composition of his autobiography may help to account for his silence on his domestic life.

Gladden's children had varied fortunes. His first child, Alice (1861–1926), early aspired to teach. While a student at Smith College, she wrote a story about an unhappy teacher who, through the discovery of her class's love for her, found joy in her vocation. After graduating from Smith in 1884, she taught Latin and mathematics in Toledo for two years and then taught history and English at the Central High School in Columbus. When controversy rocked the high school in 1899, she resigned and joined the staff of the Columbus University School. In 1903 she became principal of the Columbus School for Girls, a preparatory school located near the Gladdens' home. In 1904 Gladden tried unsuccessfully to get her a deanship

---

[115] Mrs. O. A. Miller, "Mrs. Washington Gladden," *First Church News*, VI (February, 1936), 5; Converse to Gladden, May 8, 1909, First Church archives; Mr. and Mrs. J. W. Barnett to Gladden, May 11, 1909, George D. Black to Gladden, May 13, 1909, First Church archives; William C. Jones to Gladden, November 23, 1914, Gladden Papers.

[116] *Ohio State Journal*, May 7, 9, 1909; Gladden to Taylor, June 19, 1918, Graham Taylor Papers (Newberry Library, Chicago).

at Oberlin College.[117] A spinster, reticent and dignified, she lived with her parents until they died and was the closest and perhaps the most dedicated of the children to her father.

The second child, Frederick (1863–1919), graduated in 1881 from the high school in Springfield, where he had been an outstanding student, attended Amherst College, and entered the School of Law at Cornell University in 1893. He loved music, sang in a local quartet in Columbus, and became treasurer in 1890 of the Musin Concert Company. In 1899 he married Carrie Cluthé, a girl from Brooklyn, the ceremony occurring in the Plymouth Church, where Gladden's friend Lyman Abbott was pastor. Frederick became a lawyer but was not very successful, for as late as 1915, his father had to lend him money. With his father's assistance, however, he obtained a position in 1916 in the Justice Department.[118]

The son who, apparently, caused Gladden the greatest worry was George (1867–1924), nicknamed "Joe." He attended the Michigan Agricultural College in the 1880's and then entered Cornell in 1886 as an "optional student," one who took courses without intending to complete a four-year degree program. He did not stay at Cornell because, as Gladden put it, he was "young and undisciplined; he made very poor use of his time, and was sent home." Between 1889 and 1891 he worked for a newspaper in Columbus and between 1891 and 1893 for one in Pittsburgh. Resolved to atone for his past, he re-entered Cornell as a special student in the summer of 1893. Gladden wrote to President Jacob G. Schurman, pleading for his

[117] *Springfield Republican*, June 17, 1880; Alice Gladden, "Miss Susan Cook," October 19, 1881, Gladden Papers; John W. Leonard, ed., *Woman's Who's Who of America, 1914–1915* (New York: American Commonwealth Co., 1914), p. 329; Henry C. King to Gladden, March 24, 1904, Gladden Papers. Birth and death dates of Gladden's children are from the Gladden family Bible. Mrs. Charles C. Shoemaker to author, June 15, 1966.

[118] *Springfield Republican*, June 24, 1880, April 19, June 24, 1881; *Ohio State Journal*, January 5, 1885, November 30, 1890, March 8, 1891, October 2, 1892, July 6, 1899; David A. Warren, associate registrar, Cornell University, to author, September 29, 1966; Frederick Gladden to Gladden, October 5, 1915, Woodrow Wilson to Gladden, November 20, 1916, Atlee Pomerene to Gladden, November 24, 1916, Joseph P. Tumulty to Gladden, December 22, 1916, Gladden Papers.

son's readmission as a regular student. Frederick was at Cornell at the time, and Gladden hoped that his sons could be together. Evidently, his request was in vain, for George worked for newspapers in Springfield, Massachusetts, and New York between 1894 and 1901. Thereafter he had a varied career in journalism, working on encyclopedias and yearbooks and writing popular articles and materials on nature, some of them for the Boy Scouts of America. Gladden tried to get positions for him with the *Century* and *Collier's Weekly*. A reclusive person, George never married, and neither his health nor his fortunes were good.[119]

Gladden's second daughter, Helen (1866–90), who went by the nickname "Nell," attended Oberlin College in the early 1880's. In 1886 she married George Twiss, a member of the First Church who had graduated from the Ohio State University in 1885, in a private ceremony at her parents' home in Columbus. The Twisses moved at once to Youngstown, where George had taken a position the previous year as a teacher. In 1890 she died, leaving a young child, Alice Gladden Twiss.[120]

Twiss returned to Columbus to teach chemistry in Central High School and became an officer in the Sunday school of the First Church. He departed again in 1894 for a position in Cleveland, leaving Alice with the Gladdens. A few years later he remarried, but Alice stayed in Columbus to be reared by her maternal grandpar-

[119] David A. Warren to author, September 29, 1966; Gladden to Jacob G. Schurman, September 11, 1893, Jacob G. Schurman Papers (Collection of Regional History and University Archives, Cornell University, Ithaca, New York); *Who Was Who in America, 1897–1942: A Companion Volume to "Who's Who in America"* (Chicago: A. N. Marquis Co., 1942), I, 459; Gladden to Robert U. Johnson, May 14, 1898, *Century* Collection; Gilder to Gladden, January 9, 1902, Richard Lloyd Jones to Gladden, February 23, 1904, George Gladden to Gladden, August 22, 1915, Gladden Papers; Frank Moore Colby to "Dear Sir," January 17, 1907, George Gladden Papers (Ohio Historical Society, Columbus).

[120] Interview with Mrs. Stanton C. Kelton, May 21, 1966; *Ohio State Journal,* March 18, June 24, 1885, March 22, 31, 1886; Records of the First Congregational Church for 1852–86, May 3, 1885, First Church archives; Records of the First Congregational Church for 1870–89, April 16, 1886, First Church archives; Gladden to children, April 11, 1890, First Church archives; *Congregationalist,* LXXV (April 24, 1890), 144.

ents. She became a member of the First Church in 1902. After attending the Columbus School for Girls, presided over by her Aunt Alice, for whom she was named, she went to Western Reserve University and Vassar College, graduating from the latter in 1910. Known as "Baby," she was adored by Gladden and treated protectively. In 1913 she married Stanton Coit Kelton, a member of a prominent family in Columbus and the nephew of Stanton Coit, the pioneer of the settlement house in America. Gladden's interest in Alice, her husband, and their children was unflagging. He visited them at their home in Cambridge when traveling in the East and wrote to Stanton, a law student at Harvard, about his friends there, Josiah Royce and Dean George Hodges. Alice later remembered his "beautiful sympathy and love for various members of his family." Even after his death, he never seemed far away from her—"just around the corner smiling gently, encouraging when there is anything hard to be done, loving always."[121]

For well over thirty years, the First Congregational Church of Columbus loyally followed a man who had none of the personal magnetism or spellbinding oratorical flourish of some of his century's clerical giants. Despite a polity that would surely bring differences to the surface, Gladden could boast that his church never had to enforce majority rule: "A more united and harmonious church than this has been I never knew."[122] Though during his first few years in Columbus, Gladden, partly because of his parishioners' intense Republicanism, thought several times of finding another church or leaving the ministry entirely, after 1890 he was convinced that he could find no more congenial position. There was no pulpit

[121] *Ohio State Journal,* January 7, 1892, April 23, 1893, September 16, 1894; Gladden to family, August 17, 1898, Percy Clarke to Gladden, November 12, 1901, October 27, 1907, July 16, 1909, Marion Clarke to Gladden, July 25, 1901, November 11, 1906, June 1, 1913, Gladden Papers; Records of the First Congregational Church for 1898–1913, January 5, 1902, First Church archives; *Ohio State Journal,* June 6, 1910; Gladden to Alice Twiss, March 6, 1910, Gladden to Alice Kelton, October 20, 1913, June 22, 1917, First Church archives; Gladden to Stanton Kelton, November 23, 1913, Gladden Papers; Alice Kelton to Maurer, January 5, 1931, First Church archives.

[122] Gladden, "Church Unity," Sermon, June 27, 1891, Gladden Papers.

in Christendom, he said at a celebration on his seventieth birthday, that he would have exchanged for that of the First Church.[123] The record is one of uncompromising preaching and solid expansion in an urban setting that challenged the established patterns of religious thought and church life. The story centers around Gladden, and very well it should, for he was the conscience, goad, and inspiration of the church. For about twenty-five years after his death, the church's weekly calendar bore the epigraph, "Here Preached for Over Thirty Years Washington Gladden."

[123] In the early 1880's Gladden revealed his discomfort in Columbus to Roswell Smith, who, though keeping him abreast of pastoral changes and openings in New York and Washington, advised him against leaving the ministry for journalism. Smith to Gladden, March 8, 29, 1881, March 17, December 26, 1885, January 27, March 29, 1886, First Church archives; Smith to Gladden, January 9, 1885, Gladden Papers; *Ohio State Journal,* February 13, 1906; *Congregationalist,* XCI (February 24, 1906), 253–54.

Five

The Broader Fellowship

Washington Gladden was neither parochial nor exclusive in his allegiance to Congregationalism. He cherished hopes of Christian unity long before the ecumenical spirit made its first inroads on denominational competition. But he did value the structure and outlook of Congregationalism, and he devoted much of his career to the promotion of Congregational causes. He frequently interpreted the nature and mission of Congregationalism both to Congregationalists, as a means of deepening their self-understanding and focusing their sense of direction, and to non-Congregationalists, as a means of informing if not proselyting them.

When the Central Ohio Congregational Conference met in Columbus in 1896 to consider its distinctive mission, Gladden gave an address on "Why I Am a Congregationalist." Only a week or so later, he spoke at Marietta on "The Contributions of Congregationalism to Theology" at the one hundredth anniversary of Congregationalism west of the Alleghenies. And when the Congregational Association of Ohio met in Columbus in 1899, he penned a letter to the public on the history and nature of Congregationalism.[1] He attempted to familiarize his own congregation with its traditions. He pressed the duties of congregational polity upon new members and emphasized

---

[1] *Congregationalist,* LXXXI (May 7, 1896), 753; *Ohio State Journal,* May 15, 1896, May 14, 1899.

the non-sacerdotal quality of baptism and communion, which were administered only by clergymen simply for the sake of order. Sermons on Congregational martyrs in the Elizabethan period and on the Leyden Pilgrims reviewed the origins of the denomination. At times, he criticized the Congregational churches for defects in perspective. A firm believer in the ideal of a "free church in a free state," which he felt was the source of America's unrivaled religious vitality, he lamented the theocratic practices of early New England Congregationalists.[2]

Gladden's best summary of the virtues of modern Congregationalism appeared in an address, "The Mission of Congregationalism," before the Central Ohio Congregational Conference. The distinctive contributions that he felt his denomination could make to American religion were: the message that salvation is a matter of character; the principle of equality in the Christian brotherhood, exemplified in a democratic polity; the ideal of the church as a body for all people, regardless of wealth or class; the promotion of education and popular intelligence; and the furtherance of liberty, equal rights, public order and improvement, political purity, and general progress.[3]

In Columbus, a city in which several other evangelical groups considerably outnumbered Congregationalists, Gladden worked strenuously to extend the witness of his denomination. When he came to Columbus in 1882 there were four English-speaking Congregational churches and a Welsh church, with a total of only 739 members. Though organized in 1837 and older than the First Church, the Welsh church was a small body. Gladden encouraged its efforts, and individual members of the First Church made substantial financial contributions, but it suffered both from its linguistic limitations and from the competition of a Welsh Presbyterian congregation.[4] The

[2] Gladden, Sermons, April 29, 1892; March 26, 1893; April 9, 1893; "Whose Are the Fathers," September 9, 1906; May 12, 1889; September 16, 1894, Gladden Papers.

[3] Ohio State Journal, October 29, 1891.

[4] Gladden, Sermon, December 18, 1892, Gladden Papers; Lee, History of Columbus, I, 850–51; Congregationalist, LXXVI (May 21, 1891), 174; Ohio State Journal, December 13, 1890.

three English-speaking churches, excluding the First Church, were small and weak.

The oldest, the High Street Congregational Church, was a decade old when Gladden arrived, but it was not until 1885 that its growth became notable. Gladden encouraged the two young pastors, Casper W. Hiatt and Alexander Milne, who in the late 1880's and the 1890's put the church on its feet. Both were recent seminary graduates, Hiatt of Oberlin and Milne of Yale, and Gladden took a paternal interest in their work. When Hiatt left in 1889, after five successful years of ministry, the High Street congregation, probably on Gladden's recommendation, called Milne without ever seeing or hearing him. Under Milne the church which in 1891 moved from High Street and changed its name to Plymouth, went forward rapidly for the rest of the century. But as late as 1909, the First Church raised money for its benefit.[5]

Though started by Methodists, the North Church was organized in 1874 as a Congregational body because of generous assistance from the First Church. It was failing rapidly when Gladden came to Columbus, and only further liberal aid enabled it in 1887 to call its first resident minister. During the 1890's it became well established under the leadership of another graduate of Oberlin Seminary, J. Porter Milligan, but it continued to receive financial assistance from Gladden and other interested members of the First Church.[6]

The Eastwood Congregational Church, the most independent of the First Church's colonies, began in 1875 as a chapel and Sunday school in a substantial residential community on the east side of the city. But its constituents organized as a church only a few months before Gladden's arrival in Columbus. Before that time the trustees of the First Church managed the Eastwood property. Although members of the First Church donated real estate and money for its work,

[5] Lee, *History of Columbus*, I, 840–43; *Ohio State Journal*, July 6, 1885, May 6, 1889; *Congregationalist*, LXXIV (April 18, 1889), 129, LXXVI (March 26, 1891), 104; *Ohio State Journal*, December 3, 1909.

[6] *Congregationalist*, LXIII (April 26, 1888), 142; *Ohio State Journal*, September 28, 1896; Records of the First Congregational Church for 1898–1913, statistics for 1901, 1903, 1904, First Church archives.

the Eastwood Church was always able to support itself with minimal
outside aid.[7]

Gladden's zeal to broaden the Congregational witness locally appeared most clearly in the organization of four entirely new congregations. Since each was planted in a district where there was a
dearth of churches, there was no hint of sectarian rivalry. Gladden
believed that their democratic organization and progressive message
would have popular appeal and assure them broad bases of support.
They were, like similar missions established by Lyman Abbott and
other pastors of large urban congregations, attempts to reach the
working class in districts where the fashionable churches of the middle and upper classes would have neither appeal nor success. Church
extension, which previously had centered on the successive frontiers
of the West, faced in the late nineteenth century a new frontier, that
of the mushrooming urban centers of America.

The first mission grew directly out of Gladden's desire to find a
new area for Congregational work. He discovered a section in the
southeastern part of Columbus that appeared, because of its rapid
growth and remoteness from existing churches, to be a fertile field.
In 1886 members of the First Church canvassed the neighborhood
and rented a vacant storeroom. A Sunday school was organized on
May 23, 1886, with ninety-nine in attendance, and, in honor of the
mission's birth date and of Congregational tradition, Gladden named
it the Mayflower Chapel. The school met at three o'clock on Sunday
afternoons, presumably so members of the First Church could participate and Gladden could preach. A tremendous burst of enthusiasm accompanied the birth of the Mayflower Chapel. Attendance
grew to well over a hundred in a few weeks, and the storeroom
became overcrowded. By the autumn of 1887 its program included
preaching services on alternate Sunday evenings, attended by more
than one hundred and fifty persons. After almost three years in inadequate quarters, the Mayflower congregation moved in 1889 into
a building that would seat about three hundred. A wealthy member

[7] Lee, *History of Columbus*, I, 846–48; *Congregationalist*, LXXVII (November 3, 1892), 382.

of the First Church, Francis C. Sessions, donated the lot and $1,000, and other members of Gladden's congregation contributed most of the remaining $2,850 expended on the new edifice.[8]

As the Mayflower Chapel grew, it assumed increasingly the character of an indigenous congregation. Gladden continued to do most of the preaching on Sunday afternoons, while qualified laymen alternated responsibility for the biweekly evening services; but the situation demanded something more. To meet the mission's growing needs and to relieve Gladden of the burden of preaching, the First Church took steps to secure an assistant who would manage the activities at Mayflower and in his remaining time assist Gladden in the larger parish. By the time the chapel was dedicated in February, 1889, Gladden had found a young man, then in his final term at Yale Seminary, who could begin the work by May. Imaginative, progressive in theology, and deeply influenced by the Social Gospel, Henry Stauffer proved a good choice. The organization and ecclesiastical recognition of the Mayflower Chapel as an independent Congregational church occurred shortly after his arrival. Although gaining autonomy, however, the chapel, probably for financial reasons, quickly put itself under the care of the First Church. Stauffer added a Sunday-morning service and did virtually all of the preaching at Mayflower, but he remained officially Gladden's assistant until his installation as pastor of the daughter church in November, 1890.[9]

The relations between the two churches continued to be close. Gladden assumed a fatherly role toward Stauffer, who left Mayflower in 1895 to work for the Columbus Union Mission Association, and toward Byron R. Long, Mayflower's pastor from 1895 to 1904. Gladden carefully guided the Mayflower congregation through its first pastoral change, and he probably directed its attention to Long,

[8] *Ohio State Journal*, May 22, 29, 1886, October 1, 1887, February 23, 1889, June 29, 1896; Lee, *History of Columbus*, I, 848; *Congregationalist*, LXXI (June 24, 1886), 212, LXXIV (March 7, 1889), 77.

[9] Of its thirty-nine charter members, twenty-one came from the First Church, three from Eastwood, eight from other churches, and only seven by profession of faith. Records of the First Congregational Church for 1870–89, November 21, 1888, First Church archives; *Ohio State Journal*, February 23, May 18, June 19, November 9, 1889, November 25–26, 1890.

who was pastor of the Christian Temple in Marion, Indiana.[10] The church served the community through a diversified institutional program. Stauffer organized several lecture courses for the winter of 1890–91: a Chautauqua course for Sunday-school teachers; a medical course taught by local physicians; a course in social science taught by Gladden and members of the university faculty who were active in the First Church; lessons on home culture under auspices of the Mayflower ladies' society; and monthly temperance lectures. In late 1891 the congregation constructed a reading room and gymnasium, which Stauffer considered steppingstones between the church and the world.[11]

After ten years of rapid growth the Mayflower Church began to suffer from the multiplication of churches in its neighborhood, and, as one newspaperman put it, "the little chapel on the back of the lot was never eclipsed by the church that should have been built." In 1915, after fifteen more years of heroic effort, the congregation relocated farther southeast in Columbus. Its ideal continued to be the "community-serving church," for the large, new building included a gymnasium, social rooms, a kitchen, and baths. Fittingly enough, Gladden laid the cornerstone.[12]

The second new Congregational church under the First Church's auspices had, if anything, an even more promising beginning than Mayflower. In the summer of 1890 Jessie L. Bright, a recent graduate of Yale Seminary who had grown up in the First Church, canvassed a large part of the south side of Columbus, where a new church seemed needed. The population of the area was overwhelmingly of German origin, and, except for a Baptist enterprise, there

[10] *Ohio State Journal,* March 2, 14, April 6, 1895; *Congregationalist,* LXXXIX (October 22, 1904), 585.

[11] *Ohio State Journal,* November 8, 1890, October 27, 29, December 12, 1891; Lee, *History of Columbus,* I, 850. Stauffer was also active in promoting dialogue between churches and labor unions, and he was largely responsible for meetings between the Columbus Pastors' Union and delegates of the Trades Assembly. *Ohio State Journal,* May 18, June 5, 1894.

[12] *Ohio State Journal,* October 18, 1915; *Congregationalist,* C (November 4, 1915), 676.

was no English-speaking Sunday school. Whether or not Bright began his work independently, Gladden quickly threw the resources of the First Church into the project. At an initial meeting on August 31, 1890, those interested in organizing the new mission more than filled a hall seating almost two hundred. By November the South Congregational Church was ready to organize with forty-nine members, three-fourths of whom joined by profession of faith rather than by transfer of membership from other evangelical churches, and construction of a temporary structure to seat five hundred was under way. Gladden preached the major sermon at the ecclesiastical council that recognized the church, ordained Bright, and installed him as pastor.[13]

The South Church took good root and made remarkable progress in a community supposedly indifferent to Congregationalism. Sunday-school attendance soon averaged over two hundred. When in April, 1891, the congregation dedicated its first building, it buried in the cornerstone a box containing a Bible, a list of members and historical sketch, and a portrait of Gladden. Two years later an edifice that cost $14,000 provided the church with ampler facilities. The First Church regularly supplied funds even after the turn of the century, although the South Church voted in 1900 that it could support itself.[14]

The launching of a third home mission met with less success. Sometime in 1889 several Congregational laymen acquired property in a working-class district northeast of the First Church and about a mile northwest of the Eastwood Church. Intending to establish a mission under the care of Eastwood, they erected a chapel, arranged for Jesse Bright of the South Church to take temporary charge, and began to hold services in September, 1890. The Eastwood Church

[13] Lee, *History of Columbus*, I, 851–52; *Congregationalist*, LXXV (September 18, 1890), 318, (November 13, 1890), 396, (December 4, 1890), 430; *Ohio State Journal*, November 8, 25, 1890.

[14] *Ohio State Journal*, April 15, 1891, July 10, 1893; Records of the First Congregational Church for 1898–1913, statistics for 1898, 1899, 1900, 1905, First Church archives; Gladden, "Pastor's Report for 1900," January 16, 1901, Gladden Papers.

supplied most of the Sunday-school teachers, but Gladden, Bright, and Alexander Milne shared the preaching.[15] Located on St. Clair Avenue, it became known as the St. Clair Chapel.

By the end of 1890 the First Church was becoming the main supporter of the mission. As he had previously secured Henry Stauffer to direct the Mayflower Chapel, Gladden now enlisted another assistant to do the same for the St. Clair Chapel. His first choice fell on W. B. Marsh, a promising young graduate of Princeton Seminary. Marsh's initial pastoral work had earned him a reputation for intellectual acumen and forceful preaching, and he had been elected moderator of the Congregational Association of Ohio in 1888. Just what he preached to the workingmen who heard him at the St. Clair Chapel is not clear, but on one occasion he addressed the First Church on "Modifications of Religious Thought, Induced by the Spirit of Scientific Inquiry." The First Church soon solidified its control over the mission by acquiring the title to its property, a proceeding initiated by Gladden and made possible by the assumption of its current indebtedness by two members of the First Church.[16]

The chapel always needed heavy support from Gladden's parishioners, frequently one thousand dollars or more annually.[17] But after Marsh left in 1892, a more serious problem arose. Despite Gladden's usual care in selecting assistants, he hired early in 1892 George P. Bethel, a man who lacked the liberality of Stauffer and Marsh. During the anti-Catholic panic of 1892–93, Bethel used the chapel to propagate the literature and views of the American Protective Association, an anti-Catholic organization of which he was a member. This organization, born in 1887 in Clinton, Iowa, but not nationally prominent until 1893, required its members to pledge neither to vote for nor employ Catholics (unless no Protestant was available), a

[15] *Congregationalist*, LXXIV (August 8, 1889), 261, LXXV (July 3, 1890), 230; Lee, *History of Columbus*, I, 852.

[16] *Ohio State Journal*, December 20, 1890, October 24, 1891; Records of the First Congregational Church, Society Records for 1871–1908, December 30, 1891, First Church archives.

[17] Records of the First Congregational Church, Society Records for 1871–1908, January 25, 1893, First Church archives.

virtual boycott of Catholics in politics and business.[18] In 1891 and 1892 it gained strength in several cities in Ohio, particularly Cleveland, Toledo, and Columbus, and by July, 1892, rumor had it that anti-Catholicism had become an "epidemic condition" in Columbus, which reportedly had fourteen branches of the A.P.A. Concentrating on the supposed Catholic threat to democratic institutions and the public schools, agitators circulated forged documents allegedly demonstrating Catholic plots to seize power: a "Pastoral Letter" of American Catholic bishops decrying the public-school system and urging the creation of a Catholic political party, and "Instructions for Catholics," promulgated in 1891 by Pope Leo XIII, commanding Catholics to massacre all Protestants and other heretics on the Feast of St. Ignatius Loyola in 1893.[19]

Gladden quickly denounced the organization in public, thus becoming involved in a prolonged fray with its spokesmen. In a sermon on "The Revival of Know-Nothingism" on October 2, 1892, he recalled the anti-Catholic hysteria generated in the 1850's by the Order of the Star Spangled Banner, denounced the customary intrigue, secrecy, and fraud of such subterranean societies, argued that a revival of anti-Catholicism was particularly ludicrous and lamentable at a time when the Roman Catholic church was moving in a liberal direction, and pronounced the aims of the A.P.A. unconstitu-

---

[18] *Ohio State Journal*, April 30, 1892; John Higham, *Strangers in the Land: Patterns of American Nativism, 1860–1925* (New Brunswick, N.J.: Rutgers University Press, 1955), pp. 62–63, 80.

[19] Ross Seymour Johnson, "The A. P. A. in Ohio" (unpublished M.A. thesis, Ohio State University, 1948), pp. 8–14; *Ohio State Journal*, July 1, November 8, 1892; Higham, *Strangers in the Land*, pp. 81–82, 85; Alma Jagsch, "Washington Gladden: A Prophet of Social Justice" (unpublished M.A. thesis, Ohio State University, 1935), p. 22; Donald L. Kinzer, *An Episode in Anti-Catholicism: The American Protective Association* (Seattle: University of Washington Press, 1964), pp. 68–70, 81–82. Gladden had been aware of a rising tide of anti-Catholicism as early as 1891 and had preached on the subject and participated in a discussion at the Congregational Club of Central Ohio. Converse Diaries, August 30, 1891, Gladden Papers; *Ohio State Journal*, February 14, 1891. When the Feast of St. Ignatius passed in 1893 without the expected bloodletting, spokesmen for the A. P. A. interpreted this as trickery by the Jesuits to get Protestants off their guard and make a later slaughter more successful. Johnson, "A. P. A. in Ohio," p. 29.

tional. Led by Adam Fawcett, pastor of the Hildreth Baptist Church
in Columbus, who became vice-president of the national organization in 1894, members and sympathizers immediately defended the
A.P.A. against Gladden's charges through the press and at public
meetings.[20] Except for Gladden, the clergy of Columbus were virtually mute; indeed, many let loose their pent-up prejudices and began
to preach on the menace of Catholicism. Before the episode was
over, supporters of the A.P.A. had brought Justin Fulton, a Baptist
minister from Boston who had been actively involved in the Know-
Nothing movement of the 1850's, to preach for a week in the Hildreth Baptist Church on topics like "Why the Priest Should Wed,"
"Romanists Not Fit Instructors for Our Youth," and "Nunneries—
Prisons or Worse."[21] And Gladden had to defend himself publicly
against rumors that he had received his information about the A.P.A.
from a Jesuit, that he spent his time with Bishop John Watterson
and other priests in Columbus, and that he had taken a bribe of
$1,000 for preaching his sermon against the A.P.A.[22]

The A.P.A. became so potent that Gladden felt constrained to
speak out frequently against it. In local elections in 1892 two Democratic candidates for county offices were defeated because they were
Catholics, while their running mates, all Protestants, were victorious.
A year later, the organization claimed 10,000 members in Columbus
and a total of 150,000 in Ohio.[23] It also exerted a powerful influence
on the state legislature. This influence had an important adverse
effect on Gladden: it destroyed an apparently good chance for him
to become president of the Ohio State University. Early in 1892,
Rutherford B. Hayes, the chairman of the school's board of trustees,
discussed the presidency with Gladden, who agreed to have his
name presented. The only condition that Gladden demanded was an
increase in the president's salary from $3,000 to $5,000. Hayes and

[20] *Ohio State Journal*, October 3, 5, 10, 1892.

[21] *Ibid.*, October 29, November 5, 7, 19, 1892, February 17, 21–24, 1893;
Kinzer, *Episode in Anti-Catholicism*, p. 22.

[22] *Ohio State Journal*, September 1, 3, 1893.

[23] *Ibid.*, November 9, 1892; Johnson, "A.P.A. in Ohio," p. 29.

most of the other trustees thought this possible but made it clear that approval for such an increase must come from the legislature. When the trustees made their request, the legislature's committee on colleges and universities urged the legislature to take favorable action. But, surprisingly, the increase was decisively defeated. It became clear afterward that the trustees' consideration of Gladden had leaked out and that the legislature, influenced by and afraid of the A.P.A., had been opposed not to the raise in salary but to Gladden.[24] Partly because of this personal defeat, but mainly because he could not tolerate the A.P.A.'s intolerance, Gladden began to prepare an article, "The Anti-Catholic Crusade," for the *Century*. In consulting Richard W. Gilder about the article, he confessed his emotional involvement in the issue: "I see the need of keeping the speech under control." Mainly an exposé of the organization and its forged documents, the article was designed to educate the public about the A.P.A.'s true nature and purposes.[25]

Against this background, Gladden's course in dealing with Bethel, an outspoken defender of the organization, is understandable. As Gladden explained the episode to Gilder, it was all very simple:

> Then I had trouble in one of our chapels with the man in charge who was an A.P.A. and I found him circulating those devilish documents, and

[24] Charles R. Williams (ed.), *Diary and Letters of Rutherford Birchard Hayes: Nineteenth President of the United States* (5 vols.; Columbus, Ohio: Ohio State Archaeological and Historical Society, 1922–26), V, 81, 94; Alexis Cope, *History of the Ohio State University, 1870–1910* (*History of the Ohio State University*, ed. Thomas C. Mendenhall *et al.* [7 vols.; Columbus, Ohio: Ohio State University Press, 1920–59]), I, 151–55; *Ohio State Journal*, January 29, February 11, 1893, May 10, 1894; Gladden, *Recollections*, pp. 414–15. Gladden also benefited from his defense of Catholicism. In 1895 he became the first Protestant ever to receive an honorary degree from Notre Dame. *Congregationalist*, LXXX (July 11, 1895), 75; *Ohio State Journal*, March 2, 1906.

[25] Gladden to Gilder, January 8, July 6, December 11, 22, 1893, January 2, 11, February 26, April 6, 16, 1894, *Century* Collection; Washington Gladden, "The Anti-Catholic Crusade," *Century*, XLVII (March, 1894), 789–95. For Fawcett's reply to Gladden's article and Gladden's rejoinder, see *Century*, XLVIII (July, 1894), 472. When anti-Catholicism became rampant again in 1914–15, Gladden published another attack on bigotry and drew parallels between the new unrest and the A. P. A. Washington Gladden, "The Anti-Papal Panic," *Harper's Weekly*, LIX (July 18, 1914), 55–56, "Anti-Catholic Agitation," LIX (September 12, 1914), 255–56.

getting the ignorant people into the order. I promptly dismissed him, (he was simply *my* hired man) and met the people in the chapel, and told them why I had done it: that I would not have a man in any pulpit for which I was responsible who had sworn a solemn oath not to employ "any Roman Catholic in any capacity."[26]

Bethel was not inclined to drop the issue so casually. In a statement issued to the press early in 1893, he offered a radically different explanation. A former Methodist minister, he had joined Gladden's church in January, 1892, and then, at Gladden's urging, taken over the work at the St. Clair Chapel. The chapel, he continued, had a very small attendance and not a single member; the trustees of the First Church refused to support it any longer. Gladden was not ready to give it up and secured funds from another source, a ladies' society in the First Church. His relations with Gladden were good, Bethel went on, until Gladden preached his sermon on "The Revival of Know-Nothingism." Sure that Gladden was misinformed, Bethel called on him to present his version of the case. After that, Bethel claimed, Gladden began "a freezing-out process until November 21, when I called and he notified me 'to look for another place after the first of the year.' This came Monday after I preached on 'The Infallible Pope and the Public Schools.' "[27]

Though he was preaching at Harvard when Bethel's explanation appeared, Gladden received a copy of it and shot back a rebuttal. Bethel's dismissal was not the result of his connections with the A.P.A. alone, Gladden maintained, although the "accidental discovery of his membership" did reinforce the decision. His appointment had been due to expire at the end of 1892 anyway, and his work had not been totally satisfactory in other respects. Then, Gladden tried to explain how he had the right to dismiss another minister. The St. Clair Chapel was not an independent Congregational church; the First Church owned it, and Gladden had sole responsibility for its management. Bethel was not even employed by the First Church; Gladden had personally employed him, paying him out of private

[26] Gladden to Gilder, December 23, 1893, *Century* Collection.

[27] *Ohio State Journal*, February 4, 1893.

funds. Consequently, Gladden concluded, the public had no legitimate concern in the matter. Not to be silenced, Bethel dragged the
dispute into the mud. In a reply to Gladden's rebuttal, he claimed
that Gladden had said, "I have more in common with the Catholics
than I have with the Methodists," insinuated that Bishop Watterson had told a parishioner that he could attend Gladden's church
but no other Protestant church, and suggested that Gladden hire a
priest to run the chapel. Moreover, he contended, there *was* a St.
Clair Avenue church with a deacon, clerk, treasurer, and sixteen
members; but, since it had begun to fall apart after his dismissal, it
might not last for long. To this scurrilous cluster of insinuations,
Gladden had only one answer, Bethel's slander demonstrated that
there were good reasons for his firing. At first, Gladden added, he
had tried to view the A.P.A. calmly, but then "letters of the most
violent and abusive character poured in upon me, threatening me
with all manner of indignity and outrage, and even with assassination—letters so vile and obscene that I have not ventured to show
them to my friends." But Bethel had the last word: these letters
that Gladden had received came obviously from Jesuits who wanted
"to stir him up to say hard things."[28]

This controversy over the A.P.A. was temporarily disastrous for the
St. Clair Chapel. Apparently, there were no services during January,
February, and part of March, 1893, and even then Gladden had to
rely on visiting preachers and laymen from the First Church to hold
services. By the end of April, however, he secured D. Fisk Harris, a
graduate of the Chicago Theological Seminary and Oberlin Seminary
and a man with pastoral experience in New York and Ohio.[29] Harris
shared Gladden's theology to a remarkable degree, and under his
leadership the chapel prospered. In December, 1893, Gladden presided over a council that recognized it as an independent Congregational church and installed Harris as its pastor. By early 1894 its
Sunday school numbered about two hundred, and by 1896 it had

---

[28] *Ibid.*, February 6, 23–25, 1893.

[29] *Ibid.*, March 18, April 8, 29–30, 1893; Lee, *History of Columbus*, I, 838.

outgrown its building.[30] At several points it appeared to be on the verge of self-support. But for some reason its growth reached a plateau and then declined. When in 1900 the First Church's trustees substantially decreased their aid, Harris was obliged to leave. Gladden offered to reduce his own salary by five hundred dollars if the trustees would allocate it to Harris, but they refused. The final years of the St. Clair Chapel are lost in obscurity, but by 1904 the trustees of the First Church gave up all hope of resuscitating it and sold the property to a congregation of the United Brethren in Christ.[31]

The organization of a fourth new Congregational church in Columbus came much later in Gladden's career. Apparently, it needed help from the First Church less than had the earlier missions. As a matter of fact, it was quite by accident that the church organized in 1910 in suburban Grandview Heights was Congregational. Several residents of Grandview surveyed their village informally to find a common basis on which they might organize a church. Finding that Congregationalism was most acceptable, they approached Gladden for guidance. He outlined the procedure for the organizers to follow and called a council of other Congregational churches to recognize the new member of their fellowship. The church called Fred L. Brownlee, a graduate of the Ohio State University, who read a decidedly liberal theological paper at his ordination. Gladden assisted in raising funds, and within a few months of its organization the church had started its first building.[32]

---

[30] *Ohio State Journal*, December 19, 1893; *Congregationalist*, LXXIX (February 22, 1894), 277, LXXXI (January 16, 1896), 111.

[31] *Ohio State Journal*, February 19, 1900; *Congregationalist*, LXXXIX (March 19, 1904), 415; Records of the First Congregational Church, Society Records for 1871–1908, January 18, 1905, First Church archives.

[32] *Ohio State Journal*, March 19, 1910, April 13, 1911; Converse Diaries, April 25, October 3–4, 1910, Gladden Papers. After four years at the church in Grandview, Brownlee left to study at the Union Theological Seminary and Columbia University. He returned to Columbus in 1916 to become director of religious education at the First Church. Fred L. Brownlee to Gladden, February 21, 1916, Gladden Papers; *Ohio State Journal*, January 7, 1917. The most successful of the churches that Gladden helped to organize, the church in Grandview, renamed the First Community Church, is at present one of the most prominent churches in Columbus and is now affiliated with the United Church of Christ.

The growth of Congregationalism in Columbus during Gladden's first decade at the First Church made the city one of the strongest centers of the denomination in Ohio. In 1882 the Congregational churches in Columbus had had 739 members; by 1892 they had 1,879. Gladden reported to his congregation that, while the city's population had increased 100 per cent, Congregational membership had leaped forward by 154 per cent. Of the eight churches in 1892, four of the five that had been in existence in 1882 were in new buildings, and the three new organizations had buildings and were almost self-supporting. By 1900 Columbus had 2,309 Congregationalists, exceeded in Ohio only by Cleveland's 6,243.[33]

Noting in 1898 how the First Church had supported younger churches, the *Congregationalist* observed, "First Church is the careful mother of all, and Dr. Gladden the modest and honored older brother to each party." Gladden himself promoted the concept of "the mother church." In an address by that title at the twenty-fifth anniversary of the Plymouth Church, he elaborated the idea that several churches of the denomination were better than one huge congregation.[34] But, for all his work on behalf of the neighborhood congregations, they suffered from the superior attractions of "the mother church." Often, members of the First Church were tied too strongly to its fellowship and Gladden's preaching to break away and join the daughter bodies, even when the latter were more conveniently located. And newcomers to Columbus might travel from the suburbs on the interurban to attend the First Church, passing one or more Congregational churches on their way.

The *Congregationalist* was also right in the second part of its observation: Gladden was "the modest and honored older brother" to the youthful ministers who, at times his personal choices, looked

[33] Gladden, Sermon, December 18, 1892, Gladden Papers; *Congregationalist*, LXXXV (June 7, 1900), 853. As of 1967, only three of the eight churches in existence in 1892 are still alive. The congregations of the Mayflower, Eastwood, Washington Avenue (Welsh), and Plymouth churches have in recent years disbanded. The First, North, and South churches, now part of the United Church of Christ, still remain.

[34] *Congregationalist*, LXXXIII (December 29, 1898), 936; *Ohio State Journal*, April 30, 1897.

to him for counsel and aid. After the turn of the century he had one of the longest records of service among Ohio's Congregational clergymen and the second longest tenure at one church.[35] If they had not come under the influence of his writings earlier, the Congregational pastors of Columbus almost always absorbed something of his liberal theology and social outlook before they left his circle. He began a Monday Club for them, which normally met at his study in the tower of the First Church. Letters from some of them, who spread his influence through many sectors of American Congregationalism, indicate that they regarded these meetings as "sitting at the feet of Gamaliel." After Byron R. Long left Columbus for Ashtabula, Ohio, he wrote that "Dr. Gladden's boys are getting pretty numerous in this neck of the woods," and that three of the most important churches in his conference were already influenced "by the spirit of Dr. Gladden."[36]

Gladden initiated two other organizations to strengthen Congregationalism in Columbus. In 1889 he helped to launch a Congregational club designed to deepen denominational fellowship. The club included members of churches in the Central Ohio Congregational Conference, but it normally met in Columbus. Patterned after similar clubs in New York, Boston, and Chicago, it often featured such leading Congregationalists as President William DeWitt Hyde of Bowdoin College and Gaius Glenn Atkins. Discussions frequently centered on current questions, such as the proper attitude of Congregationalists toward Roman Catholicism and Hawaiian annexation.[37] The second organization, a Congregational Union, arose out of the need to co-ordinate the financing of the chapels and smaller churches

[35] *Ohio State Journal,* January 4, 1907; *Congregationalist,* LXXXIX (November 12, 1904), 704.

[36] *Congregationalist,* LXXIV (September 12, 1889), 304; Converse Diaries, July 27, 1908, Gladden Papers; J. W. Barnett to Gladden, January 30, 1905, Thomas H. Derrick to Gladden, April 17, 1914, Byron R. Long to Gladden, August 14, September 2, 1904, Gladden Papers.

[37] *Congregationalist,* LXXIV (December 26, 1889), 449; *Ohio State Journal,* October 16, 1894, December 21, 1906; Converse Diaries, February 13, 1891, Gladden Papers; *Congregationalist,* LXXVIII (April 27, 1893), 673.

and to safeguard their property interests.[38]

Gladden's support of Congregational work reflected his belief that its distinctive emphases were essential to a complete statement of the case for Christianity, and that, especially in days of intellectual ferment, many people would respond only to its message.[39] But in Ohio the denomination's effectiveness was limited by its lopsided geographic spread. Despite striking gains in Columbus, its greatest numerical strength and, consequently, the center of its power structure continued to be in northern Ohio, where settlement from New England had been heaviest. In 1894 two-thirds of its 257 churches in Ohio were in the Western Reserve. The Congregationalist compared Congregationalism in Ohio to Nebuchadnezzar's image, "stately and golden above, with the weaker parts below."[40] Though this disproportion weakened Gladden's position, he participated in a wide range of state activities, especially those designed to strengthen the "weaker parts."

Soon after his arrival in Columbus, he became prominent in the Central Ohio Conference, which in 1884 represented over two thousand members in eighteen churches. He delivered sermons at both semiannual sessions in 1883 and thereafter addressed the conference almost every year. A broad gamut of religious topics claimed his attention: "The New Congregational Creed," "The Evils of Sectarianism," "How to Reach Men," and "City and Country Boys."[41] He helped to organize the Ohio Congregational Sunday School Association, spoke at its first convention in Akron on "The Sunday School as an Evangelical Agency," and welcomed its second convention to

---

[38] *Congregationalist,* LXXVI (March 12, 1891), 86; Converse Diaries, May 11–12, 25, 29–30, June 8, 11, 1891, Gladden Papers.

[39] Washington Gladden, "Our Shortcomings for the Last Fifty Years," *Congregationalist,* LXXXVII (October 4, 1902), 472–74.

[40] *Congregationalist,* LXXIX (May 17, 1894), 703.

[41] *Ibid.,* LXVIII (May 3, 1883), 155, (October 25, 1883), 367, LXX (October 15, 1885), 347, LXXV (October 23, 1890), 367, LXXIX (October 25, 1894), 562; *Ohio State Journal,* April 30, May 1, 1884.

his own church in Columbus.[42] He was elected in 1883 to the board of the Ohio Home Missionary Society, which promoted Congregational church extension within the state, a position he held for over two decades.[43]

Whenever his schedule permitted, he attended the semiannual meetings of the Congregational Association of Ohio, frequently leading discussions or giving addresses. As early as May, 1884, the *Congregationalist* noted his participation in a discussion on temperance.[44] For many years he was the association's delegate to the American Missionary Association, which worked mainly with the non-white races in the United States. In 1891 the Congregational Association of Ohio elected him its moderator. His address to it in 1894, "The Church and the Kingdom," later published because of popular demand, was a classic statement of the Social Gospel. He spoke before the association again in 1897, 1898, and 1899. He continued to be active after the turn of the century, even though he once protested that younger men should have a chance.[45] His addresses usually stressed the challenges of modern thought and social conditions.[46]

But his role in Congregationalism in Ohio cannot be appreciated without consideration of the informal services that he performed for local churches and ministers. Especially after he had been in Ohio for several years, he was deluged with requests for advice: churches wanted to know about ministers whom they considered calling; and ministers looking for new positions wanted information or recom-

[42] *Congregationalist*, LXXII (October 20, 1887), 358; *Ohio State Journal*, October 15, 1887, November 8, 1890.

[43] J. G. Fraser to Gladden, February 24, 1904, Gladden Papers.

[44] *Congregationalist*, LXIX (May 15, 1884), 161.

[45] *Ohio State Journal*, May 14, 1891; *Congregationalist*, LXXIX (May 17, 1894), 703, (October 25, 1894), 556, LXXXII (May 27, 1897), 767, LXXXIII (June 2, 1898), 820, LXXXIV (May 25, 1899), 765–66; G. L. Smith to Gladden, December 20, 1910, Gladden Papers.

[46] *Congregationalist*, LXXXV (May 24, 1900), 781, LXXXVI (June 8, 1901), 932, LXXXVII (May 24, 1902), 756, LXXXIX (May 28, 1904), 757; Charles S. Mills to Gladden, April 29, 1903, Burton to Gladden, April 8, 1913, Gladden Papers.

mendations. In addition, he was in constant demand to preach at ordinations, church dedications, and meetings of Congregational clubs.[47]

Gladden's rise to leadership in American Congregationalism was gradual, until by the 1890's he was one of his denomination's most valuable and representative pastors. Recent historians of American Congregationalism consider the last decades of the nineteenth and the first decade of the twentieth century its "golden age" in terms of Christian social thought and theology.[48] If their judgment is correct, Gladden's prominence in this period is particularly significant. Congregationalism's heritage of humanitarian reform, its exposure to the liberal impulses of Unitarianism early in the nineteenth century, its concentration in industrial New England, and its relative freedom from any hierarchy that might oppose change combined to "produce a church open . . . to new ideas and willing to espouse them with vigor."[49] Gladden was a key figure in this emergence of a Congregationalism thoroughly imbued with liberal theology and the Social Gospel. Saturation occurred on two fronts: official denominational agencies accepted the progressive ideology and social orientation favored by a growing party within the church; and congregations and the clergy informally imbibed this spirit of modernity.

The officers of specialized agencies could always enlist Gladden in their work. Shortly after he moved to Columbus, his church entertained the annual meeting of the American Board of Commissioners for Foreign Missions, the nation's oldest foreign-mission organization. In 1888 he was elected a member of the American Board, which, though a closed corporation and not representative of the

[47] *Congregationalist*, LXXIX (December 6, 1894), 839; *Ohio State Journal*, December 19, 1896; E. A. King to Gladden, June 26, 1900, W. H. Baker to Gladden, January 12, 1901, Dwight M. Pratt to Gladden, November 26, 1902, October 29, 1906, Frederick L. Fagley to Gladden, August 26, 1912, Gladden Papers.

[48] Gaius Glenn Atkins and Frederick L. Fagley, *History of American Congregationalism* (Boston: Pilgrim Press, 1942), p. 181.

[49] Henry F. May, *Protestant Churches and Industrial America* (New York: Harper & Bros., Publishers, 1949), p. 188.

churches, administered the entire foreign-mission program of American Congregationalists. In 1904 he became particularly responsible for its activities in Ohio by appointment to the district committee for that state.[50] He gave addresses occasionally at its annual meetings, welcomed its missionaries to his church, and actively supported its fund-raising campaigns.[51] He worked for closer ties between the American Board and the churches and for an enlightened approach to other world religions.

The Congregational Home Missionary Society, particularly in its urban work, appealed to him. In addresses to the society he called for recognition of the complex problems that obstructed religious work in the cities and urged the churches to relate themselves to the unchurched. The Congregational Church Building Society, founded in 1854 to assist churches in need of building funds, elected Gladden a vice-president in 1907, and he addressed its annual meetings on several occasions. For several years he was vice-president of the American Missionary Association, and from 1901 to 1904 he served as its president.[52]

But Gladden participated most consistently in the less-specialized activities of Congregationalism's representative national councils, and it was in these councils that he reached the pinnacle of ecclesiastical prominence. Congregationalists in New England had held

[50] *Ohio State Journal,* July 31, October 7–11, 1884; *Congregationalist,* LXXIII (October 11, 1888), 337; Frank H. Wiggin to Gladden, March 31, 1904, Gladden Papers. Though not represented as a church, the First Church had two members on the American Board, Francis C. Sessions and Walter A. Mahony. *Congregationalist,* LXXII (September 15, 1887), 311; *Ohio State Journal,* October 11, 1890.

[51] *Ohio State Journal,* October 12, 1894, April 6, 1909; John McCarthy to Gladden, October 29, 1909, Cornelius H. Patton to Gladden, September 4, 1909, Charles C. Creegan to Gladden, January 6, 1900, January 15, 1901, June 12, 1903, Samuel B. Capen to Gladden, October 24, 1903, Creegan, C. J. Ryder, and T. M. Shipherd to Gladden, July 12, 1909, Gladden Papers.

[52] *Congregationalist,* LXXXIII (June 16, 1898), 887–88; Marybelle O. Prince to Gladden, June 9, 1905, Charles H. Richards to Gladden, January 22, 1907, January 2, 1909, Clarence W. Bowen to Gladden, January 2, 1908, Gladden Papers. Gladden's role in the American Missionary Association receives more detailed treatment in chap. x.

councils as early as 1637, when John Cotton and Thomas Hooker presided over the "Newtowne" Synod, but these bodies adjourned sine die when they had achieved their limited aims. The practice disappeared in the seventeenth century, and it was not until 1865 that a council approximately representative of American Congregationalists assembled in Boston. In 1871 a council at Oberlin adopted a constitution and organized permanently as the National Council of the Congregational Churches. The councils had no binding authority over the churches or the local and regional associations that sent delegates. English Congregationalists had organized forty years earlier without jeopardizing the autonomy of local congregations, but their American brethren harbored fears of ecclesiastical machinery well into the twentieth century.[53]

Gladden did not attend the council at Oberlin in 1871, but he went to the triennial sessions at New Haven (1874), Detroit (1877), and St. Louis (1880) and rarely missed a council after that. The preoccupation of these early councils with administrative machinery distressed him. Attempts to overhaul the benevolent societies stirred up hard feelings and rivalry, but he thought the gravest danger to be the intensification of sectarianism. Speaking as one who wished to be "always first a Christian and secondly a Congregationalist," he told his congregation in Springfield: "Any movement which tends to build Congregational fences and broaden Congregational phylacteries, and emphasize Congregational shibboleths bodes no good to me."[54] Nevertheless, his first important activity at a council involved administrative reorganization, the consolidation of the periodicals of seven benevolent societies. As chairman of a special committee to explore the matter, Gladden recommended that the council at Worcester (1889) appoint a committee to confer with representatives of the societies. The council appointed the committee, making Gladden chairman; and in April, 1890, the committee produced an elaborate

[53] Atkins and Fagley, *American Congregationalism*, pp. 183–84, 205, 208, 210, 214, 219–20; *Congregationalist*, LXXXII (December 9, 1897), 923.

[54] Gladden, "The St. Louis Council," Sermon, November 21, 1880, Gladden Papers.

scheme for a single periodical, to be called the *Christian Nation*. But the effort was futile, for the benevolent societies had little interest in consolidation; about a month after the committee's recommendations appeared, one society enlarged its periodical and another issued an entirely new magazine.[55]

It was at this same council in Worcester that Gladden gave an address indicative of the increasing involvement of Congregationalists in current social questions. Previous councils had endorsed temperance and prison reform, but Gladden's paper on "Christian Socialism" probed for the first time the question of the churches' relationship to the industrial order. Opening his address with the question "Is Christianity in any sense socialistic?", he answered that Christianity certainly did not mean individualism, and that it had "encountered no deadlier foe during the last century than that individualistic philosophy which underlies the competitive system." He favored extending the powers of the state to destroy the saloon, stop Sunday labor and child labor, regulate hours of labor, and promote education.[56]

The council was not prepared, however, to plunge into social action. There was no provision for the discussion of social questions by the council that met at Minneapolis in 1892, and only the Homestead strike, which ended while the council was in session, shocked it into appointing a five-member Committee on Capital and Labor. Gladden headed the committee, which included three other ministers and President David Starr Jordan of Stanford University. When the council met at Syracuse in 1895, Gladden presented a report that established guidelines for subsequent action. The committee had studied the opinions of employers and employees, and its report urged impartiality toward both sides. It tentatively questioned the compatibility of the existing wage system with the Christian values that it thought should govern the economic order.[57] The

[55] *Congregationalist*, LXXIV (October 17, 1889), 344; LXXV (April 3, 1890), 121, (May 29, 1890), 188.

[56] *Ibid.*, LXXIV (October 17, 1889), 341.

[57] Atkins and Fagley, *American Congregationalism*, pp. 252–53; May, *Protestant Churches and Industrial America*, pp. 187–88.

report came during the final session of the council at Syracuse, and, though it was well received, the council's only action was to reappoint the Committee on Capital and Labor. Whether the return of prosperity in 1896 or some other cause was responsible, the committee fell into desuetude. Gladden was originally to be a delegate to the council of 1898 at Portland, Oregon, but he went to Europe that summer, and another minister from Columbus filled his place. The committee did not report at Portland, and the only reference to social questions came in a paper, "The Church and Social Problems," by William E. Barton of Illinois.[58]

In 1901 the council, meeting at Portland, Maine, took its first official steps toward a permanent social service program in response to a memorial from the Massachusetts General Association's Committee on Labor Organizations, which had been appointed after the Homestead strike. The council appointed a Committee on Labor, with Frank W. Merrick of Massachusetts, who had presented the memorial, as chairman and Gladden, William Jewett Tucker of Dartmouth College, David N. Beach of Colorado, and William A. Knight of Massachusetts as members.[59] Since the Labor Committee conducted most of its business by correspondence, Merrick had the difficult task of co-ordinating the suggestions of individual members. The first official meeting occurred in March, 1902, when Gladden was in New Haven to lecture at Yale Seminary. Gladden suggested that the committee get the opinions of working people toward the churches through labor periodicals, but Knight, the pastor of Berkeley Temple, a large institutional church in Boston, maintained that many labor leaders said one thing in print and quite another thing to their confidants. The committee decided to follow two courses in collecting opinions from labor: to read the periodicals and to solicit statements from leaders of labor whom its members knew personally. It also planned to approach a commission on labor established in 1901 by the General Convention of the Protestant Epis-

[58] *Congregationalist*, LXXX (October 3, 1895), 501; LXXXIII (March 10, 1898), 357, (March 24, 1898), 438, (June 23, 1898), 928.

[59] Atkins and Fagley, *American Congregationalism*, p. 253; Hopkins, *Rise of the Social Gospel*, p. 286.

copal Church. This commission included Bishop Henry C. Potter, Dean George Hodges, Seth Low, and Jacob Riis.[60] But it is not clear that the Congregational committee actually made any overtures.

Merrick outlined the committee's aims in a report printed in the *Congregationalist* shortly after its first meeting. The committee interpreted its primary duty to be the stimulation of the churches to deeper interest in labor problems. It secured an entire morning session at the next council, scheduled for 1904 at Des Moines, to present its report and addresses. This report, written by Merrick with suggestions by Gladden and the other members incorporated, embodied two convictions: that industrial problems were not transitory phenomena and could only be solved by justice; and that only by accepting the principles of the Gospel could capital and labor satisfactorily achieve their legitimate aims.[61]

The council at Des Moines exhibited greater social concern than had its predecessors. Reading their fifteen-page report at each of two sectional meetings, members of the committee told of extensive correspondence with leaders of labor, of steps taken to form auxiliary committees on the state level, and of the study of industrial strife through Gladden's visit to the troubled mining areas of Colorado and Knight's visit to Fall River during a textile strike. Graham Taylor addressed one sectional meeting, and Gladden presided over the other, at which E. E. Clark, Grand Chief Conductor of the Order of Railway Conductors, spoke. The entire council attended a Sunday-afternoon meeting of the Des Moines Trades and Labor Assembly and heard another address by Taylor.[62] After the council reappointed the committee, renaming it the Industrial Committee, the work of investigating industrial problems and arousing the churches became

[60] Frank W. Merrick to Gladden, March 5, 19, 1902, Gladden Papers; Hopkins, *Rise of the Social Gospel*, p. 284.

[61] Frank W. Merrick, "Congregationalists and the Workingman," *Congregationalist*, LXXXVII (July 26, 1902), 123; Merrick to Gladden, February 12, September 17, 1904, Gladden Papers; Atkins and Fagley, *American Congregationalism*, pp. 253–54.

[62] *Congregationalist*, LXXXIX (October 22, 1904), 572–73; Atkins and Fagley, *American Congregationalism*, p. 254.

more diversified. Merrick was again chairman and Gladden a member. The committee organized itself into five subcommittees—on child labor, organized labor, immigration, industrial organization, and socialism—and appointed several of its members, including Gladden, to arrange local conferences.[63]

At the council in Cleveland in 1907 Gladden, who had been elected moderator of the national council in 1904, delivered an address on "The Church and the Social Crisis" that gave the social orientation of the denomination its greatest prominence yet. The address was a stirring statement of the Social Gospel. The Industrial Committee recommended the appointment of an industrial secretary to supervise the denomination's activities more effectively than a committee would do. The action of the Presbyterians in appointing Charles Stelzle to a similar position four years earlier undoubtedly prompted the committee's action.[64] But, although the council accepted the recommendation, it stopped short of appropriating funds for a secretary, and the Industrial Committee had to mark time.

The council at Cleveland did approve the formation of the Congregational Brotherhood of America, which eventually absorbed the denomination's program of social service. The brotherhood quickly took hold in the local churches and tried vigorously to stimulate public-service activities on the part of Congregational laymen. Gladden worked closely with the movement from its inception. His own church organized a strong brotherhood, which became a model for others; one of its directors, a local merchant, became a member of the executive committee of the national organization.[65] The list

---

[63] *The National Council of the Congregational Churches of the United States: Addresses, Discussions, Minutes, Statements of Benevolent Societies, Constitution, etc. of the Twelfth Triennial Session, Des Moines, Iowa, October 13–30, 1904* (Boston: Published by Order of the National Council, 1904), p. 570; *Congregationalist,* XC (September 2, 1905), 313.

[64] Gladden, "The Church and the Social Crisis," October 8, 1907, Gladden Papers; *Congregationalist,* XCII (October 12, 1907), 494–96, (October 19, 1907), 532–35, (October 26, 1907), 563–64; Hopkins, *Rise of the Social Gospel,* pp. 280–83.

[65] Gaius Glenn Atkins to Gladden, January 16, 1908, Frank Dyer to Gladden, February 12, 1908, Gladden Papers; *Congregationalist,* XCIII (February 29, 1908), 275, XCIV (October 30, 1909), 572; *Ohio State Journal,* January 24, 1909.

of speakers at the national brotherhood's first convention, held in 1908 in Detroit, included General O. O. Howard, President James B. Angell, Graham Taylor, Gladden, and other prominent Congregational ministers and laymen. Gladden helped to plan the brotherhood's activities and spoke at its second and third annual conventions.[66]

The Industrial Committee of the national council, with Graham Taylor as chairman after 1907, worked closely with the Congregational Brotherhood. In 1910 the committee appealed to the council to implement its earlier proposal for a secretary, and the council in turn delegated this responsibility to the brotherhood. The brotherhood elected a minister, Henry A. Atkinson, to the new secretarial post, and he immediately initiated educative and investigative activities. Finally, in 1913 the national council reorganized its Industrial Committee, on which Gladden had continued to serve, as the Commission on Social Service and placed the Congregational Brotherhood under its direction. Gladden was an active member of the reorganized commission for several years after 1913.[67]

The greatest honor that American Congregationalists could bestow on one of their number came to Gladden in 1904, when the national council elected him moderator. He had been nominated for the position in 1895, but his name was subsequently withdrawn, "inasmuch as it was found that he had not yet arrived." It appears that neither the Central Ohio Congregational Conference nor the Congregational Association of Ohio, which were represented proportionally in the national body, elected him a delegate in 1904; and only the resignation as a delegate of Byron R. Long, one of "Dr. Gladden's boys," opened a place for him. Both Long and J. W. Barnett, who had also worked with Gladden in Columbus, forewarned Gladden that there was a movement under way to elect

---

[66] *Congregationalist*, XCIII (April 4, 1908), 443; XCIV (October 30, 1909), 572; XCV (October 22, 1910), 582.

[67] Henry M. Beardsley to Gladden, November 25, 1910; Henry A. Atkinson to Gladden, December 19, 1910, April 18, May 2, 1914; Hubert C. Herring to Gladden, October 31, 1913, Gladden Papers.

him. Occasional references to Gladden in Congregational papers in the months before the council met indicated that he would have widespread support.[68]

When the council convened in Des Moines, President Henry C. King of Oberlin College nominated Gladden, calling him "the first citizen of Columbus, orator, author, ideal pastor, civilian, saint." Gladden took a decisive lead on the first ballot over two other nominees and won on the second ballot. Deeply moved, he declared that no honor he had ever won compared with this. He then presided over the council's sessions with remarkable aplomb and in his direction of congregational singing proved himself an "admirable preceptor,"[69]

Gladden became moderator at a crucial time in the evolution of modern Congregationalism. The council at Des Moines was by common consent an extraordinary one, both for the large attendance of denominational leaders and for the importance of its agenda. Gladden joined in celebration of the council's achievements:

> In its unity, its enthusiasm, its high purpose, its hopeful outlook it has left all its predecessors far behind. Something has certainly happened to our Congregational brotherhood.

A growing sense of denominational self-consciousness and loyalty prevailed.[70]

Gladden made significant contributions to the moderatorship itself. Since 1871, the national council had met regularly and was regarded as a permanent institution; it was continuous, and its triennial sessions were merely phases of a single, ongoing entity. The modera-

---

[68] *Congregationalist*, LXXX (October 17, 1895), 569; Barnett to Gladden, October 6, 1904, Long to Gladden, October 7, 1904, Gladden Papers; Sydney H. Cox, "For Moderator—Dr. Gladden," *Congregationalist*, LXXXIX (June 18, 1904), 867.

[69] *Congregationalist*, LXXXIX (October 22, 1904), 571, (October 29, 1904), 605.

[70] Samuel B. Capen, "Our First Duty as Christians and Congregationalists," *ibid.*, LXXXIX (October 1, 1904), 458; LXXXIX (October 29, 1904), 600, 604–11.

torship, however, had achieved no such permanence. At the end of each triennial session the moderator laid aside his functions. Gladden's predecessor, Amory H. Bradford, the pastor of the influential First Congregational Church of Montclair, New Jersey, responded to the need for greater cohesiveness among Congregationalists by writing annual letters to the churches and making addresses as moderator. He claimed that the moderator, as "servant of the churches," should interpret to them current developments in the Congregational fellowship.[71]

Bradford's activities frightened many who saw in his conception of the office the roots of hierarchical power. The *Congregationalist* quoted a denominational paper in Nebraska that called for election of a layman who would not know how to write an "encyclical" and would not think that he was moderator after the council adjourned.[72] One of the most resolute opponents of a strong, continuous moderatorship, F. A. Noble, who had been moderator in 1898, argued that Congregationalists had gotten along well enough without it. The innovators, according to Noble, considered

> the moral bond which held the primitive churches together in a quench-less love and in a service which is still the marvel of the ages, and which has held the churches of our faith and order together from the strenuous days of Plymouth and Salem until now, and under which they have become a mighty band of witnesses and workers, . . . only "a rope of sand." They want to change it into "a rope of hemp or of steel."[73]

Gladden felt that a stronger moderatorship would increase Congregational unity, and he endorsed Bradford's use of the office. After heated discussion, the council at Des Moines also approved Bradford's course. It granted the moderator a "representative function," but declared

---

[71] Atkins and Fagley, *American Congregationalism,* pp. 219–21; Amory H. Bradford, "The Moderator to the Churches," *Congregationalist,* LXXXIX (January 9, 1904), 56.

[72] *Congregationalist,* LXXXIX (September 10, 1904), 379.

[73] F. A. Noble, "A Rope of Sand," *ibid.,* LXXXIX (September 17, 1904), 396.

that all his acts and utterances shall be devoid of authority and that for
them shall be claimed and to them given only such weight and force as
there is weight and force in the reason of them.[74]

The *Congregationalist,* which had not committed itself in the pre-
conciliar discussion, pointed out the denomination's need for "leadership that is conservatively but surely progressive," and rejoiced that
Gladden, a man who had the churches' confidence, was the first
to be specifically entrusted with this larger role.[75]

Some dissenters were not satisfied with the council's decision. William E. Barton of Oak Park, Illinois, a vocal critic of the new policy
during the council's discussion, defended his position in the *Advance*.
When Gladden answered him effectively, the *Congregationalist*
endorsed the new position and argued for change to meet new situa-
tions.[76] Gladden received encouragement to make liberal use of the
office from Congregationalists all over the country. Bradford assured
him of general support from churches in the East. President Charles
F. Thwing of the Western Reserve University declared: "I am a
believer in a strong Congregational system. I shall be glad to think
of you as my Bishop." Hubert C. Herring, minister of the First Congregational Church of Omaha, wrote: "Since you are now Archbishop (I refuse to acknowledge you as Pope) you must bend your
back to the burdens." Others who endorsed Gladden's acceptance of
Bradford's view were President Henry Hopkins of Williams College, Henry H. Proctor, minister of the First Congregational Church
of Atlanta, a Negro congregation, James L. Barton, corresponding
secretary of the American Board, Frank P. Woodbury, an officer of
the American Missionary Association, and William Horace Day,
minister of the First Congregational Church of Los Angeles.[77]

[74] *Congregationalist,* LXXXIX (October 22, 1904), 573.

[75] *Ibid.,* LXXXIX (October 22, 1904), 561.

[76] *Ibid.,* LXXXIX (December 3, 1904), 811.

[77] Amory H. Bradford to Gladden, November 29, 1904; Charles F. Thwing
to Gladden, October 26, 1904; Herring to Gladden, November 11, 1904; Hopkins to Gladden, November 12, 1904; Henry H. Proctor to Gladden, November
29, 1904; James L. Barton to Gladden, December 9, 1904; Frank P. Woodbury
to Gladden, December 12, 1904; William Horace Day to Gladden, December
23, 1904, Gladden Papers.

The moderatorship greatly increased the demands on Gladden for addresses and advice. He did not continue Bradford's practice of writing annual letters to the churches, but he wrote special devotional articles for the *Congregationalist*.[78] Invitations to speak to local churches, Congregational clubs, denominational colleges, and associational meetings flooded his correspondence. At the end of his three years in office he assured his successor of a strenuous schedule. He visited twenty-five states and the national capital, crossed the continent twice, and delivered about seventy-five addresses to Congregational groups. Early in 1906, he already had to warn readers of the *Congregationalist* that he was "unable to undertake the work of a ministerial bureau."[79]

Gladden's activity in his denomination did not end when he relinquished the moderatorship. He continued to attend national councils and to participate in their deliberations. The last one that he attended met in Columbus in 1917, less than a year before his death, and offered profuse tributes to the "grand old man" of Congregationalism.

Gladden's role in the emergence of modern Congregationalism extended into one other important field, the establishment of ties between English and American Congregationalists. In 1888 he attended the International Missionary Conference in London, in which members of his denomination figured largely.[80] While in England, he preached in several important Congregational churches, among them the Queen Street Church in Wolverhampton, probably the strongest Congregational church outside London; and he began a friendship with the family of Percy Clarke, publisher of the *Christian World*, the leading Congregational organ in the British Isles. Many of his books subsequently went into English editions with the

---

[78] Washington Gladden, "Foundations," *Congregationalist*, XCII (February 9, 1907), 178; "Character Building," XCII (March 2, 1907), 278; "Following on to Know," XCII (March 16, 1907), 346; "The Homeward Way," XCII (July 27, 1907), 111.

[79] Gladden, "The Church and the Social Crisis," October 8, 1907, Gladden Papers; *Congregationalist*, XCI (March 17, 1906), 401.

[80] *Congregationalist*, LXXIII (September 6, 1888), 298.

imprint of James Clarke and Company. In 1891 he was one of a hundred American delegates to the first International Congregational Council, which met in London. He focused his participation in the council on the two topics for which he had become well known, liberal theology and the Social Gospel. In brief informal remarks he summarized the tendency in American theology toward "a more ethical statement of Christian truth—away from the doctrine of sovereignty toward the doctrine of righteousness." And in a paper on "The Relations of Labor and Capital" he pointed to the social philosophy of Christ as the remedy for industrial disorder.[81]

The international council deepened Gladden's sense of Congregational unity and his appreciation for congregational polity. He chafed against the disadvantages under which English Congregationalists had to work. An incident that he related to his congregation in Columbus illustrates his reaction to the Established Church. One morning a clergyman of the Church of England began to converse with him, and when he discovered Gladden's vocation he remarked, "You are a Nonconformist, I take it!" Gladden replied that he was a Congregationalist. "O well, that's the same thing," the Anglican replied.

> I beg your pardon [Gladden retorted]. It is not the same thing at all. The term would be an impertinence, if applied to any one in the country where I was reared; but if it had any significance at all, the Episcopalians and not the Congregationalists would be entitled to it.

According to Gladden, the clergyman did not think it would be very pleasant to be called a Nonconformist.[82]

Gladden also attended the second International Congregational Council, which met in 1899 at Tremont Temple in Boston. He had no formal part in the program, but, after a paper on social reform by

---

[81] *Ibid.*, LXXVI (January 15, 1891), 23, (March 19, 1891), 97; *The International Congregational Council, London, 1891: Authorised Record of Proceedings* (London: James Clarke & Co., 1891), pp. 96, 177–81. He also delivered a course of lectures on social questions at Mansfield College, a Congregational institution. *Congregationalist*, LXXVI (July 2, 1891), 224.

[82] Gladden, Sermon, October 18, 1891, Gladden Papers.

Graham Taylor, President Angell, who was chairman of the meeting, called on Gladden for impromptu remarks. Once again, Gladden affirmed his conviction that the Sermon on the Mount contained the essential message of Christianity and that it was an adequate guide for social conduct.[83] When American Congregationalists met at Cleveland in 1907, Gladden entertained his English friends, the Clarkes, who came as official observers for the English Congregational churches.[84] It appears that he intended to visit Edinburgh in 1908 for the third International Congregational Council, and he received invitations to preach at the council and in British churches, but Mrs. Gladden's rapidly deteriorating health prevented him from going.[85]

By the beginning of the twentieth century Gladden's name was a household word for American Congregationalists, and it was known to many abroad. His appearance on important denominational platforms for several decades, his constant availability for services small and great, and the publication of many of his books and articles by the Congregational presses of England and America established him as a loyal son of his church. He reflected the currents of the day, but he also influenced them. And he made an inestimable contribution to the emergence of modern Congregationalism as a liberal, socially-conscious, and cohesive force in American religion.

[83] *Proceedings of the Second International Congregational Council, Held in Tremont Temple, Boston, Massachusetts, September 20–29, 1899* (Boston: Press of Samuel Usher, 1900), p. 151; *Congregationalist*, LXXXIV (September 28, 1899), 430.

[84] *Congregationalist*, XCII (November 2, 1907), 637; Percy Clarke to Gladden, October 21, 1907, Gladden Papers.

[85] Richard J. Wells to Gladden, January 9, 1908; Hugh S. Griffiths to Gladden, February 11, 1908; E. S. W. Moore to Gladden, April 12, 1908, Gladden Papers.

Six

Evolution of a Theological Liberal

Theology was important to Gladden throughout his career. His own theological development falls into two principal categories of events, which occurred in approximate chronological order. First, finding it impossible to reconcile the primary tenets of the Calvinism that prevailed in the evangelical churches in his youth with Bushnell's ethical test for theology, he gradually divested himself of them. His experience was not isolated, but was part of a widespread movement away from Calvinism in the evangelical churches. Second, he attempted to adjust his thought to modern biblical criticism and evolutionary science and to reformulate what he regarded as the cardinal elements of Christian theology in terms that were acceptable to the modern mind. Thus, his own experience encompassed a complete transition from the modified Calvinism of the mid-nineteenth century to a full-blown liberalism in the early twentieth.

Gladden was not an original theologian. By standards of systematic theology, he was not a theologian at all. He had no substantial theological training. Moreover, accepting Bushnell's contention that language was an inadequate instrument for precise statements of truth, he distrusted speculative theology except as a provisional basis for religious dialogue. In addition, influenced by the romantic movement, he considered intuition to be as valid a source of truth as reason and usually took little interest in purely logical discussions. He was also pragmatic, in that he subordinated theology to the demands of religious experience. Consequently, his theological writings and sermons were expressions of personal faith rather than comprehensive systematic treatises. Nevertheless, in their breadth, clarity, and cogency, and as writings that were extremely popular in their day, they are superb examples of the intellectual adjustments that many Christians felt compelled to make in a period well described as an "ordeal of faith."

Guided by Bushnell and Robertson, Gladden began in the 1860's to overhaul the beliefs that he had inherited. Although his preaching was conventional, his rejection of doctrines that he found ethically unacceptable became increasingly apparent. Total depravity, original sin, predestination, and the substitutionary atonement—the hallmarks of Calvinism—were absent. He was not alone in his theological restiveness, as several tests of strength in the 1870's between conservative Calvinists and a growing party of revisionists reveal.

Gladden used the *Independent* to defend the progressives against those who insisted that they subscribe literally to the Calvinist creeds. In one of his early editorials, "Come-outers and Stay-inners," he argued that, since the areas of agreement were normally much more important than those of disagreement, the churches should allow minor lapses from theological standards. Later in 1871, when an ecclesiastical council in North Adams refused to ordain a young man who apparently had been one of Gladden's parishioners there, the *Independent* decried its greater concern for doctrinal orthodoxy than for the character of the candidate.[1] Gladden defended liberal Congregationalists against the charge of a Unitarian periodical that they were hypocrites for staying in a conservative denomination:

> They believe in its principles; they are at home in its associations; they have always worked by its methods and cannot do their work in any other way. They believe in prayer-meetings, in revivals, in earnest work

[1] [Washington Gladden,] "Come-outers and Stay-inners," *Independent,* XXIII (June 22, 1871), 6; *Independent,* XXIII (December 14, 1871), 4; George A. Jackson to Gladden, February 2, 1896, Gladden Papers.

of evangelization. The kind of religion they believe in is not the kind which is generally in vogue in the so-called Liberal churches.[2]

Gladden also espoused Bushnell's principle that doctrine must conform to enlightened human ethical norms. In "The Offense of the Cross," an editorial based on a sermon he had preached in North Adams, he argued that the scriptural reference to man's creation "in the image of God" implied a correspondence between human morality and God's nature. Doctrines that imputed to God acts that would be immoral for men must be rejected. The sovereignty attributed to God by strict Calvinists, Gladden argued, was that of "sheer self-will," not that of "righteousness." And he accused those who, in his own, thus portrayed God as a capricious monarch of actually driving sensitive people to atheism.[3]

During 1873 and 1874 the *Independent* devoted extensive space to theological discussions and to debates with other religious papers on the questions of original sin, predestination, and future punishment.[4] Many years later, Gladden recalled a meeting of Sigma Chi, the ministerial club in New York City to which he belonged during his years with the *Independent*, where the question of the possible salvation of the heathen arose. Gladden timidly suggested that those would be saved who were in a state of mind that, if they were to hear the Gospel, they would accept Christ. The only one who agreed with Gladden was sure, however, that this would not apply to very many of the heathen.[5]

One of the papers that opposed the *Independent* most vigorously was the *Interior*, a Presbyterian organ published in Chicago and edited by Professor Francis L. Patton of the Presbyterian Seminary

---

[2] [Washington Gladden,] "Liberal Orthodoxy," *Independent*, XXV (July 17, 1873), 908.

[3] [Washington Gladden,] "The Offense of the Cross," *Independent*, XXVI (August 6, 1874), 16; *Independent*, XXV (July 24, 1873), 936, (August 14, 1873), 1020.

[4] *Independent*, XXV (August 7, 1873), 992, (August 28, 1873), 1076, (September 4, 1873), 1105, (September 25, 1873), 1201; XXVI (June 18, 1874), 16.

[5] Gladden, Sermon, July 27, 1913, Gladden Papers.

of the Northwest (McCormick Theological Seminary). Patton soon found a heretic nearer home, David Swing, the pastor of the Fourth Presbyterian Church of Chicago. As early as February, 1873, the *Independent* had noted Swing's departure from "the form of ortho- doxy" and his similarity to Bushnell, Beecher, and Robertson; but its appraisal was sympathetic.[6] A few months later, Patton critically reviewed one of Swing's published sermons, and Swing replied in his own defense, questioning not only orthodox Calvinist views on original sin and future punishment but also the *Interior*'s theory of the inspiration of the Bible, an extremely sensitive point among Presbyterians. Patton accused Swing of important departures from the Westminster Confession (1648), the doctrinal standard for Pres- byterians, and in April, 1874, preferred charges of heresy against him before the Presbytery of Chicago.[7]

Swing was a mild, poetic man of irenic temper, and Patton was unable to prosecute him effectively. The *Independent* followed the trial and accurately predicted that, since he had the unswerving sup- port of his own church and the confidence of most of his ministerial brethren, Swing would be acquitted. It was probably Gladden who wrote that Swing did accept

> . . . the inspiration of the Holy Scriptures, the Trinity, the divinity of Christ, the office of Christ as a mediator when grasped by an obedient faith, conversion by God's spirit, man's natural sinfulness, and the final separation of the righteous and wicked.

In Gladden's view it was "a good Providence which . . . called him to stand as the defender of a rational faith against the assaults of medieval superstition."[8]

After the Presbytery supported Swing by a vote of more than three to one, Patton appealed the case to the Synod of Illinois. Op-

[6] *Independent*, XXV (February 6, 1873), 176.

[7] Lefferts A. Loetscher, *The Broadening Church: A Study of Theological Issues in the Presbyterian Church since 1869* (Philadelphia: University of Penn- sylvania Press, 1957), p. 13.

[8] *Independent*, XXVI (March 5, 1874), 16, (May 14, 1874), 16–17.

posed to further controversy, Swing immediately resigned his church and at the urging of a group of laymen began to hold independent services in Chicago's Music Hall that led to the organization of the Central Church. Gladden lamented Swing's decision. In an editorial in the *Independent*, "A Good Fight Declined," he charged that Patton and his supporters were trying to hold Presbyterianism to a creed that less than half of its ministers could accept without equivocation and asserted that Swing might have won a great victory for liberty by staying in the fray. Gladden thought that acceptance of the Westminster Confession as a "historical symbol," with broad freedom of private interpretation, would be a feasible compromise.[9]

Swing's trial was important to Gladden for several reasons. It manifested his own aversion to doctrinal restraint and reflected the issues then uppermost in his own theological development. It demonstrated his willingness to identify himself with those under the ban. It accented and forced him to rethink the question of denominational standards.[10] His vulnerability on the questions under debate gave his editorials a partisan quality and led him to ignore the grounds of orthodox fears. With blurred historical vision he dismissed the controversial parts of the Calvinist creeds as "medievalism," an unfortunate confusion of terms that he repeated to the end of his career. His discussions in *Recollections* of this and similar episodes are, as one writer has put it, "still a little hot to the touch."[11] An interesting aftermath to the trial occurred in 1894, when Gladden, who subsequently had become acquainted with Swing, negotiated with the Central Church to succeed Swing as its pastor. However, nothing came of his widely-publicized visit to Chicago for consultations.[12]

After Gladden left the *Independent* for the North Church in

---

[9] Loetscher, *The Broadening Church*, p. 14; Gladden, *Recollections*, pp. 227–31; [Washington Gladden,] "A Good Fight Declined," *Independent*, XXVI (May 28, 1874), 16.

[10] *Independent*, XXVI (June 25, 1874), 16 (October 22, 1874), 16; Gladden, *Recollections*, p. 230.

[11] Atkins and Fagley, *American Congregationalism*, p. 177.

[12] *Ohio State Journal*, November 11, 13, December 11, 1894; *Congregationalist*, LXXIX (November 22, 1894), 736.

Springfield, his involvement in theological disputes became more
direct and more heated. In 1877 he again entered the lists to defend
Bushnell's theory of the atonement. He took issue with Joseph Cook,
a popular lecturer who attempted to modernize Calvinism. In 1874
Cook began a series of "Monday Lectures" in Tremont Temple in
Boston that continued for over twenty years. These lectures were
widely reported and published in book form. Cook regarded his
restatement of the doctrine of the atonement as his theological mas-
terpiece. He tried to reconcile the current orthodox view that Christ
suffered punishment as a judicial substitute for sinful mankind with
Bushnell's theory that Christ voluntarily suffered to demonstrate con-
clusively the love of God. But his emphasis was on the substitutionary interpretation, and he criticized Bushnell for giving insufficient
attention to its biblical foundation. He visited Springfield to address
the congregation of the South Church and meetings of the clergy,
and Gladden undoubtedly heard him in person.[13]

Gladden was not satisfied that Cook's views met his ethical test
for theology; accordingly, in May, 1877, he published a pamphlet
based on a series of four sermons he had preached on one of Cook's
lectures on the atonement. Its title, *Was Bronson Alcott's School a
Type of God's Moral Government?*, was taken from Cook's reference
to an experimental school founded by Alcott, the transcendentalist
and educational reformer, in which, as Cook put it, Alcott would
"substitute his own voluntary sacrificial chastisement" for a guilty
pupil's punishment.[14] Cook saw this rule, which supposedly had
transformed behavior in the school, as a "type of God's moral government." He claimed, moreover, to have used it in Alcott's presence
to illustrate his theory of the atonement. This transfer of "obligation
to satisfy the demands of a violated law" from pupil to master and
from sinner to savior was, in his view, "the highest possible dissua-

[13] Theodore D. Bacon, "Joseph Cook," *Dictionary of American Biography*,
IV, 371–72; *Springfield Republican*, April 29, May 13, June 5–6, 17, 1876.

[14] *Springfield Republican*, May 7, 14, 21, 28, 1877; Washington Gladden,
*Was Bronson Alcott's School a Type of God's Moral Government? A Review of
Joseph Cook's Theory of the Atonement* (Boston: Lockwood, Brooks, & Co.,
1877), p. 33.

sive from the love of sin."[15]

But Gladden took issue with the analogy on two grounds. First, he doubted that Cook's version of the rule was accurate; he thought it more likely that Alcott had said, "Boys, if you whisper, I shall not whip you, but I shall make you whip me." Second, he insisted that such a rule, even in Cook's form, actually disproved Cook's point. If it was in fact the rule of the school, there was no substitution of another rule involved, but simply the rigorous enforcement of its own prescription:

> . . . The penalty threatened against the transgressor was literally and exactly visited upon him; he was made to strike his master, and it hurt him so badly to do it that he would never want to be made to do it again.[16]

Cook used Alcott's school simply to illustrate and popularize a theory that was complex and subtle. Gladden examined twenty-seven "self-evident" propositions that Cook had put forward to prove from reason and conscience the need for the atonement. Cook's main contention, which was reflected in his reference to Alcott's school, was that, though "personal blameworthiness" for sin could not be imputed to Christ, as some advocates of the substitutionary theory held, it was morally defensible to believe that Christ had voluntarily assumed man's "obligation to satisfy the demands of a violated law." By this distinction Cook hoped to preserve the substitutionary aspect of the atonement, which the scriptures seemed to require, without incurring the charge by the followers of Bushnell that he was attributing to God an ethically impossible transfer of personal guilt. Gladden flatly rejected Cook's crucial distinction. Neither guilt nor "obligation to satisfy the demands of a violated law" was transferable:

> Others may suffer on account of my sins; others may voluntarily take upon themselves suffering in seeking to save me from my sins; in this

---

[15] *Springfield Republican,* March 15, 1877; Gladden, *Alcott's School,* p. 28.
[16] Gladden, *Alcott's School,* pp. 33–37.

manner Christ does suffer for me; but to affirm that any part of my obligation to satisfy the law which says, "I ought," can be transferred to any
other being, is to contradict one of the first principles of morality.[17]

Gladden's elaboration of his own theory, an inheritance from
Bushnell, was more important than his refutation of Cook's argument. Violation of God's law, he asserted, brought spiritual death.
Sin dulled the moral senses, unleashed the "malignant passions and
the selfish desires and the animal cravings," and led straight to further sin; the penalty for sin came into operation at the moment of
violation, not at some future judgment, and only the sinner could
bear it. Thus, Christ's suffering could not be a substitute for that of
the sinner. He did not die to change God's attitude to man by paying a judicial penalty for sin, but to change man's attitude to God.
Because of his sin, man felt that God was angry with him; and as
sin debilitated man, his estrangement from God grew. Demonstrating that God loved and forgave man, Christ's suffering and death
had the "moral influence" of removing man's fear and convincing him
of divine compassion. Reconciliation restored man to his rightful
share in the divine life and reversed the process of disintegration.[18]
Reconciliation and the cessation of sin, not vicarious punishment,
abrogated spiritual death. Sin and its penalty were related, in Gladden's view, as cause and effect, and the forensic terminology of the
substitutionary theory was grossly inappropriate.

Reactions to Gladden's pamphlet varied. Appreciative reviews
appeared in such liberal religious papers as the *Universalist Quarterly* and the *Unitarian Review,* while the *Christian Register* (Unitarian) called it "one of the ablest and most trenchant pamphlets of
modern times." David Swing's *Alliance* commended Gladden's outspoken course. The *Watchman* of Boston declared that his views on
this and kindred topics would be unwelcome in the Baptist denomi-

---

[17] *Ibid.,* pp. 28–30.

[18] *Ibid.,* pp. 44–50, 53–59, 62. Gladden developed this same view in a number of sermons in the late 1870's. Gladden, Sermons, "Christ Our Ransom,"
November 14, 1877; "Redemption by the Precious Blood of Christ," May 2,
1879, Gladden Papers.

nation. The *Congregational Quarterly* implied that it was less than honest for one who held Gladden's view of the atonement to remain in his denomination, and Gladden felt obliged to defend himself in the *Congregationalist*.[19]

Gladden was never in personal danger of ostracism by his fellow Congregationalists, but a few months after he published his critique of Cook, a controversy occurred in Springfield that reverberated in Congregational circles for many years. It centered in the Congregational church in Indian Orchard, an industrial suburb of Springfield, which had called James F. Merriam, a bright young graduate of Yale College and Andover Seminary, to be its pastor. Merriam had served a church in Connecticut with distinction. His family, the prominent publishers of Springfield, had an old and honored Congregational lineage. George S. Merriam, his brother, had been Henry Ward Beecher's chief editorial assistant on the *Christian Union* from 1870 to 1876. Merriam resuscitated the congregation in Indian Orchard, and on November 7, 1877, an ecclesiastical council, which included Gladden, met to examine and instal him.[20]

After examining him with unusual rigor for several hours, the council voted 8–6 against installation. Though Merriam's doctrinal statement skirted controversy, several of the local clergy, led by W. T. Eustis of the Memorial Church of Springfield, pressed the question of future punishment, on which they had heard that he was unsound. The *Springfield Republican* characterized Eustis and his party as "thorough inquisitors": "The pursuit was close, the breath of the gospel hounds puffed hot on their quarry when it surrendered." Merriam's heresy was mild indeed. He declared that since the Bible left the question open, he would not teach any particular view of future punishment, although annihilation of the wicked seemed more acceptable than their endless, conscious tor-

[19] *Springfield Republican*, August 21, June 16, May 26, June 26, October 20, 1877.

[20] *Ibid.*, February 19, November 28, 1876; *Congregationalist*, XCIII (February 8, 1908), 175; Brown, *Abbott*, pp. 67, 69; *Springfield Republican*, October 30, 1877.

ment. The council's bill of particulars against him also referred to his view of the atonement, against Gladden's protest that it was not an issue.[21]

Despite the council's vote, a minority of its seventeen members actually defeated Merriam. One member left early, and two others, Merriam's uncle, Homer Merriam, and his former pastor, Dr. Buckingham of the South Church, though present, did not vote. Since Buckingham spoke in Merriam's favor, his abstention is inexplicable. The clerical members, who voted 5–2 against installation, were more sensitive to heresy than were the lay members. Only Gladden and Charles L. Morgan of the Hope Church supported Merriam. The *Springfield Republican's* survey of the Congregational clergy in western Massachusetts shortly after the council showed a similar consensus against tolerating divergent views on eternal punishment.[22]

In congregational polity, installation was highly desirable, but not mandatory for continued fellowship with sister churches. Congregationalists in Massachusetts were particularly individualistic in ecclesiastical procedure and even allowed pastors who had not received formal installation to participate in councils to instal others. According to one report, only 275 of the state's 642 Congregational ministers had been regularly installed. Consequently, the church in Indian Orchard was within its rights when it retained Merriam in the face of conciliar rejection. Its action was unanimous and enthusiastic. Though crushed by the council's action, Merriam stayed until 1879, when illness and nervous collapse forced his resignation. Suspicion and prejudice, however, continued to hamper his ministerial labors for several decades.[23]

The council at Indian Orchard had more than local significance. It was the point of departure for a debate over future punishment that lasted for about two decades within Congregationalism and eventually affected the foreign mission work of the denomination.

[21] *Springfield Republican,* November 8, 17, 1877.

[22] *Ibid.,* November 8, 27, December 3, 1877.

[23] *Ibid.,* December 4, November 9, 1877, April 21, May 12, October 25, 1879; James F. Merriam to Gladden, June 10, 1904, Gladden Papers.

But the spread of debate did not eclipse protracted friction in Springfield. Booksellers there reported a lively interest in works on eternal punishment, especially those that took Merriam's position.[24] The local Unitarian and Universalist ministers of Springfield lauded the minority's bravery and explained the majority's action as a logical result of adherence to Calvinism, while the ministers of the First, Olivet, and Memorial churches defended the doctrine at issue. The *Springfield Republican* noted the response of one religious paper to Eustis' defense of "the great doctrines of salvation": "We thought it was the 'great doctrine' of damnation that was at the bottom of Mr. Eustis's difference with Rev. Mr. Meulum." At the meeting in November the Hampden Congregational Association scheduled a discussion on the question "Is belief in future punishment essential to ordination?" for its session in February, which, contrary to custom, it planned to close to the public. Discussion spread to other denominations, and controversial sermons aroused sleepy congregations in the rural districts of western Massachusetts. According to the *Springfield Republican*, even the "high-toned livery-stable loafers joined with the churches . . . in discussing the popular theme."[25]

Gladden and Morgan withheld comment the first week after the council, but on November 18, 1877, Gladden vigorously defended his course, arguing that Congregationalists had no authoritative creed and that few ministers actually preached eternal punishment, and Morgan joined the fray the following Sunday. E. A. Reed of the First Church and Eustis of the Memorial Church continued to preach on the subject. Interest centered on Gladden and Reed as the best representatives of the opposing views. On November 25

---

[24] *Congregationalist*, XCIII (February 8, 1908), 175; *Springfield Republican*, November 13, 1877. Two of the most popular writers on eternal punishment were George S. Merriam and James M. Whiton. Whiton, a friend of Gladden's, came under fire for his views and soon after the council at Indian Orchard had to resign as principal of the Williston Academy in Easthampton. *Springfield Republican*, April 19, 1879; James M. Whiton to Gladden, January 21, 1910, Gladden Papers.

[25] *Springfield Republican*, January 26, 1878, November 12, 14, 26, 1877.

Gladden avoided the subject, but Reed examined his sermon of the previous week point by point.[26]

What really troubled many of the conservatives was the recognition that local churches persisted in giving to Merriam. According to Merriam, Reed and Eustis were more perturbed by his decision to stay at Indian Orchard and the approbation he received than by his doctrinal dissent. In early December a church in neighboring Chicopee Falls invited Merriam to an installation council, but when Gladden tried to read a letter from him, in which he stated that he would avoid contention and would not claim ministerial recognition, the council, indignant that he had been invited, refused to allow the reading. This action, however, was an exception to the widespread respect accorded him. In Springfield, for example, Gladden exchanged pulpits with him on January 13, 1878, and Dr. Buckingham honored him with the pulpit of the South Church in February.[27]

Gladden continued to insist that Congregationalists had no creed —except possibly the antiquated Savoy Confession of 1658, which was similar to the Westminster Confession—and could not require doctrinal uniformity. The council that installed Theodore T. Munger in the Congregational church in North Adams on December 11, 1877, despite Munger's equivocation on eternal punishment, vindicated somewhat Gladden's position. There was sharp disagreement among the council's members, but, because of several abstentions, the decision was unanimous. The council included Gladden, President Noah Porter of Yale, and President Mark Hopkins of Williams. Being therefore more representative geographically than Indian Orchard, it was an important triumph for an inclusive policy among Congregationalists. Gladden repeatedly brought Munger to Springfield during the next few years to demonstrate the acceptability of the views that had caused Merriam's rejection. Grateful for Gladden's stout support, Munger likened himself to "the man in the Bear-fight who slid into the garret while his wife fought the beast—

[26] *Ibid.*, November 19, 26, December 1, 1877.

[27] Merriam to Gladden, June 10, 1904, Gladden Papers; *Springfield Republican,* December 6, 1877, January 14, February 23, 1878.

he was very encouraging but not very helpful."[28]

The repudiation of the decision at Indian Orchard by many prominent Congregationalists led Reed to resign from the First Church. In his final sermon on July 14, 1878, he avowed his appreciation for congregational polity but denied that it freed the churches from collective responsibility for doctrinal purity. In a sermon the following Sunday Gladden disputed Reed's appeal to the doctrines of "historic Congregationalism" and argued for orientation to the present rather than to the past. Gladden focused his remarks not on the issue of eternal punishment but on the question of fellowship.[29]

Outside of Springfield the doctrinal issue merely added intensity to the argument over denominational limits. The conservatives forged a new weapon, the idea that heretics should practice "self-discipline" and get out of the denomination voluntarily. But this weapon shattered on the convincing assertion of the progressives that Congregationalism was not really a denomination but only a fellowship based on common polity. Even before Merriam's case arose, Gladden had censured the *Congregational Quarterly's* enumeration of doctrines on which ministers, in its opinion, must be orthodox. His militant remarks in the *Congregationalist* brought encouraging approval from ministers all over the country:

> I do not care to be in a ministry in which I have not equal rights with every other minister. Such rights I suppose myself to possess, and I shall continue to exercise them until I am advised by some competent tribunal that they have been abrogated.[30]

It was not long before Gladden had a fight on his hands with the editor of the *Congregationalist*, Henry M. Dexter, an ardent member of the orthodox party. During the controversy over Merriam the

[28] *Springfield Republican*, December 10, 13, 1877; Gladden, "Theodore Thornton Munger," Sermon, n.d., Gladden Papers; Gladden, *Recollections*, p. 265; *Springfield Republican*, May 18, 1878, July 19, 1879, February 28, 1880; Theodore T. Munger to Gladden, January 30, 1878, Gladden Papers.

[29] Charles L. Morgan to Maurer, April 6, 1928, First Church archives; *Springfield Republican*, July 15, 22, 1878.

[30] Gladden, *Recollections*, p. 267.

paper supported the decision of the council as "painful, but necessary," and criticized Gladden's broad views on congregational polity, though Dexter did print a defensive letter from Merriam. Dexter's position, however, was weak. The *Independent* observed that "Dr. Dexter's troops all fight on Mr. Gladden's side."[31] As the battle dragged on, Dexter's willingness to print communications from Gladden slackened. He based his refusal to print one article on its length, whereupon Gladden accused him of discrimination. Gladden then got the *Springfield Republican* to print the article, together with a condemnation of Dexter's course. The article clarified a recent prediction by Gladden that the minority view of future punishment would eventually prevail, which the *Congregationalist* had taken to prophesy the conversion of Congregationalists to Universalism. The *Congregationalist* apologized lamely for misinterpreting Gladden's statement but continued to criticize his utterances, despite the widespread disapproval of other religious papers.[32]

The Vermont Congregational Convention's passage in June, 1879, of what became known as the "historic resolution" prolonged the controversy over fellowship. The resolution called for the voluntary withdrawal of those who rejected "any substantial part" of the doctrines "commonly called evangelical." An amendment excepting those who felt themselves worthy of fellowship and who had not been rejected by "a competent ecclesiastical tribunal" was voted down. When a well-known minister in Hartford, George L. Walker, defended the convention in the *Springfield Republican*, Gladden again denied the existence of suitable doctrinal standards by showing that Walker himself deviated in important respects from the Savoy Confession. Walker did not reply to Gladden, but he answered

---

[31] *Springfield Republican*, November 17, December 22, 1877, February 23, April 20, 1878; *Independent*, quoted in *ibid.*, January 19, 1878.

[32] Henry M. Dexter to Gladden, October 12, 22, 1878, Gladden to Dexter, October 18, 1878, Gladden Papers; *Springfield Republican*, October 19, 26, November 9, December 12, 1878.

other critical letters, among them one by Theodore T. Munger.[33]

Gladden was in close consultation with George B. Safford and Lewis O. Brastow, two leaders of the minority in Vermont.[34] In July, 1879, a little over a month after the convention in Vermont, he wrote an important letter, which the *Springfield Republican* and other papers printed, defending Safford, Brastow, and their supporters. He called for an equilibrium between the two key ideas of congregational polity—independence and fellowship. While he abhorred atomistic independence and recognized the need for associational ties among local congregations, he felt that these ties should be for co-operation in Christian work, not for the enjoinment of important creeds. The action of the Vermont Congregational Convention provided a way, he feared, by which a minister's standing could be damaged without regular ecclesiastical procedures:

> It denies to every man who may be suspected of heresy the right of private judgment respecting himself, and gives to every one who may choose to accuse him the right of private judgment upon him.[35]

This cluster of events that disturbed the otherwise peaceful course of Gladden's ministry in Springfield greatly troubled him. But it also inspired one of his most lasting contributions to American religion. One night after a prayer meeting at the North Church, he penned the words to "The Great Companion," known since the 1880's as "O Master, Let Me Walk with Thee," an enduring hymn in all of the Protestant denominations. The first and last of the poem's three stanzas have each been divided for musical purposes, making a four-stanza hymn. The second stanza, which has always been omitted from hymnals, reflects most clearly Gladden's experience in the late 1870's:

---

[33] Gladden, *Recollections*, pp. 268–69; *Springfield Republican*, June 14, 17–18, 27, July 1, 1879.

[34] George B. Safford to Gladden, June 21, 28, October 27, 1879; Lewis O. Brastow to Gladden, June 14, 19, 1879, Gladden Papers.

[35] *Springfield Republican*, July 26, 1879.

O Master, let me walk with Thee
Before the taunting Pharisee;
Help me to bear the sting of spite,
The hate of men who hide Thy light,
The sore distrust of souls sincere
Who cannot read Thy judgments clear,
The dullness of the multitude
Who dimly guess that Thou art good.[36]

The theological disputes of the late 1870's continued to trouble Congregationalism. When the National Council of the Congregational Churches met in St. Louis in 1880, there was a strong demand for a theological statement that would represent current thinking in the denomination. Embarrassed by the lack of an authoritative standard, the conservatives were eager to secure a firm creedal position, while many progressives, though less anxious to engage in creed-making, were more than willing to break the ambiguous hold of the Savoy Confession. The council appointed a commission of twenty-five and authorized it to publish an informal declaration of what its members felt most Congregationalists believed. This solution to the doctrinal problem probably pleased the progressives more than the conservatives. At least, it received Gladden's public approval.[37] The commission appointed at St. Louis did not settle the questions raised at Indian Orchard. It refused to state that all who died impenitent would suffer eternal punishment, thus tacitly vindicating the position for which Merriam and Gladden had contended. To Gladden, who was fond of quoting John Robinson's assurance to the first band of Pilgrims to leave Leyden that "the Lord had more truth and light to break forth out of his holy word," the Creed of 1883 was an admirable tribute to theological progress.[38]

---

[36] Gladden, *Fifty Years in the Ministry*.

[37] *Springfield Republican*, November 16, 1880; Gladden, "The St. Louis Council," Sermon, November 21, 1880, Gladden Papers.

[38] Atkins and Fagley, *American Congregationalism*, p. 60. According to one authority on Congregational history, Robinson had reference to church polity, not doctrine. Walker, *A History of the Congregational Churches*, p. 64.

In 1883, the year of the creed, the council that met in Columbus to instal Gladden was quite concerned with his views on future punishment. After Gladden presented a statement of his beliefs, ending with the Nicene Creed, Dr. James Brand of Oberlin raised the issue of "second probation," the theory that those who never heard of Christ in this life might have another chance after death. He answered Brand adroitly. Then someone else asked bluntly, "Is there any chance after death?" Gladden's reply, "Not that I know of," brought a round of applause from the audience.[39] Gladden was, in fact, frankly agnostic on future punishment and did not believe in either universal salvation or "second probation." He simply refused to believe in eternal punishment.

During the 1880's and early 1890's the controversy over future punishment centered around Andover Seminary and the American Board of Commissioners for Foreign Missions. For about a decade after 1884 a group of professors at Andover expressed their views on "second probation" and other theological questions through the *Andover Review,* which became a highly controversial journal. When several candidates for foreign missionary service were found to hold the doctrine of "second probation" espoused by the professors, the American Board refused to appoint them to foreign fields. Gladden took his stand with the candidates in a sermon, "Probation for the Heathen," to a packed opera house in Columbus. He denied that they believed in a "second probation"; they merely insisted on one probation for everybody, which, for those who had never heard of Christ, might come after death. Even their conservative critics believed that God would judge the heathen by a different standard than the one He applied to citizens of Christian lands. On another occasion he stated that Robert A. Hume, one of the candidates, had "simply maintained the right to think for himself on a subject concerning which nothing is clearly revealed. . . . "[40]

The controversy ended in victory for the proponents of the new

[39] *Congregationalist,* LXVIII (March 29, 1883), 111.

[40] Loetscher, *The Broadening Church,* p. 12; *Ohio State Journal,* October 18, 1886, February 18, 1887.

views. Gladden made "a vigorous liberal speech" at the annual
meeting in Chicago in 1892 at which the American Board began to
adopt an inclusive policy.[41] It was only in 1892–93 that the turmoil
that began at Indian Orchard was quieted. Reviewing the episode,
Gladden claimed that the American Board had been "out of line
with the whole trend of thought in the Congregational churches,
and with the consensus of intelligent evangelical opinion in all
lands." He suggested that Peter's reference to Christ preaching to
"the spirits in prison" might offer scriptural support for the idea of
a future probation for those who never had heard the Gospel, but
his receptivity to this view was the result of the tolerant spirit of
his age rather than of biblical exegesis.[42] Subsequent theological
changes have given the issues an appearance of unreality, but they
seemed crucial to the participants in these controversies. Gladden
worked persistently for the ideal of a broad church, and no small
part of his contribution to Congregationalism is to be found in its
modern tolerance of diversity.

Throughout his career Gladden preached a non-Calvinistic theology. He recognized Calvin's contributions to civil liberty but
deplored his doctrines of predestination, original sin, and eternal
punishment. The affinity between God and man, the cornerstone
of Gladden's thinking, received frequent emphasis. Emphatically
rejecting definitions of original sin that implied imputed guilt, he
spoke of man inheriting only "a condition of moral disability and
disorder" that would lead to sin if he lived to the age of discretion.[43]

But the new intellectual challenges of the late nineteenth century
required a different adjustment in Gladden's theology. Two major
forces, biblical criticism and evolutionary science, conditioned the
nature and direction of this adjustment. Biblical criticism forced a

[41] *Ohio State Journal*, October 8, 1892.

[42] I Peter 3:19; Gladden, Sermon, October 29, 1893, Gladden Papers.

[43] Gladden, Sermons, "John Calvin," June 15, 1890, February, 1889, "God's
Thoughts and Man's Thoughts," April 7, 1889, "Original Sin," February 10,
1889, "Old Facts with New Faces," June 24, 1894, Gladden Papers; H. Shelton
Smith, *Changing Conceptions of Original Sin: A Study in American Theology
since 1750* (New York: Charles Scribner's Sons, 1955), pp. 175–77.

re-examination of the commonly accepted source of religious authority for Protestants. For Gladden, who was nurtured on the "proof
text" approach to an infallible Bible, this re-examination was liber-
ating: it made the Bible more intelligible and reasonable. Evolution
challenged theology on a different level—that of the basic presuppo-
sitions on which the Christian *Weltanschauung* of the nineteenth
century rested. Evolution raised questions not only about the conditions under which the world came into being but also about the
validity of theology itself. Did it not offer a convincing naturalistic
cosmogony whose philosophical implications obviated the necessity
of positing God and a supernatural order? Whereas biblical criticism
struck at the traditional method of religious inquiry (the discovery
of truth in the Bible), evolution threatened to invalidate religion
itself.

After 1880 these forces—evolution to a greater extent than biblical criticism—provided the fundamental issues in theological reconstruction. Progressives reached a consensus, known variously as
liberal theology, the New Theology, and Modernism, which signified
their attempt to reconcile these new trends with what they regarded
as the essentials of Christian faith. This liberal theology had representatives in all of the major Protestant denominations, but Congregationalists, because of their freedom from rigid theological
standards, were especially receptive to it.

Gladden's role in the liberal movement was not that of creative
thinker, but rather that of simplifier and popularizer. Popularization
was his avowed goal. The subtitles of several of his books declared
that they were "books for the people." His extensive use of quotations indicates that he borrowed heavily from other thinkers and
that, though he was receptive to contemporary intellectual currents,
he was not himself an original theologian.

In the early 1870's Gladden was already sensitive to new developments in the study of the Bible. Incorporating the findings of textual
criticism into his preaching, he pointed out verses that were not in
the most ancient manuscripts. According to his own testimony, he
was in the vanguard of the clergy in this practice. At one meeting

of Congregational ministers in Springfield he was the only one who thought it safe to tell laymen that a certain verse was an interpolation, although the other ministers agreed that the verse was spurious. In *Sunday Afternoon* he urged honest discussion of the latest biblical knowledge. He commended the work of British and American scholars on the Revised Version, which incorporated manuscripts older than those possessed by the translators of the King James Version,[44] and he used the Revised Version rather than the King James Version in his preaching. In one sermon toward the end of the century on the final words of the Lord's Prayer in the King James Version, "For thine is the kingdom, and the power, and the glory, for ever," which the Revised Version omitted, Gladden introduced his remarks in these words:

> My text is not in my Bible. It may be in yours, but it is not in mine. The oldest and best manuscript copies of the New Testament do not contain it. . . . [But] they are inspired words, for the spirit of truth is in them.[45]

Agreeing with Matthew Arnold's dictum that the Bible must be treated not as dogma but as literature, Gladden also encouraged puting a natural construction on the Bible's words. He wrote, ". . . It is not by etymological microscopy nor by logical practice upon words that we get the true meaning, but simply by trying to put ourselves in the writer's place. . . . "[46]

The challenge to the traditional view of the Bible came from that branch of scholarship known as higher criticism, which went beyond textual criticism to questions of composition and authorship—in short, to the historical origins of the Bible. Gladden was reluctant at first to endorse the higher criticism, and in 1882 he defended the Mosaic authorship of the Pentateuch in an article for the *Independ-*

[44] *Springfield Republican,* October 25, 1880; Gladden, *Recollections,* pp. 260–61; *Sunday Afternoon,* III (July, 1879), 665.

[45] Gladden, Sermon, March 8, 1898, Gladden Papers.

[46] Washington Gladden, "How to Use the Bible," *Sunday Afternoon,* II (November, 1878), 451–56.

ent.[47] The introduction of the higher criticism from its German home into American theological circles during the 1880's threatened the dogma of biblical infallibility that most American clergymen and almost all laymen still held. Though many ministers suspected the higher critics of infidelity, Gladden began in the early 1880's to welcome their conclusions. When an unsigned article in the *Century* on "The Bible in the Sunday-school," which Gladden appears to have written, suggested the abandonment of the principle of biblical inerrancy in religious education, some conservatives reacted sharply. A prominent Southern Presbyterian, Robert L. Dabney, citing the familiar text, "All Scripture is given by inspiration of God . . . ," apparently denounced the magazine for fostering infidelity. Dabney, a diehard ex-Confederate who defended religious orthodoxy and the southern way of life with equal ardor, had only a few months earlier succeeded in ousting Professor James Woodrow, an uncle of Woodrow Wilson, from the Presbyterian Theological Seminary at Columbia, South Carolina, for teaching evolution. In a letter to Richard W. Gilder, editor of the *Century*, Gladden noted that the Revised Version's rendering of the text, "Every Scripture, inspired of God," materially changed its meaning, and he charged Dabney with duplicity. "What can you do with such a man?" he exclaimed. "All I have to say is that, if there isn't a hell for such, there ought to be." Gladden's first line of argument against the idea of biblical infallibility continued to be a denial that the Bible claimed infallibility for itself. In the introduction to a sermon on George Eliot's novel *Romola,* he told his congregation that "several of the best books of the Old Testament are works of fiction."[48]

[47] Munger to Gladden, March 27, 1882, Gladden Papers. Munger, himself an early friend of biblical criticism, agreed with Gladden that Moses had written the Pentateuch. He was surprised to find Gladden taking that position.

[48] Walter F. Peterson, "American Protestantism and the Higher Criticism, 1870–1910," *Transactions of the Wisconsin Academy of Sciences, Arts, and Letters,* L (February 26, 1962), 321–24; [Washington Gladden,] "The Bible in the Sunday-school," *Century,* XXIX (November, 1884), 146–48; Harvey Wish, *Society and Thought in Modern America: A Social and Intellectual History of the American People from 1865* (2d ed.; New York: David McKay Co., 1962), p. 36; Gladden to Gilder, March 5, 1885, *Century* Collection; Gladden, "Romola," Sermon, April 16, 1899, Gladden Papers.

While Congregationalists were preoccupied with speculative theological issues, such as eternal punishment, Presbyterians were engulfed in controversy over the accuracy of the Bible and the authorship of its component parts. During the 1880's Professor Charles A. Briggs of Union Theological Seminary gained recognition as the leading Presbyterian exponent of critical views. His appointment in 1890 to the seminary's new chair of biblical theology, and particularly his inaugural address in 1891 on "The Authority of Holy Scripture," brought the nascent conflict over the Bible into the open and precipitated formal charges of heresy against Briggs. His trial, which lasted until 1893, culminated in his suspension from the Presbyterian ministry and the voluntary disaffiliation of Union Seminary from the Presbyterian Church. By 1893 Presbyterians had another trial for heresy on their hands. Professor Henry Preserved Smith of Lane Theological Seminary in Cincinnati, a friend of Gladden's, espoused critical views, and the Presbytery of Cincinnati took action against him. Like Briggs, he was suspended from the ministry.[49]

Gladden drew his congregation's attention to both trials. In 1891, before the proceedings against Briggs began, he sympathetically appraised Briggs's approach and conclusions in a sermon on "The Theological Crisis and Its Issues." And in a sermon in 1893 on "Heresy Trials and What They Prove" he observed that the views for which Briggs and Smith were under fire were no different from those he had preached for years: that the Bible contained scientific and historical errors; that parts of the Old Testament reflected an imperfect morality; and that many of its books were of composite authorship. He doubted that the ecclesiastical majorities that suspended Briggs and Smith meant much, since the verdict of a scholar was worth more than that of "some illiterate ruling elder." The conservatives were foolish to fear biblical criticism, not only because the new views were "substantially true" and bound to prevail, but also because there was "no book in the world" that could "so well

[49] Loetscher, *The Broadening Church*, pp. 49, 55–62, 65–68.

afford to have the truth about it all told." Though an "earthen vessel," the Bible clearly contained the Word of God. Before Briggs's trial ended in 1893, Gladden had him preach in the First Church for both services on one Sunday. At the evening service, which Henry Preserved Smith attended, ushers had to turn away almost as many as they were able to seat in the spacious auditorium.[50]

Gladden believed that he could propagate the findings of biblical criticism without diminishing respect for the Bible. Indeed, he was sure that these findings made the Bible more remarkable than ever. He brought outstanding biblical scholars, such as George Adam Smith, a Scottish critic, to lecture at the First Church. About 1900 Gladden based a series of midweek studies on a guide to proper use of the Bible by William Newton Clarke, the outstanding Baptist theologian of the period. Clarke's theme, that the Bible, a progressive revelation, must be filtered by its Christian element, was not new to Gladden's congregation.[51] Ancient civilization had conditioned the morality of the Old Testament. According to Gladden,

> the revelation given by God to half savage men must needs be morally imperfect. They are given as much as they can receive, and as their natures are gradually purified and enlarged they are given more.[52]

He maintained that the early Hebrews had been henotheistic, not advancing to pure monotheism until the time of the later prophets. In an imaginative sermon on Abraham's attempted sacrifice of Isaac, Gladden refused to admit that God had commanded the act, which was morally acceptable to the heathen but not to Christians; instead, he thought, Abraham's primitive conscience had prompted him to demonstrate devotion to his God equal to that of his neighbors to

[50] *Ohio State Journal,* May 23, 1891; Gladden, "Heresy Trials and What They Prove," Sermon, January 8, 1893, Gladden Papers; *Ohio State Journal,* February 13, 1893.

[51] *Ohio State Journal,* May 27, 1899; Gladden, Sermons, January 19, 1902, February 14, 1904, December 3, 1905, Gladden Papers.

[52] Washington Gladden, *How Much Is Left of the Old Doctrines? A Book for the People* (Boston: Houghton, Mifflin & Co., 1899), p. 75.

their gods, and, because he was faithful to the light that he had,
God gave him more light.[53]

Although the Bible was not of uniform value, it was a unique
revelation of God. It was not a revelation in the sense of a verbally
inspired communication from God to men, but in the sense of a
record of God's self-revelation in past ages. If studied properly, with
recognition of its errors, understanding of its setting, and unforced
construction of its words, the Bible would yield vital religious truth.
One could give up the theory of inerrancy, he thought, without surrendering the authority of the Bible. Its "complete utterance" on
any question of religion or morality would be authoritative and true.
In "The Bible as Literature," part of a series in the *Outlook* that
included articles by Dean Farrar of Canterbury, Dean Fremantle
of Ripon, and Lyman Abbott, Gladden, citing Bushnell's treatise on
language in *God in Christ,* urged study of biblical language as symbol and classification of the biblical writings by literary type as
methods of extracting the Bible's meaning.[54]

Gladden tried to calm popular fears by stressing the conservatism
of much criticism and the attachment to the Bible of many higher
critics. He thought that "those who are in constant panic for fear
that the influence of the Bible will be impaired, show themselves
to be profoundly skeptical as to the real worth of the Bible." He
denounced as absurd the organization in 1904 of a protective league
to defend the Bible.[55] The Bible was its own best defense. In 1898
he lamented a "bibliophobia which now affects a certain class of
minds," but in an address ten years later to the International Student Bible Conference in Columbus he hopefully predicted the

[53] Gladden, *The Interpreter,* p. 45; Gladden, Sermon, July 8, 1906, Gladden
Papers.

[54] Gladden, Sermons, May 27, 1900, February 14, 1904, Gladden Papers;
Washington Gladden, "The Bible as Literature," *Outlook,* LIII (June 27, 1896),
1207–8.

[55] Washington Gladden, "The New Bible," *Arena,* IX (February, 1894), 304;
Gladden, "Friends and Enemies of the Bible," Sermon, June 19, 1904, Gladden
Papers.

reversal of a tendency to sully the Bible.[56] Lamenting a growing ignorance of the Bible, Gladden argued for the inclusion of literary study of the Bible in the public schools. Though he recognized that the perfunctory reading of a few verses was inadequate and that a cultural approach would not satisfy many supporters of religious instruction in the schools, he advocated experimentation toward an acceptable compromise. He also participated in the activities of the Religious Education Association, organized in 1903 to orient biblical education to modern educational techniques, and became its president in 1917. And in the last years of his ministry he spoke of the Bible as "a dear old comrade" that had been richer to him in recent years than ever before.[57]

Gladden's popularization of biblical criticism reached far beyond his congregation. In fact, he and Lyman Abbott might be considered the major interpreters of critical studies to laymen. He wrote articles for such journals as *McClure's Magazine* and the *Biblical World*, edited by Shailer Mathews of the University of Chicago, and for newspaper syndicates.[58] He frequently gave a popular address, Dare We Tell the Truth about the Bible?", to churches and religious societies.[59] But his most important contributions were two books, *Who Wrote the Bible?* (1891) and *Seven Puzzling Bible Books* (1897). Both grew out of series of Sunday evening sermons.[60]

---

[56] Gladden, Sermon, October 16, 1898, Gladden Papers; *Ohio State Journal*, October 23, 1908.

[57] Washington Gladden, "Religion and the Schools," *Atlantic Monthly*, CXV (January, 1915), 57–68; Henry C. King to Gladden, November 18, 1907, Henry F. Cope to Gladden, January 7, 1908, January 27, 1915, March 5, 1917, Gladden Papers; *Ohio State Journal*, June 22, 1914.

[58] Gladden and Abbott took similar approaches to the Bible. Brown, *Abbott*, pp. 150–60. An article that Gladden wrote for *McClure's Magazine* was apparently never published. S. S. McClure to Gladden, April 16, 1900, April 2, 1902; Shailer Mathews to Gladden, April 18, 1914; Joseph B. Bowles to Gladden, April 7, 1914, Gladden Papers.

[59] Gladden, "Dare We Tell the Truth about the Bible?", Sermon, [1914,] Gladden Papers.

[60] The series on "Who Wrote the Bible?" ran from September to December, 1890, and that on "Seven Puzzling Bible Books" ran through May and early June, 1897. Church notices in the *Ohio State Journal* carried announcements of each sermon.

Ladies' societies, Sunday-school classes, and study groups used both books as manuals, and Gladden even received requests to allow translation of *Who Wrote the Bible?* into French and Italian. W. S. Rainsford, rector of St. George's Church in New York City and a prominent social gospeler in the Protestant Episcopal church, used this book and gave scores of copies to friends and parishioners.[61]

In some ways both books were conservative. Gladden announced on the first page of *Who Wrote the Bible?* that he believed the Bible contained supernatural elements, and in the concluding chapter, "How Much Is the Bible Worth?", he stressed the need for a reverent as well as a rational approach to its contents. He rejected the views of the radical critics who, in his words, "started out with the assumption that these books are in no respect different from other sacred books . . . " and who bent their energies "to discrediting, in every way, the veracity and the authority of our Scriptures." He rejected likewise the orthodox assumption that Moses wrote all of the Pentateuch, but, as one reviewer noted, he was not prepared to "dethrone Moses from his high seat as the organizer and lawgiver of Israel. . . . " He incorporated the consensus of most contemporary critics that the Pentateuch grew out of four documentary sources, but he was impatient with patchwork attempts to fragment verses according to documentary origin.[62]

On the New Testament Gladden was even more cautious. Granting that the first three Gospels, though compiled by the individuals whose names they bear, were collections of oral and written memoranda, he contended that John wrote his narrative without such aids. In *Who Wrote the Bible?* and other writings he defended the historical integrity and philosophical unity of the Gospels.[63] Gladden's

[61] Houghton Mifflin Company to Gladden, April 20, 1909; Pasquale Vocatura to Gladden, January 4, 1914; W. S. Rainsford to Gladden, January 26, 1900, Gladden Papers.

[62] Washington Gladden, *Who Wrote the Bible? A Book for the People* (Boston: Houghton, Mifflin & Co., 1891), pp. 1, 5, 56, 380–81; *Ohio State Journal,* April 25, 1891.

[63] Gladden, *Who Wrote the Bible?,* p. 260; Gladden, "The Christ I Serve," Sermon, March 20, 1885, Gladden Papers; Washington Gladden, *Burning Questions of the Life That Now Is and of That Which Is to Come* (New York: Century Co., 1890), pp. 197–218.

views on the New Testament, however, paralleled the advances of the higher critics, who extended their studies to the New Testament later than to the Old Testament.

But while *Who Wrote the Bible?* was not conservative enough for the *Congregationalist*, which denied the conclusiveness of Gladden's views, a reviewer for the *Nation* accused him of taking the traditional position whenever in doubt, branding as "enemies of the Bible" those only a little more radical than himself, and surrendering only the most implausible assumptions in his treatment of the New Testament. The *Nation* touched on a crucial aspect of Gladden's breezy dismissal of the more radical German scholars. It questioned whether he had ever read them at first hand.[64] Indeed, he had not. He relied on translations and on the original works of British and American scholars, who were considerably less daring than the German pioneers. Comforted by the thought that their faith need not crash on the rocks of modern knowledge, laymen were unaware of the limitations of Gladden's approach, but his potpourri of opinions and conclusions not only contributed nothing to contemporary scholarship but was actually based on fragmentary knowledge of that scholarship.

His second work on biblical criticism, *Seven Puzzling Bible Books*, designed to supplement *Who Wrote the Bible?*, covered seven books of the Old Testament in detail. The same assumptions—the evolution of reason and morality and the progression of revelation—ran through both volumes. But in *Seven Puzzling Bible Books* Gladden concentrated on elucidating meaning rather than on delving primarily into questions of authorship. In his first and most important chapter he argued persuasively that ministers were obligated to "tell the truth about the Bible." He re-emphasized his preference for the "reverent" critics, as well as his conviction that the Bible would have more value to laymen if approached historically than if veiled with sacrosanctity.[65]

[64] *Congregationalist*, LXXVI (May 21, 1891), 173; review of *Who Wrote the Bible?* in *Nation*, LIII (September 17, 1891), 222.

[65] Washington Gladden, *Seven Puzzling Bible Books: A Supplement to "Who Wrote the Bible?"* (Boston: Houghton, Mifflin & Co., 1897), chap. i.

Biblical criticism challenged accepted views of the Bible's origins and raised questions about its historical accuracy. Evolution challenged its scientific veracity. These two forces were closely related. The higher critics reconstructed the development of the Old Testament on the basis of evolutionary theory. They replaced the idea of revelation as a divine activity occurring at certain intervals in the past with an evolutionary explanation of religion in which concepts of God and morality were refined through historical circumstances and progressive revelation. Both forces seemed to undermine the authority of the Bible, and those who reacted against one also normally reacted against the other. Liberal theology incorporated both, while fundamentalists found in them key targets for the attack that they mounted with increasing vigor in the twentieth century. When Billy Sunday and Gladden clashed in 1912–13 in Columbus, two principal causes of friction between them were biblical criticism and evolution. Though biblical criticism strongly colored Gladden's preaching, its influence was less pervasive than that of evolution. Evolution became the leaven of his religious and social thought, and the authority of its philosophical implications was, for him, unchallenged.

Gladden was neither the first nor the most important of the Protestant clergymen who adjusted theology to evolution. Unitarians, although initially disturbed by this new concept, were first to prove hospitable to it. Henry Ward Beecher, a Congregationalist, startled the religious world with his forthright acceptance of evolution in the early 1880's. Lyman Abbott, Beecher's successor as editor of the *Christian Union* and as pastor of the Plymouth Church, developed a more elaborate evolutionary theology and wrote more widely on the subject than Gladden did.[66] But Gladden's early and continued sensitivity to scientific currents and his popularization of the liberal theological consensus give his views importance.

In the early 1870's he began to give sympathetic attention to evo-

[66] Francis P. Weisenburger, *Ordeal of Faith: The Crisis of Church-going America, 1865–1900* (New York: Philosophical Library, 1959), pp. 66 f.; Brown, *Abbott,* pp. 139–49.

lutionary theory. It was probably Gladden who, as religious editor of the *Independent,* recalled the day when doubt concerning a literal six-day creation branded one as an infidel and asserted that "now, no Christian, unless he also be a blockhead (a not impossible combination), so interprets it." In an address at Amherst College on "The Conditions of Religious Inquiry" shortly after the council at Indian Orchard, he pronounced respect for the facts of history and science an essential ingredient of the search for truth. The geologic record, he said, was as much God's revelation as the Decalogue.[67]

To reconcile apparent conflicts between science and religion, he posited the unity of truth; there could be no real conflict because both agree with a united creation. But to preserve this theoretical concord between science and religion, it was necessary for him to relegate them to separate spheres of inquiry—science, to facts ascertainable by the senses, and religion, to the realm of the spirit. Thus, he dismissed the literal interpretation of the account of creation in Genesis as a strained attempt to turn a religious book into a scientific treatise. Denying that the Bible meant to teach geology or astronomy, he tried "to separate its religious elements from the imperfect scientific and historical conceptions in which they are often imbedded."[68] The truths that these "folk-stories of the Hebrews" taught were the presence of God in the world and the consequent sacredness of man and his environment. Science could not contravene them. Moreover, the account in Genesis testified that the universe was not self-originated, that it was unified, that its development was orderly and progressive, that its consummation would be beneficent, and that man was pre-eminent among its creatures.[69]

Gladden's first major attempt to bring religion and science to terms was a series of lectures in 1886 at the Ohio State University. The lectures were published in England and the United States as *Burning Questions of the Life That Now Is and of That Which Is to Come* (1890). During the winter of 1887–88 he gave a supplemen-

---

[67] *Independent,* XXIV (May 16, 1872); *Springfield Republican,* June 24, 1878.
[68] Gladden, Sermons, September, 1892; January 7, 1900, Gladden Papers.
[69] Gladden, Sermon, February 4, 1894, Gladden Papers.

tary series at the same institution on the "Relations of Religion to Modern Thought."[70] In *Burning Questions* he discussed fundamental Christian doctrines in the light of modern science, restating each doctrine in terms of a spiritual interpretation of the universe. In his first chapter, "Has Evolution Abolished God?", he argued that while science could explain how matter had reached its present forms, it could not explain existence itself, and that evolution actually made the universe more mysterious and divine than did the clockmaker theory of Paley's *Natural Theology*. In addition, he contended that evolution presupposed a purposive, not a chaotic, theory of the origin of the universe.[71]

Gladden's scientific authorities in *Burning Questions* and later writings were Herbert Spencer and his American popularizer, John Fiske. Fiske's adaptation of Spencerian ideas to the needs of theism suited Gladden's non-scientific temper. Whereas Spencer saw only an unknown and unknowable reality behind the universe, Fiske espied a God of personality and intelligence, knowable and accessible. In *The Idea of God*, published the year before Gladden's initial lectures at the Ohio State University, Fiske had declared frankly: "The infinite and eternal Power that is manifested in every pulsation of the universe is none other than the living God." Gladden agreed with Spencer that men must not conceive of God in the form of a human person, but he did not think that Spencer's unknown reality was an "Omnipotent It." Similarly, Gladden refused to accept a naturalistic view of man. He argued from consciousness and the requirements of morality to human freedom. Every man knew that he was free and responsible, whatever the theories of materialistic scientists and philosophers.[72]

Gladden saw no conflict between evolution and the concept of natural law. According to him, natural law was the governance of

[70] *Ohio State Journal,* February 20, 1886; *Congregationalist,* LXXII (December 15, 1887), 440.

[71] Gladden, *Burning Questions,* pp. 25–32.

[72] John Fiske, *The Idea of God as Affected by Modern Knowledge* (Boston: Houghton, Mifflin & Co., 1885), p. 166; Gladden, *Burning Questions,* pp. 62, 89–90; Gladden, Sermon, December 20, 1903, Gladden Papers.

God in the physical world, and its uniformity and inevitability were more convincing proofs of an intelligent deity than its ostensible interruptions by so-called miracles might be.[73] Presupposing natural law, he accepted quite automatically the cosmological deduction, a traditional link in the chain of Christian apologetics, that order bespoke a prior and transcendent intelligence. Natural law was, for him, a logical necessity, not an inductive conclusion. Accordingly, he frequently emphasized that science itself proceeded on faith in a rational and orderly universe. But he tried to give natural law an evolutionary direction, by suggesting the possibility of grades and combinations of laws. As evolution progressed, higher laws would void lower ones, and new combinations of laws would introduce dimensions of development previously unknown. He was thus able to justify miracles and prayer in a structured universe without violence to uniformity—they were supernatural, not antinatural or unnatural occurrences—and to enlist evolution in behalf of the whole framework.[74]

Gladden repeated and expanded the main lines of thought established in Burning Questions in later books and sermons. His one basic assumption was that the universe was rational. Not only did science assume this, but to deny rationality was to plunge into intellectual chaos.[75] His use of evolution as a defense and explanation of theism became more explicit in the writings that followed Burning Questions, particularly How Much Is Left of the Old Doctrines? (1899). Instead of weakening the validity of religion, the idea that religion itself was evolutionary strengthened, in his thinking, the argument for the existence of God. He borrowed the reasoning of Fiske's Through Nature to God (1899) that man's universal religious instincts evolved because of a corresponding reality behind the universe, just as the eye evolved because there was something to

[73] Gladden, "The Religion of To-day," Sermon, January 11, 1880, Gladden Papers.

[74] Gladden, Burning Questions, pp. 108–11; Gladden, "Christ as Healer," Sermon, April, 1886, Gladden Papers.

[75] Gladden, Sermon, July 1, 1900, Gladden Papers.

see. In *How Much Is Left of the Old Doctrines?* he wrote that if there was nothing to satisfy "this hunger which evolution has taken so many centuries to develop . . . then all that is fundamental in the philosophy of evolution is discredited and set at naught."[76] William James's analysis of the common features of all religions in *The Varieties of Religious Experience* (1902) substantiated for Gladden mankind's spiritual quest.[77]

Gladden also argued for the doctrine of immortality from Fiske's interpretation of evolution. In *How Much Is Left of the Old Doctrines?* he declared: "So far as I have a reasoned theory of the existence of God and of the future life, it rests, very largely, on the truth brought to light by the evolutionary philosophy." Fiske, particularly in *The Destiny of Man* (1884) and *Through Nature to God* (1899), suggested two grounds for belief in immortality: the universal expectation of a future life; and the incompleteness of evolution without an opportunity for man to attain perfection. The first ground was similar to Fiske's argument for the existence of God: in Gladden's words, "faculties as deep-seated, as persistent, as universal as the religious faculties must have something corresponding to them in the universe." The second ground required the assumption that evolution, to justify itself to reason, must promise "an endless future for the human race." Man must become more than he is for the promise of perfection inherent in evolution to be realized. Otherwise, "the whole process of gain and advance by which he has become what he is turns on itself and reverses its order."[78] In a popular pamphlet written after the death of two close friends, Gladden reaffirmed this line of reasoning. If man went into nonentity, this would be a "lying universe," one that gave him powers that he could never use and longings that he could never satisfy. But Fiske did not believe that science could prove or disprove immortality.

[76] Gladden, "Through Science to Faith—the Life of John Fiske," Sermon, July 21, 1901, Gladden Papers; Gladden, *How Much Is Left of the Old Doctrines?*, p. 23.

[77] Gladden, Sermon, September 7, 1902, Gladden Papers.

[78] Gladden, *How Much Is Left of the Old Doctrines?*, pp. 286, 292–93.

Likewise, Gladden used this reasoning from evolution only to support the moral probability of a future life.[79] Both Fiske and Gladden assumed that man was the end product of evolution and that, though evolution would introduce new possibilities of human development, the universe would remain constantly anthropocentric.

For Gladden, evolution was not only rational, but also religious. Christian theology had always represented God as the sustainer as well as the creator of the universe. Although in delineating God's continuing relation to creation theology had veered widely between deism and pantheism, the orthodox norm had been the doctrine of omnipresence, which, while maintaining His otherness, accented His actual and providential control. The deism of the eighteenth century, which profoundly affected orthodox theology, was based on a mechanistic conception of the universe that modern science made archaic. But the reaction in the nineteenth century against mechanistic philosophies was more than scientific. In philosophy, literature, and religion there was a new emphasis on the immanence of God in nature, history, and human consciousness. His thinking saturated in the writings of Carlyle, Coleridge, Wordsworth, and Bushnell, Gladden found even pantheism a "more rational, and inspiring theory than that deistic carpenter theory of God, which separates him wholly from nature." "Nature and the supernatural," he wrote in his last comprehensive work on theology, *Present Day Theology* (1913), "are no longer conceived to be opposite poles of thought, they are seen to be inseparably related; different sides of the same phenomena."[80] Deism was clearly incompatible with the evolutionary idea of process, while the doctrine of divine immanence explained how God revealed himself and achieved his purposes. The doctrine of immanence was the natural theological counterpart of evolution.

---

[79] Washington Gladden, *The Practice of Immortality* (Boston: Pilgrim Press, 1908), pp. 22–23; Milton Berman, *John Fiske: The Evolution of a Popularizer* (Cambridge: Harvard University Press, 1961), pp. 162, 237–38.

[80] Gladden, "The First Temptation," Sermon, February 8, 1885, Gladden Papers; Washington Gladden, *Present Day Theology* (Columbus, Ohio: McClelland & Company, 1913), p. 44.

It was the rationale for cosmic process. It made evolution both rational and religious. In evolution Gladden saw, as did Tennyson,

> . . . one God, one law, one element,
> and one far-off divine event
> toward which the whole creation moves.

The universe, Gladden declared in *Where Does the Sky Begin?* (1904), was a "revelation of the Eternal Reason": " . . . There is not a substance that we can touch, not a force whose operation we can see or feel, not a vibration of the air, not a pulsation of the light that does not reveal to us God." He thought that this conception, which "transfigured" the whole world, might be "the very deepest truth of the Bible." And in *Present Day Theology* he proclaimed that the immanence of God was "the central truth" of liberal theology.[81]

Evolution without belief in God would be a barren theory. Like those who rejected evolution altogether, Gladden feared an alliance between evolution and atheism. He criticized scientists who dismissed Christianity because of what he considered an antisupernaturalistic bias. They failed to realize the power of free personalities to supervene fixed law and achieve their own intelligent purposes, which was the essential postulate of supernaturalism.[82] According to Gladden, Thomas H. Huxley had "adopted a philosophy by means of which he shut himself out of one of the hemispheres of human experience, and made himself incapable of dealing with . . . Religion. . . . " Gladden's own inability to share in the scientific temper became very clear in a sermon on the life of Matthew Arnold. Arnold's greatest failing, Gladden said, was his preoccupation with analysis:

[81] Gladden, *How Much Is Left of the Old Doctrines?*, p. 42; Washington Gladden, *Where Does the Sky Begin?* (Boston: Houghton, Mifflin & Co., 1904), p. 22; Washington Gladden, *Ruling Ideas of the Present Age* (Boston: Houghton, Mifflin & Co., 1895), p. 281; Gladden, *Present Day Theology*, p. 14.

[82] Gladden, *How Much Is Left of the Old Doctrines?*, pp. 46–50, 58; Gladden, Easter Sermon, 1898, Gladden Papers.

. . . Not content with liking things, it takes them to pieces to see why it likes them; . . . its spirit is, essentially, scientific; and its product must therefore be anything but nutritious, for the spiritual nature.

In another sermon, in which he judged John Fiske the man most fit to "utter the verdict of evolutionary science," Gladden remarked that proof of God was not nearly so clear in minute analyses "as in those large views which we gain when we follow the great laws of evolution, and note the increasing purpose that runs through the ages."[83]

Such "large views" suffused Gladden's writings and gave them sustained optimism. His approach to science was not inductive. The broad conclusions that he drew came not from the practitioners of science but from theistic popularizers like Fiske. For Gladden, evolution was primarily a philosophy; his understanding of evolutionary science was imprecise. He could easily describe heredity as "God, working in us," and environment as "God, working round about us."[84] Pointing out that biological variation operated within certain well-defined limits, he concluded that limitation meant law and that law signified purpose. To say that environment conditioned variation was not to deny the control of law, since environment was rational "from top to bottom, from center to circumference." He proclaimed too quickly that evolution was bringing a "mighty reinforcement" to religious faith.[85] And it was easy for him to see the immanence of God in Benjamin Kidd's principle of "projected efficiency," which meant simply that evolution operated purposefully for the good of the future. Kidd united evolution and social progress in *Social Evolution* (1894), a book that greatly influenced Gladden.[86]

Early in the twentieth century Gladden thought he saw the alli-

[83] Gladden, Sermons, "Thomas H. Huxley," July 14, 1895; "Matthew Arnold," December 13, 1891; May 6, 1894, Gladden Papers.

[84] Gladden, *How Much Is Left of the Old Doctrines?*, p. 131.

[85] Gladden, Sermons, "Louis Agassiz," May 26, 1907; June 2, 1907, Gladden Papers.

[86] Gladden, Sermons, "Posteritism," November 21, 1901; April 20, 1902; June 2, 1907, Gladden Papers.

ance between atheism and science dissolving and a reunion of religion and science taking place. For one thing, Christians had been forced to re-examine their beliefs in the light of modern knowledge, and the result had been a more rational faith. Gladden recalled that he himself had questioned some aspects of Christianity until, as he put it, "I found out that they are no part of the Christian religion—nothing but fabrications of the system mongers which have been fastened upon it." The "truths of Christianity," Gladden observed at the close of Lyman Abbott's preaching mission at the First Church in 1905, "when stripped of all extraneous matter, and presented in their simplicity approve themselves to the human mind as rational and credible."[87] By abandoning what Gladden and other liberals considered "extra-belief" about the Bible's relevance on scientific questions, and by interpreting the Bible in terms of the current evolutionary theory, Protestants had, in his opinion, removed a major barrier between science and religion.

Second, Gladden saw science itself, together with philosophy and social science, turning to a spiritual interpretation of the universe. "Scientists," he wrote, were "dealing with the forces of nature and pushing their investigations further and further back into her mysteries," till they stood "confronted with the Infinite and Eternal Energy from which the whole universe proceeds. . . . "[88] There were few exponents of the materialism of the mid-nineteenth century, and as the twentieth century progressed scientists seemed to be turning away from the rejection of religion typified by Ernst Haeckel's *The Riddle of the Universe* (1899). Sir Oliver Lodge argued in *Science and Immortality* (1908) that religion and science were not only compatible but that they were actually only different aspects of the same reality. Rudolph Eucken interpreted the universe from a Christian and idealistic viewpoint, while Henri Bergson emphasized intuition and unity in his book, *Creative Evolution* (1907), which confirmed Gladden's conviction "that evolu-

[87] Gladden, Sermons, March 17, 1895; "Finally, brethren," April 30, 1905, Gladden Papers.

[88] Gladden, Sermon, December 17, 1899, Gladden Papers.

tion is in its essence creative, and that creation is in its essence evolutionary. . . . "[89]

By the beginning of the twentieth century liberal theology had rather widely displaced the orthodox consensus, rooted for the most part in Calvinism, that had prevailed fifty years earlier in most of the large evangelical denominations. Significantly, Gladden's career spanned this period of rapid change. A child of orthodoxy, he had been a theological pioneer in the decades after the Civil War, and he lived to enjoy many years of liberalism's supremacy. For Gladden, liberalism included:

> the idea of the immanence of God; the idea that God's method of crea-
> tion is evolution; the idea that nature in all its deepest meanings is
> supernatural; the idea of the constant presence of God in our lives;
> the idea of the universal divine Fatherhood and of the universal human
> Brotherhood.[90]

But theological liberalism was not all of a piece. It had no authoritative or uniform statement of faith, and within it there were important differences of emphasis and intent. One recent writer has distinguished two basic types of liberalism. Evangelical liberals, he says,

> stood squarely within the Christian tradition and accepted as normative
> for their thinking what they understood to be the essence of historical
> Christianity. These men had a deep consciousness of their continuity with
> the main line of Christian orthodoxy and felt that they were preserving
> its essential features in terms which were suitable to the modern world.

Their thought was highly Christocentric: the revelation of God in Christ was, for them, the core of religious truth. Modernistic liberals, though recognizing some "elements of permanent significance in the Christian tradition," judged them by the assumptions of modern thought. Their approach was less Christocentric, and they were not as committed as the evangelical liberals to the idea of continuity.[91]

[89] Gladden, Sermons, January 12, 1908, "A Student's Religion," September 17, 1911, October 12, 1913, Gladden Papers; Gladden, *The Interpreter*, p. 29.

[90] Gladden, *Present Day Theology*, p. 6.

[91] Kenneth Cauthen, *The Impact of American Religious Liberalism* (New York: Harper & Row, Publishers, 1962), pp. 27–30.

Gladden belongs in the category of evangelical liberalism. His sermons and books reveal a preoccupation with adjusting Christianity to modern conditions—in short, an interest in continuity. Forms and language change, he argued, but not the great facts of existence. He illustrated his conviction that the church must "keep firm hold of the facts" behind changing formularies with the idea of original sin. The church could no longer believe, as it once did, that God had imputed Adam's guilt to the human race, but it knew that man did inherit "a diseased moral nature—a tendency to sin." The truth that it had long misunderstood was the "solidarity of moral history," man's propensity to sin because the first man had sinned.[92] Similarly, Gladden saw moral evolution in the church's successive theories of the atonement, culminating in the view that "Christ 'bore our sins,' in fellowship with us, not in substitution for us," a view that took into account the teachings of the New Testament and yet avoided modern ethical objections to the idea of judicial transfer of guilt or merit.[93]

Gladden's consciousness of continuity can also be seen in his attitude toward creeds. Although as early as the 1870's he opposed using creeds as tests, he felt that they had value as "provisional statements of religious truth."[94] He liked President William DeWitt Hyde's idea of substituting a platform of purposes for a statement of doctrines, but he also favorably reviewed contemporary statements of faith,

[92] Gladden, "Old Facts with New Faces," Sermon, June 24, 1894, Gladden Papers.

[93] Gladden, *How Much Is Left of the Old Doctrines?*, p. 192. Gladden's concentration on the atonement further demonstrates his desire to retain as the core of his theology the cardinal doctrines of Christianity. His principal discussions of the atonement, all of which reveal the continuing influence of Bushnell, appear in: Washington Gladden, "The Central Doctrine of Protestantism," in *Things New and Old in Discourses of Christian Truth and Life* (Columbus, Ohio: A. H. Smythe, 1883), pp. 69–82; Gladden, *Where Does the Sky Begin?*, pp. 150–66; Gladden, "The New Theology: The Atonement," Sermon, July 7, 1907, Gladden Papers; Gladden, *Present Day Theology*, pp. 149–98.

[94] *Good Company*, IV (1879), 188–89; Gladden, Sermon, October 18, 1891, Gladden Papers.

such as one formulated by William Hayes Ward.[95]

Moreover, Gladden repeatedly declared that the supreme revelation of God came through Christ. In a chapter, "Who Is Jesus Christ?", in *Burning Questions*, he pronounced it impossible to class Christ with the founders of other religions because He differed from them "not merely in degree but in kind." "Jesus was not the founder of a religious system," he insisted, but "simply the Revelation to men of the Living God, of the Life of God, of the truth concerning their relations to God and the duties growing out of those relations." Commenting on a book by John Watson, an English clergyman, Gladden agreed that the teachings of Christ, and especially the Sermon on the Mount, were central and normative for Christianity.[96] To be sure, since he was more concerned with ethics than with speculative theology, Gladden placed greatest importance on Christ's ethical teachings, but his approach was nevertheless Christocentric. His interest in the "search for the historical Jesus," a Jesus freed from the encrustations of "extra-belief," was another aspect of this Christocentric approach to theology.

Gladden was neither uncritical nor doctrinaire in his allegiance to liberalism. With its major features, as he interpreted them, he was heartily in accord: its ethical quality; its emphasis on the unity of the human and the divine, the sacred and the secular; and its belief in man's "immediate access to the Source of all truth and life."[97] But he felt that liberals often reacted excessively against orthodoxy. He feared that some of them, rejecting the doctrine of total depravity, slurred over the fundamental reality of sin, the fact

[95] *Congregationalist*, XCI (November 17, 1906), 645–46; *Ohio State Journal*, November 26, 1906; Washington Gladden, "Dr. Ward's Credo: A Review of 'What I Believe and Why?'", *Independent*, LXXXIV (October 18, 1915), 105–6.

[96] Gladden, *Burning Questions*, pp. 167, 169; Gladden, "Ian Maclaren's Creed," Sermon, April 22, 1900, Gladden Papers.

[97] Gladden, "The Heart of the New Theology," Sermon, July 14, 1907, Gladden Papers.

that man was in rebellion against God.[98] Furthermore, when liberalism exhausted its energies in criticizing orthodoxy, he wrote in the *Congregationalist,* it became as dead as orthodoxy. He tried to avoid such negative criticism himself. One liberal who knew him well maintained that he "always sweetened his liberalism with a deeply reverent spirit. Free and fearless as he was, he was no iconoclast." Liberalism could not afford to ignore the past; if it did, it would be "only a little less absurd than the traditionalism which finds no revelation in the present." Without roots in the past it would be "fruitless."[99] Finally, Gladden felt that liberals, obliged to construct a new theology for themselves, theorized too much instead of preaching a practical religion: "What ordinary human beings want most," he asserted, "is not the philosophy of religion but religion itself. . . . "[100]

This was, after all, the heart of Gladden's liberalism. His first steps away from Calvinism in the mid–ninteenth century were necessitated by his own religious experience. Unable to believe in the God portrayed in contemporary preaching, he found in Bushnell's writings an interpretation of the Bible that made God seem real and near and a faith related to the common concerns of life. The challenges presented by biblical criticism and science made it imperative for him to establish a new intellectual framework for this faith, a framework that would make Christianity reasonable to the modern world. But the framework itself was less important than the experience of religion. Consequently, Gladden could work with those both more radical and more conservative than himself. He co-operated with evangelists who based their preaching on a literal interpretation of the Bible, as well as with Unitarians and Universalists, who did not share his view of Christ. Those who loved God

[98] Gladden, Sermons, "Christ's Fulfillment of Life," January 10, 1886; "The New Theology: God and Man," June 16, 1907, Gladden Papers.

[99] Washington Gladden, "Congregationalism and the Unchurched Classes," *Congregationalist,* LXXXIV (September 7, 1899), 308–9; Buckham, *Progressive Religious Thought,* p. 248; Washington Gladden, "Laissez Faire in Religion," *Atlantic Monthly,* CXIV (October, 1914), 501.

[100] Gladden, Sermon, December 11, 1892, Gladden Papers.

and their neighbors, he concluded in *Present Day Theology,* were saved from sin, regardless of their creeds.[101] The validity of their religious experience could not be denied. He judged men by their works, not by their creeds, and theology was, for him, always the handmaiden of religion.

[101] Gladden, *Present Day Theology,* p. 83.

Seven

Ideology of the Social Gospel

For Gladden liberal theology and the Social Gospel were inseparable. As a major interpreter of both movements has written:

> . . . The Christianity to be applied was very clearly conceived by Dr. Gladden. Behind his social mission there has been from the first not only Christian motive, but a definite, tangible, clear-cut idea of what Christianity means. . . . And all his thinking has been conscientiously and avowedly allied with the New Theology.[1]

The relationship was reciprocal. The humanitarianism of the pre-Civil War years contributed to the liberalization of theology. The key figure in the transformation of theology in the mid-nineteenth century from its concentration on individual piety to a social orientation was Horace Bushnell.[2] But the new theological structure erected in the last decades of the nineteenth century, markedly social in its orientation, quickened the spirit of reform, deepened its dimensions, and channeled it into new areas of need. The social gospelers were normally also theological liberals. Gladden, Lyman Abbott, Graham Taylor, Walter Rauschenbusch, George A. Gordon, and Dean George Hodges exemplified the conviction that faith and social reform were related aspects of the same Christianity.

[1] Buckham, *Progressive Religious Thought*, p. 222.

[2] Atkins and Fagley, *American Congregationalism*, pp. 248–49.

The conservative reaction against liberal theology, especially as embodied in the fundamentalist movement, which became a well-defined and potent force in American religion early in the twentieth century, was often also a reaction against the social preoccupation of the liberal churches. In calling for a return to the "simple Gospel," fundamentalism appealed to an individualistic pietism uncorrupted by either humanistic theology or organized Christian social reform.[3] The identification of social service with a theology that they regarded as apostate may have led some religious conservatives to react against a social involvement of the churches against which they had no innate bias. To reject liberal theology seemed to require opposition to the Social Gospel with which it was so closely allied.

It is clear that liberal theology provided an intellectual framework for the Social Gospel. In addition to reconstructing the historical origins of the biblical writings, biblical criticism sought their historical meaning. It focused on the social orientation of the Old Testament prophets, especially their pronounced emphases on justice, social purity, and righteousness, which had been obscured by preoccupation with their predictive utterances and their teachings on individual piety. The message of Jesus, especially the Sermon on the Mount, likewise took on social significance. Moreover, liberal theology's cardinal doctrines, the fatherhood of God and the brotherhood of man, were inherently social. Human brotherhood became co-ordinate with, and concomitant to, divine fatherhood: American Protestants could no longer consider their vertical relations with God complete without practicing brotherhood in their horizontal relations with other men. Liberalism had no monopoly of either of these features—emphasis on the social implications of the teachings of Jesus and the prophets and on the necessity of right relations with God issuing in right relations with men. It did, however, ex-

---

[3] In a provocative chapter on "The Social Meaning of Fundamentalism," the historian of the Social Gospel from 1920 to 1940 probes the relationship between fundamentalism's reaction against both theological and social liberalism. Paul A. Carter, *The Decline and Revival of the Social Gospel: Social and Political Liberalism in American Protestant Churches, 1920–1940* (Ithaca, N. Y.: Cornell University Press, 1956), pp. 46–58.

press them with distinctive singularity and force. A third feature of theological liberalism also contributed to the ideology of the Social Gospel. Its incorporation of evolutionary theory led naturally to a doctrine of progress that presupposed the melioration of both the social organism and its environment.[4]

The Social Gospel had other, less direct sources. Though largely independent of English social movements, it drew inspiration from their example and literature, as did many other reform movements in the progressive period.[5] This was particularly true of Gladden, whose mild Anglophilia stemmed from a sense of spiritual and intellectual affinity among Anglo-Saxons rather than from racial consciousness. "Gladden knew his Carlyle and Ruskin," wrote Gaius Glenn Atkins. "I can hear him still reading nobly from *Sartor Resartus*."[6] He began reading Ruskin while in college, and, though he rejected Ruskin's paternalistic feudalism and denunciation of modern capitalism, he thought the English writer's deprecation of dehumanizing economic forces entitled him to primacy among writers on economics.[7] Gladden also knew his Carlyle, and he considered him a major inspirer of English social reform. The English Christian Socialists provided the most important example for the Social Gospel, although there was no linear connection between the two movements. Gladden admired their attempts to mediate between social

[4] James Dombrowski asserts that the Social Gospel had "a decidedly antitheological bias," and it is true that Gladden disliked theology as a purely speculative enterprise. But theology, loosely construed as an intellectual framework for religious thought and action, was not absent from the Social Gospel, although there was little interest in metaphysical questions. James Dombrowski, *The Early Days of Christian Socialism in America* (New York: Columbia University Press, 1936), p. 14.

[5] Arthur Mann examines the specific ties between British and American reform thought in "British Social Thought and American Reformers of the Progressive Era," *Mississippi Valley Historical Review*, XLII (March, 1956), 672–92.

[6] Atkins, *Religion in Our Times*, p. 48.

[7] *Good Company*, V (1880), 87–88; Gladden, "John Ruskin," Sermon, March 12, 1899, Gladden Papers. Gladden included Ruskin in a series of lectures given at the First Church and then as the William Belden Noble Lectures for 1903 at Harvard. They were published as *Witnesses of the Light* (Boston: Houghton, Mifflin & Co., 1903). Cf. pp. 263–79.

classes, and he gave his congregation biographical sketches of Maurice, Kingsley, and Hughes, and reviews of their writings. He immersed himself not only in the primary writings but also in standard biographies of Ruskin, Carlyle, and the Christian Socialists. In Carlyle's case, for example, he used the sympathetic study by James A. Froude.[8]

Although the dual forces of industrialization and urbanization created conditions that contributed to the growth of social concern in the churches, explanations of the Social Gospel that deal solely with these factors or that offer purely causative hypotheses, such as the suggestion that progressive reform stemmed from a "status revolution," are inadequate.[9] They reject, ordinarily, the possibility of disinterest and neglect the influence of ideology on human behavior. For Gladden it is not enough to posit a reaction against existing evils. Social problems did condition the nature and direction of reform, but reform itself rested on an ideology compounded of personal pragmatism, philosophical idealism, romanticism, and the American faith in democratic institutions. Above all, though he tended to underrate this aspect of his heritage, he built on a strong foundation of "this-worldliness" in Christian thought. Temperament, Christian faith, social conditions—all are necessary to an understanding of why Gladden joined with the pioneers of the Social Gospel in social reform that was distinctively religious.

Theological liberalism and the Social Gospel shared so completely a common ideology that it is often difficult in reading Gladden's sermons and books to decide whether his ideas belong more properly to theology or social theory. Fundamental to both was a broadening

[8] Gladden, Sermons, "Frederick Denison Maurice," January 15, 1888; "Charles Kingsley," January 22, 1888; "Thomas Carlyle," February 26, 1899; "Alton Locke," June 4, 1899; "Thomas Hughes," March 28, 1896, Gladden Papers.

[9] Richard Hofstadter's suggestive hypothesis, which is, of course, more complicated than the phrase "status revolution" intimates, is elaborated most clearly in his panoramic study, *The Age of Reform: From Bryan to F. D. R.* (New York: Alfred A. Knopf, Inc., 1955), pp. 131–73. Samuel P. Hays offers industrialism as the central factor behind such reform movements as the Social Gospel in *The Response to Industrialism, 1885–1914* (Chicago: University of Chicago Press, 1957), pp. 77–78.

of the Protestant view of God's relationship to human society, and, consequently, of the applicability of the Christian message. The philosophical foundation of this broadening was a unitary view of the universe as the sphere of divine activity. This enlargement of the Christian view of God vis-à-vis man and society occurred in two ways. With respect to the individual it gave universal application to the doctrine of the fatherhood of God. Orthodox theology, both Roman Catholic and Protestant, had maintained that, apart from the act of creation, God was the Father only of those who became partakers, by faith and/or the sacraments, of divine grace. Although some were willing to equivocate concerning enlightened pagans like Socrates, theologians normally restricted this relationship to Christians. In Calvinist theory and practice, and particularly in the religious world of Gladden's childhood, only those who had experienced a new birth, their entry into the spiritual family of God, could justifiably consider themselves "sons of God" in the scriptural sense. Rejecting any limitations on the fatherhood of God, Gladden emphasized the kinship rather than the alienation of God and man.[10]

Gladden began as early as his pastorate in Springfield to preach that God was the Father of all men in a spiritual as well as creative sense. The effect of his books on the Christian life, *Being a Christian* and *The Christian Way,* was to minimize the obstacles to fellowship with God and thus to diminish the consciousness of radical alienation that orthodox Protestants felt must accompany conversion. In *The Lord's Prayer* (1880), another book written in the same period, he stated the germinant idea of the universal fatherhood of God more explicitly. When Jesus taught this prayer to men—and here Gladden evaded the contention of some orthodox theologians that Jesus taught the prayer only to His disciples—He introduced to them "the true constructive idea in all theological science." If the encrustations of theology, which in the past had pictured God as the

---

[10] In *Progressive Religious Thought,* pp. 255–56, Buckham contends that, in thus stressing kinship rather than alienation between God and man, Gladden and most of the social gospelers, with the notable exception of Walter Rauschenbusch, adopted an idea common to Greek but not to Latin theology.

autocratic ruler of a governmental universe, could be removed, Jesus' message that God was the head of a family could be grasped. This idea not only softened human conceptions of God, but also suggested the dignity of man.[11]

That all men were sons of God did not mean, however, that all men were aware of or accepted their sonship. Gladden used the Parable of the Prodigal Son both to defend and to elucidate this doctrine. Though he squandered his resources, forsook his father's table, and abdicated his familial prerogatives, the prodigal never ceased to be his father's son. And when he decided to return to his father's house, the fact of sonship made him immediately welcome.[12] At times Gladden improvised on the parable and described a son who, still living in his father's house, was an alien to its prevailing spirit. The need for repentance and obedience was always an integral part of Gladden's appeal to men to accept their rightful place in the divine-human family: there could be no personal union with God that was "merely sentimental and emotional." To ascribe to God "an easy going good nature, which makes no strenuous demands on us for conduct and character, which lets us do about as we will, and takes care that we do not suffer," was as bad as to make Him a stark and relentless judge. Browning was right, in Gladden's opinion: "all's love, yet all's law!"[13]

Gladden argued repeatedly that the Bible clearly taught the fatherhood of God, particularly in the Parable of the Prodigal Son and in the Sermon on the Mount, and that this doctrine was an ade-

---

[11] Washington Gladden, *The Lord's Prayer: Seven Homilies* (Boston: Houghton, Mifflin & Co., 1880), pp. 25–27. The centrality of the fatherhood of God in Gladden's thinking remained constant. In a sermon in 1907 he reaffirmed his conviction that it was the "constructive idea" of theology. Gladden, "The Heart of the New Theology," Sermon, July 14, 1907, Gladden Papers.

[12] Gladden, "Heirs of God," Sermon, November 2, 1884, Gladden Papers. Interestingly, Gladden interpreted infant baptism as a declaration that God was the Father of all, though the children baptized might later, like the Prodigal Son, forfeit the benefits of sonship. Gladden, "What is Baptism?", Sermon, May 18, 1884, Gladden Papers; Gladden, *How Much Is Left of the Old Doctrines?*, pp. 254–56.

[13] Gladden, Sermons, December, 1899; November 27, 1904, Gladden Papers.

quate summation of the Gospel.[14] Scriptural references that implied
limited sonship were not to be taken as "sober prose statements" but
as expressions of "heightened religious feeling." The central point
of Christian faith, the atonement, was the loving sacrifice of the
"All-Father" to win back His erring children.[15] This vicarious suffering—not vicarious punishment—was the supreme demonstration of
fatherhood. To reach the seat of estrangement in the hearts of men,
the "moral influence" of the atonement was necessary:

> The father's suffering may reveal to the son the father's love and his own
> sin, and may bring him to hate the sin as his father hates it, and to accept
> the love that seeks to save him from it.[16]

But though Gladden often spoke as if Christianity was requisite
for the realization of sonship, he also urged a sympathetic understanding of other religions, all of which had elements of truth in
them. Moreover, he envisaged God leading His children who were
beyond the Christian fold to fuller light. Though non-Christians
were sons of God, their religions often obscured that fact; Christianity was the special vehicle by which the Father communicated it.
Nevertheless, Gladden believed that men who had never heard of
the "historic Jesus" might know the "essential Christ," through
whom God's attributes were made known in creation and in human
conscience. The World's Parliament of Religions, held in 1893 in
conjunction with the Columbian Exposition, was to Gladden a cheering recognition of the common divine sonship of all men. It was not,
however, a recognition of the equality of all religions. Gladden felt
that by maintaining friendly relations with other religions Christianity would refine them.[17] Toward the end of his life he simplified

[14] Washington Gladden, "Theology in the Council," *Congregationalist*,
LXXXIV (November 9, 1899), 684–85; Gladden, Sermons, October 15, 1899,
1900, Gladden Papers.

[15] Gladden, Sermon, September 13, 1891, Gladden Papers.

[16] Gladden, *Where Does the Sky Begin?*, p. 162; Gladden, "The New Theology: The Atonement," Sermon, July 7, 1907, Gladden Papers.

[17] Gladden, Sermons, June, 1891; September 10, 1893, Gladden Papers.

his view of the relationship between God and men even further: "Religion is friendship," he declared, and "the supreme friendship" was the divine-human friendship.[18]

Two aspects of the broadening of the doctrine of the fatherhood of God require further emphasis. First, it epitomized Gladden's optimism concerning human nature. Universal fatherhood meant for Gladden "that goodness, the most glorious and perfect goodness, is, in the deepest sense of the word, natural to man." Since evil was not natural, but "a false, an artificial self, which has usurped . . . power," it could be vanquished by "the restoration of clear thinking" and the comprehension by man of his real identity.[19] Second, Gladden assumed that, since human society was in fact a brotherhood, ideal social relations would correspond to ideal family relations. If men could learn subordination to their Father's will and consideration for each other, social order, peace, and common welfare would ensue. Writing on "The Social Problems of the Future" in 1897, Gladden illustrated how brotherhood could solve such problems as taxation, monopoly, labor relations, poverty, and crime. "Of all our social questions," he declared, "this is the one: Do we believe in Christ's law of brotherhood?" He saw the growth of brotherhood in the extension of democracy and in the elevation of the working classes, and, predicting its invasion of all social relations, he called it "the ruling idea of modern civilization."[20] But the practice of the Sermon on the Mount, particularly the Golden Rule, was the essential ingredient for well-being, whatever the economic or political system.

The second way in which liberal theology and the Social Gospel broadened the Christian view of God's relationship to man and society involved society collectively. The idea of the Kingdom of God was extended to include every facet of human activity. Gladden

[18] Gladden, "The Supreme Friendship," Sermon, [ca. 1910,] Gladden Papers.

[19] Gladden, *Ruling Ideas*, pp. 23–25.

[20] Washington Gladden, "The Social Problems of the Future," *Outlook*, LVII (December 11, 1897), 904–11; Washington Gladden, *Christianity and Socialism* (New York: Eaton & Mains, 1905), pp. 9–57; Gladden, *Ruling Ideas*, pp. 33–35.

rejected all distinctions between the sacred and the secular, which he said had plagued Christianity since the time of the Gnostic heresy, and insisted that the whole world was God's province of activity and that all was potentially and ideally sacred.[21] The petition "Thy Kingdom come," the most comprehensive clause in the Lord's Prayer, excluded nothing from the sphere of divine influence. The Kingdom was neither a future celestial state nor "any material or earthly organization with a visible head." It was, nevertheless, both a "spiritual condition" and a "social fact," and it found expression in manners, fashions, laws, and social relations.[22] It was a kingdom of law, and its law was love. Consequently, its progress depended on the triumph of love in the individual; because of God's unwillingness to coerce men, it could be a social fact only when all men voluntarily obeyed the law of love.[23] The law of love prescribed by Jesus was twofold: love for God and love for men. Thus, men could not maintain the right relation to their Father, according to Gladden, "except as it issues in right relations with men," and "a religion which has no room in it for social questions cannot be the Christian religion."[24]

The Kingdom of God, Gladden said, included "the whole social organism so far as it is affected by divine influences."[25] If mankind would put itself "under the benign sway of the King of love," government, education, the arts, philanthropy, industry, and commerce would be transformed by the law of love.[26] This law, the redemptive force in human life, was not always clearly defined. Some social

[21] Gladden, *Ruling Ideas*, pp. 110–16.

[22] Gladden, "The Coming Kingdom," Christmas Sermon, 1877, Gladden Papers; Gladden, *Lord's Prayer*, pp. 62–63, 71.

[23] Gladden, *Burning Questions*, pp. 225–28; Gladden, Sermon, July 28, 1901, Gladden Papers.

[24] Washington Gladden, *The Church and Modern Life* (New York: Houghton, Mifflin & Co., 1908), pp. 83–84.

[25] Washington Gladden, *The Church and the Kingdom* (New York: Fleming H. Revell Co., 1894), p. 6.

[26] Gladden, *The Interpreter*, pp. 258–63; Gladden, *The Church and Modern Life*, p. 85.

gospelers emphasized love as self-sacrifice to an extent that Gladden considered unbalanced. That it was not self-love—the unbridled self-interest of laissez faire economics and of much pietistic religion, the latter, in Gladden's opinion, a major support of the former—he was sure. The sin of Cain had been a bad social philosophy, thorough-going individualism. The world had tried individualism ever since, and it had failed.[27] But neither was the law of love sheer altruism. The precept, "Thou shalt love thy neighbor as thyself," presumed a safe and rational self-regard and the defense of personal rights and dignity. Indeed, Gladden held that altruism would follow a proper understanding of one's own worth. Furthermore in the right light of man, there could be no antithesis between the well-being of an individual and that of his fellows.[28] Egoism and altruism must complement and check each other. Much of Gladden's preaching and writing, however, was directed against the lack of altruism in the ethical balance.

Gladden's reliance on altruism as the force that would bring in the Kingdom, rather than on environmental reform, received reinforcement from the interpretation of evolution offered by Henry Drummond, a Scottish philosopher. Gladden did not know Drummond, though he tried once to visit him in Scotland, but he read his works and heard him lecture in Boston. In *Natural Law in the Spiritual World* (1883) Drummond drew analogies between natural and spiritual phenomena and tried to demonstrate that identical laws operated in both realms. In *The Ascent of Man* (1894), following this same assumption, he contended that the law of love operated everywhere in the universe, even in biology, and that it was replacing the struggle for survival. Instead of being purely a struggle for life, nature was also in its very structure a "struggle for the life of others"; instead of competition, co-operation was the ruling principle

---

[27] Gladden, "Sinners of the Olden Time—Cain," Sermon, January 5, 1902, Gladden Papers; Gladden, *Where Does the Sky Begin?*, pp. 120–28.

[28] Gladden, *The Church and the Kingdom*, pp. 46–67; Gladden, *Ruling Ideas*, pp. 258–59.

of evolution. Drummond's argument was the antithesis of conservative Social Darwinism, the justification by Herbert Spencer, William
Graham Sumner, and others of individualistic ethics and laissez
faire economics as the social expression of the "survival of the fittest"; and Gladden, who had always rejected conservative Social
Darwinism, accepted Drummond's work as conclusive.[29]

Gladden also took heart from the conclusion of Prince Kropotkin
that, even among animals and primitive men, there had never been
a perpetual, pitiless struggle for life. Reproduction demonstrated
the social nature of all creatures; love, sacrifice, and co-operation
were to be found in primitive parentage and childhood.[30] With co-
operation clearly in the ascendancy, Gladden was sure that "the
next step in evolution" would be "the kingdom of the spiritual man."
He spoke of this "struggle for the life of others" as the "Christ-life
imbedded in the very order of creation, and in the long processes
of evolution," and, quoting an unidentified author, as "the shadow
of the cross lying upon the whole domain of creature existence."[31]

If altruism was at the very heart of nature, Gladden reasoned, it
must certainly be applicable to human society. He considered it, in
fact, the central pillar of a framework of laws governing the universe, just as inflexible and certain in its results as the laws of gravi-
tation. Not simply an ideal for social conduct, it was the norm for
all harmonious personal and social existence, and, precisely because
it was an absolute law, violation of it was the cause of all discord,
strife, and evil. Gladden used William Allen White's first social
novel, *A Certain Rich Man* (which, incidentally, White described
as the story of a modern prodigal son), to illustrate his point. In it,
after John Barclay successfully opposes improvement of his city's
water supply, his wife dies of typhoid fever caused by bad city

[29] Gladden, Sermons, March 21, 1897, May 22, 1898, Gladden Papers; Washington Gladden, "Why I Am Thankful," *Congregationalist*, LXXXII (November 18, 1897), 734–35.

[30] Gladden, Sermon, June 2, 1907, Gladden Papers.

[31] Gladden, Sermons, February 28, 1897; "The Next Step in Evolution,"
March 1, 1903, Gladden Papers.

water.[32] Hardly "obscure and mysterious," such punishment was "involved in the very nature of things." "There is only one way for men to live together," Gladden asserted, "and when they will not live together in that way they must take the consequences." The law of love would go on pulverizing even world systems of selfishness until they submitted to its sway.[33] Those who argued that the law of love would not work in society missed the point, in Gladden's opinion, for it was constantly at work. What he urged was not that men put it in operation but that they put themselves into conformity with it. Of course, the idea that nature itself was on the side of the Christian ethic of altruism greatly bolstered Gladden's optimism.

Optimism pervaded another important aspect of liberal theology's concept of the Kingdom—and, more broadly, of human history. The Kingdom was not only all-encompassing, but also a present reality. The spread of evangelicalism in the early nineteenth century had given wide currency to premillennialism, the doctrine that the second advent of Christ would precede his millennial reign on earth. This was the spiritual pabulum of Gladden's youth. The Millerite movement in the 1840's was a radical expression of the premillennialist conviction that the world was getting worse and could be saved only by a cataclysmic reversal of its downward tendencies. Gladden rejected premillennialism as an admission of the failure of spiritual forces. It would not be necessary, he asserted, for Christ "to descend upon the world with a great physical demonstration, flashing his omnipotence in men's faces, annihilating his enemies, overawing the populations of the earth by a great display of power."[34] Though

---

[32] Gladden, Sermons, September 23, 1888, September 5, 1909, Gladden Papers; William Allen White, *The Autobiography of William Allen White* (New York: Macmillan Co., 1946), p. 374. Gladden sent White a copy of his sermon on *A Certain Rich Man*, whereupon White assured Gladden that there was no one in America whose commendation he prized more than Gladden's. White to Gladden, September 29, 1909, Gladden Papers.

[33] Gladden, Sermon, December 12, 1897, Gladden Papers.

[34] Gladden, Sermon, September 23, 1900, Gladden Papers. In 1878 Gladden criticized the members of a premillennialist prophetic conference in New York City for the mistaken notion that the physical presence of Christ would be more effective than His spiritual presence. *Springfield Republican*, November 29, 1878; *Sunday Afternoon*, II (December, 1878), 565–66.

he did not insist on a literal millennium, his view came closest to postmillennialism, the theory that the second advent would climax, rather than commence, a thousand-year period of peace established by the forces of good. Postmillennialists expected progress, not regress.

Gladden's view of human progress was not very different, apart from its Christian framework, from the systems of linear progress to which the Enlightenment gave birth. He believed in "no second comings" but "in one continuous kingdom of law and of love, with no breaks, nor interregnums, nor cataclysms." "Those who take pains to find out the truth about the good old days are not under any illusions," he declared.[35] Rather than looking back to a lost golden age, he turned his eyes to the future in the faith "that it is better farther on." The world was improving slowly under divine guidance. "God's way of mending the world," as evolution illustrated, was not destruction and reconstruction but life and growth—the development and perfection of the individual and the social organism. Evil was by nature self-destructive and impermanent. Obviously, however, men must not wait for it to vanish; they must abolish ignorance, vice, and poverty to facilitate the spread of Christian principles. But the good in society was "immortal"; political and economic forms would change from age to age, but progress was accumulative and would carry over into each new form, giving each successive age an advantage over its predecessor.[36]

Gladden saw signs of progress all around him. World history furnished him with proof of "the steady increase of light and truth."[37] At the beginning of each year he preached a sermon surveying the previous year's events for hopeful tokens. As early as the 1870's, he often preached series of sermons on long-range progress in reli-

[35] Gladden, Christmas Sermon, 1893, Gladden Papers.

[36] Gladden, Sermons, "God's Way of Mending the World," May 8, 1898; "Society-Building," April 9, 1883; "Social Immortality," April 5, 1885, Gladden Papers.

[37] Gladden, "Taking Your Bearings," Sermon, December 28, 1875, Gladden Papers.

gion, society, morals, aesthetics, and justice.[38] Those who thought their own age to be worse than previous ages were not aware of the course of history. Assuming that knowledge of history and optimism were inseparable, Gladden wrote: "I have never known a competent historical scholar who was at all disposed to pessimism."[39] Furthermore, genuine pessimists negated, in Gladden's opinion, the primary postulate of a sound ethical system—"that that which ought to be will be"—and in so doing negated rationality. Such thoroughgoing pessimism was normally rooted in bodily and mental disorders. But it also hastened the process of mental disintegration: "The goal of pessimism is the insane asylum."[40] Because of his a priori assumption of progress, Gladden would not acknowledge any serious holdbacks, but only eddies in otherwise linear improvement. He confessed his personal expectation "to see through the shadow of an impending calamity, the path to a great deliverance."[41]

His standards for progress—the material and moral values of the nineteenth century in general, and his theological and social values in particular—were subjective. He was delighted to think that religion was becoming less dogmatic and ritualistic and more ethical and tolerant. The elevation of women and the purification of the family were unmistakable evidences of Christianity's leavening influence. In society he saw an "increase of love as a practical power."[42] Belief in progress was itself a vital force for progress. The progress of Western civilization rested on the apex of Christian optimism. While in Buddhist lands a philosophy of resignation had retarded progress,

---

[38] *Springfield Republican,* January 27, 1879.

[39] Gladden, *Where Does the Sky Begin?,* p. 45.

[40] Gladden, Sermons, "City of Dreadful Night," June 19, 1898; "Friedrich Nietzsche," January 10, 1915, Gladden Papers.

[41] Gladden, "A New Day for Religion," Sermon, September 18, 1910, Gladden Papers. For example, in 1913 he stated his faith in "a steady and orderly progress toward righteousness guided by the Creator himself—a movement in which there are many local and apparent pauses and eddies, but which is, nevertheless, as certain and resistless as the flight of time." Gladden, Sermon, May 25, 1913, Gladden Papers.

[42] Gladden, Sermons, December 16, 1900, April 30, 1893, Gladden Papers; Gladden, *Burning Questions,* pp. 231–35.

Christianity had made men believe that salvation was possible, that they could resist evil and destruction. The cumulative effects of this faith were becoming apparent in the nineteenth century.[43] His own age was "one of those sublime periods in history of which men will read in coming ages with thrills of wonder and joy"; never before were there "such swift and mighty forward movements toward justice and truth and love."[44] Since the time of Christ, when social conditions were such that "they cannot be told in any decent company," the Kingdom had been coming "with fuller light, with larger liberty, with increasing love"; but, according to Gladden, "there never was a time when it was moving as to-day, with stately and victorious tread, to take possession of the earth."[45]

He pointed to Benjamin Kidd's *Social Evolution* (1894), "the most masterly historical generalization that has yet been given to the world." If anyone doubted the existence of that accumulating "great fund of altruistic feeling" to which Kidd testified, Gladden

> . . . bid him study the great movements of human society . . . I show him the thousand wars of old . . . gradually disappearing from history,— with lengthening periods of universal peace; I point to the broken and rusted fetters of the slaves . . . I show him the black specters of famine and pestilence slinking away into the darkness of the past; . . . more than all I desire him to fashion his attention upon that great spectacle of the toiling millions of the race, so long chattels and menials, slowly rising up . . . to manhood, to citizenship, to sovereignty. . . .[46]

To Gladden, human progress was the strongest proof of the truth of the Christian religion. Indeed, he often hinted that if the world did not show improvement under the impact of Christianity, there would be no valid reason for any man to be a Christian. For one thing, a religion that failed to improve the world in nineteen cen-

[43] Gladden, Sermons, "The Pessimist's Creed," March 14, 1897; January 7, 1912, Gladden Papers.

[44] Gladden, "Repent Ye," Sermon, March 12, 1888, Gladden Papers.

[45] Gladden, Sermons, "The Kingdom of Christ," November 17, 1889; September 23, 1900, Gladden Papers.

[46] Gladden, Sermon, April 19, 1908, Gladden Papers.

turies could not claim the world's faith. Nor could the world believe in a confused, helpless God who had created a social order that He could not purify.[47] But Gladden himself was not prepared to abandon his faith, even should regress become unmistakable. He used progress as an apologetical device rather than as the final test of Christianity. Christianity meant too much to him personally for him to subject it to such a test. Furthermore, he measured progress over many centuries; the events of a single lifetime, however discouraging, could not overbalance the gains of the Christian Era.

Gladden did not identify the Kingdom of God with the church. He compared the Kingdom to a biological organism. The church was its motive force—what the brain is to the body. But the church could not live apart from the rest of the body. Its health depended on the health of the whole organism. What Gladden envisioned was a social order inspired and guided by religion and a religion dedicated to the service of society. When this ideal, typified by the physical organism, became reality the Kingdom of God would be complete.

To bring humanity under the law of love, there must be a specialized institution to cultivate religious ideas and feelings.[48] It was simply because religion was the one force that could arrest selfishness and stimulate altruism—in short, reach the seat of evil and disorder in the will—that it was essential to the growth of the Kingdom. Since evil was in the spiritual nature of man, legal and social coercion, though they might "beat it down, drive it into holes, check, for a time, its manifestation," could never exterminate it. Force was futile. In giving man personality and free will, God had refused to use coercion; His method, demonstrated by the Incarnation, was to change the human heart by truth and sacrificial love. The church had erred badly, Gladden thought, by failing to grasp the divine method and relying on other forces than truth and love.[49]

[47] Gladden, *Christian Pastor*, p. 105; Gladden, Sermon, May 25, 1913, Gladden Papers.

[48] Gladden, *The Church and the Kingdom*, pp. 9–13.

[49] Gladden, Sermon, February 26, 1893, Gladden Papers; Gladden, *The Church and Modern Life*, pp. 104–5, 116, 122.

In his address as moderator to the National Council of the Congregational Churches in 1907 Gladden asserted that it was the church's responsibility to permeate society with "a better morality." Although lauding Theodore Roosevelt's reforms, he insisted that even after the government had exhausted its resources, the roots of evil would still be alive and shooting up new sprouts. No form of political or social organization could change human nature:

> Instead of it being true that democracy will transfigure egoism, we have found that no form of society can march hellward faster than a democracy under the banner of unbridled individualism.[50]

Pointing on another occasion to the exposures of the muckrakers, he observed that only "the revival in the hearts of men of the sense of the presence of God, of a righteous God," could cure such "mighty mischiefs."

> Does a man believe in God who organizes or joins a ring in the city council or a legislature to sell legislation by which the people are fleeced? Does a man believe in God who buys such legislation? Does a man believe in God who artfully vends millions or hundreds of millions of inflated stock which he knows must collapse in the hands of its purchasers and spread suffering and calamity far and wide?[51]

Ethics and religion were, in Gladden's opinion, inseparable. Ethics must find its inspiration in religion; and religion must result in ethical living and service to humanity. What contemporary society needed most was not a better ethical rule—it had the Golden Rule —but "an impulse, an inspiration, an energy of life which shall prompt it to act upon the truth it knows already." That inspiration could come only through the vital communion of the church with God.[52]

But was the church capable of filling this role? Gladden answered affirmatively, confessing the church's "mistakes and failures, with-

[50] Gladden, "The Church and the Social Crisis," October 8, 1907, Gladden Papers.

[51] Gladden, Sermon, December 11, 1904, Gladden Papers.

[52] Gladden, Sermon, August 5, 1906, Gladden Papers.

out despairing of its life."[53] He vigorously opposed the criticisms of organized religion made during the 1890's by George D. Herron of Iowa College (Grinnell). Herron thought thorough reconstruction rather than reform to be the only solution to society's ills, and he even claimed it impossible to practice the Christian life in contemporary society. Denouncing organized religion for compromising with the existing order, he declared that the "entrenchments of custodial religion" often made "the most stubborn resistance to the will of God."[54] Writing of "The Conflict of Christ with Christianity," Herron suggested that accepting the Christian religion might be "very remote from accepting Christ and the order of things for which he stood."[55] After the turn of the century he dropped this Christian phraseology of his earlier writings and took up the cause of socialism outside of the churches.

Gladden denied that Christian inspiration could exist without religious institutions: the "principle of organization" operated wherever there was life, and though there was danger of institutions replacing inspiration with "the cake of custom," the remedy was not to destroy organization but to "replenish its vital energies."[56] Though the church had "very imperfectly understood the teachings of Christ," it was still the agency for God's continuing "revelation through incarnation." Herron also failed to see the loyalty to Christ that existed in the church and overestimated the loyalty to His principles that existed outside of it.[57] And as for the hopelessness of the contemporary environment, Gladden asserted that even radical social reconstruction would not solve the problem of individual behavior. He insisted that it was more realistic to begin with individual regeneration and to co-ordinate environmental change with moral progress

---

[53] Gladden, Sermon, September 23, 1906, Gladden Papers.

[54] George D. Herron, *The Christian Society* (New York: Fleming H. Revell Co., 1894), p. 56.

[55] George D. Herron, *Between Caesar and Jesus* (New York: Thomas Y. Crowell & Co., 1899), p. 184.

[56] Washington Gladden, "Shall We Abolish Institutions?", *Congregationalist*, LXXIX (June 7, 1894), 791.

[57] Gladden, Sermon, March 3, 1897, Gladden Papers.

than to reconstruct the social structure in anticipation of individual improvement. But he minimized the influence of the social environment both on individuals and on the church and expected too much of the church's moral influence.[58]

Gladden was probably more important as a popularizer of the Social Gospel than as a theoretician, although he followed an independent ideological course. He spread the social message in his own denomination, and he was connected in some way with almost all of the major co-operative organizations of the Social Gospel. He participated with Lyman Abbott, Graham Taylor, and Richard T. Ely in the Interdenominational Congress called in 1885 by Josiah Strong, whom he had met in 1883 at his installation in Columbus, to discuss urban church work. The urban concentration of America's social problems was the theme of Stong's extremely popular book *Our Country* (1885), published the same year as the Interdenominational Congress met. In 1886 Strong became secretary of the Evangelical Alliance, an early Protestant ecumenical venture, and he quickly made it an important forum for the Social Gospel. Gladden attended meetings of the alliance and in 1888 gave a major address at its sessions in Montreal.[59]

Gladden was one of the founders in 1885 of the American Economic Association and was on the committee, which included such progressive economists as Richard T. Ely and John Bates Clark, that drafted its platform. Though it lost some of its reforming ardor during the 1890's, it began as a bold challenge to laissez faire economics.[60] In 1889 Gladden, Ely, Lyman Abbott, and others launched

---

[58] Gladden, Sermon, March 19, 1899, Gladden Papers; Washington Gladden, *Social Salvation* (Boston: Houghton, Mifflin & Co., 1902), pp. 15–30.

[59] Hopkins, *Rise of the Social Gospel*, p. 113; Josiah Strong, *Our Country* (New York: Baker & Taylor Co., 1885), p. 138; May, *Protestant Churches and Industrial America*, p. 194; *Ohio State Journal*, October 27, 1888.

[60] Hopkins, *Rise of the Social Gospel*, pp. 116–17; Richard T. Ely, *Ground Under Our Feet: An Autobiography* (New York: Macmillan Co., 1938), pp. 140–43; John L. Shover, "The Attitude of American Intellectuals toward the Labor Movement, 1890–1900" (unpublished Ph.D. dissertation, Ohio State University, 1957), p. 146. In 1904 Ely tried to enlist Gladden's aid in raising funds for a projected volume by Ely and John R. Commons on American labor. Ely to Gladden, February 7, 1904, Gladden Papers.

Chautauqua into the stream of the Social Gospel, and Gladden lectured there in subsequent years. According to the foremost historian of the Social Gospel, Chautauqua made an important contribution to the propagation of social Christianity. Ely remembered Gladden as one of those who "high-lighted" Chautauqua's parade of illustrious speakers.[61] In 1893 the American Institute of Christian Sociology was founded at Chautauqua, with Ely as president. The institute sponsored a Summer School of Applied Christianity, and when the summer school met at Oberlin in 1894, Gladden presided and read a paper on "Religion and Wealth."[62] This was evidently the same paper he had given the year before at the World's Parliament of Religions. The institution gave a prominent place to presentations of the Social Gospel by Gladden, Ely, and other representatives of the movement.[63]

Gladden also supported the American Institute of Social Service, which Josiah Strong founded in 1898 after the Evangelical Alliance failed to endorse his broad plans for popular education in social issues. Gladden was a member of the National Committee for Studies in Social Christianity, which carried on this institute's primary work.[64] He also spread the Social Gospel through appearances before organizations that were not strictly devoted to its propagation, such as the National Social and Political Conference and the American Association for the Advancement of Science.[65] But, inter-

[61] Hopkins, *Rise of the Social Gospel,* p. 163; Ely, *Ground Under Our Feet,* p. 80.

[62] May, *Protestant Churches and Industrial America,* p. 254; *Ohio State Journal,* November 15, 1894; *Congregationalist,* LXXIX (November 22, 1894), 737–38; Washington Gladden, "Religion and Wealth," *Bibliotheca Sacra,* LII (January, 1895), 153–67.

[63] *Ohio State Journal,* September 23, 1893; *Congregationalist,* LXXVIII (September 28, 1893), 415–16; John Henry Barrows, *The World's Parliament of Religions* (2 vols.; Chicago: Parliament Publishing Co., 1893), II, 1068–70; Hopkins, *Rise of the Social Gospel,* pp. 115–16.

[64] Hopkins, *Rise of the Social Gospel,* p. 260; Josiah Strong to Gladden, September 11, 1908, November 6, 1913, Gladden Papers.

[65] *Ohio State Journal,* May 23, August 24, 1899.

estingly enough, though he had read his books, Gladden did not meet Walter Rauschenbusch, the foremost Baptist social gospeler and one of the movement's most incisive thinkers, until 1908, when they appeared together before a joint meeting of Congregationalists and Baptists in Boston's Tremont Temple.[66]

Moreover, Gladden's writings appeared in a variety of journals devoted to the spread of social Christianity. He contributed to the *Dawn,* a monthly paper founded in 1889 by W. D. P. Bliss and the Society of Christian Socialists. And he served on the editorial board of the *Kingdom,* established in 1894 as the successor to the *Northwest Congregationalist.* The *Kingdom* became the most important organ of the Social Gospel from 1865 to 1915. This position meant not that he performed editorial duties for compensation, but only that he contributed articles fairly regularly.[67]

The Social Gospel presupposed the applicability of the Golden Rule to all spheres of human activity, whether domestic, ecclesiastical, political, economic, or international. In his preaching and writing Gladden developed the ramifications of this presupposition. Most characteristically, however, the Social Gospel focused on the problems resulting from industrialization and urbanization. But, as Gladden's wide-ranging thought and far-flung activities reveal, there was no social, economic, or political disease for which the social gospelers did not think that the Golden Rule was an adequate cure. It was the unifying thread that ran through his interest in industrial organization, charity, Negro education, urban politics, and international peace.

[66] Frank Gaylord Cook to Gladden, November 2, 1908, Gladden Papers; Gladden, "The Church and the Social Crisis," Address, [November 30, 1908,] Gladden Papers.

[67] Hopkins, *Rise of the Social Gospel,* pp. 175–76, 194–95.

Eight

Christianization of the Economic Order

Gladden began to consider the relationship between religion and the economic order very early in his career and continued to devote his attention to it for nearly five decades. In 1870, for example, in response to Wendell Phillips' criticism of the otherworldliness of the churches, Gladden called for the application of Christian principles to business life and for social service on behalf of the working classes.[1] But, apart from such isolated incidents as the importation of Chinese strikebreakers by a leading shoemaker, the industrial scene in North Adams was quiet during his years there. Later, while on the editorial staff of the *Independent,* he was preoccupied with literary affairs and current religious events.

After he became pastor of the North Church of Springfield in 1875, however, Gladden's awareness of economic disorder gained depth and breadth. In a popular lecture on "Drummers" he traced an increase in the number of traveling salesmen to unsound business conditions: excessive competition, a fluctuating currency, and the restless, feverish spirit of the age. He attributed the political corruption of the Gilded Age to an inordinate love of money generated by rapid economic growth.[2]

[1] Washington Gladden, *Salt Without Savor* (North Adams, Mass.: James T. Robinson & Co., 1870).

[2] *Springfield Republican,* March 6, 1875, June 26, 1876.

The unprecedented expansion of industry after the Civil War was broken in 1873 by a severe depression. This depression turned Gladden to his initial study of the problems of labor. Beginning in May, 1875, he preached a series of sermons on topics of interest to working people. Gladden later admitted that these sermons, published as *Working People and Their Employers* (1876), were neither profound nor radical. Their significance, however, as a brave attempt to apply Christian principles to the industrial order is clear. Charles Howard Hopkins has called *Working People* "the most important discussion" prior to 1880 of the profits of labor and "one of the first mileposts set by American social Christianity."[3]

"Now that slavery is out of the way," Gladden declared, "the questions that concern the welfare of our free laborers are coming forward. . . . It is plain that the pulpit must have something to say about them." Although unemployment was widespread, Gladden used strong terms to stress the duty and sanctity of work: "Idleness is . . . immoral; and whoever, man or woman, is living without occupation, is leading a life of immorality."[4] Gladden's analysis of the depression revealed a superficial understanding of economic forces. He insisted that machinery not only improved wages but also stimulated employment by cheapening products and increasing demand. The causes of the depression were, in his opinion, the destruction of property by war and great fires, the debts resulting from war, extravagant and wasteful living (including consumption of liquor), a fluctuating paper currency, and overexpansion.[5] He referred to overexpansion only in passing. His solutions for distress were equally simple: the unemployed should take any work that was available (and if none was available in the cities, they should go back to the farms); all who were hard pressed should econo-

---

[3] *Ibid.*, May 17, 24, June 7, 14, 21, July 5, 12, 19, 1875; Gladden, *Recollections*, p. 255; Hopkins, *Rise of the Social Gospel*, p. 27.

[4] Washington Gladden, *Working People and Their Employers* (New York: Funk & Wagnalls Co., 1894), pp. 3, 10.

[5] *Ibid.*, pp. 18, 54–59; Robert R. Roberts, "The Social Gospel and the Trust-Busters," *Church History*, XXV (1956), 239–41.

mize by wearing simpler clothes, staying away from "circuses and nigger-minstrel shows," and using less tobacco and rum. He sided with the Republican party in its demand for a firm gold standard and resumption of payment in specie. He also discussed the home, divorce, the values of friendship and social intercourse, and the question of "rising in the world." His tone was strongly moralistic. He felt that, "of all the enemies of the workingmen, the worst is strong drink."[6]

His most important observations concerned the relations between employers and employees. He traced three historical systems of organizing labor: slavery, the wages system, and co-operation In the first there had been no conflict between capital and labor but also capital had owned labor. Christianity had made slavery impossible and set the stage for the wages system, which was a state of conflict. "Slavery first," he declared, "then war. All the kingdoms of the world's industry are now in a state of war." Contrary to the claims of the laissez faire economists, the wages fund depended not only on supply and demand but also on the will of the capitalist. Consequently, there could be equity and peace, even under the wages system, "if the capitalist would measure his profits, and the workingman his wages, by the Golden Rule." That was, in Gladden's analysis, "the only way to secure peace on the basis of the wages system."[7]

In *Working People* Gladden gave qualified approval to labor unions. Workingmen had a right to combine for protection against combinations of capital, but reason and moral influence should be their primary weapons. He considered strikes defensible, though often unwise, unprofitable, and injurious to the community. The ideal of "free labor" meant the open shop. He condemned violence and the intimidation of non-unionists and deprecated the "large proportion" among union members of "ignorant men, whose passions are easily excited, and who may be led to take very fanatical and

[6] Gladden, *Working People,* pp. 60, 62–70, 165.
[7] *Ibid.,* pp. 34, 37, 43.

absurd views of the labor question." They often willingly followed leaders who were "noisy, crazy, crack-brained creatures."[8]

Influenced by Ruskin's appeal for personal bonds between employers and employees, Gladden lamented their growing social separation and condemned as barbarous policies that would array class against class. He believed that the employer who tried to apply the Golden Rule to his business would care for the health, comfort, intellectual improvement, and moral and religious welfare of his workers. He would provide lectures and libraries and might even rent pews in his church for them, as did several of Gladden's parishioners. Above all, he would respect them and treat them politely. The relations between capital and labor must be personal, not those based on class; and they must be moral, not simply economic.[9] The tendency of Gladden's discussion, which he later regretted, was to exaggerate the dangers of unionism. His deprecation of class solidarity also handicapped labor, which, as the case proved, could achieve its aims only by countering management's power with an equivalent unity and power of its own.

Though he felt that the application of the Golden Rule might redeem the wages system, Gladden expected economic salvation to come through the reorganization of industry on a co-operative basis. Socialism, or any other system of redistributing and equalizing wealth, would be "simply pillage." Moreover, private property was essential to the perfection of character. Socialism lacked the discipline and the appeal to individual initiative inculcated by the management of private property. He regarded the identification of capital and labor in a joint ownership of industry as having few of the defects of either the wages system or socialism. It could take two forms: profit-sharing plans, by which employers would give workers an interest in the business and a proportion of the profits in addition to their wages; and the co-operatives like Rochdale in England, in which workers would go into business for themselves,

[8] *Ibid.*, pp. 40–42, 137–38.
[9] *Ibid.*, pp. 166–83, 190–92.

furnishing the capital from their savings and managing and performing the labor. Gladden thought that profit sharing was more practicable, since American workers, because of their relatively high wages, had little disposition to set up their own workshops, and since workers normally lacked the mutual trust, the spirit of concession, and the intelligence necessary for independent enterprise. But profit sharing might be the intermediate step between the wages system and full co-operation. Gladden doubted that the warfare inherent in the wages system would ever end until that system was "abolished or greatly modified." Confident that co-operation was "the arrangement of the essential factors of industry according to the Christian rule," he maintained that ultimately it would prevail.[10] Shortly after he wrote *Working People,* Gladden had a firsthand example of co-operative enterprise in Springfield. The Sovereigns of Industry, a national labor organization started in 1874, operated a co-operative store in Springfield; but though initially successful, it had a difficult existence in the 1870's.[11] Unfortunately, Gladden did not record his impressions of this experiment.

During his pastorate in Springfield Gladden continued to maintain from his pulpit and in *Sunday Afternoon* that Christianity was relevant to all social life. He criticized the exclusiveness of many churches and pointed out that even they needed Christianization.[12] He urged employers to divide a larger share of their profits with their employees; he concluded that competition was a destructive as well as a beneficent force; and he explained the violence of strikers as "the natural fruit of a policy that steadily impoverishes and degrades them."[13] He began to realize that the immobility of labor, both geographical and vocational, increased the inequality between capital and labor.[14] But he opposed the intervention of gov-

[10] *Ibid.,* pp. 44–48, 50, 198–200.
[11] *Springfield Republican,* September 11, 1875, January 14, 1878.
[12] *Sunday Afternoon,* III (May, 1879), 473–74.
[13] *Ibid.,* I (January, 1878), 86–87; III (January, 1879), 87–88.
[14] *Ibid.,* II (September, 1878), 277–78, (November, 1878), 470–71.

ernment to relieve unemployment. Beyond reducing its own expenditures, ceasing to subsidize corporations, and protecting workers' savings, government could do little to alleviate distress. Unemployment, after all, was not an insoluble problem: "All that is needed is that the Christian law be put in force."[15] Inequality of condition was inevitable, he claimed, because God gave men unequal powers and opportunities. He did not interpret inequality of opportunity in economic terms, however, for he was still sure that "the boy who belongs to what are called the working classes has quite as good a chance of becoming a 'bloated bondholder' before he dies, as the boy who is born with a silver spoon in his mouth."[16]

Gladden's ideal was an industrial society based on co-operation, permeated by the spirit of the Golden Rule, and geared to human welfare rather than to profits. But the individualism in his thinking died slowly. Individual employers and small groups of workingmen were to practice co-operation; regenerated individuals were to apply the Golden Rule; and individual employers were to safeguard the welfare of their employees. Believing that opportunity was virtually unlimited, Gladden minimized the structural limitations on social justice.

After Gladden moved to Columbus in 1883 industrial problems pressed themselves even more urgently upon him. In the great coal regions of southeastern Ohio smoldering unrest erupted in 1884 into a labor war of volcanic character and proportions. Strikes occurred in 1884–85 in many mining areas, but the strike in the Hocking Valley was the largest and most publicized. Contrary to a popular misconception, Gladden had no major part in the settlement of the strike against the Columbus and Hocking Valley Coal and Iron Company, a syndicate formed in 1883 to eliminate excessive competition. But two vice-presidents and the treasurer of the company were members of the First Church. The two vice-presidents, Walter Crafts and Thaddeus Longstreth, were on the church's board of trus-

---

[15] *Ibid.*, II (October, 1878), 376–77.
[16] *Good Company*, IV (1879), 282–83; VI (September, 1880), 94–95.

tees. Wages and recognition of the miners' union, the Ohio Miners' Amalgamated Association, were the main issues. Gladden defended labor's right to organize, but when he attempted to persuade Crafts and Longstreth, one of them flatly told him that the company would kill the union if it cost half a million dollars. Longstreth was particularly hostile to unionism, and the mines he owned before the syndicate was formed had a bad record of labor relations. Crafts was less tyrannical and, as Gladden recalled, he thought that he was doing the miners a service by opposing the union. Although Gladden's position must have piqued them, the officers stayed in the First Church, and Gladden later enjoyed pleasant relations with at least Crafts.[17]

In March, 1884, the company won temporarily and forced the returning workers to sign an "ironclad oath." But within a few months the union, functioning more vigorously than before, renewed the strike. Both sides suffered severely. The cost to the operators overbalanced their temporary victory. Recognizing the miners' determination and the advantages of dealing with a union rather than with an unorganized mob, the operators finally accepted a wage-fixing and arbitration agreement in the Hocking Valley, which Gladden regarded as a model for industrial relations. Gladden claimed no credit for the company's change of heart, and, though one economist, John Bates Clark, believed that his counsel hastened the settlement, it is not clear that it actually had this effect.[18]

In a series of sermons in 1884–85 Gladden studied a variety of social questions, ranging from "The Strength and Weakness of Socialism" to "Christianity and Popular Education" and including such

[17] Gladden, *Recollections*, pp. 291–93; John W. Lozier, "The Hocking Valley Coal Miners' Strike, 1884–1885" (unpublished M.A. thesis, Ohio State University, 1963), pp. 35–37, 44, 57, 59.

[18] *Ohio State Journal*, March 2, 1883; Gladden to Ely, December 6, 1887, Richard T. Ely Papers (State Historical Society of Wisconsin, Madison); Gladden, *Recollections*, pp. 291–93; Gladden, "Greetings to Miners," Sermon, January 22, 1911, Gladden Papers; Lozier, "Hocking Valley Coal Miners' Strike," pp. 89–90, 93; John L. Shover, "Washington Gladden and the Labor Question," *Ohio Historical Quarterly*, LXVIII (October, 1959), 337.

topics as intemperance, gambling, and the family. Several of the
sermons appeared in the *Century*, and, with the encouragement of
Roswell Smith, Gladden published the series under a title suggestive
of its theme, *Applied Christianity* (1886).[19]

"Is It Peace or War?", probably the most important address in the
collection, had an interesting background. During a strike in Cleveland early in 1886, a man identified by Gladden simply as a "philanthropist of that city" invited both sides in the conflict to attend a
mass meeting at which an impartial outsider would speak. Selected
to make this conciliatory address, Gladden spoke on March 25, 1886,
at Cleveland's Music Hall on the question, "Peace or War between
Capital and Labor?" He later recalled the surprised expressions on
the strikers' faces and the rousing cheer that they gave him when
he endorsed unionism. But "they were compelled to listen to quite
a number of things after that which did not make them cheer."
Within a few weeks he delivered the same address to the Law and
Order League of Boston and to a large audience of workingmen,
both of which met in Tremont Temple. He claimed to have received
an enthusiastic reception on each occasion.[20]

Combinations of capital and labor, Gladden asserted in his address, meant war. They were fighting organizations. But though war
was a great evil, it was not the greatest of evils: "The permanent
social degradation of the people who do the world's work would
be a greater evil." If capitalists could combine, it was only fair to
allow laborers the same right for self-defense: "If war is the order

[19] Washington Gladden, "Three Dangers," *Century*, XXVIII (Midsummer,
1884), 620–27, "Christianity and Wealth," (October, 1884), 903–11, "Christianity and Popular Amusements," XXIX (January, 1885), 384–92, "The Strength
and Weakness of Socialism," XXXI (March, 1886), 737–49, "Is It Peace or War?"
XXXII (August, 1886), 565–76; Smith to Gladden, May 22, 1886, First Church
archives. Particularly interested in divorce during the 1880's, Gladden wrote an
analytical article on the subject and was a vice-president of the Ohio Divorce
Reform League. Washington Gladden, "The Increase of Divorce," *Century*,
XXIII (January, 1882), 411–20; *Ohio State Journal*, December 7, 1883.

[20] *Ohio State Journal*, March 26, April 10, May 10, 1886; Gladden *Recollections*, pp. 300–304; Gladden to Gilder, [May 9, 1886,] *Century* Collection.

of the day, we must grant to labor belligerent rights."[21] Gladden's recognition of the necessity for labor to be able to juxtapose organized power against capital was a significant advance over his paternalistic attitude toward workingmen in *Working People*.

But, as in the earlier book, he declined to accept the finality of conflict. There must be industrial peace. And as the first steps toward peace, employers must recognize the justice of labor's demands and share the rewards of industry more equitably with labor. Industrial partnership—probably in the form of profit sharing—was "the next step in the evolution of our industrial system."[22] Arguing that, according to all economists, increased efficiency enlarged profits, Gladden claimed that experiments in profit sharing had shown that forms of industrial organization to increase efficiency. Employers who insisted that they could not pay higher wages could, if they adopted profit sharing, enlarge wages and still maintain their own profits. Peace would not come, Gladden predicted, until industrial partnership prevailed. It was the economic expression of human brotherhood; men were made to live not as enemies but as co-workers and friends. Gladden's enthusiasm for profit sharing was shared by other social reformers, such as Richard T. Ely, who edited a history of co-operation in the United States, and Lyman Abbott, who popularized the idea through the *Outlook* and his books.[23]

During the 1880's Gladden became more alert to another aspect of industrial disorder, the growing alienation of the working classes from the churches. Like many other clergymen in this decade, he made a survey of church attendance and found that, compared to other social classes, wage earners attended the Protestant churches in disproportionately small numbers. His investigations, conducted in April, 1885, showed that only about one-third of the manual

---

[21] Washington Gladden, *Applied Christianity: Moral Aspects of Social Questions* (Boston: Houghton, Mifflin & Co., 1886), pp. 124–25.

[22] *Ibid.*, pp. 131–32, 136–37.

[23] Shover, "Gladden and the Labor Question," pp. 341–42; Lyman Abbott, *Christianity and Social Problems* (Boston: Houghton, Mifflin & Co., 1896), pp. 209–10.

workers in Columbus attended church and that many of these were
Roman Catholics. Examining his own church, he found that, while
the working classes constituted nearly one-fourth of the total population, wage earners accounted for only one-tenth of his congregation.
Later that year at Josiah Strong's interdenominational conference on
"Problems of the Cities," Gladden contended that economic issues
often caused this alienation. Some wage earners feared that because
of their dress they would feel uncomfortable in the Protestant
churches, which they supposed were all fashionable. But an even
more fundamental reason for alienation was the identification of the
churches with their employers. This trend could only be reversed,
Gladden argued, if the churches demonstrated that they were not on
the side of capital by endorsing unionism, industrial arbitration,
and profit sharing.[24]

He applied this remedy in his own church, but, despite his obvious
sympathy for labor, working people never joined his congregation in
large numbers. The First Church was, after all, a downtown church,
and it was associated in the popular mind with the professional and
commercial families that were its chief supporters. Gladden was
strongly influenced by *The Workers* (1897–99), a two-volume study
by Walter Wyckoff, a young professor at Princeton who traveled
across the country in the guise of a workingman. Wyckoff found
among non-churchgoing workers a widespread feeling that they
were not welcome in the fashionable churches on the avenues and a
strong resentment against mission chapels. Many had tenuous ties
with the churches, however, and few considered themselves real
opponents of religion. In fact, workers often criticized the churches
while expressing admiration for Christ.[25] Gladden always thought
that by preaching on themes of interest to wage earners and evinc-
ing sympathy with their lot he could restore them to the fold. In

[24] Abell, *Urban Impact on American Protestantism*, p. 61; Winthrop S. Hudson, *Religion in America* (New York: Charles Scribner's Sons, 1965), pp. 314–15;
Ohio State Journal, April 11, 25, 27, 1885; *Congregationalist*, LXX (December
17, 1885), 429.

[25] Gladden, Sermons, "The Workers," December 11, 1898; "Non Church
Goers," May 15, 1901, Gladden Papers.

1905, for example, he began to preach a monthly sermon especially for working people. Some sermons viewed Jesus and Paul as workers, and one series was on "Great Friends of the Working Classes."[26] He usually placed the burden of the estrangement between the churches and the working classes on the churches. "The coming reformation," he wrote in 1908, "will be signalized by a great change in the attitude of the church toward the toiling classes."

> It will not turn its back on them, as it did in Luther's day; it will not maintain toward them an attitude of kindly patronage, as it has done in our day; it will recognize the fact that its welfare is bound up with them . . . that it needs them quite as much as they need it; that it is a monstrous thing even to conceive that a church of Jesus Christ could exist or a class institution, with the largest social class in the community outside of it.[27]

While Gladden's analysis of industrial society grew increasingly realistic during the 1890's, he continued to hope for a peaceful resolution of strife, particularly through profit sharing. His most important book on labor problems after *Working People, Tools and the Man: Property and Industry under the Christian Law* (1893), appeared first as a series of lectures in 1887 under the Lyman Beecher Foundation at Yale Seminary. Gladden was the first lecturer under that foundation to discuss labor problems.[28] He subsequently delivered this course at Cornell University, Mansfield College at Oxford, and Meadville Seminary. He began with the declaration that Christianity had a twofold end: perfect men in a perfect society. The salvation of men and of society were inseparable. Gladden then directed his attention principally to the salvation of society. The social and economic philosophies that exalted self-interest, especially the laissez faire school of economics erected on

---

[26] Gladden, Sermons, "Religion of Workingmen," February 12, 1905; "Jesus the Carpenter," May 7, 1905; "Paul the Tent-Maker," June 4, 1905; "Workingman's Family," October 1, 1905; "William Lloyd Garrison," December 10, 1905, Gladden Papers.

[27] Gladden, *The Church and Modern Life*, pp. 146–47.

[28] *Congregationalist*, LXXII (February 10, 1887), 44.

the doctrines of Adam Smith, had not only created unprecedented conflict in social relations but had also weakened the message and influence of Christianity. The Christian rule for society was not "sheer altruism" but a blending of altruism and egoism.[29] Social salvation would follow implementation of the Golden Rule.

Gladden's view of property in *Tools and the Man* underscored his reaction against laissez faire economics. Agreeing with Orestes Brownson that "property is communion with God through the material world," he drew the following conclusions: "That God is the absolute owner of the material universe. . . . There are no absolute rights of property except his rights"; that, since property was also communion with man through the material world, no man could accumulate it without incurring a heavy debt to society; and that property was power, both its production and consumption vitally affecting the lives of others.[30]

The influence of Henry George, whose *Progress and Poverty* (1879) had stimulated Gladden's social thought since the time of its publication, was clear in Gladden's contention that the rights of the state were superior to those of private landholders. Gladden's judgment on George's specific proposals, however, was still suspended nearly twenty years after he had first read *Progress and Poverty,* and he never accepted George's cardinal tenet, the single tax. Since communistic landholding antedated private ownership, Gladden thought it ridiculous to consider private property "something peculiarly sacred and indefeasible." The nation must regulate ownership of land by social use and the public welfare; every man's right to the means of life transcended any man's right to property. Gladden favored a combination of private ownership and public contro!

[29] Washington Gladden, *Tools and the Man: Property and Industry under the Christian Law* (Boston: Houghton, Mifflin & Co., 1893), pp. 1–2, 26, 31, 34 41–42.

[30] *Ibid.,* pp. 86, 90, 101, 106, 110. Gladden had been strongly influenced by Brownson's mystical statement since at least the mid-1870's, when he quoted i in a sermon on the moral obligations of property-holding. Gladden, "Rights o Property," Sermon, August 7, 1876, Gladden Papers.

for the present but predicted an ultimate return to some system of common property.[31]

The labor question, Gladden's major concern in *Tools and the Man*, was, in his words, "the most urgent question before the country." Unrestricted competition between employers, which led to reductions in wages, first by the most rapacious employers and then by those who followed suit to stay in the market, had broken down. The rapid growth of such combinations as the Hocking Valley coal syndicate was a natural reaction against the damaging effects of such competition. It was utter folly, Gladden thought, to suppose that there could be real freedom of contract between industrial combines and individual laborers. Workingmen could safeguard their welfare only through unions. But fighting combinations of labor and capital were intolerable. Only arbitration, the "substitution of moral law for physical law in the distribution of the product of industry," could save the wages system, and for arbitration to succeed, public opinion must force employers to accept unionism.[32]

Gladden still hoped that co-operation would supplant both competition and combination. Resting on the cornerstone of brotherhood, and cemented by the spirit of the Golden Rule, co-operation would be the economic temple of Christianity. Gladden had visited the National Co-operative Festival at the Crystal Palace during one of his trips to England, and he marshaled an impressive array of statistics in the defense of co-operative production and distribution. But strongly influenced by the ideal of *noblesse oblige* and doubting the ability of American workingmen to organize co-operative stores and workshops without the leadership and initiative of captains of industry, he still believed, as he had stated in *Working People*, that profit sharing was the most practicable form of co-operation for American industry. Several years later, he asked why co-operatives had hardly taken root in America, while the movement had suc-

---

[31] Gladden, "The Life and Work of Henry George," Sermon, November 7, 1897, Gladden Papers; Gladden, *Tools and the Man*, pp. 63, 71–79, 81–85.

[32] Gladden, *Tools and the Man*, pp. 116, 152–69.

ceeded in England. The heterogeneity of the American working class was a partial answer. However, he thought a more fundamental reason was that Americans relied on political freedom to the neglect of economic freedom. "Political democracy is a delusion," he maintained, "when it rests on economic feudalism."[33]

After writing *Tools and the Man*, Gladden continued to commend experiments in profit sharing and co-operatives, but he realized that changes in industrial relations were not likely to take these forms. His next book on industrial problems, *Social Facts and Forces* (1897), revealed his growing concern for the improvement of existing conditions. *Social Facts and Forces* originated in 1896 as lectures for the Ryder Foundation in Chicago; Gladden repeated them as the E. A. Rand Course on Applied Christianity at Iowa College and to his congregation.[34]

Gladden held that "the principle of association," a major force in modern life, had revolutionized industry in the last half-century. On the whole, the factory system had benefited modern society, but certain evils, which were not essential to the system, must be eliminated. He suggested, though less sanguinely than before, that co-operatives or profit sharing might correct the worst evil, the division of the community into warring classes.[35] But he gave more attention to working hours and woman and child labor, calling for legislation to end child labor and arbitration (or, if arbitration would not work, legislation) of working hours. While he sympathized with the movement for an eight-hour day, he preferred to have labor win shorter working hours gradually from management—for example, by achieving first a nine-hour day and a Saturday half-day—than by legislative enactment of a universal eight-hour day. When labor was actually working eight hours a day, legislation could register

[33] *Ibid.*, pp. 176, 181, 197, 203 f., 237; Gladden, "Social Progress of the English People," Sermon, [October 2, 1898,] Gladden Papers.

[34] *Congregationalist*, LXXXI (January 30, 1896), 171, LXXXII (February 25, 1897), 267; *Ohio State Journal*, January 25, 1896.

[35] Washington Gladden, *Social Facts and Forces* (New York: G. P. Putnam's Sons, 1897), pp. 5, 26.

this advance, but legislation ought not anticipate the movement of society. Good will, "the one thing needful," was his basic panacea.[36]

Gladden criticized labor unions for opposing contract prison labor and limiting apprenticeships, and again condemned labor violence; but *Social Facts and Forces* was more sympathetic to unionism than any of his earlier books. Whereas previously he had cautioned the unions against intimidating non-unionists, he now comprehended their indignation. He argued, however, that they must learn human solidarity, not proletarian solidarity. The "true trades-union" was

the union of employers and employed—of guiding brains and willing hands—all watchful if each other's interests, cooperating each other's welfare, working together for the common good.[37]

Although he was never reluctant to castigate unions for abusing their power, Gladden's defense of unionism became increasingly emphatic in the twentieth century. In 1901 he told the Retail Grocery Clerks' Union of Columbus that he wished "that all the working men in every trade were included in the union representing that trade, and that all the bargaining were collective bargaining." And in *Christianity and Socialism* (1905) he stated: "The rights of life and liberty are more sacred than the rights of property. The life and liberty of the workingmen depend on their right to combine." Moreover, warning employers against encouraging non-unionists, he urged them to accept collective bargaining and arbitration without equivocation. When both sides were firmly organized, there could be mutual respect and effective negotiation.[38]

In his most vigorous defense of unionism, *The Labor Question* (1911), Gladden admitted that industrial relations were worsening

[36] *Ibid.*, pp. 14–15, 29–31, 36, 39–41; *Ohio State Journal*, May 5, 1890; Gladden, Sermons, [January, 1890,] "The Workingman's Pleasures," November 5, 1905, Gladden Papers.

[37] Gladden, *Social Facts and Forces*, p. 81.

[38] Gladden, "Strengths and Weaknesses of Organized Labor," Sermon, January, 1900, Gladden Papers; *Ohio State Journal*, April 29, 1901; Gladden, *Christianity and Socialism*, pp. 85, 92–101.

and that profit sharing and co-operatives were dead issues.[39] Labor unions were not above reproach: they imposed petty restrictions on work, opposed contract prison labor, deliberately reduced speed, perpetrated violence, and called normally unjustifiable sympathetic strikes and secondary boycotts. He granted, however, that reduction of speed was defensible on piecework, for which only the fastest workers received a living wage, and he blamed non-unionists for much violence attributed to the unions. And since the other practices were perversions of the unions' true functions, "excrescences which may be purged away," he considered it unjust to condemn the movement because of them. Unionism was the only safeguard against the degradation of labor: "The fact that unorganized labor is steadily forced down toward starvation and misery is a fact which no student of industrial conditions would dream of denying."[40] Workers wanted economic freedom, not the protection of the state or the paternalism of employers, and the union was their means of obtaining it.

Gladden insisted that partnership between capital and labor was the answer to industrial disorder. But he no longer conceived of partnership through profit sharing or other paternalistic schemes, though the responsibility for achieving it still rested mainly on the captains of industry. Partnership meant industrial democracy—"giving the wage-workers, through collective bargaining, a voice in the determination of their share of the joint product." To change the metaphor, as Gladden often did, the barons of "economic feudalism" must surrender their vested privileges and recognize the equality of labor, or else the forces of democracy, "the great fact of the age," would trample them in the dust. Gladden imagined that the democratic employer would address his employees thus:

[39] Washington Gladden, *The Labor Question* (Boston: Pilgrim Press, 1911) pp. 3–13. This book first appeared as a series of highly controversial articles in the *Outlook*. Washington Gladden, "The Case against the Labor Union," *Outlook*, XCVII (February 25, 1911), 465–71; "Reasons for the Unions," (March 4, 1911), 497–502; "Industry and Democracy," (March 18, 1911), 589–95. "Cross-Lights and Counter-Claims," (April 15, 1911), 827–32; "The Church and the Labor Question," XCVIII (May 6, 1911), 35–40.

[40] Gladden, *Labor Question*, pp. 13–39, 55.

Certainly, men, you must organize. . . . And I want all the men in this shop to join this union. . . . This is not my business, not your business, it is our business. I shall study your interest and you will study mine; we will consult together about it all the while. . . . If we must fight we stand on the level and fight fair. I hope that there will be no fighting.

If the employer took this stance toward the union, the open shop would be a virtual impossibility. Gladden stated that he would feel obligated, if a wage worker, to join the union in his trade.[41]

The Labor Question marked an important change in Gladden's prescription of the church's responsibility in economic affairs. In 1895 he had declined to have the church discuss the economic aspects of industrial problems. But in 1911 he thought that the enunciation of ethical principles was no longer adequate. The church could and must deal concretely and explicitly with the problems of labor. It would be better for it to err in applying Christian principles than to give the impression that those principles were not relevant to industrial relations.[42] The doctrine of brotherhood, which was the source and inspiration of democracy, belonged to the church, and the church not only had much to gain from public recognition of this fact, but it also had an obligation to guide democracy and to replenish its inspiration.

Behind all of Gladden's pleas for better relations between capital and labor were the fundamental assumptions that society was an organic entity and that its lineaments were not primarily economic. The ideology of the Social Gospel was an implicit rejection of Marxian economic determinism and of the necessity of class struggle. Moreover, the use of biological concepts to sustain an optimistic interpretation of history, rather than a completely objective appraisal of economic realities, may, as Dombrowski argues, have led to a faulty conclusion that the interests of the working class and the owning class were fundamentally harmonious. It was certainly true that Gladden, like most of those in the mainstream of the Social

---

[41] *Ibid.*, pp. 98, 109–10, 136–40.

[42] *Congregationalist*, LXXX (October 24, 1895), 613; Gladden, *Labor Question*, p. 161.

Gospel, believed that the·church should exercise an impartial, mediating role between labor and capital. His attempts at impartiality resulted, by his own testimony, in employers regarding him as "a regular walking delegate" and in workers accusing him of "being a mere tool of the capitalists." His a priori assumption of the harmony and organic unity of society was almost as rigid as the laws of the laissez faire economists that he rejected.[43]

If social classes could only come together in amity, they would discover that their differences were more imaginary than real. As Gladden saw it, the development of the social organism in the nineteenth century had been excessively rapid and unhealthy. The process of differentiation had outdistanced that of integration; material progress had created abnormal social differences and weakened the bonds of society. But though differentiation was rooted in the economic order, Gladden proposed a spiritual remedy, brotherhood, which he was sure would socialize men's thinking and correct economic injustice.[44]

Gladden promoted dialogue between labor and capital within the limits of his own influence and commended wider efforts at rapprochement. In 1892, for example, as chairman of the Ohio Congregational Association's labor committee, he helped to organize one-day conferences in Columbus and Toledo for employers, labor leaders, and churchmen. Despite some initial suspicion among labor leaders, there were amicable discussions of working conditions, profit sharing, arbitration, and the nationalization of industry.[45] In 1894 Gladden delivered an address on industrial arbitration at a conference on labor held by the Chicago Civic Federation, an organiza-

[43] Dombrowski, *Early Days of Christian Socialism,* p. 23; Gladden, "Strengths and Weaknesses of Organized Labor," Sermon, January, 1900, Gladden Papers; Shover, "The Attitude of American Intellectuals toward the Labor Movement," pp. 116–17, 122.

[44] Gladden, Sermons, "Wickedness Proceedeth from the Wicked," 1886, "The Potency of Spiritual Forces," January 31, 1893, September 10, 1893, Gladden Papers; Gladden, *Social Facts and Forces,* pp. 192–96.

[45] *Ohio State Journal,* January 14, 18–19, 1892; Gladden, Sermon, January 24 1892, Gladden Papers.

tion that tried unsuccessfully that same year to arbitrate the Pullman strike. The Civic Federation's conference was influential in rallying the support that brought about a state arbitration law in Illinois.[46] Gladden praised the aims of the National Civic Federation, an organization representing employers like Mark Hanna, John D. Rockefeller, Jr., and Charles M. Schwab, labor leaders of the stature of Samuel Gompers of the American Federation of Labor and John Mitchell of the United Mine Workers, and other public figures like Grover Cleveland, President Charles W. Eliot of Harvard, and Archbishop John Ireland. Created in 1896 to promote voluntary arbitration, the National Civic Federation was the most notable manifestation of a short-lived but auspicious courtship between labor and capital. Gladden also served for many years on the labor committee of the National Council of the Congregational Churches and had a large part in its important sessions in 1904 on labor problems. And in 1912 he became a member of a committee, composed of such prominent figures as Jane Addams, Louis D. Brandeis, Paul U. Kellogg, Florence Kelley, Owen R. Lovejoy, Lillian D. Wald, and Rabbi Stephen S. Wise, to persuade Congress to establish a federal commission on industrial relations.[47]

Gladden's attitude toward specific strikes over a long period reflected a tendency, moderated by his attempt at impartiality, to favor the cause of labor. He denounced the anarchists who were convicted of contributing to the murder of a policeman during the riot in 1886 at the Haymarket Square in Chicago. Although the question of anarchism made this episode more than an ordinary conflict between capital and labor, it was significant of Gladden's horror of violence that he approved the death sentence on men who had only preached anarchism, not actually killed the policeman, while

[46] *Ohio State Journal*, November 13, 1894; Wade, *Taylor*, pp. 76, 188–89.

[47] Gladden, Christmas Sermon, 1901, Gladden Papers; Foster Rhea Dulles, *Labor in America: A History* (3d ed.; New York: Thomas Y. Crowell Co., 1966), pp. 186–87; Stephen S. Wise to Gladden, January 2, 1912, Edward T. Devine to Gladden, January 22, February 8, 27, May 15, 1912, Pomerene to Gladden, March 18, 1912, Gladden Papers.

he said little or nothing about the death of several workers in the disturbance at the McCormick Harvester plant that had initially prompted the protest at the Haymarket.[48]

He found it impossible to sympathize with either capital or labor in a series of strikes in 1892. In the Homestead strike, particularly, he felt that labor had made unreasonable demands and then had forfeited public sympathy by such "barbarous and brutal conduct" as attacking Pinkerton detectives. He argued that, though the unions may not have directly perpetrated violence, they were, nevertheless, responsible for controlling their forces in industrial conflict. By 1894 he was more inclined to justify the violence of strikers by comparing it to the malpractices of the unscrupulous heads of "soulless corporations."[49] He commended President Cleveland for sending federal troops, over the strong protest of Governor John Peter Altgeld of Illinois, to quell the Pullman strike. But he questioned the judicial decision that jailed Eugene V. Debs, the head of the American Railway Union, for violation of the Sherman Anti-Trust Act, when the combinations of capital against which that law had been aimed had so far escaped its reach. The *Ohio State Journal*, gleefully twisting his remarks, branded him a defender of Debs. A strong reply from Gladden re-established his impartiality.[50]

The succession of strikes that disturbed the American scene during the 1890's convinced Gladden that some comprehensive method of resolving industrial conflict must be found. Arbitration seemed to be the only recourse in a democratic society. During the anthracite strike in 1900 he drafted a petition, which his congregation endorsed, urging the governor of Pennsylvania to promote voluntary arbitration.[51] But Gladden was already entertaining the idea of compulsory arbitration. After careful study he favorably surveyed New

[48] *Ohio State Journal*, October 17, November 25, 1887.

[49] Gladden, Sermon, January 1, 1893, Gladden Papers; *Ohio State Journal*, September 10, 1894.

[50] Gladden, Sermon, [January, 1895,] Gladden Papers; *Ohio State Journal*, June 27–30, 1895.

[51] *Ohio State Journal*, September 24, 1900.

Zealand's experiment with compulsory arbitration in a sermon, "A Country without Strikes." Industrial wars injured the entire community, and, in his view, the community had a right to end them. Interestingly, the Machine Trades and Professions Association, a local organization dedicated to the principle of arbitration, attended the First Church to hear the sermon and afterward passed a resolution favoring compulsory arbitration. One of the organizers of this new body was Robert N. Jeffrey, an officer in the Jeffrey Manufacturing Company and the son of its founder. The Jeffreys, who lived just a few doors from Gladden on Town Street, one of Columbus' most elegant avenues, were members of the First Church. Starting with a little capital and a good invention, Joseph A. Jeffrey had made his company one of the world's largest manufacturers of mining machinery. His company was noted for its progressive management and freedom from strikes. The Machine Trades and Professions Association attracted favorable attention, and within a few months branches appeared in other cities. The extent to which Gladden participated in its organization is unclear, as is his influence on Robert Jeffrey. He did address a mass meeting under the association's auspices early in 1901, declaring once again his commitment to compulsory arbitration. And it was evidently at Jeffrey's urging that he tried in 1907 to get the various religious bodies in Columbus to establish a society to maintain industrial peace locally.[52]

In the years after 1900 Gladden espoused arbitration as the only possible alternative to mutual destruction by powerful combinations of capital and labor. In 1901 he favored the unsuccessful strike against the United States Steel Corporation and, criticizing their unwillingness to arbitrate, maintained that the steel kings must make "a very decided change in their attitude and their policy."[53] And in

---

[52] Gladden, "A Country without Strikes," Sermon, October 7, 1900, Gladden Papers; Robert N. Jeffrey to Gladden, August 3, 1900, Gladden Papers; *Ohio State Journal,* February 11, 1911, June 24, 1894, October 5, 8, 12, November 2, 16, 23, December 16, 1900, January 25, 1901; Jeffrey to Gladden, May 27, 1907, Gladden Papers; *Ohio State Journal,* October 8, 1907.

[53] Gladden, Sermons, "The Great Industrial Conflict," August 18, 1901; "Good News from the Wide World," September 22, 1901, Gladden Papers.

the anthracite strike of 1902 he acted directly to secure arbitration. At the suggestion of the editor of the *Cincinnati Post* he framed a petition calling on President Roosevelt to intervene, not in his official capacity, but as "First Citizen" of the country. Many newspapers printed the petition, and, as Gladden later recalled, it was one of numerous influences that induced Roosevelt to take the desired action.[54] When the operators rejected the proposal of arbitration, Gladden was incensed. He declared that if they persisted in ignoring the claims of the miners, there were only two alternatives, compulsory arbitration and nationalization of the mines. Having expected Roosevelt's intervention to end the strike speedily, Gladden could hardly believe that the operators had rejected all overtures for settlement. The public, twenty millions of whom faced the onset of winter without fuel, confronted the most appalling social crisis ever.[55] Finley Peter Dunne's "Mr. Dooley" satirized the consumers' dilemma:

> Iverybody will have plinty iv fuel this winther. Th' rich can burn with indignation, thinkin' iv th' wrongs inflicted on capital, th' middle or middlin' class will be marchin' with th' milishy, an' th' poor can fight among thimsilves an' burn th' babies.

But Gladden's faith in Roosevelt's ability to end the strike proved to be well founded. When the President passed through Columbus in November, 1902, Gladden met him at the station and congratulated him on his success.[56]

This was an isolated success, however, and Gladden's frustration grew as employers mounted a telling counterattack against unionism after 1902, and hostility intensified. He predicted that, if the captains of industry did not make peace with moderate union leaders, revolutionaries would push those leaders aside and create unimag-

[54] *Congregationalist*, LXXXVII (September 27, 1902), 429; *Ohio State Journal*, October 3, 1902, October 13, 1909; Gladden, *Recollections*, pp. 395–97.

[55] *Ohio State Journal*, October 5, 1902; Gladden, Sermon, October 12, 1902, Gladden Papers.

[56] *Ohio State Journal*, October 12, November 13, 1902.

ined violence. An investigative trip in 1904 to the strife-torn mining regions of Colorado further impressed the reality of conflict upon Gladden. He made the trip for the Newspaper Enterprise Association, which paid him $500 for a series of articles on conditions in Colorado. Both sides received his thorough condemnation: the Western Federation of Miners, which in 1905 was to participate in the organization of the revolutionary Industrial Workers of the World, for its lawlessness; and John D. Rockefeller's Colorado Fuel and Iron Company and other operators for fomenting retaliation by a citizens' alliance. The state's enlistment of its resources on the side of the operators he denounced forcefully.[57] A few months later, reviewing strikes in the textile mills of Fall River and the shipyards of Chicago, he decried continued unrest:

> This witches' caldron is still bubbling and steaming; probably it will never cease to boil, until those who are dancing around it suffer enough from its scalding waters, to be willing to join in putting out the fires beneath it. For the present, the majority of both contending parties seem to think that the only remedy is found in increasing the fuel which keeps it boiling.[58]

Gladden's emphatic espousal of compulsory arbitration after 1900 came in response to the failure of both employers and unions to accept voluntary arbitration. Relations between labor and capital were much less friendly in the 1900's, he observed perceptively in a sermon on Hutchins Hapgood's *The Spirit of Labor* (1907), than they had been even in the 1890's.[59] While he preferred voluntary, private agreements, he was prepared to enlist the state in the protection of the rights of society. However, his growing realism about industrial conditions did not diminish his appeal to good will and

[57] Gladden, "Social Unrest," Sermon, May 3, 1903, Gladden Papers; Sam T. Hughes to Gladden, April 21, 1904, Gladden Papers; *Ohio State Journal,* April 18, June 8, 1904. He also wrote articles on the troubles in Colorado for the *Congregationalist* and *Cincinnati Post.* Howard A. Bridgman to Gladden, May 10, 1904; Charles F. Mosher to Gladden, June 14, 1904, Gladden Papers.

[58] Gladden, "Labor War," Sermon, September 18, 1904, Gladden Papers.

[59] Gladden, Sermon, March 1, 1908, Gladden Papers.

brotherhood. The state might enforce peace, but it would be an illusory solution unless the men in both camps had a change of heart.

A streetcar strike in Columbus in 1910, which in a sense climaxed the long series of conflicts that frustrated his hopes for social unity, drew Gladden into direct participation in industrial arbitration. The strike began on April 29, after the Columbus Railway and Light Company refused to reinstate four men whom it had discharged in March for participating in the organization of a union. The company refused both to recognize the union and to increase wages substantially. Mayor George S. Marshall immediately proposed arbitration by Governor Judson Harmon and himself, but the company flatly refused.[60]

Marshall then enlisted Gladden, who on May 3 held conferences in his study with representatives of business, labor, and the company. The union, a local of the Amalgamated Association of Street and Electric Railway Employees of America, was willing to submit the dispute to Gladden, President William Oxley Thompson of the Ohio State University, and Foster Copeland, a local banker, but the company remained obstinate. After these negotiations failed, the company imported strikebreakers and rioting and violence broke out. The state's Board of Arbitration took the dispute under review in July, but just before it announced its decision, which it appeared would favor the union, the company declared that it would not be bound by the decision. The strike resumed on July 24, bringing new violence in its wake. Rioting mobs battled policemen, stoned and beat non-unionists, attacked streetcars, and tore up tracks, whereupon the company's employees began shooting from streetcars into the streets. On July 28 Governor Harmon sent in five regiments of state troops, but violence continued.[61]

Many businessmen blamed Mayor Marshall for not taking stern action against the strikers, but Gladden, though supporting demands for law and order, refused to join the chorus of denunciation. Early

[60] *Ohio State Journal*, April 30, May 1, 1910.

[61] *Ibid.*, May 2–5, July 14, 22, 26–28, 1910.

in August, Gladden, William Oxley Thompson, and the president of the Columbus Chamber of Commerce drafted a proposal for arbitration, which Thompson presented to the company and Gladden to the union; but the company, emphatically refusing to recognize the union, rejected it.[62]

On August 7 Gladden faced this impasse in a sermon on "The Path to Peace." Deprecating violence, he declared: "If men or associations of men have business differences, they must settle those differences by legal and peaceful methods; they must not go to war in our streets. . . . " But his sympathy was with the union. Violence on the streets was not the worst violence in industrial society, it was an understandable reaction against the heartlessness and contempt engendered by wealth. Nor would the suppression of violence for which businessmen were clamoring eliminate the causes of conflict. Brotherhood was the only fundamental remedy.

> How easy it would be to settle all the trouble, if all these men on both sides would only say, "Come! let us be friends." Is that, brother men, a hard thing to say?[63]

Violence continued. A mass meeting composed primarily of unionists went on record for municipal ownership of the streetcar lines. Thirty-two demoralized policemen mutinied, refusing to ride and guard the company's cars; the company hired Pinkerton detectives to protect its property, and citizens talked of forming vigilance committees. In a sermon on August 14 Gladden called on employers to compensate for the loss of personal relations in modern industry by considering foremost the welfare of their employees. "The making of men" was more important than the building of granaries, hotels, factories, machines, and "money, money, money,—the mighty symbol that represents them all, that commands them all."[64]

[62] *Ibid.*, August 6, 1910.

[63] Gladden, "The Path to Peace," Sermon, August 7, 1910, Gladden Papers.

[64] *Ohio State Journal*, August 12–13, 1910; Gladden, "Faith in Men," Sermon, August 14, 1910, Gladden Papers.

On August 18 Gladden appealed for arbitration through the local press. He accused the company of prolonging the strike by refusing to arbitrate, when the union had been willing even before the strike began. The company, moreover, was not simply a private organization, but a public-service company holding a franchise from the city. It had no right to disregard the public. Gladden was not alone in demanding a change of posture by the company. Other unions pledged support to the strikers, and a large delegation of Ohio's labor leaders urged Governor Harmon to exert pressure on the company. He refused to interfere beyond sending troops to preserve order and instructing the attorney-general to investigate the rioting. On September 10 Theodore Roosevelt appeared with Gladden before a crowd of twelve thousand to advocate compulsory arbitration.[65]

The company's obduracy, the refusal of Governor Harmon to intervene, and public antagonism to the strikers because of violence resulted in the frustration of Gladden's appeals and defeat for the union. In *The Labor Question,* the pro-unionism of which partly reflected his disgust with the streetcar company, Gladden suggested that the failure of the carmen to follow his advice to patrol the car lines and prevent violence was a major cause of their defeat. The union's defeat had an unexpected but important effect on politics in Columbus. It contributed to the astounding strength, especially in working-class wards, of Socialist candidates in the county election in November. Little more than nine hundred in 1906 and 1908, the Socialist vote leaped to over ten thousand in 1910.[66]

The effects of Gladden's strong stand on his relations with parishioners and other townspeople are not easy to determine. According to one writer who interviewed Gladden after the strike, the businessmen and employers of Columbus, "like a pack disturbed in full cry, turned upon the minister in rage." There were "wrath and revilings upon the head of the devoted old man; the cooling of friend-

---

[65] *Ohio State Journal,* August 18, 24, 31, September 3, 11, 1910.

[66] Gladden, *Labor Question,* p. 33; *Ohio State Journal,* November 10, 1910.

ships, the straining of church relationships almost to the bursting and the saying of bitter, reproachful things. . . . " These strong words may have been largely journalistic embellishment. A letter to Gladden from a parishioner who owned the Central Ohio Paper Company, the only relevant piece of evidence, indicates that at least one member of the First Church was hostile to the union.[67] But there is no hint of a serious rupture in the church at this or any other time.

In the autumn of 1911 one of the most frustrating incidents of his career raised the question of his congregation's loyalty. Anticipating the arrival of Charles E. Burton, who was to be his associate and probable successor, Gladden sent out a pastoral letter urging "those who seem to have lost their interest in the buying and the work of the church to renew their commitment. He cast no aspersions on the devotion of the congregation as a whole. But a reporter obtained a copy of this confidential letter and construed it as a resignation in discouragement due to empty pews and humiliating indifference among the people. The report spread rapidly, and Gladden received letters of condolence from friends all over the country. In an attempt to correct the false report he asserted that his congregation had never been larger or more enthusiastic than in the past six months and that his preaching had never been more satisfying to him than in recent years. Unable to undo completely the damage caused by the press, he called this "the greatest injury" he had ever suffered: "One who is drawing near to the end of a busy life does not like to be reported to the world as confessing that his life has been a failure."[68] One thing is certain. The streetcar strike was neither a happy

---

[67] Peter Clark MacFarlane to Gladden, March 8, 1912, Gladden Papers; MacFarlane, "Washington Gladden: The First Citizen of Columbus," *Collier's Weekly*, XLIX (June 29, 1912), 20–21; Orlando A. Miller to Gladden, August 1, 1910, Gladden Papers.

[68] *Ohio State Journal*, September 1, 1911; Whiton to Gladden, September 3, 1911, Wallace M. Short to Gladden, September 5, 1911, Ross W. Sanderson to Gladden, September 11, 1911, William Rice to Gladden, September 16, 1911, Gladden Papers; *Congregationalist*, XCVI (September 16, 1911), 387; Washington Gladden, "An Experience with Newspapers," *Outlook*, XCIX (October 14, 1911), 387–88; Washington Gladden, "Tainted Newspapers, Good and Bad," *University of Kansas News-Bulletin*, XV (November 30, 1914).

climax to his lifelong desire for industrial peace nor a reassuring fulfilment of his optimistic appeals for brotherhood.

Gladden's willingness to enlist the state in the establishment of economic justice grew out of his realization that without a radical conversion of humanity to the social ideal, economic injustice would not right itself. As he put it, laissez faire meant not only "let well-enough alone," but also "let ill-enough alone." It assumed "that ill-enough, if let alone long enough, will turn to well-enough." Originally a justifiable reaction against "the meddlesome interference of government with private industry," it had become the shibboleth of those who stood to gain by being "let alone." The government did interfere in significant ways with the private affairs of citizens: it imposed education, protected private property, and operated a postal service. The government was just the people, who in a democracy had the right to manage their own affairs. The preamble to the Constitution, Gladden pointed out, included the promotion of public welfare.[69] He rejected the theory that laissez faire was a law of nature:

> The industrial conditions are largely the product of human volition; legislation and associated action of all kinds have greatly affected them; tariffs, and currency laws, and the laws regulating contracts and inheritance have had much to do in establishing them. . . . And what man has done he may be able . . . to undo or mend, if it prove to be not well done.[70]

Gladden maintained that the defenders of economic freedom on laissez faire principles were often themselves responsible for the loss of freedom by others. What freedom did a workingwoman have in bargaining with a wealthy employer or corporation? Freedom merely to accept the employer's conditions or to starve! Freedom in terms of laissez faire was an inadequate safeguard of human welfare. The Kingdom of God rested not only on liberty but also on jus-

[69] Gladden, Sermon, January 23, 1898, Gladden Papers.

[70] Washington Gladden, "Moral Tendencies of Existing Industrial Conditions," *Outlook*, LXIII (December 9, 1899), 871–72.

tice, co-operation, and truth; its cornerstone was opportunity rather than liberty. According to Gladden, "the social justice which Christ has ordained, and of which his Kingdom is the organic expression," would not allow the "vast accumulations and consolidations and encrustations of privilege and power, by which the sphere of effort is circumscribed and individual growth is impeded."[71] The laissez faire economists had overextended the protection of property, making it sacred and justifying it solely on the basis of possession rather than by integrity of acquisition and social use. Gladden would defend wealth, the honest accumulation of initiative and industry; but he regarded many fortunes as "illth," a curse to both their pos-sessors and society [72] The state must act to remove the building of injustice and to restore opportunity.

Though Gladden would link political and economic freedom, he viewed with alarm the socialist program for identifying them with the state. Like most of his fellow social gospelers, he thought that socialism neglected the personal regeneration essential to a genuine social reformation. An excessive reaction to individualism, socialism was likely to make the state not a "Guardian of Liberties" and "Guarantor of Equal Opportunities" but a "Colossal Providence." Gladden told his congregation, "The trouble with the socialistic scheme is that it proposes to do what the infinite Benevolence refuses to do. It is not worth while to try to be kinder and better than God."[73]

Similarly, he criticized the socialist state proposed by Edward Bellamy in *Looking Backward, 2000–1887* (1888): "I do not believe that the government of nature, which is the government of God, is administered on that plan." It was not equitable to give an equal stipend to all, regardless of talent and contribution. Besides, Bel-

[71] Gladden, "The Gospel of the Kingdom," Sermon, January 27, 1889, Gladden Papers.

[72] Gladden, "Wealth and Illth," Sermon, January 28, 1894, Gladden Papers; Gladden, *Ruling Ideas,* p. 150; Gladden, *New Idolatry,* pp. 255–56.

[73] Hopkins, *Rise of the Social Gospel,* p. 75; Gladden, Sermon, September 23, 1894, Gladden Papers.

lamy's presumption that the thorough social transformation envisioned in *Looking Backward* could occur in about a century was too optimistic. Unlike political revolution, moral progress was "silent and gradual"; Bellamy would have been sanguine to predict that his ideal state could appear after a thousand years. Furthermore, Bellamy stressed changes in the economic structure more than individual regeneration, and, to Gladden, that was like putting the cart before the horse.[74]

Though warning against the idea that the state could become "a good fairy that shall empty the horn of plenty at every man's door and let him consume without care what has been gathered without toil," Gladden did welcome increasing governmental promotion of public welfare. As the culmination of individualism under the democratic ideal had occurred in the nineteenth century, cooperation and fraternity grounded in religion would triumph in the twentieth. The role of religion as a socializing force was crucial: without it, men would be "trying to build industrial socialism on moral individualism."[75]

Gladden, however, displayed calmness, fairness, and sympathy toward socialism that were uncommon among the Protestant clergy of his day. In *Tools and the Man* he declared that socialism was the "reaction of a scourged and outraged humanity against the greed and rapacity of the individualist regime." Unfortunately, like most reactions, it flew to the opposite extreme. Socialists made two basic mistakes: underrating the importance of inventors and organizers, they would deny them their special just rewards; and they proposed the nationalization of all industries, a program that "nothing short of omniscience could compass." Gladden held that neither individualism nor socialism furnished an adequate basis for industrial society. But in *Tools and the Man* he announced that if forced to choose between the two, he would choose socialism. Besides protecting its citizens and their property and furnishing education, the

[74] Gladden, Sermon, September 1, 1889, Gladden Papers.

[75] Gladden, Sermons, May 27, 1894, January 6, 1901, Gladden Papers; *Ohio State Journal,* November 13, 1911.

state should suppress the saloon, prohibit Sunday labor, limit hours of labor, enforce the sanitary inspection of factories and mines, encourage industrial arbitration (and require it in cases involving public-service corporations), and regulate or own virtual or natural monopolies.[76]

Gladden repeated these principles in *Christianity and Socialism,* a collection of lectures delivered in 1905 at Drew Theological Seminary. Reasserting the importance of private property for the development of character, he predicted the evolution of a compromise between capitalism and socialism. Private and collective industry would exist side by side, with no clear distinction or logical stopping-point to socialization. He doubted, however, that public ownership would extend beyond the railroads, telegraph lines, mines, and public-service industries, a degree of socialism that he favored. But the economic system itself was less important than brotherhood, which was attainable under either capitalism or socialism. In one very interesting sermon Gladden contrasted "Two Types of Socialism," that of Jack London's *The Iron Heel* (1907) and that of H. G. Wells's *New Worlds for Old* (1908). London's arraignment of capitalistic society, with its pictures of violence and hate, he considered worthless, while Wells's hope for a co-ordination of private and collective ownership struck him as rational and wholesome.[77]

Aware of the widespread popular confusion of political and economic ideologies, Gladden always carefully distinguished socialism from anarchism. Anarchism he could not tolerate. After President McKinley's assassination by Leon Czolgosz, he called for the extermination of anarchism in America: " . . . There is simply nothing to do but to turn on these people and crush them." As in the case of the Haymarket anarchists, it did not matter whether or not anarchists had actually instructed Czolgosz, "whose name no American should ever try to pronounce." They had at least inspired him. Gladden maintained that socialism and anarchism were at opposite

---

[76] Gladden, *Tools and the Man,* pp. 255, 260, 264–66, 280, 282–99.

[77] Gladden, *Christianity and Socialism,* pp. 51, 122–25, 126 f.; Gladden, "Two Types of Socialism," Sermon, May 10, 1908, Gladden Papers.

poles. Anarchism was "individualism gone to seed," and anarchists were blind to the irresistible modern tendency toward economic and social co-operation for the common good. It was the recognition of this sign of progress that made socialism preferable to anarchism and all other extremely individualistic philosophies.[78]

Gladden gave frequent and prolonged attention to economic problems because he believed that the Christian message had social as well as personal implications and that his vision as a Christian minister must be universal. Considering his special province to be the moral aspects of economic issues, he emphasized at first such individualistic values as frugality, temperance, industry, and self-restraint rather than structural limitations on justice. Conflicts between labor and capital could be resolved, he thought, by application of the Golden Rule and by minor changes in the economic order itself, principally in the direction of profit sharing and, where practicable, workers' co-operatives. His primary assumption was that since workers and employers were brothers, their fundamental interests must be harmonious. This assumption led him to minimize, especially in his early writings, the economic causes of strife and to prescribe a moral remedy, the spirit of brotherhood, for what he was sure was a moral problem.

However, his thought was not static. The aims of the practical unionism pursued by Samuel Gompers and his American Federation of Labor—better working conditions, shorter hours, higher wages, recognition of the unions, and collective bargaining—gradually replaced the panacea of profit sharing in his prescription for economic ills. Moreover, while he continued to abhor violence as a denial of brotherhood, he became increasingly aware that labor had to assert and protect its rights by pitting its strength against the strength of capital. In the 1870's he sharply criticized labor for abuses of what little power it then had and exaggerated the dangers posed by unions, but toward the end of the century he sided more definitely with labor against employers who appeared unwilling to grant the

[78] Gladden, Sermons, "The Roots of Anarchy," September 8, 1901; "The Philosophy of Anarchism," September 29, 1901, Gladden Papers.

most reasonable demands. There could be no doubt that he considered violence essentially a product of injustice and therefore less censurable than injustice. He became one of the earliest American clergymen to appeal consistently for the equality and independence of organized labor.

Because Gladden conceived of society as a brotherhood, not a collection of hostile and warring interests, he was willing to sanction co-operation through the state for the achievement of economic justice and common welfare. Though not a socialist, he repeatedly sanctioned public ownership of natural or virtual monopolies; he did not, however, attempt to defend it on economic grounds. A gradual nationalization of certain monopolies and services, like his other remedies for economic ills, was a moral and spiritual, more than an economic, necessity. Through many years of hope and frustration, covering profound changes in industry, his emphasis was always on the religious dimension of economic relations and on what he considered the ultimate goal of the church—the Christianization of the economic order.

Nine

"Tainted Money"

Gladden criticized the capitalist economic order and favored mildly socialistic measures to mollify the unhealthy effects of modern industrialism. But he wanted the purification, not the destruction, of capitalism. He enjoyed the friendship of businessmen and industrialists in his church and neighborhood, and, though mingling with all sorts of people and endearing himself to some workingmen, he was most comfortable with the well-to-do and refined. He cautioned his parishioners against serving Mammon, but he never questioned their patrician way of life. Perhaps contradictorily, he preached both equalitarianism and *noblesse oblige* in social relations.

His salary ranged from $2,000 in North Adams to over $5,000 in Columbus, and he had other income from lectures and royalties, while many of his colleagues in parishes in small towns and rural areas received only one-quarter as much. Living modestly but comfortably, he husbanded his resources and invested in solid securities in firms located in Columbus. At the time of his death his estate totaled $39,361.94. In addition to a lot valued at $10,000, a savings account of $759.21, and personal effects and insurance worth $7,332.73, he had $21,270.00 in stocks.[1] He obviously had no animus

---

[1] His stock investments were as follows: fifteen shares in the Kilbourne and Jacobs Manufacturing Company, $1,500.00; twenty shares in the Ohio Cities Gas Company, $1,500.00; forty-five shares in the State Savings Bank and Trust Company, $5,625.00; twenty-seven shares in the Scioto Valley Traction Com-

against stockholding, capitalism, or wealth.

Wealth that represented honest labor, inventiveness, or organizational ability he considered justifiable. But the fruits of exploitation or parasitism were a curse to a democratic society, in which every man's right to his just reward—but no more—was sacred. Gladden knew that many of the great fortunes of his day did not accrue from hard work and integrity. Furthermore, he realized that the economic structure itself was largely responsible for the disturbing contrast between great wealth and glaring poverty. The breakdown of free competition and the emergence of corporations and trusts aggravated the imbalance between capital and labor, enhanced the opportunities for exploitation, and put the public at the mercy of impersonal and irresistible forces.

Although Gladden was cognizant of the threats posed by great combinations of capital, he opposed their rigorous repression by the state. He tended to agree with the ideas appropriated by Theodore Roosevelt in 1912 as the New Nationalism rather than those of Woodrow Wilson's New Freedom. About 1890 he marveled at an "apparently irresistible movement toward combination," of which ten years earlier he had had no hint. He saw potential advantages in combination, such as the lowering of the costs of production, the stabilization of prices, and the prevention of destructive competition. But there were also disadvantages and dangers. Some trusts, especially those in oil and sugar, made no appreciable reductions in prices. Moreover, corporations might use their power to create stability to suppress wholesome competition, and they would certainly tend to suppress individuality. Finally, he took alarm at their influence on the legislative and judicial systems. Deprecating state control of corporations, he felt, nevertheless, that only regulation by public tribunals with complete access to the records of corporate

pany, $2,160.00; thirty-seven shares in the Citizens Trust and Savings Bank, $3,885.00; ten shares in the Midland Mutual Life Insurance Company, $2,100.00; thirty shares in the Wolfe Brothers Shoe Company, $3,000.00; and fifteen shares in the Columbus School for Girls Company, $1,500.00. Washington Gladden Estate, #35501, Franklin County (Ohio) Probate Court, Document 23.

operations would prevent economic and political tyranny. If socialism came, Gladden observed, Americans would have John D. Rockefeller and his associates to thank.[2]

He repeatedly warned against unregulated combination, as well
as against too severe restriction of a natural economic force. In an
address in 1895 on "The Relation of Corporations to Public Morals"
at the Oberlin Summer School of Christian Sociology, he stressed
the failure of personal ethical standards to restrain corporations.
Though corporations created undeniable material benefits, their
effects on public morality were primarily negative: they cheapened
breadstuffs but killed "individuality and enterprise." Regulation was
necessary, and for quasi-public corporations, at least, the government must require publicity of operations. But regulation must be
cautious, since the corporation was not an "unmitigated evil, that
ought to be discouraged," but "a great blind Samson that needs
guidance."[3] In 1897 he repeated these ideas in a chapter on corporations in *Social Facts and Forces*, emphasizing especially the limitations that corporate organization imposed on individual freedom.
But even their moral influence was not entirely nefarious, for they
taught men to co-operate, forced them to curb their conceit, and
developed fiduciary virtues. In both his address at Oberlin and
Social Facts and Forces he declared:

> These corporations must find out whether they have souls or not. If they
> have and will demonstrate the fact by a conscientious administration of
> their trusts, there will be no disposition to interfere with them.[4]

Quasi-public corporations presented a special problem to a democratic society. Since they received great advantages from the state
and in effect taxed the community for their own maintenance, they

[2] Gladden, Address, n.d., Gladden Papers; Washington Gladden, "The Spread
of Socialism," *Outlook*, LXII (May 13, 1899), 116–22.

[3] Washington Gladden, "The Relation of Corporations to Public Morals,"
Bibliotheca Sacra, LII (October, 1895), 607–28.

[4] Gladden, "Choice of Calling and Chances of Success," Sermon, October 24,
1898, Gladden Papers; Gladden, *Social Facts and Forces*, pp. 82–114.

must avoid socially injurious practices. The railroads especially could never operate on a competitive basis. They were natural monopolies that the government must "either own or firmly control." Gladden pronounced regulation by the Interstate Commerce Commission, created in 1887, a failure and called for stronger legislation. Creation of a stronger regulatory tribunal, enforcement of publicity, imprisonment of any official who speculated in the stock of his own railroad, legal provision for the representation of minority stockholders on boards of directors, and establishment of uniform rates and abolition of the pass and half-rate systems would be important steps in the rectification of abuses; but governmental owner ship and control, though not necessarily management, would be the only permanently adequate solution.[5]

Though he grew increasingly alarmed at the revelations of corporate malfeasance, Gladden retained his faith that the economic order could be purified without radical structural changes. He saw industrial combination as a natural and, consequently, divine force. Even though capitalists were unaware of it, they were working with God to prepare a great foundation of industrial co-operation on which a real spiritual unity of mankind might rest. But they were not always willing co-workers. Though not disabused of his faith in the eventual triumph of justice, Gladden decried alliances of businessmen with corrupt public officials, stock-watering, and "the overlordship of Mammon that gives rise to those stupendous combinations whose purpose it is to despoil the many for the enrichment of the few." "King Monopoly," he declared, "is well-seated upon a throne which we have prepared for him, and from which it seems difficult to dislodge him." The great fortunes of the day were heaped up by monopolistic schemes that laid millions of people under tribute, extorting small tolls from each of them. Because of this diffusion of injustice, its enormity often escaped notice.[6]

[5] Gladden, *Social Facts and Forces*, pp. 135, 139–40, 145, 148–51.

[6] Gladden, Sermons, June 30, 1901; July 5, 1903; "The Education of Conscience," October 18, 1905, Gladden Papers.

Gladden's protest in 1905 against acceptance by the American Board of Commissioners for Foreign Missions of a gift of $100,000 from John D. Rockefeller, the best-known episode in his career, focused his interest in economic justice on the relations between the churches and corporate wealth. Because Rockefeller's Standard Oil Company popularly epitomized ruthless exploitation, Gladden's attack on his "tainted money" quickly captured public attention, which had been awakened to injustice by the revelations of the muckrakers and the trust-busting activities of Theodore Roosevelt. Though unable to prevent the American Board from taking Rockefeller's money, Gladden did succeed in marshaling an impressive number of Congregationalists, as well as many people outside the denomination, in his cause and in influencing the American Board to scrutinize more carefully the sources of its funds.

Gladden's protest in 1905 was not fortuitous. He had long singled out Rockefeller as the worst of the "malefactors of great wealth." Interestingly enough, as boys Gladden and Rockefeller had lived simultaneously in Tioga County, New York, and, for several years before his family migrated to Ohio, Rockefeller had lived in Owego itself. Although it does not appear that they were personally acquainted, in so small a community they certainly must have known about each other. Gladden's first public passage at arms with the Standard Oil Company occurred in 1889, when in a course of lectures on "Social Forces" at Chautauqua, he attacked several trusts, particularly the oil trust. He condemned the Standard's use of railroad rebates to crush competition and its failure, despite economies, to reduce substantially the price of refined oil.[7] George Gunton, an economist from New York, hurried to Chautauqua to dispute Gladden's statements, and a full-scale debate ensued. Although the authorities at Chautauqua informed Gladden that the Standard Oil Company was sending a man to answer him, and the public believed that Gunton spoke for the company, Gunton announced, according

---

[7] Gladden repeated the lecture on trusts in Columbus, and the press reported it extensively. *Ohio State Journal,* October 25, 1889.

to Gladden, that "he was there on his own hook purely and had no connection with any trust."[8]

As a resident of Columbus, Gladden was acutely aware of the dissolution proceedings against the Standard Oil trust, begun in 1890 by Attorney-General David K. Watson of Ohio, that dragged on during the 1890's before the state's Supreme Court.[9] He also followed Henry D. Lloyd's campaign against the Standard, which, after a series of articles in the 1880's, culminated in his famous *Wealth against Commonwealth* (1894). Despite the controversial nature of Lloyd's evidence, Gladden accepted the book as the damning arraignment that Lloyd intended it to be. He wrote in a private letter, "I wonder that Lloyd's Book has not caused more excitement. I hope and trust that it is doing its work silently; but it surprises me that it does not cause an insurrection."[10] Whether or not Gladden and Lloyd were acquainted earlier, by 1895 they were friends and regular correspondents.

Gladden also criticized churches and colleges for accepting gifts from dubious sources long before 1905. As early as 1879, he objected to the deference that many colleges paid questionable contributors. By 1895, when in an article for the *Outlook* he coined the phrase "tainted money," he had developed a comprehensive critique of philanthropy based on the fruits of exploitation. Lloyd, whose own writings had sharpened Gladden's antagonism to the Standard Oil Company, praised Gladden's article, which he found to be the topic of conversation wherever he went. Gladden saw the question of "tainted money" as one of the most important that Americans would have to face. "Money," he asserted, "is not a mere material entity. Its character is symbolic and representative." Money obtained by

---

[8] *Ohio State Journal*, October 19, 1889; *Congregationalist*, LXXIV (August 29, 1889), 285; Henry D. Lloyd to Gladden, August 20, September 10, 1895, Gladden Papers; Gladden to Lloyd, September 11, 1895, Henry D. Lloyd Papers (State Historical Society of Wisconsin, Madison).

[9] *Ohio State Journal*, May 9, 1890.

[10] Gladden to unidentified correspondent (fragment), December 11, 1895, Lloyd Papers.

unjust methods was "corroded with a rust which eats the flesh like fire." The seal of silence on great social and moral issues would cover the lips of churches and schools that accepted "the reward of iniquity." The givers of "tainted money" polluted the entire stream of public opinion; though "pirates of industry" and "spoilers of the state," they received deference and honor from the very institutions that ought to censure them.[11] Gladden's article in the *Outlook* probably stemmed from John D. Rockefeller's lavish gifts to the University of Chicago. A few months before the article appeared, Professor Edward Bemis had resigned from the university, presumably because his criticism of trusts offended Rockefeller. At any rate, President William Rainey Harper considered the article an assault on his institution and sent a copy to Rockefeller.[12]

Gladden and Lloyd collaborated on the best means of arousing popular indignation against the Standard Oil Company. When Gladden visited Chicago, Lloyd invited him to his home in Winnetka, Illinois, and Gladden commended Lloyd's writings from his pulpit in Columbus.[13] In 1896 Gladden rejected a proposal that a panel of ministers investigate the company under the guidance of its solicitor, Colonel S. C. T. Dodd. The idea apparently originated with the company, after Dodd had successfully converted B. Fay Mills, a prominent evangelist whom Gladden had praised only a few months earlier for a scathing attack in Columbus on the Standard. Foreseeing a whitewash that would mollify public indignation, Gladden spurned Mills's overtures with the argument that, since ministers were not qualified judges, a verdict on the company must come from the courts and investigating commissions, and cautioned Lloyd

[11] *Sunday Afternoon,* III (August, 1879), 761–62; Lloyd to Gladden, December 24, 1895, Gladden Papers; Washington Gladden, "Tainted Money," *Outlook,* LII (November 30, 1895), 886–87.

[12] *Ohio State Journal,* August 10, 1895; Nevins, *Rockefeller,* II, 210.

[13] Lloyd to Gladden, January 14, April 14, 1896, October 5, 1899, Gladden Papers; Gladden to Lloyd, October 23, 1900, Lloyd Papers.

against being taken in.[14] Never doubting Lloyd's contribution to American reform, Gladden wrote after his death in 1903: " . . . He has done a great work—a work that will endure. The New America will be different from what it would have been . . . if he had not lived."[15]

After the publication of his article in 1895 several incidents drew Gladden's attention to the influence of "tainted money" on educational and religious institutions. The forced resignation in 1897 of President E. B. Andrews of Brown University, allegedly because of his public advocacy of free silver, was a case in point. Gladden lamented the incident in an article for the *Outlook* and in a strong sermon on freedom of opinion, "God or Mammon—a Question for Colleges and Churches." His congregation applauded when he urged such institutions to spurn gifts intended to muzzle them, and he in turn praised his parishioners for the freedom they allowed him to say things "that must have been rather unwelcome to rich men." In *The Christian Pastor and the Working Church*, which appeared in 1898, he declared:

> Money that has been gained in extortion, in grinding the face of the poor, by the unmerciful treatment of rivals in trade, by corrupting officers of the government, is not the Lord's money and the Lord wants none of it. . . .

On the other hand, it appears that he encouraged Henry C. King, a professor (and later president) at Oberlin, to remain at his institution and exert his influence for good, despite an impending gift from Rockefeller. When Shailer Mathews, a professor at the University of

<hr/>

[14] Gladden to unidentified correspondent (fragment), December 11, 1895; Lloyd to Gladden, April 28, 1896; Gladden to Lloyd, April 30, 1896, Lloyd Papers. A rumor that Gladden investigated and exonerated the company did get out, for in 1905 the president of the Rochester Theological Seminary (Baptist) asked Gladden whether he had made such an investigation and since changed his mind, or the report was fictional. Augustus H. Strong to Gladden, March 26, 1905, Gladden Papers.

[15] Gladden to Mrs. Henry D. Lloyd, September 29, 1903, Lloyd Papers.

Chicago and an ardent social gospeler, invited him to contribute to *Christendom,* a new religious journal identified with the university, Gladden first questioned him about Rockefeller's connections with the paper before assenting.[16]

Ida Tarbell's articles in *McClure's Magazine* in 1902–3 on the Standard Oil Company, published in 1904 in two volumes, further convinced Gladden of the gross injustice of Rockefeller's business career. Neither her personal hostility to the Standard, growing out of her childhood in the oil regions of Pennsylvania, nor her use of disputed evidence caused him to question her reliability.[17] Moreover, he probably found her analysis of the country's economic maladies as resulting from the unethical business practices of capitalists more palatable than Lloyd's general arraignment of capitalism. He would have agreed with the statement in her autobiography: "I never had an animus against their size and wealth, never objected to their corporate form. I was willing that they should combine and grow as big and rich as they could, but only by legitimate means." In a sermon on "Some Common Ways of Cheating and Stealing," in which he noted Tarbell's articles in *McClure's,* he accused the Standard Oil Company of "the most stupendous, the most monumental robbery known to modern history." Yet, he lamented, college presidents bowed down before Rockefeller, thousands of churches mentioned his name with awe, and hundreds of

---

[16] Washington Gladden, "Protestants at Providence," *Outlook,* LVI (August 14, 1897), 937–39; Gladden, "God or Mammon—a Question for Colleges and Churches," Sermon, September 12, 1897, Gladden Papers; Gladden, *Christian Pastor,* pp. 372–73; Henry C. King to Gladden, January 25, February 19, April 17, 1901, December 9, 1902, Gladden Papers; Shailer Mathews to Gladden, April 4, 7, 1903, Gladden Papers.

[17] Ida M. Tarbell, *All in the Day's Work: An Autobiography* (New York: Macmillan Co., 1939), p. 203. The fact that Gladden's copies of Tarbell's work, now in the possession of a resident of Columbus, have many uncut pages prompts speculation about whether Gladden actually read her work in its entirety. Because of his repeated references to it and his confidence in her results, it seems likely that he had read it in *McClure's Magazine* or had access to other copies. Frederic Heimberger to author, December 28, 1964.

thousands of Sunday-school children were taught that he was a very religious man and a great benefactor.[18]

The controversy over "tainted money," which heightened long-standing public resentment against Rockefeller and made Gladden's epigram a household word, began in March, 1905, following an announcement that the American Board had received a gift of $100,000 from Rockefeller. Gladden's crusade against acceptance of the gift rode the crest of the wave set up by Tarbell's muckraking study; and, as Gaius Glenn Atkins, one of Gladden's supporters, later wrote, it "flamed across the continent." Tarbell herself supplied the protestants, as they were called, with information and encouragement, although she later claimed to have regarded as unjust their charge that Rockefeller intended to silence criticism by his gifts.[19]

By March 18, when the *Congregationalist* officially heralded "Good News for the American Board," Gladden had made his opposition known privately and a group of pastors in and around Boston had begun to plan a protest. Just when Gladden learned of the gift is unclear, but he claimed to have conferred with officials of the American Board in Boston only ten days before the announcement without being informed. "This is the most painful feature of the affair," he said.[20]

It was not easy for Gladden to decide how best to protest. On the one hand, the leading protestants, badly in need of men of stature in the denomination for their side, urged him to rush a statement into print. On the other hand, some of his oldest friends defended receipt of the gift. His position as moderator, complicated by flickering resentment over the national council's formal endorsement in 1904 of a perpetual moderatorship, required deliberation and delicacy.

[18] Tarbell, *All in the Day's Work*, p. 230; Gladden, "Some Common Ways of Cheating and Stealing," Sermon, November 29, 1903, Gladden Papers.

[19] Atkins, *Religion in Our Times*, p. 52; Ida M. Tarbell to Gladden, April 27, 1905, Gladden Papers; Tarbell, *All in the Day's Work*, p. 243.

[20] *Congregationalist*, XC (March 18, 1905), 349; George P. Morris to Gladden, March 16, 22, 1905, Gladden Papers; *Ohio State Journal*, April 2, 1905.

Whatever his qualms, he decided to make a public statement, and by March 20 he had sent an article to A. E. Dunning, the editor of the *Congregationalist*. Dunning explained that though normally he would send anything from Gladden directly to the printing room, in this case, because it seemed unfair to address the American Board's officers through the press, he was withholding the article and sending it instead to an officer of the board. In addition, he advised Gladden that the national moderator should not become leader of a faction. After Gladden agreed to delete two objectionable statements, Dunning scheduled the article to appear on April 1 alongside a defense of the gift by Amory H. Bradford, Gladden's predecessor as moderator.[21]

Apparently dissatisfied with the delay, Gladden denounced Rockefeller and acceptance of his money in a sermon on March 26 on "The Religion of a Gentleman." The gift, he said, came from "a colossal estate whose foundations were laid in the most relentless rapacity known to modern commercial history." Rockefeller represented "more perfectly than anyone else, the system of brigandage by which our commerce has been ravaged for many years"; he had "taught the other plunderers most of what they know." It would be wrong to take his money with one hand and smite him with the other; it would be worse to take his money if it was designed to prevent the smiting. Gladden issued a formal protest on March 28 through the Associated Press and another public statement on March 31, so that his views were broadcast all over the country before his article appeared in the *Congregationalist*. He also presented a formal protest directly to the Prudential Committee, the American Board's fifteen-member executive body, which had arranged the details of the gift.[22]

In his article in the *Congregationalist*, "A Dissenting View,"

[21] Daniel Evans to Gladden (telegram), March 23, 1905; Morris to Gladden, March 22, 1905; Bridgman to Gladden, March 29, 1905; A. E. Dunning to Gladden, March 20, 25, 1905, Gladden Papers.

[22] Gladden, "The Religion of a Gentleman," Sermon, March 26, 1905, Gladden Papers; *Ohio State Journal*, March 29, 31, 1905; E. E. Strong, Clerk of the Prudential Committee, to Gladden, March 29, 1905, Gladden Papers.

Gladden objected to acceptance of the gift "because the money thus bestowed does not rightfully belong to the man who gives it; it has been flagitiously acquired, and all the world knows it." The facts could be found, he asserted, in the reports of legislative commissions, judicial records, Lloyd's exposures, and "the calm, judicial, relentless revelations of Miss Tarbell." He still assumed that the Prudential Committee had been the passive recipient of the gift, as did the thirty ministers from the vicinity of Boston whose protest appeared in the same issue. Defending the Prudential Committee on the same premise, Dunning and his editorial associate, Gladden's warm personal friend Howard A. Bridgman, argued that, although "a board may discriminate with regard to those from whom it solicits gifts," it should not turn down an unconditioned gift simply because the giver is popularly disliked."[23]

Amory H. Bradford's article, "An Approving View," removed all doubt about the gift's origins. Far from being an attempt at self-justification on Rockefeller's part, the situation

> was that of a noble enterprise in its extreme need making its appeal to him. To that appeal he yielded, not in any way making the Board his partner, and not asking it to give him any approval.[24]

In fact, Bradford had been party to the Prudential Committee's decision to ask Rockefeller to replenish its empty coffers, and he had been instrumental in securing the gift. It gradually became clear that the committee had actually requested the gift through Frederick T. Gates, the co-ordinator of Rockefeller's benevolences and a member of Bradford's church in Montclair, New Jersey, and then had attempted to conceal its role.[25]

In his biography of Rockefeller, Allan Nevins states that the con-

[23] *Congregationalist*, XC (April 1, 1905), 424.

[24] *Congregationalist*, XC (April 1, 1905), 424.

[25] Frederick T. Gates to Gladden, December 20, 1909, Gladden Papers. According to a member of Bradford's church, another of Rockefeller's aides, Starr J. Murphy, was also a parishioner of Bradford's. Charles J. Ives to Gladden, April 7, 1905, Gladden Papers.

troversy over "tainted money," a "three months' wonder," "died away when the most excited participants found, to their chagrin, that the Board had actually solicited the money."[26] But just the reverse happened. The Prudential Committee's involvement gave the protestants an even stronger case than they had originally surmised. Although they had to retreat for practical reasons from their opposition to passive acceptance of morally objectionable gifts, their contention gained intensity. It was the Prudential Committee that was chagrined, not its critics.

The controversy captured public interest and imagination to an amazing extent. Journalists, clergymen, and politicians applied the concept of "tainted money" to every conceivable situation and often aligned themselves either with the American Board or with the protestants. In Columbus, Gladden received support from the press, other clergymen, including at least one rabbi, and Frank S. Monnett, who as attorney-general of Ohio had tried in vain to dissolve the oil trust. It appears that Gladden's church stood almost solidly behind him.[27] The editors of the *Congregationalist*, except for George P. Morris, defended the Prudential Committee, while the editor of the *Advance*, Chicago's Congregationalist paper, supported the protestants.[28] Both the secular and the religious press printed polls of various groups and statements from more or less well-known figures. The *Congregationalist* quoted numerous clergymen. Graham Taylor, an old friend of Gladden's, flatly stated, "I do not approve of the protest." Charles H. Parkhurst, the most sensational clerical reformer in New York, thought the question "too involved for a categorical answer." Robert S. McArthur, editor of the New York *Examiner* (Baptist) and a constant apologist for Rockefeller's gifts to Baptist causes, considered the protest "nothing but an insult to Mr. Rockefeller's generosity, especially when one considers that Mr.

[26] Nevins, *Rockefeller*, II, 345.

[27] *Ohio State Journal*, March 30, April 8, 1905; Frank S. Monnett to Gladden, March 31, 1905, George W. Knight to Gladden, March 28, 1905, William E. Barton to Gladden, September 21, 1905, Gladden Papers.

[28] J. A. Adams to Gladden, March 29, 1905, Gladden Papers.

Rockefeller is a Baptist."[29] Another friend of Gladden's, Charles E. Jefferson, pastor of the Broadway Tabernacle in Manhattan, said he would accept the money, as would the majority of the clergy in any denomination. He argued that instead of attacking a single man, Gladden "ought to be arraigning the entire competitive system as it is conducted by the men of our generation." Jane Addams later recalled that many invitations came to her to write and speak on the question.[30]

Many prominent eastern clergymen seemed to favor the churches' accepting money from any source. Russell Conwell, pastor of the Baptist Temple in Philadelphia, lauded Rockefeller's Christian character, while Talmage favorite Hale admitted that he would take the money.[31] Lyman Abbott, another of Gladden's old friends and a leading social gospeler, argued in the *Outlook* that ministers lacked judicial prowess and power. Conducting evangelistic services for Gladden a month after the controversy broke out, Abbott announced to the papers in Columbus: "I am on record as approving the American Board's acceptance from any one, no matter from whom it comes or what the character of the giver." Later in 1905, he contradicted Gladden's assertion that no one thought it right to take money from gamblers and prostitutes: "But that is just what I do think is right. . . . In brief, I would co-operate with the wickedest person in doing good . . . one of the very best ways of leading him to repentance."[32]

In a further defense of his position in the *Congregationalist*, Gladden expressed bewilderment at the quality of the men defending the committee's action; he knew their intelligence and sincerity but had no doubt about his own path of duty. The same issue of the paper carried further proof that relatively few prominent Congre-

[29] *Congregationalist*, XC (April 1, 1905), 425.

[30] Charles E. Jefferson to Gladden, May 16, June 29, 1905, Gladden Papers; Addams, *Twenty Years at Hull-House*, p. 108.

[31] Nevins, *Rockefeller*, II, 347.

[32] *Ohio State Journal*, April 19, 1905; Abbott to Gladden, October 3, 1905, Gladden Papers.

gationalists opposed the gift. The Prudential Committee denied its responsibility for the sources of its funds—it had received gifts from Mohammedans, Parsees, and Hindus—and stated that it was merely a trustee for gifts designated for specific objects. A long list of corporate members of the American Board, including William Hayes Ward, with whom Gladden had worked on the *Independent,* and Charles H. Richards, who had been in Gladden's circle during the theological turmoil of the late 1870's, endorsed the gift.[33]

But Gladden could console himself with the flood of letters and telegrams that by a ratio of twenty to one encouraged him to maintain his stand. People in small towns and rural areas and urban workers who had had their own bitter experiences with the trusts were glad to see Rockefeller attacked. One woman, who thought Rockefeller a threat to "the very life of the nation," reported to Gladden that her neighbors in a small town in Illinois could feel "the tightening pressure of his 'human leach like' methods," which closed the avenues of opportunity to honest businessmen. A railroad employee in Columbus told Gladden of long hours, poor pay, and merciless company rules; with pathos he wrote that "the golden days are slipping away." A professor at Antioch College in Yellow Springs, Ohio, who had known Gladden for several years wrote: "Wherever I go I hear the Board's action ridiculed. At the cross-roads, in the village store, on the street, everywhere the comments . . . are severely condemnatory."[34]

Not all of Gladden's supporters were exploited wage-earners or farmers. Professor Lewis O. Brastow of Yale Seminary, a member of the minority in Vermont with whom Gladden had sided during the theological battles of the 1870's, came to his side early in the controversy. So did Josiah Strong, who was then president of the American Institute of Social Service, and Charles M. Sheldon, pastor of the Central Church in Topeka and author of the best-selling novel

[33] *Congregationalist,* XC (April 8, 1905), 465–67.

[34] Margaret D. Brewer to Gladden, March 30, 1905; E. M. Williams to Gladden, May 4, 1905; George D. Black to Gladden, April 1, 1905, Gladden Papers.

of the Social Gospel, *In His Steps* (1896). Friends outside the Congregational fold offered encouragement and public support. I. L. Kephart, editor of the *Religious Telescope* of the United Brethren in Christ, wrote in Gladden's defense. The best-known rabbi in the country, Stephen S. Wise, commended the protest. Whether accurately or not, Gladden and the protestants claimed that the best secular papers, if not the religious journals, were on their side.[35]

The controversy also had humorous aspects, particularly in the imaginative vocabulary that it engendered. The *Congregationalist* extracted the following variations on "tainted money" from one article in a Boston paper: "greasy gold," "soiled silver," "tarnished till," "filthy treasure," "villainy pelf of criminal donations," "censurable coin," "suspicious specie," "penitential pesos," "reprehensible rocks," "malodorous mazuma," "opprobrius opulence," "nefarious nuggets," "disreputable dough," and "degraded ducats."[36]

During April, 1905, both parties to the dispute stepped up their campaigns for denominational approval. The Prudential Committee confronted its critics with a partial *fait accompli* by announcing that it had already forwarded $41,500 of the total gift to the mission fields for which it was earmarked. The protestants met in Boston on April 3 and framed an address "To the Corporate Members of the American Board and the Ministers of our Congregational Churches." Endeavoring to preserve peace in the denomination, the *Congregationalist* praised both sides for sounding the "high ethical note," albeit its commitment to the Prudential Committee was unwavering.[37]

[35] Brastow to Gladden, April 9, 1905; Strong to Gladden, April 5, 1905; Charles M. Sheldon to Gladden, March 31, 1905; I. L. Kephart to Gladden, April 8, 1905; Wise to Gladden, April 5, 1905; Morris to Gladden, March 25, 1905, Gladden Papers.

[36] *Congregationalist*, XC (May 6, 1905), 625.

[37] *Ibid.*, XC (April 8, 1905), 465; Committee for the protestants, "To the Corporate Members of the American Board and the Ministers of Our Congregational Churches," April 4, 1905, Taylor Papers; Evans to Gladden, April 4, 1905, Herbert W. Gleason to Gladden, April 4, 1905, Gladden Papers; *Congregationalist*, XC (April 8, 1905), 459–60.

Gladden continued to discuss the gift in his pulpit and to give striking statements to the press. Losing his usual balance, he declared that the issue was "the most serious . . . that this nation has ever faced"; that the gift was part of "an organized, persistent and tremendously successful attempt to overthrow the industrial liberty of the American people"; and that the honor given men like Rockefeller was "a reflection of the dark ages, when robber barons whose trade was murder and pillage won laudation from the priests for their gifts to monasteries."[38] In a sermon on "The Religion of the Lawyer" he decried in passing the perversion of legal talent to the defense of "gigantic plunderers." He wrote an article defending his position, which Lyman Abbott, though supporting the Prudential Committee, printed in the *Outlook*. And in an article on "The Church and Social Problems" in the *International Quarterly* for April, 1905, he interjected the question in his closing sentence: "If she [the church] unfits herself for it [her social mission] by taking bribes of tainted money she ought to perish with her money, and she will."[39]

After the revelation of the committee's solicitation of the gift, some of the protestants began to suspect a master plan involving the officials of all of the denomination's societies (who were centered, significantly, in New York) to replenish their treasuries from the same source. One fearful pastor, William A. Knight, sought Gladden's advice on the propriety of forming a "Vigilance League." Concerned particularly about the reputation of the American Missionary Association, Gladden inquired of Amory H. Bradford, his successor as its president, if there were plans to get money for it from Rockefeller. Bradford's reply, that there were no concrete plans, but that

[38] *Ohio State Journal*, April 1, 3, 1905; Gladden, Sermon, April 2, 1905, Gladden Papers.

[39] *Ohio State Journal*, April 10, 1905; Washington Gladden, "Rockefeller and the American Board," *Outlook*, LXXIX (April 22, 1905), 984–87; Washington Gladden, "The Church and Social Problems," *International Quarterly*, XI (April, 1905), 147.

he would not oppose such action, was not reassuring.[40]

With most of the denominational machinery at its disposal, the Prudential Committee had a decided advantage over the protestants. In a lengthy public reply to the protestants' formal criticism, the committee reported that of 189 voluntary messages from corporate members of the board 164 wished to retain the gift, while only 25 desired to return it. Charles L. Noyes, a protesting pastor near Boston, sensing "a reaction of something like sympathy, towards the Prudential Committee and even toward Rockefeller," despaired of getting general support for any resolution censuring the committee.[41]

One of the most significant features of the controversy was the willingness of people connected with the Standard Oil Company, contrary to previous policy, to answer criticisms. Henry H. Rogers, the company's vice-president, publicly ridiculed Gladden. He averred that Gladden could not trust his deacons for ten days with the Ten Commandments, "because they would surely break some of them and bend the rest." He likened Gladden before one audience to an old whaling captain whose scattered pains a doctor diagnosed as "a case of bewildered wind."[42] Gladden refused to reply to personal calumny. Colonel Dodd, the company's solicitor, issued a rejoinder to the protestants, and the *Congregationalist* printed it on the page following one of their pronouncements. And when Gladden elaborated his opposition to the gift in an article for the *Independent*, "The Church and the Reward of Iniquity," Starr J. Murphy, Rockefeller's personal counsel, wrote "A Reply to Dr. Gladden" for the same journal. Undaunted, Gladden countered Murphy's criticisms of his accuracy with a discussion of "Mr. Rockefeller as a Truth Teller." William Hayes Ward, the editor of the *Independent*, admitted to Gladden that Murphy's reply was dis-

---

[40] Charles L. Noyes to Gladden, April 13, 1905; William A. Knight to Gladden, April 11, 1905; Bradford to Gladden, April 18, 1905, Gladden Papers.

[41] *Congregationalist*, XC (April 22, 1905), 556; Noyes to Gladden, April 18, 1905, Gladden Papers.

[42] *Ohio State Journal*, April 1, 22, 1905.

courteous but reflected, "perhaps yours did not challenge courtesy."[43]

On a broader scale, the controversy over "tainted money" helped to break down Rockefeller's former opposition to official public defenses of his career. Frederick T. Gates was particularly influential in convincing him that the public interpreted silence as an admission of guilt. This was true of Gladden, who felt that Rockefeller, if innocent of their charges, would have sued Lloyd and Tarbell for libel. Murphy, Dodd, and Rogers revolted against Rockefeller's silence, and he finally yielded and allowed them to hire Joseph I. C. Clarke, a staff writer for the New York *Herald*, as perhaps the first publicity agent for a corporation in American history. After the battle over "tainted money" the Standard Oil Company struck back at its critics in a concerted effort to create a better public image.[44]

Despite the odds against them, the protestants would not be silenced. On April 26 they met at Young's Hotel in Boston to plan their strategy. Gladden read an important paper and on April 27 issued a statement to the press reiterating the grounds of opposition to the gift. Disputing the Prudential Committee's assertion that "responsibility begins with the receipt of the gift," he argued that it should reject gifts from those against whom creditable charges had been made. In Rockefeller's case, judicial records and the findings of investigating commissions, coupled with Lloyd's and Tarbell's books, provided sufficient evidence to impugn his character.[45]

The meeting at Young's Hotel decided to send copies of a reprint of Gladden's address in the Boston *Transcript*, a sermon by Artemus J. Haynes, another protesting minister, and an explanatory paper, "The Issue Before the Churches," to every Congregational minister

---

[43] *Congregationalist*, XC (April 15, 1905), 495–96; Washington Gladden, "The Church and the Reward of Iniquity," *Independent*, LVIII (April 20, 1905), 867–70; Starr J. Murphy, "A Reply to Dr. Gladden," *Independent*, LVIII (May 18, 1905), 1097–99; Gladden, "Mr. Rockefeller as a Truth Teller," *Independent*, LVIII (June 8, 1905), 1290–91; William Hayes Ward to Gladden, May 11, 1905, Gladden Papers.

[44] Nevins, *Rockefeller*, II, 349–50; Bill Arter, "Tainted Money and PR," *Columbus Dispatch*, March 7, 1965.

[45] *Congregationalist*, XC (May 6, 1905), 624.

in the country. A long list of names accompanied this packet: President David N. Beach of Bangor Seminary and President William Jewett Tucker of Dartmouth College, Professor Lewis O. Brastow of Yale Seminary and Professor John W. Buckham of the Pacific Theological Seminary, Josiah Strong, Gaius Glenn Atkins, John Bascom, Newell Dwight Hillis, pastor of Plymouth Church in Brooklyn, Charles R. Brown, pastor of the First Congregational Church in Oakland, California, who later became president of Yale Seminary, Charles M. Sheldon, and Gladden. The meeting also decided to organize regional committees to focalize the protest much as the coterie in Boston was doing. Gladden was to compile a list of key men in the middle and interior states, and Charles R. Brown was to do the same for the Pacific Coast.[46]

But after their meeting in Young's Hotel the protestants found their way more thorny than before. Daniel Evans, a minister in Cambridge, complained to Gladden that the *Congregationalist* refused to publish statements from John Bascom, himself, and others. And Dunning even closed the editorial door to Gladden, explaining that he did not object to Gladden's expressing himself, but to his "assuming the leadership of a party in the denomination while Moderator of the National Council." He disliked Gladden's appearance at Young's Hotel most of all. He resented the meeting's secrecy, its partisan tone, and the issuance of a manifesto interpreted by the press as a "rebuke to the denomination" of which Gladden was "popularly regarded as the official head." Dunning even went on to question Gladden's "desire to exercise a representative function for the denomination." Others called on Gladden to govern his statements by his role as moderator, and one prominent New York minister suggested that this might mean "proper silence."[47] A wide range

[46] Gleason to Gladden, April 27, 28, 1905, Gladden Papers; Circular letter of protestants to Congregational ministers, issued by Herbert W. Gleason, secretary of the committee, May 6, 1905, Taylor Papers; *Congregationalist*, XC (May 13, 1905), 646; Gleason to Raymond Calkins, April 28, 1905, Gladden Papers.

[47] Evans to Gladden, May 13, 1905; Dunning to Gladden, May 9, 1905; Reuen Thomas to Gladden, May 13, 1905; Henry A. Stimson to Gladden, March 31, 1905, Gladden Papers.

of criticisms descended on Gladden. There were dispassionate suggestions that his church, which in 1904 had given less than three hundred dollars to the American Board, minimize the board's need to turn to wealthy contributors by increasing its donations. One critic generalized that "the men prominent in the protest have never been prominent as helpers of foreign missionary work." An anonymous writer slurred, "If you can find a hole big enough, it would please many good people to have you crawl in and pull the hole after." Another correspondent informed Gladden several months later that someone had sent copies of the New York *Examiner* (Baptist) containing denunciations of Gladden to all Congregational clergymen in the country.[48]

Many critics insinuated that Gladden was a hypocrite. A frequent but unfounded charge was that he accepted clerical passes, loosely comparable to rebates, from railroads. He had stopped using them about 1890 and usually told agents who offered them that they had no right to do so.[49] The Standard Oil Company's manager for central Ohio reported to the press that a member of Gladden's church was a stockholder and had held a responsible position in the company for years.[50]

Gladden's greatest embarrassment probably derived from the presence in his congregation of Samuel B. Hartman, founder and owner of the Peruna Patent Medicine Company. Although the first exposé of Peruna did not appear in the *Ladies' Home Journal* until September, 1905, and *Collier's* did not carry Samuel Hopkins Adams' devastating attack until 1906, Peruna was already suspected to be

---

[48] Roy E. Bowers to Gladden, April 10, 1905; R. C. De Forrest to Gladden, May 1, 1905; Edward F. Williams to Gladden, April 4, 1905; Anonymous to Gladden, April 2, 1905; Samuel W. Dike to Gladden, July 12, 1905, Gladden Papers.

[49] *Ohio State Journal*, January 10, 1895; Charles E. Perkins to Gladden, April 1, 1905, L. C. Beatty to Gladden, May 8, 1905, Gladden Papers; Gladden, *Social Facts and Forces*, p. 152; *Congregationalist*, XC (February 25, 1905), 245.

[50] B. S. Mathews to Gladden, April 4, 1905, Gladden Papers; *Ohio State Journal*, April 6, 1905.

only cheap whiskey.[51] As early as May 8, a Congregationalist in Oberlin declared, "Congregational *Peruna* should find less favor with you certainly than Baptist *oil*." In June a pastor in Missouri informed Gladden that W. A. Waterman, a corporate member of the American Board who had visited his parish, besides calling Gladden a socialist, had told of a prominent member of Gladden's church who manufactured Peruna. Waterman repeated his charges in a letter to Gladden, in which he not only chronicled the nefarious effects of Peruna but also inferred that other capitalists of questionable reputation were heavy contributors to the First Church. The issue of Peruna spread rapidly in Congregational circles.[52]

Unfortunately, scanty evidence leaves several important questions unanswered: What was Gladden's attitude toward Hartman? To what extent did Hartman contribute to the First Church and participate in its activities? And how did Gladden justify his relations with Hartman? Hartman had been a member of Gladden's church since at least 1895, although, apparently, he never held any office. Gladden had officiated at the marriage of his daughter, Mary Belle, to Frederick W. Schumacher, whom Hartman had brought to Columbus from Texas to undertake the promotion of Peruna on a vast scale. Though Schumacher, Hartman's successor as head of the Peruna empire, did not join the church, his wife was a member, and the church's directories listed him as a supporter.[53] At the annual meeting of the society of the First Church previous to the controversy over "tainted money," a meeting that Gladden did not attend, Schumacher was elected a trustee, an action that seemed to one parishioner "to show the money power very strongly." And it appears that as late as 1912, when Schumacher sought a federal appointment, Gladden addressed President Taft on his behalf.

[51] Stewart H. Holbrook, *The Golden Age of Quackery* (New York: Collier Books, 1962), pp. 101–5.

[52] Albert J. Swing to Gladden, May 8, 1905; Edgar H. Price to Gladden, June 20, 27, 1905; W. A. Waterman to Gladden, October 2, 1905; William A. Bartlett to Gladden, October 2, 1905, Gladden Papers.

[53] *Directory of the First Congregational Church, Columbus, Ohio* (Columbus: Nitschke Press, 1895, 1904); Gladden, "Pastor's Record, 1883–1897," First Church archives; Holbrook, *Golden Age of Quackery*, pp. 99–100.

Certain that Gladden's recommendation would carry considerable weight, Schumacher thanked him for that and other unspecified favors.[54]

It is not clear whether Gladden ever accepted the evidence against Peruna. In 1914 Samuel Hopkins Adams sent him a copy of his latest novel, *The Clarion* (1914), and, recalling a conversation with him about patent medicines, suggested that he might "recognize in it the portrait of an eminent fellow townsman."[55] On the other hand, Gladden and Hartman lived only a block apart on Town Street, and it is reasonable to assume that Gladden would be more generous in his attitude toward a parishioner and neighbor, who was noted for his geniality and kindness, than he would be toward a remote symbol of corporate greed, who was diffident and cold in public. Even if Gladden accepted the evidence, however, he may have distinguished between Rockefeller's gift and Hartman's contributions, which, given the budget of the First Church, could never have been large. What Hartman dropped silently into the collection plate was neither personally solicited nor publicized.

Ministerial groups and Congregational associations were almost as quick to take sides in the controversy over Rockefeller's gift as were individual members of the American Board, denominational officials, and leading pastors. The Central Ohio Congregational Conference, meeting in Columbus late in April, after brisk debate passed a resolution supporting Gladden by name, although several pastors from Columbus objected to a specific declaration against Rockefeller's gift, and Walter A. Mahony, a member of the First Church and a corporate member of the American Board, opposed any resolution at all.[56] A pastor in Illinois reported to Gladden that, though there was no vote, "a seemingly large majority" at the annual meeting of the Chicago association were against the gift. And the Sacra-

---

[54] Clara G. Orton to Gladden, April 2, 1905; Frederick W. Schumacher to Gladden, April 27, 1912, Gladden Papers.

[55] Samuel Hopkins Adams to Gladden, October 3, 1914, Gladden Papers.

[56] *Ohio State Journal,* April 27, 1905; E. Lee Howard to Gladden, April 28, 1905, Gladden Papers; *Congregationalist* XC (May 6, 1905), 624.

mento Valley association sent a resolution against solicitation of such gifts to the secretaries of all Congregational benevolent societies.[57] On the other side, every Congregational pastor in New Haven but Artemus J. Haynes signed a formal rebuttal to the materials sent out by the protestants who had met at Young's Hotel.[58]

More important than these actions, resolutions adopted by the Congregational associations of Massachusetts and Ohio represented strategic victories for the American Board's critics. Although it did not specifically refer to Rockefeller's gift, the Massachusetts resolution called for serious consideration of the effects on public morals and on the church's influence of financial dealings "with persons whose character and business methods are in serious question."[59] The resolution passed by the Ohio association, which met on May 23–25 at Oberlin, was an even clearer triumph for Gladden. He was strongly supported by Byron R. Long and J. W. Barnett, two of his "boys," and by delegates from his own church. Edward J. Converse, his assistant, had led a movement to assure Gladden loyal delegates from the First Church by electing Professor George W. Knight and William E. Jones and excluding Walter A. Mahony.[60] The association endorsed the resolution passed in Massachusetts; condemned "all such methods of business men and business corporations as are working injustice, embittering classes, and destroying that confidence which is the foundation of all abiding prosperity"; and affirmed its confidence in the American Board, which it urged member churches to support more energetically.[61]

[57] M. N. Darling to Gladden, May 3, 1905; George H. DeKay to Gladden, May 6, 1905, Gladden Papers.

[58] *Congregationalist*, XC (May 20, 1905), 684.

[59] *Ibid.*, XC (May 27, 1905), 712; Noyes to Gladden, May 18, 1905, Gladden Papers.

[60] Converse Diaries, May 23–25, 1905, January 14, 1907; Long to Gladden, May 2, 1905; Barnett to Gladden, May 26, 1905, Gladden Papers. Gladden had kept the issue out of his pulpit for the most part, although he did preach at least one sermon on it and referred to it in several others. One Sunday his parishioners found copies of his address at Young's Hotel in their pews. *Ohio State Journal*, May 8, 1905.

[61] *Congregationalist*, XC (June 3, 1905), 767.

Although the *Congregationalist* wanted to consider the Massachusetts association's resolution a proper end to the controversy, Gladden and the protestants had planned almost from the beginning to press the issue at the autumn meeting of the American Board in Seattle. The plan that emerged was for Gladden, one of the few protestants who was a member of the board, to present an address and resolution. By late August Gladden had formulated his statements, and in a reply in the *Congregationalist* to a statement from the Prudential Committee he publicized his resolution:

> That the officers of this society should neither solicit nor invite donations to its funds from persons whose gains are generally believed to have been made by methods morally reprehensible and socially injurious.[62]

Both sides divided over the wisdom of this plan. Charles R. Brown, one of Gladden's supporters, thought it unwise to carry the protest to the board, while Lyman Abbott, though opposed to Gladden's resolution, agreed that the board should formulate a clear policy.[63] In September Gladden circulated his paper among the leading protestants for advice and criticism. Charles L. Noyes thought that it admirably avoided the trap of endorsing all unsolicited gifts, while William Jewett Tucker liked all but its suggestion that large fortunes could normally be linked with unethical business practices. John Bascom, Lewis O. Brastow, and David N. Beach gave unqualified approval.[64]

Gladden faced overwhelming odds as he boarded the train for Seattle. The *Congregationalist* had maintained a steady editorial barrage against the protestants. During the months of discussion the Prudential Committee and most of the American Board had formed a solid phalanx. Many of the protestants anticipated defeat

[62] *Ibid.*, XC (August 26, 1905), 276.

[63] *Ibid.*, XC (September 9, 1905), 341; Abbott to Gladden, August 21, September 11, 1905, Gladden Papers.

[64] Noyes to Gladden, September 11, 1905; William Jewett Tucker to Gladden, September 11, 1905; John Bascom to Gladden, September 12, 1905; Brastow to Gladden, September 12, 1905; David N. Beach to Gladden, September 13, 1905, Gladden Papers.

in Seattle, and, according to one report, some of Gladden's friends had tried to get him to abandon a fool's errand. But, having taken an unyielding ethical stand, he could not retreat. One of the many cartoons on the controversy had pictured Gladden, sword in hand, in crusader's garb, and astride a charger, leading an army with standards inscribed "For God and Humanity" against a medieval castle, atop whose parapets flew banners with dollar signs.[65] While Gladden did not entertain so quixotic an interpretation of his cause, he realized that he must carry his protest to the final arbiter of missionary policy, the full council of the American Board. Furthermore, it would have been out of character for him to embarrass the board publicly without pressing the issue through channel of communication provided by the board.

When the board met during the second week of September, Gladden took the first opportunity to introduce his resolution. A layman from Chicago produced a counterresolution, and the board delegated a special committee of seven, including two protestants, Gladden and Philip S. Moxom, pastor of Gladden's former church in Springfield, Massachusetts, to examine both resolutions and make recommendations. Since Gladden and Moxom stood adamantly against any dilution of Gladden's resolution, the committee made two reports. Gladden read them to a crowded church on Friday, September 15, then introduced a printed address of his own, from which, after announcing that free copies were at the door, he read extended selections.

His address, "Shall Ill-gotten Gains Be Sought for Christian Purposes?", criticized the Prudential Committee's statements of policy and defended the concept of "tainted money." In a day when the churches were trying "to bridge the chasm that divides the great masses of the working people of this country from the church," he declared, they could ill afford to ally themselves even more closely than before with the rich. The members of the board, seated in the center section of the church, listened "patiently and respectfully,"

[65] *Ohio State Journal,* April 9, 1905.

while visitors, filling the sides and rear of the auditorium, broke into "ardent and sometimes prolonged" applause.[66]

The parties to the dispute interpreted the effect of Gladden's presentation differently. The president of Whitman College moved to table both resolutions, and his motion carried by a vote of forty-six to ten. Four of the ten who opposed tabling were reportedly against Gladden's resolution but wanted a direct vote on the issue. The vote and the re-election of the board's officers and the Prudential Committee led the *Congregationalist* to assert that Gladden's position had few friends on the board.[67] But Gladden claimed the victory. In a sermon after his return to Columbus and in his *Recollections* he declared that, by tabling *both* resolutions, the board had recoiled from both defense and public censure of its Prudential Committee. The Prudential Committee, he insisted, had never presented the real issue—solicitation of gifts—to the board. When at Seattle the board's members saw that this was the central question, they were unwilling to vote against Gladden's resolution.[68] Convinced that he might yet win formal recognition for his position, Gladden continued to agitate the issue. In November, for example, he addressed the New York State Conference of Religion, directed by James M. Whiton, who had shared his theological battles in the 1870's, on "The Relations of Moral Teachers to Predatory Wealth."[69]

Within a few months after the meeting at Seattle, Gladden and the protestants secured a pledge from the Prudential Committee that it would not solicit gifts from dubious sources. Two factors contributed to their success. One factor was the return from Europe of George A. Gordon, who startled everyone with an attack on the

[66] A. E. Dunning, "The American Board at Seattle," *Congregationalist*, XC (September 30, 1905), 445–46.

[67] *Ibid.*

[68] Gladden, "A Long Journey and a Lively Debate," Sermon, September 24, 1905, Gladden Papers; Gladden, *Recollections*, p. 407.

[69] Whiton to Gladden, September 19, 27, 1905, Gladden Papers; Washington Gladden, "The Relations of Moral Teachers to Predatory Wealth," in *Addresses before the New York State Conference of Religion* (Series IV, April, 1906), reprint in Taylor Papers.

Congregationalist's course and a demand that the board define its position. As minister of the Old South Church in Boston, the largest regular contributor to the American Board, Gordon was able to assume a mediatorial role. The other factor was the board's urgent need for unanimous support for a mammoth fund-raising drive, the million-dollar Haystack Campaign.[70]

By October 10 a member of the Prudential Committee had called Daniel Evans to assure him that doubtful sources of funds would be avoided; however, Evans refused to accept assurances "given in a corner when the principles . . . had such wide publicity." Then, Gordon conferred with representatives of the committee and reported to Gladden that the protestants could obtain an honorable solution without publicly humiliating the committee.[71] For several weeks in late October and early November the situation was delicate. Friends in Boston discouraged Gladden from making an address there under the auspices of A. A. Berle, minister of the Crombie Street Congregational Church in Salem and an uncompromising critic of the Prudential Committee.[72] On November 1 Gordon held another private conference, this time with several protestants present. Members of the Prudential Committee clearly stated that they would not solicit funds from doubtful sources, and, though declining to make a public statement, they agreed that those attending the conference might make private assurances. They also acceded to Gladden's request for authorization to make an announcement to his congregation, but, as Gordon reported the meeting, there were to be no statements to the press.[73]

[70] *Congregationalist*, XC (October 14, 1905), 539; Morris to Gladden, October 9, 1905, Gladden Papers.

[71] Evans to Gladden, October 10, 1905; George A. Gordon to Gladden, October 12, 23, 1905, Gladden Papers.

[72] Morris to Gladden, October 24, 1905; Evans to Gladden, October 24, 1905; Noyes to Gladden, October 24, 1905; A. A. Berle to Gladden, October 30, 1905, Gladden Papers.

[73] Evans to Gladden, November 1, 1905; Noyes to Gordon, November 1, 1905; Noyes to Gladden, November 2, 1905; Gordon to Gladden, November 2, 1905, Gladden Papers.

Gladden made his public statement in a sermon on November 12 and, true to a pledge to support the Haystack Campaign, urged his congregation to increase its contributions to foreign missions. Unfortunately, whether by prior arrangement with Gladden or not, the Associated Press reported the sermon.[74] Gladden had wanted permission to give these assurances in his addresses as national moderator, and when he received Gordon's authorization to cite the Prudential Committee's revision of policy, but not to make statements for the press, he replied that he could hardly keep his public addresses out of the papers. His sermon on November 12, delivered before he received an answer from Gordon, astounded the committee, which refused to corroborate it. As late as April, 1906, Gladden threatened to withdraw his personal aid from the American Board unless the Prudential Committee would publish its policy, but by then the controversy over "tainted money" had worn thin among Congregationalists.[75] The committee accepted the protestants' principles, and Gladden loyally promoted the American Board's program.

Although this was the most famous controversy over "tainted money," the question was not restricted to Congregational foreign missions. Gladden included his arguments in *The New Idolatry*, issued late in 1905 by S. S. McClure and John S. Phillips, the muckraking publishers. He sent the manuscript, which included the article he had written in 1895, "Tainted Money," and his address in 1905 before the American Board, "Shall Ill-gotten Gains Be Sought for Christian Purposes?", to Ida Tarbell, who favored immediate publication. McClure and Phillips also arranged for an English edition, which carried the question of the ethics of philanthropy

[74] *Ohio State Journal*, November 13, 1905; *Congregationalist*, XC (November 18, 1905), 733. Within a few weeks the First Church had sent $510.63 to the American Board; the board's secretary wrote, "You are backing up your words in the most effective way, and surely no one can question the sincerity of your interest in this work." Cornelius H. Patton to Gladden, December 6, 1905, Gladden Papers.

[75] Edward C. Moore, H. A. Wilder, John Hopkins Denison, Samuel B. Capen, Francis O. Winslow, and Edward M. Noyes to Gladden, April 7, 1906; Gladden to Moore, Wilder, Denison, Capen, Winslow, and Noyes, April 12, 1906, Gladden Papers.

abroad.[76] For awhile at least there was a wave of reaction against "tainted money." It was reported that the International Juvenile Association, led by Judge Ben Lindsey of Denver, spurned a gift of five million dollars from Rockefeller. In 1906 William Jennings Bryan warned a committee that was planning a reception for him in New York City not to accept money from questionable sources. In 1907 an officer of Colgate University announced that his school would no longer accept money from Rockefeller and that, except for some western schools, no Baptist college would. In 1911 the freshman class at Wellesley College objected to a gift from Rockefeller for construction of a new heating plant. And as late as 1964, Governor Orval E. Faubus, in his campaign for the governorship of Arkansas, accused his opponent, Winthrop Rockefeller, a grandson of John D. Rockefeller, of trying to buy office with "ill-gotten gains."[77]

Gladden never flinched in his opposition to "tainted money." In a sermon in 1910, "Charity on the Grand Scale," he criticized plans for a Rockefeller foundation and called the economic order that permitted the growth of huge fortunes abnormal. "When the path to life is kept open before every man and the strong are not permitted to plunder the weak," he declared, "there is no call for vast gratuities." In fact, "there never could be any such colossal accumulations to distribute."[78] The whole system of modern philanthropy was at odds with the principles of self-help and self-respect essential to democratic society. In addition, he objected to gifts in the form of securities, which were in effect "charges on the industries" they represented and reduced for years to come the funds available for wages. Gladden's fear of corporate control of educational institutions through foundations appeared to be well founded when in 1915 Basil M. Manly, director of research for the United States Commission on

[76] Tarbell to Gladden, October 6, 10, 16, 1905, Gladden Papers; Gladden, *New Idolatry*, pp. 15–63; Robert McClure to Gladden, February 16, 1906, Gladden Papers.

[77] *Religious Telescope*, LXXII (July 4, 1906), 835; *Ohio State Journal*, July 27, 1906, February 22, 1907, May 9, 1911; *New York Times*, October 25, 1964.

[78] Gladden, "Charity on the Grand Scale," Sermon, April 3, 1910, Gladden Papers; *Ohio State Journal*, April 4, 1910.

Industrial Relations, reported that two professors had recently lost their positions under business pressure.[79]

Gladden's protest had obvious weaknesses—its emphasis on gifts as bribes, when Rockefeller gave the money only after two years of solicitation, and the lameness of its apparent distinction between the inconspicuous gifts of a Hartman and the much larger, public gifts of a Rockefeller. But it also had the strength of Gladden's own consistent devotion to social justice and the qualities of disinterest and good will. His goal achieved, he was able to promote again the work of the American Board and to maintain with undiminished ardor old friendships with opponents in the controversy.

The controversy over "tainted money" did not permanently deter the growth of philanthropy by wealthy capitalists. Foundations such as the one created by Rockefeller became a permanent part of American life, and after the demise of the progressive movement there was less disposition among educators, clergymen, or the public at large to question the sources of financial support for colleges, religious institutions, and charitable agencies. The protest that Gladden rightfully represented had general significance as a heightened reaction against the exploitative forces that threatened, in the progressive mind, not only economic freedom and democratic institutions but also the spiritual and moral vigor of the nation. Without the pervasive enthusiasm of the crusading milieu, such a protest might appear futile at best and petty or vindictive at worst. It also had personal significance as an exemplification of Gladden's willingness to follow the dictates of conscience with no apparent possibility of personal advantage and against the judgment of a large segment of the Protestant public, including avowed proponents of the Social Gospel. Adhering to an ethical purism that would not admit compromise, he minimized the contradictions of his own position, created arbitrary standards for judging the acceptability of gifts, and overlooked the complexity of industrial society and the culpability of society itself for injustice. These blind spots, and particularly his

[79] *Ohio State Journal,* August 26, 1915.

concentration on one figure as a scapegoat, were not typical of his social message. But on the other hand, Gladden may have sensed the inherent strength of a protest that focused on one narrow object, especially when public wrath against that object was already at the boiling point and when the moral sensitivity of the American people, white-hot with the fires of reform, was ready for social purification.

Ten

The Challenges of Poverty and Race

The forces shaping American society in the years after the Civil War created two other social problems to which Gladden attempted to apply the Social Gospel. Poverty, which in 1905 he called America's most portentous social problem, confined unprecedented numbers to lives of squalor and deprivation.[1] Like many other reformers, he began to discover the symptoms of poverty in the 1870's as depression upset antiquated forms of charity; by the end of the century his understanding had broadened to include the conditions and causes of poverty itself. The continued disfranchisement and degradation of American Negroes, the second problem, was more remote and, complicated by racial prejudice, more perplexing. Both problems challenged at times his faith in progress, though he never gave up hope that they could be solved. In both cases he sought remedies that would improve the moral as well as material condition of the unfortunate. Writing with reference to poverty, but with relevance to any social problem, he declared: "Suffering is not the greatest evil; moral unworthiness is the greatest evil." Moreover,

> To care for bodily needs, and ignore the effect of what we are doing upon the manhood of the recipient, is a curious way of imitating Christ.

[1] Gladden, "The Church and Social Problems," *International Quarterly*, p. 143.

Now, if Christ did not come primarily to relieve suffering, then it is not
the Christian's first business to relieve suffering.[2]

Social work consistent with the spirit of brotherhood would not make
men comfortable in a quagmire, but would strive to get them out
of it.

When Gladden confronted the prolonged national depression of
the 1870's, he shared the attitudes of the most progressive reformers.
Appalled by the indiscriminate and unco-ordinated forms of aid that
had prevailed earlier in the century, the foremost charitable workers
in England and America attempted in the last half of the nineteenth
century to put charity on a systematic and fiscally sound basis,
Gladden agreed with those who thought that previous charitable
work, though inspired by Christian motives, had actually increased
pauperism.

The tramps who thrived on handouts from soft-hearted individuals
confirmed this conviction. Their ranks swelled by both the Civil
War and the depression that began in 1873, these rootless wan-
derers threatened to establish perpetual beggary in the streets of
many cities. A major center in western Massachusetts, Springfield
attracted large contingents of itinerants, and the city fathers were
at odds over how to deal with them. Most felt that making tramps
work for food and lodging would discourage them from coming
to Springfield. But providing work was a major difficulty for the
authorities, who were reluctant to employ them on public projects.
Their solution, letting tramps sleep in the lockup and making them
chop wood or clean gutters for their breakfast, was not entirely satisfactory, mainly because the city could not always find enough suitable chores. By late 1876, however, Springfield was successfully
diverting the unwelcome travelers from her gates.[3]

In *Sunday Afternoon* Gladden urged rigorous measures against
tramps: "First, we must stop feeding these tramps . . . "; "Second,

[2] Gladden, *Ruling Ideas,* pp. 40, 45.

[3] *Springfield Republican,* July 16, December 22, 1875, December 19, 1876,
January 27, 1877.

we must have, in every state, some such system . . . by which every vagrant beggar shall be arrested, placed in confinement and compelled to work for his living not less than ninety days for the first offense and not less than six months for the second. . . . " Following Mrs. Josephine Shaw Lowell's suggestions for effective police repression of begging, he claimed that "speedy and adequate punishment" would virtually eliminate tramps from the streets.[4]

Gladden had the same antipathy to random private charity to resident paupers, although his attitude toward their predicament was more equivocal. The cumulative effects of the depression made 1876 Springfield's worst year for unemployment. While public officials debated the problem, the unemployed grew restive. In August, 1876, these "Irishmen of the pick and shovel," after meeting in the police court to petition the city for jobs, submitted lists of those wanting work to a special committee appointed by the city council. At the request of the leader of the unemployed petitioners, Gladden addressed one of their meetings. Though he frankly told them that the city probably could not provide employment, they received him cordially and accepted his invitation to hear him address his congregation, which included many of the city's employers. Preaching on "Our Duty to the Unemployed," he "deprecated the idea of the city furnishing work" but appealed to his parishioners to create employment by remodeling their houses and initiating new building. He did not fail to point out the relative cheapness of such projects during a depression.[5]

Although some of his parishioners followed his advice, the city's failure to provide employment and the prolongation of depression kept poor relief in the forefront of public discussion. The city's almoner and the overseers of the poor were equipped to administer various forms of charity under normal circumstances, but the crisis

---

[4] *Sunday Afternoon,* I (March, 1878), 277; *Good Company,* VII (July, 1881), 479–80.

[5] *Springfield Republican,* August 4–5, 10, 12, 16, 26, September 16, 25, 1876. Gladden later described the leader of the unemployed as a man of "impulsive and reckless temper"; he recalled, however, that the man eventually became one of his "most loyal parishioners." Gladden, *Recollections,* pp. 249–50.

of the 1870's, aggravated in 1874 by a state law lowering the residence requirement for municipal relief from ten to five years, made havoc of their work. Criticism of their administration focused on outdoor relief, the assistance given to people who continued to live outside the almshouse. The *Springfield Republican* led the attack, calling outdoor relief "the most dangerous form in which the poor can be aided." It reported that, while the total expenses of the pauper department had increased 150 per cent between 1870 and 1876, the cost of outdoor relief had trebled or quadrupled.[6]

The *Republican*, edited by Gladden's friend Samuel Bowles, began in 1876 to call for a new charitable organization that would co ordi nate public and private agencies and reduce the cost of poor relief.[7] Gladden had recognized the disarray of private organizations for some time and in 1875 had urged the YMCA to systematize them. Consequently, he responded immediately to the *Republican's* proposal. At an exploratory meeting in the South Church he stressed the need for methodical elimination of unworthy applicants for aid. Because of his interest and outspokenness, he became chairman of the committee that drew up the new agency's constitution and was a member of its first board of managers.[8]

Gladden's committee incorporated the new ideals of scientific charity in its plan of organization. His report predicted an increase in pauperism, due to immigration, the rise of a native and often hereditary pauper class, and the increasing specialization of modern industry, and concluded that outdoor relief, by actually encouraging mendicancy, did more harm than good. Citing Charles Loring Brace, founder of the Children's Aid Society of New York and author of the term "the dangerous classes," he propounded three cardinal principles of the new charity: that the able-bodied should never receive outdoor relief, but should earn their keep in public workhouses; that the state should never provide work outside its workhouses; and

[6] *Springfield Republican,* February 4, October 7, December 20, 1876, March 19, 1877.

[7] *Ibid.,* December 22–23, 1876, January 13, 1877.

[8] *Ibid.,* November 22, 1875, January 31, February 14, June 6, 1877.

that the city should never dispense outdoor relief but only private charities. Like the English poor-law reformers, Gladden and his committee believed that a grudging dispensation of public relief was best for the recipients, as well as for society. The objectives of the organization were "the discouragement of mendicancy and of indiscriminate alms-giving, the judicious relief of those who are destitute and helpless, and the assistance of those who need employment." Members pledged "to abstain from indiscriminate giving of food, money or clothing."[9]

Gladden hammered away at the same ideas in *Sunday Afternoon*: abandonment of public outdoor relief; hard labor in workhouses for those who could work; a strict regimen of work, rest, food, and moral stimulation to restore "chronic and incorrigible paupers" to social usefulness; and private charity for "worthy persons in temporary want." What the poor needed most was not material aid but "moral stimulus and nourishment." By helping the poor to help themselves, public and private charities would not only reduce their expenses, they would also correct defects of character and thus eliminate the primary sources of pauperism.[10]

The new organization, the Union Relief Association, rapidly gained public support during the early months of 1877. Noting some reluctance to plunge into relief work during preparation for a revival, Gladden argued in a sermon on "Holiness and Charity" that such work would assure a religious awakening. The association obtained a room in city hall for its central office, and a flood of applicants immediately appeared. A corps of friendly visitors, prototypes of

[9] *Ibid.*, February 14, 1877; Robert H. Bremner, *From the Depths: The Discovery of Poverty in the United States* (New York: New York University Press, 1956), p. 47; Washington Gladden *et al.*, *Constitution and By-Laws of the Union Relief Association, also, Report on Organization* (Springfield, Mass.: Atwood & Noyes, Printers, 1877).

[10] *Sunday Afternoon*, I (January, 1878), 85–86, (April, 1878), 378–79, III (March, 1879), 283–84, (June, 1879), 569–70; *Good Company*, IV (1880), 567–68. Gladden defended his opposition to public outdoor relief in a letter to the *Republican*: " . . . I have come to see that the government bungles pretty much everything that it puts its hands on." *Springfield Republican*, February 21, 1877.

the modern caseworker, each assigned to a city district, investigated applicants, suggested suitable assistance, and filed detailed questionnaires in the central office for future reference. Charitable organizations had begun to use friendly visitors several decades earlier, on the theory that the personal ties they established could promote moral uplift.[11]

Gladden supported the association constantly. He instructed the friendly visitors, before their second winter's work, to be firm but tender. At the beginning of each winter he participated in meetings in various churches to win popular support. These meetings featured prominent charitable workers and theorists, such as Professor Francis Wayland of Yale, C. C. Amsden of Germantown, Pennsylvania, where the first such organization in the United States had originated in the early 1870's, and William Burnet Wright of Boston. In 1878 Gladden was on a committee that investigated the city's lockup and urged administrative reforms and construction of a new jail.[12]

The association appears to have achieved its goals, although providing employment was a persistent problem. At first its officers reported that many applicants were either "unworthy" or made false claims, but after several weeks both the total number of applications and the proportion of "unworthy" applicants declined, much to the delight of the organization's economy-minded backers.[13] Investigations of the city's almshouse, hospital, and lockup led to corrective measures.[14] During its second winter of activity the Union Relief Association collaborated more closely with the city's pauper department, and by 1882 it had assumed complete management of outdoor relief in Springfield.[15] An attempt to promote migration from the city to rural areas, during which Gladden extolled the joys of rural

[11] *Springfield Republican,* February 19, 26, March 1, 15, 1877; Bremner, *From the Depths,* p. 36.

[12] *Springfield Republican,* December 29, November 19, 1877, November 25, 1878, December 13, 1879, December 26, 1878.

[13] *Ibid.,* April 14, 20, 1877.

[14] *Ibid.,* September 28, 1877, October 8, 11, 1878.

[15] *Ibid.,* December 22, 1877, January 3, February 7, 1882.

life and its conduciveness to "the Anglo-Saxon love of home and children," failed largely because there was no greater demand for agricultural labor than for industrial labor.[16] The expenses of the pauper department declined, though probably more because of the return of prosperity than because of the association's investigative work. The association itself spent $1,890.65 in assistance to 241 families over its first four years; and during this period families aided and money expended declined regularly.[17] Its supporters regarded this decrease in the demand for its services as proof of the association's effectiveness.

The association was a pioneer in applying the principles advocated by reformers like Mrs. Lowell and Charles Loring Brace. The movement to organize public and private charity had begun in London in 1868, but in the United States it was still in an experimental stage. Under the stimulus of depression many cities established such agencies during the late 1870's, and several took the Union Relief Association of Springfield as their model.[18]

Gladden's experience in Springfield established the guidelines for his persistent subsequent efforts to make charity serve the moral as well as material needs of the poor. Apart from a deeper understanding of the causes of poverty, his thinking underwent little change. However, the almost immediate success that followed his and Samuel Bowles's efforts in Springfield did not repeat itself in Columbus.

In 1883 Columbus had no central organization to co-ordinate its multifarious private charities. Gladden co-operated with existing agencies, such as the Female Benevolent Society, the oldest philanthropic organization in the city. Many of his parishioners were

[16] *Ibid.*, February 17, 1877, February 9, September 26, 1878.

[17] *Ibid.*, December 27, 1877, September 25, 1879, December 2, 1880.

[18] Amos G. Warner, *American Charities* (New York: Thomas Y. Crowell Co., Publishers, 1894), pp. 442–43. Both Boston and Hartford investigated Springfield's organization while planning their own. *Springfield Republican*, March 5, 1877, January 29, 1879.

active in local charities, giving him a natural interest in their work and access to their councils. Recognizing the need to eliminate overlapping and to promote co-operation between public and private agencies, he called in November, 1885, for an organization similar to those in Springfield, New York, Buffalo, and other cities. He first made his plea to the pastors' union and then, at their request, to the officers of the charitable societies. The report of the city's infirmary director, showing that in 1884 about one-ninth of the population had applied for outdoor relief, indicated a "rapid and alarming" growth of pauperism. And judging by the number calling at his door every day, he concluded that Columbus was a "paradise of tramps and bummers."[19]

Impressed by Gladden's experience in Springfield, businessmen, ministers, and charitable workers organized the Associated Charities of the City of Columbus and appointed him chairman of a committee to draft a constitution. His report provided for a central office for registration and records, a voluntary staff of district visitors, an employment agency, and such provident schemes as a penny bank and a coal fund. He was also chairman of a committee to organize popular support, and at a mass meeting he read and explained the agency's constitution. He participated in all of the planning, became a member and temporary chairman of the advisory council, and was a member of the council's committee on employment and police. By his own admission, he yielded to pressure to participate only because he feared that the organization would need all the support it could get. But despite his efforts, lack of public support did cripple the Associated Charities. Membership remained small, and the council, dependent on subscriptions for revenue, ended its first year in debt.[20]

The Associated Charities struggled through another winter with some success and then, apparently, died. That it lived that long was due largely to Gladden. The council met in October, 1886, and

[19] *Ohio State Journal*, January 6, 8, November 9, 1885.

[20] *Ibid.*, December 5, 14–15, 22, 1885, March 5, June 2, 1886; Gladden, "Good Morals in Columbus," Sermon, March 21, 1886, Gladden Papers.

debated whether to continue, whereupon the *Ohio State Journal* lamented that a city of 75,000 people had scarcely been able to meet the previous year's budget of about five hundred dollars. A month later, the same paper observed that the organization was "believed now to be among the things of the past." But in a letter in the same issue Gladden claimed that the agency had received several hundred dollars and that, since its machinery was intact, it could renew the work that had "pretty well cleared" the city of tramps. His plea led to another large public meeting, at which he raised $1,300.[21] Precariously begun, the second year of operations was more successful than the first. One new feature was a "friendly inn," managed by a superintendent and matron, that fed and lodged those willing to saw and split wood, which was sold to augment the association's income.[22]

The persistence of poverty, especially in Columbus, troubled Gladden. Despite undeniable economic growth, a large proportion of the city's population—in 1892 he estimated it at one-eighth—required public assistance. In 1891 he analyzed "The Problem of Poverty" before audiences in Columbus and New York, and in 1892 he got Richard W. Gilder, editor of the *Century*, to publish his conclusions in a series of "Present-Day Papers" by "The Sociological Group," which included Bishop Henry C. Potter, Theodore T. Munger, Seth Low, Richard T. Ely, and Francis G. Peabody. Noting such recent literature on poverty as Jacob Riis's *How the Other Half Lives* (1890), Helen Campbell's *Prisoners of Poverty* (1887), and Charles Booth's *Life and Labor of the People of London* (1891), Gladden deplored popular ignorance of the life of the poor. He emphasized the economic causes of poverty, such as irregularity of industrial employment, competition of women and children, who would work for substandard wages, indiscriminate charity, immigration, and migration from country to city, rather than the personal

---

[21] *Ohio State Journal*, October 13, November 25, 29, 1886
[22] *Ibid.*, January 12, February 4, March 12, 1887.

causes that had occupied his attention previously. He considered intemperance more frequently a result than a cause of poverty and attributed most physical debility to environment. Still, he noted that many simply did not want work.[23]

Early in 1893, as if prophetic of the impending depression, he severely criticized the administration of public and private charities in Columbus, which he labeled "The Beggar Factory of Ohio," and called for an agency to co-ordinate them and for the abolition of outdoor relief. His appeals went unheeded until October, when civic officials, businessmen, and ministers finally established the needed organization. They adopted Gladden's proposals for a central office for application and records, bureau to investigate and counsel applicants, the provision of employment whenever possible, and aid in food, clothing, and fuel rather than in cash. Amasa Pratt, head of the state's Deaf and Dumb Asylum and one of Gladden's parishioners, became the organization's secretary and major administrative officer. During the first month the organization spent several thousand dollars to help nearly fifteen hundred families.[24]

To promote systematic charity on a broader scale, Gladden joined the Ohio State Conference of Charities and Correction, organized in 1891 as an affiliate of the National Conference of Charities and Correction, and served on its committee on associated charities. In 1895–96 he was president of the state conference. He addressed the National Conference of Charities and Correction in 1893, counterpoising as "The Perfect Law of Charity" two principles inherent in Christianity, mutual aid and self-help, and rejecting "the sentimen-

[23] *Ibid.*, November 9, 16, 1891; Gladden to Gilder, January 25, 1892, *Century* Collection; Washington Gladden, "The Problem of Poverty," *Century*, XLV (December, 1892), 245–56. Gladden familiarized his own congregation with works on poverty by referring to them in sermons and, as in the case of Campbell's study of workingwomen, by entire sermons. *Ohio State Journal*, May 28, 1887; Gladden, "My Neighbor in the Slum," Sermon, November 27, 1904, Gladden Papers.

[24] *Ohio State Journal*, January 14, 16, October 27–28, 31, November 2, 5, 10, 14, December 14, 1893.

tal charity which has no sense of the values of character."[25]

Although he sensed the reality of economic crises for genuine working people, Gladden entertained a basic distrust toward the motives of the poor. For example, he condemned the march on Washington of Jacob Coxey's "army" in 1894. Unlike Wat Tyler's rebellion in 1381 and the Chartist uprising of 1848 in England, it had no justification. Whereas Tyler's followers and the Chartists lacked political recourse, Coxey's adherents could vote. Moreover, both English movements had definite propositions to make, but, Gladden maintained incorrectly, Coxey's "army" had none. Finally, while Tyler's peasants and the Chartists were workingmen who wanted employment, Coxey's "straggling company" was filled with "people who are always looking for work, with both eyes tightly bandaged."[26] According to the *Ohio State Journal*, at the request of a newspaper in Philadelphia Gladden gave this satirical advice on "how to be happy, though poor":

1. Move three times a year.
2. Throw up your job whenever it becomes the least bit disagreeable.
3. Run in debt to everybody who will trust you.
4. Take a drink whenever you haven't anything else to do.
5. Make up your mind that the world owes you a living and that your woes are all due to the oppression of your neighbor.[27]

Believing that employment was the best charity for the able-bodied, as well as "the only charity they crave," Gladden appealed to his congregation in November, 1893, as he had done in Springfield, to create jobs for the worthy. Helping the needy to help them-

[25] General R. Brinkerhoff, Chairman, "Report of Committee on Prisons," Board of State Charities Circular No. 4 (Norwalk, Ohio: Laning Printing Co., State Printers, 1893); *The Ohio Bulletin of Charities and Correction,* Board of State Charities Circular No. 7 (Columbus, Ohio: Board of State Charities, 1893); *Ohio State Journal,* August 21, 1896; Washington Gladden, "The Perfect Law of Charity," in Isabel C. Barrows, ed., *Proceedings of the National Conference of Charities and Correction, 1893* (Boston: Press of George H. Ellis, 1893), pp. 263–78.

[26] Gladden, Sermon, April 22, 1894, Gladden Papers.

[27] *Ohio State Journal,* June 14, 1893.

selves, he asserted, was the "first principle of true charity." Those who could work and would not, even if the work was shoveling potatoes for fifty cents per day, did not deserve pity. And after the winter of 1893–94, discouraged by his own charitable efforts, he became even harsher toward those who balked at the work test. Speculating that probably nine-tenths of the unemployed would not work if they could avoid it, he declared that there were very few "really industrious, sober, thrifty, independent people among the unemployed."[28]

In an article in 1894 in the *Review of Reviews* he advocated the temporary provision of work by cities. Without sympathy for those who would refuse menial work at low wages he said, "such beggars should be permitted to choose starvation." The state should impose indeterminate sentences in workhouses, the only effective remedy against chronic poverty, on those whose alcoholism or incorrigible indolence made them socially undesirable. To the charge that the provision of work by government was socialistic, he replied that it was no more socialistic than were gratuitous handouts.[29] In informal remarks in 1899 at the National Conference of Charities and Correction he underscored the necessity of state employment in economic crises. Charity without work fostered pauperism, and if forced to choose between pauperism and socialism, he declared, "I shall go for socialism every time."[30] He once asked his congregation,

> Who of us would not a thousand times rather see any one dear to us die of starvation than see him sink into that abject condition where he would rather grovel as a mendicant for bread than earn it by honest work?[31]

The "workless man," he told his parishioners in 1898 and the National Conference of Charities and Correction in 1899, should be defined as the man who does not desire to work, "who prefers to eat his

[28] Gladden, Sermons, November 19, 1893; April 22, 1894, Gladden Papers.

[29] Washington Gladden, "Relief Work—Its Principles and Methods," *Review of Reviews,* IX (January, 1894), 38–40.

[30] Isabel C. Barrows, ed., *Proceedings of the National Conference of Charities and Correction, 1899* (Boston: George H. Ellis, 1900), pp. 413–14.

[31] Gladden, Sermon, October 28, 1894, Gladden Papers.

bread in the sweat of some other man's brow." Having dealt with the unemployed for over thirty years, he claimed to know their real weaknesses better than did the social theorists who saw their problems as mainly environmental. Those not willing to work deserved pity more than censure, however, and the workhouses should be educational, not penal, institutions.[32]

Gladden's constant prodding during the depression of the 1890's resulted in a revival of the Associated Charities of Columbus. It declined temporarily after about 1895, and, when in 1897 the city's poor fund was depleted, Gladden participated in an unsuccessful attempt to reactivate it. Thorough reorganization followed another crisis in 1899. Gladden continued to support the organization and served on its board of directors. After a pastorate in Ashtabula, Ohio, Byron R. Long, the former minister of the Mayflower Chapel, became director of the Associated Charities of Columbus. In 1916 the organization was still giving outdoor relief to the sick and crippled and providing work for the unemployed; it supervised sixty-three co-operating agencies and had a budget of over twenty-four thousand dollars and a staff varying from fourteen to eighteen employees.[33]

Three fundamental emphases marked Gladden's approach to poverty after the depression of the nineties. In the first place, he advocated a clear division of responsibility between public and private relief agencies. The state should provide suitable temporary employment, with compensation in provisions and at a lower rate than current wages, for those able to work; it should maintain work-

[32] Gladden, "What to Do with the Workless Man," Sermon, February 13, 1898, Gladden Papers; also in *Proceedings of the National Conference of Charities and Correction, 1899*, pp. 141–52. Like workhouses, prisons should seek the rehabilitation of the inmate. The indeterminate sentence, in both workhouse and prison, would insure the return of morally sound and socially useful individuals to normal roles in political and economic life. Gladden, Sermons, October 24, 31, 1897, January 17, 1909, Gladden Papers; Gladden, *Social Salvation*, pp. 112–19.

[33] *Ohio State Journal*, November 27, 1897, September 27, October 24, 1899, January 24, February 7, 1900, May 26, 1916. Gladden evidently remained a director for well over a decade. *Ibid.*, October 2, 1908, May 27, 1911.

houses for those unwilling to work and trade schools for those unfit for any vocation. Private agencies and churches, which alone had the manpower to establish helpful relations with the poor and the equipment for moral stimulation, should manage all outdoor relief.[34]

In the second place, despite his harsh judgments on the motives of the unemployed, he maintained that society itself created much poverty and distress. In 1896 he denied that the tariff, defects in the currency, political corruption, or unjust combinations of capitalists, though undoubtedly factors, were the basic causes of depression. The "abuse of credit" and the "reckless extravagance of the people," which "begins in the boulevards and goes down to the slums " were the real causes of the collapse. Though his economic analyses were hardly profound, he did recognize the effects of full occupation of western lands, inflation, technological unemployment, and inequitable division of profits.[35] "Somehow or other," he declared,

> we must establish different conditions and furnish larger opportunities. Our civilization is a failure if it cannot somehow put the opportunity of earning an honest living within the reach of every human being who is willing to work.[36]

Instead of allowing men to "eat the bread of charity," a preposterous exigency in a rich land, the state must "see to it that the ground is clear, that the course is open, that every man who wants to work shall have a fair chance. . . . " The parasites in the upper echelons of society created many of the conditions on which the parasites at the bottom thrived. In a just social order both would work for equitable rewards. Gladden favored industrial education to relieve technological unemployment. And he thought that the state might devise projects, such as road-building, irrigation, land reclamation, and other public works, that would both reduce unemployment and in-

---

[34] Gladden, *Christian Pastor,* pp. 454, 465–68; Gladden, *Social Salvation,* pp. 60, 83–88; Gladden, Sermon, September 13, 1908, Gladden Papers.

[35] Gladden, Sermons, November 8, 1896; September 26, 1897, Gladden Papers.

[36] Gladden, "The Workers," Sermon, May 15, 1898, Gladden Papers.

crease the national wealth.[37] Confident that poverty need not be permanent in America, he looked to the state to find creative remedies and, in the long run, to remove the structural roots of poverty, while the churches and private agencies planted the seeds of self-help, thrift, and personal dignity.

Gladden's third major emphasis was that charitable work must rest on a religious foundation. He urged the churches to broaden their charitable activities and, acknowledging the religious orientation of many social workers, encouraged non-religious private and public agencies to study more thoroughly the spiritual needs of the poor. Consequently, when in 1910 the National Conference of Charities and Correction established a committee on the church and social work and appointed Gladden chairman, he regarded its action as a step toward bringing the churches more directly into social work and restoring a religious dimension to the entire movement. He worked closely with Frederic Almy, secretary of the Charity Organization Society of Buffalo, in planning the committee's sectional meetings for the national conference in 1911 in Boston. Reporting the conference in Boston to his congregation, Gladden concluded that the churches must first study social work, then stimulate, guide, and supplement it. The churches could learn from social work that the imperative of brotherhood was mutual aid; social workers could learn from the churches that the salvation of character was the most elemental of human needs.[38] His interest in the National Conference of Charities and Correction—particularly in its committee on the church and social work, of which John M. Glenn of the Russell Sage Foundation became chairman—continued unabated. Though the committee ceased to function after a few years, at its reorganization in 1917 as the National Conference of Social Work, the conference,

[37] Gladden, Sermons, January 17, 1897; "Industrial Education," January 8, 1899; June 10, 1900, Gladden Papers.

[38] *Ohio State Journal*, September 4, 1910; Frederic Almy to Gladden, March 8, May 12, June 24, 1911, Gladden Papers; *Congregationalist*, XCVI (June 17, 1911), 817; Gladden, Sermon, June 25, 1911, Gladden Papers.

then led by Frederic Almy, established a permanent section on the church and social work.[39]

Gladden linked his conviction that the churches should undertake more extensive charitable activities to his long-standing appeal for federation of the churches. In 1879 he described the church in the New Testament as the body of all Christians in a given city, though for practical purposes they met in separate congregations; and as early as 1880, he thought that local congregations might co-ordinate their work through such a "Municipal Church."[40] His idea was similar to that of W. T. Stead, who used the British *Review of Reviews*, which he had founded in 1890, to promote an alliance of reformers and churches in a Civic Church. In 1892, about a year before Stead helped to organize the Civic Federation of Chicago during a visit to the United States, Gladden addressed his own congregation on "The Municipal Church" and contributed an article to the American *Review of Reviews*, founded by Stead and Albert Shaw.[41]

Despite repeated expositions of the potential values of a municipal church, Gladden did not achieve his goal in Columbus until 1910.[42] By then, church federation had taken great strides in the organization of local councils of churches and the Federal Council of Churches; but Gladden still felt the need for a local body that, unlike the conciliar movement, would include Roman Catholics and Jews, and that would concentrate on social work. By uniting to investigate social problems and to ameliorate human suffering, the churches "would recover that sacred and vital function which, in their divisions, they have suffered to lapse," and "would regain the opportu-

[39] John M. Glenn to Gladden, September 19, 1913; Almy to Gladden, June 12, 1917, Gladden Papers.

[40] *Sunday Afternoon*, III (February, 1879), 185–86; Gladden, Sermons, "The St. Louis Council," November 21, 1880, October 20, 1889, Gladden Papers.

[41] Joseph O. Baylen, "A Victorian's 'Crusade' in Chicago, 1893–1894," *Journal of American History*, LI (December, 1964), 418–21; *Ohio State Journal*, September 17, 1892; Washington Gladden, "The Municipal Idea of the Church," *Review of Reviews*, VI (October, 1892), 305–7.

[42] Gladden, Sermons, January 15, 1899; January 13, 1901, Gladden Papers.

nity of exercising that friendship which is the primary reason of their existence."[43]

Gladden devoted considerable energy in 1910 to popularizing the idea of the municipal church. He addressed the local ministerial council, the Central Ohio Congregational Conference, and, at the invitation of the evangelist J. Wilbur Chapman, who heartily approved the idea, an audience of over fifteen hundred at the Victoria Theater in Dayton. By the end of May a movement to organize a municipal church was under way in Columbus, with Gladden as chairman of a planning committee.[44]

Attributing the failure of the churches to reach the poor, the very classes that had followed Jesus eagerly, to barriers erected by the churches themselves, he wrote in the *Century* for May that the municipal church could become "the chief promoter of philanthropy" in every community. Christianity had created, in Benjamin Kidd's words, "a great fund of altruistic feeling," which had inspired the state to assume charitable work itself. But Gladden doubted that Christianity had permeated the state sufficiently for it to "minister in Christ's name," and that the churches could afford to relinquish this ministry. If they restored their ties with the poor, the churches could still the hisses of those who, while damning them, held Jesus in the highest regard. The municipal church might promote better housing, sponsor playgrounds, find substitutes for the saloon, check prostitution, prevent child labor, operate employment bureaus, and mediate industrial disputes. Its motto would be non-creedal, "The union of all who love in the service of all who suffer."[45]

Although Gladden hoped to have the municipal church operative in Columbus before his article appeared in the *Century*, it was not until October, 1910, that pastors and delegates of twenty churches

[43] *Ohio State Journal*, February 22, 1910; Gladden, Sermon, February 21, 1910, Gladden Papers.

[44] *Ohio State Journal*, March 4, April 21, 30, May 30, June 14, 1910.

[45] Washington Gladden, "The Municipal Church: The Crying Need of It, and a Program of Its Possible Work," *Century*, LXXX (August, 1910), 493–99; *Congregationalist*, XCV (August 20, 1910), 245.

ratified a constitution prepared by Gladden's committee and organized the General Council of the Churches and Religious Societies of Columbus. Accepting the presidency, Gladden remarked: "I am glad and willing to take this office, because I would like to employ a large share of my energies for a few years in working along this line."[46] The council, which included the minister and two lay delegates from each co-operating religious body, appointed standing committees for each public and private charitable institution and for such issues as housing and sanitation, immigrants, popular amusements, industrial peace, child labor, and unemployment. These committees reported in rotation at monthly meetings of the council, and in addition, there were frequent public meetings.[47] Gladden offered to send copies of the constitution to those interested in forming similar organizations elsewhere, and he received many queries, as well as invitations to address such groups as the pastors' union in Toledo and the Twentieth Century Club of Boston.[48]

Re-elected president for four years, Gladden led the council into a wide variety of activities. During its first year it drew public attention to unsanitary conditions in the city's prison and abuses of the contract system in the workhouse, fostered the planting of gardens in vacant lots, took a leading part in getting the city council to pass a new building code, and criticized the Anti-Saloon League for failing to promote substitutes for the saloon. The next year, faced with growing unemployment, it secured a pledge from the mayor to accelerate public works and asked ministers to urge their congregations to create employment. It attempted to regulate nickelodeons and to prevent the opening of saloons near schools. In 1912 the Men and Religion Forward Movement, an interdenominational organization based on the idea that religion and social service were comple-

---

[46] Gladden to Robert U. Johnson, April 2, 12, 1910, *Century* Collection; *Ohio State Journal*, October 1, 4, 25, 1910.

[47] Gladden, Sermon, [1911,] Gladden Papers.

[48] William Newton Clarke to Gladden, August 22, 1910; Edward H. Chandler to Gladden, September 13, 1910; Ernest Bourner Allen to Gladden, July 15, 1910; Hubert D. Gallaudet to Gladden, November 14, 1910, Gladden Papers.

mentary, made the council's executive committee its official social service arm in Columbus.[49]

In the 1870's Gladden had shared the concern of reformers with the relief of pauperism rather than with the conditions of poverty. To find temporary work for the unemployed, to remove the unworthy from public relief, and to eliminate dependency were their primary aims. But as the century drew to a close, they began to define the problem of poverty, in the words of one historian, "in terms of insufficiency and insecurity rather than exclusively as a matter of dependency."[50] Appropriately, Gladden became a student of a variety of social problems related to poverty.

Whatever the reformers might think of the moral qualities of the poor, they could not attach any opprobrium to their children. One of the earliest modern charities, the Children's Aid Society of New York, was founded in 1853 to transplant indigent children from urban slums to rural communities, where they would have fresh air, wholesome domestic life, and agricultural training. Elsewhere, homes for orphans, ladies' benevolent societies, and religious agencies attempted to save the children from the debilitating effects of the slums. Gladden's Bethel Sunday School offered religious instruction, entertainment, and opportunities for friendship to the children of the unchurched poor near downtown Columbus, and the West Side Social Center began as a community center for the youth of another depressed neighborhood. Gladden supported local kindergartens, fresh-air campaigns, and the Big Brother movement.[51]

William R. George's "Junior Republic" at Freeville, New York, also captured Gladden's interest, and he publicized its work. Each summer "Daddy" George took about two hundred children from the slums, especially in New York, to his "Republic," where they practiced self-government within a complete civil and industrial frame-

[49] *Ohio State Journal,* September 17, 19, 1911, February 20, March 19, May 21, 1912.

[50] Bremner, *From the Depths,* pp. 123–25.

[51] *Ohio State Journal,* June 28, July 7, 1890, September 14, 1908, March 12, 1911.

work that included a congress, civil and criminal courts, a police force, military organization, prison, bank and currency, and tariffs. Gladden first visited the "Republic" in 1896, while at his summer home in Owego, which was less than forty miles south of Freeville. Enthusiastic about the project, he told his congregation, "I do not know that I have seen anything that touched me more deeply," and wrote a descriptive article for the *Outlook*. Another visit the following summer impressed him even more, and in a sermon on "The Boys' Republic and the Boy Anarchists" he contrasted the traits cultivated by George with a growing disrespect for authority among other children. Continuing his interest in the "Junior Republic," he had George speak in the First Church and apparently induced a movement to establish a Republic in Ohio.[52]

Gladden became aware of conditions in the slums only gradually. During the early 1890's he read about slums in New York and London in the popular books of Jacob Riis and Charles Booth, and in the middle of the decade he made personal, though cursory, investigations in both cities. One of the founders of Mansfield House guided him through neighborhoods around the London docks, and Alderman Fleming Williams, a Congregational minister and chairman of the Housing Committee of the London County Council, showed him other slums. During vacations in New York he ventured alone into tenement districts and the Jewish ghetto. Charles Dickens' portrayal of the mixed squalor and heroism of the slums strongly influenced him.[53] But, largely because the poor in Columbus, both Negro and white, lived, not in sprawling slums, but in alleys and courts adjacent to the principal residential streets, he was slow to appreciate

[52] Gladden, "Junior Republic," Sermon, September 13, 1896, Gladden Papers; Washington Gladden, "The Junior Republic at Freeville," *Outlook*, LIV (October 31, 1896), 778–82; *Ohio State Journal*, September 6, 1897; Gladden to William R. George, September 27, October 8, 1913, Virginia M. Murray to George, October 8, 30, 1913, George Junior Republic Records, 1859–1958 (Collection of Regional History and University Archives, Cornell University, Ithaca, New York).

[53] Gladden, Sermons, "Mansfield Settlement," September 30, 1894; September 11, 1896; "My Neighbor in the Slum," November 27, 1904; "Dickens as Preacher," February 4, 1912, Gladden Papers.

conditions at his own doorstep. When in 1910 he accompanied Lawrence Veiller, secretary of the National Housing Association, on an
investigation of housing in Columbus, his discoveries made him
heartsick.[54]

Gladden realized that slums perpetuated the poverty that the
Associated Charities and public relief department tried futilely to
relieve. Though men made slums, slums also made men. Calamity,
sickness, or accident might reduce people to poverty, but the conditions under which they then had to live made their poverty permanent. His program for obliterating slums was threefold. First,
churches and public agencies must take the initial step by encouraging and helping slum-dwellers to move. Besides benefiting the poor
directly, this would make slum property unprofitable. Second, model
tenements, built by philanthropists or the city and operated for a
modicum of profit (he suggested 4 per cent), could provide healthy
conditions for as little as half the rental on slum property. And third,
law and public sentiment must grant the right of the city, either
by strict housing regulations or by condemnation and purchase, to
abolish slums.[55]

Although Gladden regarded immigration as a contributor to unemployment and the swelling ranks of the poor, he never censured the
newcomers to American shores. In the spirit of *noblesse oblige*, he
appealed to the native middle class to assimilate the immigrants to
the American democratic tradition and to American standards of
thrift, industry, and cleanliness—in short, to Christianize them. He
had no doubt that they could become an integral part of American
life.

Fitting the immigrants for citizenship was primary. Gladden
deplored their manipulation by urban political machines and in 1888
suggested a moratorium on naturalization papers between July and

[54] *Ohio State Journal*, September 16, 1910.

[55] Gladden, Sermons, 1884; "Present Needs of the City," Thanksgiving, 1902;
"My Neighbor in the Slum," November 27, 1904; "What I Would Do with
a Million Dollars," May 28, 1905, Gladden Papers. Gladden, *Social Facts and
Forces*, pp. 170–72.

November in presidential election years. Though it had been a mistake to give the ballot to the ignorant, whether immigrants or newly-
freed slaves, it was too late to take it away. But by imposing certain
tests, such as reading the Constitution in English, the country might
avert repetition of the mistake. In addition, Gladden thought that
there should be tests of moral character, and that perhaps paupers
should be denied the franchise. As improvements were made in the
admission of immigrants, however, his optimism about their prospects for citizenship grew, and just before his death he appeared
to favor a reduction in the five-year residence requirement for
naturalization.[56]

Gladden's relative inattention to immigration may have been due
to the small numbers of the foreign-born who settled in Columbus.
There was a large German community on the south side of the city,
but many of them had arrived in the middle decades of the nineteenth century, and they were on the whole sturdy citizens; there
was no tidal wave of immigrants from southern or eastern Europe.
In 1904 the foreign-born constituted less than 10 per cent of the
city's population. Though Gladden believed that there were good
elements among the Poles, Russians, Italians, Greeks, and other
"new" immigrants who came to America in increasing numbers
after 1880, he declared that their "average of intelligence or of efficiency" was not high. Unskilled, often unambitious, and concentrated in ethnic ghettoes in large cities, they intensified the struggle
for life in the lower ranks of society and produced a disproportionate
number of paupers and criminals. Gladden favored stronger immigration laws to eliminate the least promising, but he thought that,
at least until there was machinery to distribute them more effectively, the kindest expedient was to discourage immigration.[57] It is
not clear how he thought this should be done.

Two friends who worked actively with immigrants contributed to

[56] *Ohio State Journal*, November 12, 1888; Washington Gladden, "Who Shall
Exercise the Suffrage?", *Congregationalist*, LXXIV (October 17, 1889), 349;
Gladden, "Citizen Making," [1917,] Gladden Papers.

[57] Gladden, Sermon, December 11, 1904, Gladden Papers.

Gladden's perception of the role immigrants might play in American life. Edward A. Steiner, a Jew who came to America from Carpathian Hungary, entered the Congregational ministry and served churches in Springfield and Sandusky, Ohio, before becoming professor of Applied Christianity at Grinnell College. Steiner's books, especially *From Alien to Citizen* (1914) and *On the Trail of the Immigrant* (1906), fostered sympathetic understanding of the immigrants' problems. He frequently crossed the Atlantic in steerage with groups of immigrants and had a profound appreciation of their customs and mores. Steiner received encouragement from Gladden in at least one trying experience, and it seems likely that Gladden gained insights into the aspirations, abilities, and problems of the immigrants from Steiner.[58]

The second friend, Robert Watchorn, brought Gladden into direct confrontation with the most recent immigrants, those at Ellis Island. Watchorn, who left England as a child, had lived in Columbus in the late 1880's and attended Gladden's evening services for about three years. He was active in unionizing the coal miners of the Hocking Valley, and, when the United Mine Workers union was organized in 1890, he became its first secretary. In January, 1905, Theodore Roosevelt appointed Watchorn, who had become commissioner of immigration in Montreal, to the post of commissioner of immigration in New York. In a preliminary interview Roosevelt had encouraged him to ask Gladden to write to Senator Chauncy Depew

[58] Edward A. Steiner, *From Alien to Citizen: The Story of My Life in America* (New York: Fleming H. Revell Co., 1914); *Ohio State Journal,* May 7, 1896, November 15, 1898, March 15, 1901, March 8, 1902. On one of his visits to Europe, Steiner brought Gladden's writings to the attention of Count Tolstoy, whom he knew personally. Steiner to Gladden, October 25, November 3, 1900, Gladden Papers. When Steiner turned to Gladden in 1902 for counsel during an unpleasant episode with his church in Sandusky involving his ethnic background, Gladden raised the possibility of Steiner becoming pastor of the Plymouth Church in Columbus. Gladden was also involved in the deliberations that led shortly thereafter to Steiner's appointment at Grinnell. Jesse Macy to Gladden, September 3, 1902; Steiner to Gladden, September 13, 16, 22, October 21, 1902, Gladden Papers. Two of Steiner's children remember a visit that Gladden paid to their father at Grinnell. Richard M. Steiner to author, May 31, 1964; Mrs. Clyde B. Hightshoe to author, October 4, 1964.

of New York, whom Gladden knew slightly and for whom the question of patronage was involved. Gladden apparently got Depew to endorse Watchorn, for Watchorn secured the post without difficulty and thereafter held himself in Gladden's debt.[59]

At the time of his appointment Watchorn promised to have "a special latch string . . . hung out" for Gladden, but it was not until January, 1909, that Gladden used it to open the door of Ellis Island. What he saw inspired him. He commended the government's refusal to have criminals, invalids, and paupers dumped on American shores. The people he saw were "strong, vigorous, wholesome folk; most of them are very decently clad; they are thrifty and industrious nearly all of them bring with them some money, . . ." If these were reliable samples, the American people had no reason to fear the immigrants. The protection offered by the federal government against "wolves and harpies" was genuinely Christian and American, an example of its capacity "to care for the larger interests of men." All that worried Gladden was that the welcome extended by the cities and states would be less salutary.[60]

Although the Social Gospel's message of brotherhood theoretically included the Negro, its exponents were for the most part strikingly silent on the problems of race in the United States. The Protestant churches had contributed much zeal and leadership to the anti-slavery movement before the Civil War, and they had been in the forefront of efforts during Reconstruction to educate and elevate the freedmen. But after Reconstruction this crusading and often equalitarian ardor waned, as northern churchmen acquiesced in the southern view of the Negro and in the southern prescription of segregation in racial relations. One social gospeler, Josiah Strong, though in some of his statements opposed to racial prejudice, actually did much to popularize pseudo-scientific racist theories of

[59] *Ohio State Journal*, May 1, 13, July 23, 1889, August 31, 1890, May 22, 1893; Robert Watchorn to Gladden, January 9, 26, 1905, Gladden Papers; John L. Sewall, "A Host with Two Million Guests," *Congregationalist*, XCII (September 21, 1907), 370.

[60] Gladden, Sermon, January 31, 1909, Gladden Papers.

Anglo-Saxon superiority, especially in his most widely circulated book, *Our Country* (1885). Others, notably Walter Rauschenbusch, found the problems of race so complex that they avoided commenting on them. The churches were not alone, however, in their neglect of the Negro after Reconstruction. The progressive movement, of which the Social Gospel was an integral part, was essentially blind to America's oldest and most persistent social dilemma.[61]

There are several plausible reasons for this ambiguity on race of otherwise progressive clergymen. In the first place, the full-blown Social Gospel was essentially a northern phenomenon, led by northern churchmen whose contact with Negroes and whose involvement in racial relations were rarely more than incidental. It is true that many social gospelers carried on their work in northern cities that already, even before the mass migration of Negroes to the North during World War I, had sizable contingents of Negroes, but they usually had few dealings with these Negro communities.

Second, progressive ministers and religiously oriented social workers were preoccupied with industrial problems and with urban concentrations of the foreign-born, and, consequently, they ignored the plight of Negroes. The literature of the Social Gospel is filled with discussions of unionism, poverty, political reform, temperance, and immigration but contains little reference to racial problems.

Third, many of the social gospelers were confused, or at least uncertain, as to the implications of evolution for racial theories. They took common ground in accepting evolution despite the objections of theological conservatives, and they did so without letting social theories based on evolution (such as the conservative Social Darwinism of Herbert Spencer and William Graham Sumner) justify the exploitation of the economically weak. But the meaning of evolution for racial theories was more perplexing and divisive. To many of them the conclusion seemed inevitable that the races were at differ-

[61] David M. Reimers, *White Protestantism and the Negro* (New York: Oxford University Press, 1965), pp. vii, 51–54; Thomas F. Gossett, *Race: The History of an Idea in America* (Dallas: Southern Methodist University Press, 1963), p. 189.

ent stages of development in the upward ascent of man. Thus, one can readily find almost casual usage of the words "superior" and "inferior" in the writings not only of Strong but also of Gladden. Sensitive to the need for the churches to assimilate the findings of modern science, the social gospelers may have felt that to attack the concept of racial superiority and inferiority would be to attack an inherent part of the evolution that they accepted.[62]

Finally, the social gospelers, like most other educated northerners at the end of the nineteenth century, succumbed to the southern judgment that Reconstruction had been a tragedy. By implication, any other northern efforts to rearrange the southern way of life would be similarly ill-fated, Gladden, whose own interest in the Negro stemmed from the antislavery movement, repeatedly expounded this view of Reconstruction as a catastrophe. As early as the end of the Civil War itself, he had called for "the utmost delicacy" in the North's treatment of the South as the basic prerequisite to the "new career of amity and concord" that he desired. He had feared that Lincoln's assassination would provoke northern severity and greatly complicate the restoration of the South. And in his *Recollections* he maintained that this was exactly what happened: the "passions engendered by that tragedy have left their blight on the whole subsequent history of this nation."[63]

The basic fallacy in Gladden's assessment of racial relations in the South was that, inverting cause and effect, he attributed the problem of race to the war and Reconstruction. Two assumptions went into this conclusion. First, Gladden minimized the racial dimensions of the causes of the Civil War by arguing, even before Professor William A. Dunning of Columbia University and his students popularized this view, that the main cause of the war had been national sovereignty. "The slavery question was incidental," he declared in 1916. To bolster this interpretation, he allowed himself to believe

[62] Gossett, *Race,* pp. 176–77, 197.

[63] Gladden, Sermons, [1865,] April 19, 1865, Gladden Papers; Gladden, *Recollections,* p. 154.

that, in idyllic racial harmony, southern soldiers marching off to the front had entrusted their wives and children to their slaves. Second, he also accepted the picture of Reconstruction popularized by Dunning and taken up by most historians of his generation. This was a picture of political dominance by corrupt and ignorant Negroes, manipulated by carpetbaggers and scalawags, over a prostrate white populace. "To imagine that it was possible, by any political device whatever," he wrote,

> to invert the natural order of society, and give to the ignorance of the community the supremacy over its intelligence, was an infatuation to which rational legislators ought not to have been subject.

It was this overturning of the natural social order that had "left the southern people angry and sullen," caused the "complete ostracism of the southern men of character and influence," and metamorphosed the mutual trust of the antebellum period into suspicion and hatred.[64]

Two major themes emerge from Gladden's appraisal of the problem of assimilating the Negro into the mainstream of American life: first, though the problem was national, responsibility ultimately belonged to southern whites, particularly those in positions of leadership; second, the Negro must establish his worthiness for full citizenship and social equality. By alienating southern whites and thrusting Negroes into positions for which they were not qualified, Reconstruction, in his opinion, violated these two cardinal principles.

From the 1870's until almost the end of his career Gladden channeled his interest in the Negro into the work of the American Missionary Association, founded in 1846 by the consolidation of several Congregational antislavery missionary societies. At first the American Missionary Association worked among northern Negroes, but when Union armies opened the South to northern influences, it quickly started schools and churches there. Hampton Institute, Tillotson Institute, Atlanta University, Howard University, Fisk Uni-

---

[64] *Sunday Afternoon*, III (August, 1879), 762–63; *Ohio State Journal*, January 10, 1916; Gladden, "Even These Least," Sermon, January 9, 1916, Gladden Papers; Gladden, *Recollections*, p. 179.

versity, Tougaloo University, Straight University, Berea College, and Talladega College were its most important educational institutions, but it also established scores of primary and secondary schools. The importance of the association in training Negro leaders is inestimable. It endeavored to allay white fears and win general southern sympathy for the religious, educational, and industrial training of Negroes. On the issue of segregation in its schools, it pursued a courageous policy at first—probably the most determined opposition to segregation of any religious agency in the South—but gradually acquiesced, like other northern organizations, in the emerging pattern of separate facilities.[65]

Gladden was a member of the association from the beginning of his ministry, and he was probably more active in it than in any other Congregational benevolent society. In an article in 1876 for the *Independent* he approved the association's broad range of activities, and in 1877 he addressed its annual meeting. In 1883 he read a paper on "Illiteracy in the South" showing that, while illiteracy was growing absolutely, it was not growing relative to the population. The same year he was appointed to a committee to work out an agreement with the American Home Missionary Association, a Congregational agency considered by the American Missionary Association to be too willing to allow segregation by planting white churches in areas where the A. M. A. had organized its own congregations. The agreement was a temporary victory for the A.M.A., recognizing its pre-eminent claims to the South.[66] The publisher of the *Century*, Roswell Smith, a liberal contributor to the association, and especially to Berea College, encouraged Gladden's interest and apparently initiated his election to Berea's board of trustees. For a number of years after 1894 Gladden was a vice-president of the

---

[65] Walker, *A History of the Congregational Churches,* pp. 401–6; Reimers, *White Protestantism and the Negro,* pp. 58, 64–65.

[66] Gladden, *Recollections,* p. 368; *Springfield Republican,* September 9, 1876, November 5, 1877; *Ohio State Journal,* November 3, 1883; Reimers, *White Protestantism and the Negro,* pp. 58–59.

association.[67] Though he welcomed a variety of Negro speakers to his pulpit, among them Bishop Benjamin T. Tanner of the African Methodist Episcopal church, most Negroes who appeared under his auspices were connected in some way with the association. They included officers of the association and its affiliated schools, the Fisk Jubilee Singers, Booker T. Washington, and Henry H. Proctor, pastor of the First Congregational Church of Atlanta.[68]

Until the 1890's Gladden sanguinely predicted the eventual triumph of racial harmony through the rise, with the assistance of enlightened whites, of a qualified Negro citizenry. In 1880 he asserted that "no other emancipated people ever made, in the same length of time, an approach to such progress as our freed people have made in the last fifteen years." He urged Negroes in Springfield to learn trades and enter farming.[69] He also condemned segregation in public accomodations both North and South. Denouncing the treatment in Kentucky of the Jubilee Singers of Fisk University, he asserted in 1880:

> If you are indifferent to the color of the barber who twists your nose and rubs your scalp you have no business to raise the question of color in an omnibus. If the color of the waiter who leans over your shoulder at dinner does not trouble you, you have no right to object to the color of some one who sits on the other side of the table.[70]

In a dispute in the mid-1880's with General John Beatty, an Ohio Republican who wanted his party to take new steps to protect Negroes' voting rights, Gladden reaffirmed almost complacently his

[67] Smith to Gladden, July 3, 1884, July 3, December 17, 1885, Gladden Papers; William G. Frost to Gladden, March 26, 1904, Gladden Papers; *Congregationalist*, LXXIX (November 1, 1894), 602, LXXXIII (November 3, 1898), 606–7; *Ohio State Journal*, October 26, 1895.

[68] *Ohio State Journal*, July 4, 1884, November 22, 1890, March 10, 1894, March 7, 1896, March 6, 1897, June 11, 1898, May 12, 1900, October 28, 1905, October 19, 1907, September 18, 1909.

[69] *Good Company*, V (1880), 381–82, VI (September, 1880), 93–94; *Springfield Republican*, June 28, 1881.

[70] *Good Company*, V (1880), 477–78.

satisfaction with racial progress in the South. Quoting Richard T. Greener, a Negro educated at Harvard, he observed that the country was rectifying the mistake of putting political ahead of social progress, and that with growing numbers, increased education, and economic prosperity, Negroes could not long be denied the franchise.[71] He based his optimism on the reports of northern educators and co-operative white southerners. James Poindexter, pastor of the Second Baptist Church and the picturesque leader of the Negro community in Columbus, joined Beatty in criticizing Gladden. Poindexter's information on conditions in the South, taken from the experiences of northern Negroes who tried to teach there, was less encouraging Gladden and Poindexter eventually became good friends, and during Poindexter's last illness Gladden called almost daily to learn his condition and, if possible, to visit with him.[72]

During the 1890's, as racial tension worsened, Gladden's faith was shaken. In 1895 he introduced to the association a resolution condemning lynching, and in 1896, speaking on "Sociological Aspects of A. M. A. Work," he stressed the urgency of dealing with conditions not much better than slavery.[73] When in 1901 he became president of the association (an office he held till 1904), the task of elevating the Negro, complicated by a tide of southern antipathy, seemed as monumental as at any time in the previous forty years. At the same meeting at which it elected Gladden president, the association felt constrained to approve formally Theodore Roosevelt's entertainment in the White House of Booker T. Washington, a product of the association's schools, a gesture that had received widespread censure.[74]

Gladden's presidential address to the association in 1902 com-

[71] *Ohio State Journal,* June 17, 25, 1884.

[72] *Ibid.,* July 1, 17, 1884, February 8, 1907.

[73] *Congregationalist,* LXXX (October 31, 1895), 660; LXXXI (October 29, 1896), 646–49.

[74] Woodbury to Gladden, July 16, September 7, October 8, 1901, Gladden Papers; *Ohio State Journal,* October 23, 1901; *Congregationalist* LXXXVI (November 2, 1901), 690.

bined urgency and reassurance. The problems the association faced in helping all of its charges—Negroes, Chinese, Indians, Puerto Ricans, and mountain whites—were never greater. But, Gladden maintained, the "great fund of altruistic feeling" that had been accumulating in Christian lands would disarm prejudice and conquer hate. Two recent events buoyed his confidence. The organization of the Southern Education Board, partly by prominent southerners, promised to accelerate the education of both Negroes and whites. And the Negro Young People's Educational Congress at Atlanta, in which Negroes trained by the American Missionary Association figured largely, demonstrated the dignity and intelligence that Negroes could attain. Gladden was confident that it could not be "the prevailing purpose of the people of any portion of this country to keep any part of its population in a permanently subject condition."[75]

The year 1903 marked an important development in Gladden's appraisal of the needs of Negroes. Invited to deliver the baccalaureate sermon at Atlanta University, to address the university's eighth annual conference on the Negro, and to preach in the First Congregational Church of Atlanta, a Negro church, he made one of his few trips to the South.[76] Two things happened on this journey. He saw living conditions among southern Negroes that he considered worse than urban slums. The state of those in rural areas was "far more hopeless than that of their fathers." And he met, apparently for the first time, W. E. Burghardt DuBois, then a young professor at Atlanta University and director of the conference.[77] On the train from Atlanta to Columbus he read DuBois' *The Souls of Black Folk* (1903). Two recent tendencies underscored by DuBois in this book alarmed him: the complete disfranchisement of Negroes in most

[75] Gladden, Address, [October 23,] 1902, Gladden Papers; *Congregationalist*, LXXXVII (November 1, 1902), 636–37.

[76] Horace Bumstead to Gladden, January 22, 1903; W. E. Burghardt DuBois to Gladden, January 24, 1903; Proctor to Gladden, April 14, 1903, Gladden Papers.

[77] Beginning in 1895 DuBois had taught at Wilberforce University in Ohio, an institution of the African Methodist Episcopal church, and it is possible that Gladden had met him during that period. *Ohio State Journal*, February 2, 1895.

parts of the South; and the disparagement of higher education for Negroes. Although the American Missionary Association had always capped its system of primary and secondary schools with colleges and universities, Gladden, without depreciating higher education, had accepted the thesis of Booker T. Washington's Atlanta Compromise of 1895 that the Negro must concentrate on industrial education and economic security, not social or political equality.[78] But after reading *The Souls of Black Folk* he agreed with DuBois that economic progress would not automatically open these other doors.

Gladden's address to the association in October, 1903, reflected increasing realism toward the problems confronting Negroes. This realism stemmed in part from such portentous events as James K. Vardaman's successful appeal to anti-Negro feeling in his campaign for the governorship of Mississippi and the murder of Laforest A. Planving, a Negro graduate of Straight University who, under the auspices of the American Missionary Association, had founded the Pointe Coupée Industrial and High School at Oscar, Louisiana. As president of the association, Gladden wrote to the governor of Louisiana, requesting an investigation of Planving's murder.[79] Gladden's keynote was that the future of the Negro was a national problem, requiring co-operation between the North and progressive southerners: "The health, the peace, the vigor of our national life are involved in the destiny of this race." While he did not think that the association should try to win southern sympathy by allowing any suggestion of Negro inferiority to penetrate its schools, he counseled against teaching Negroes to demand social equality, opposed interracial contacts that might lead to intermarriage, and defended sepa-

[78] Gladden, Sermons, "The Race Problem," May 31, 1903; "Booker Washington," November 17, 1901, Gladden Papers.

[79] *Congregationalist*, LXXXVIII (September 12, 1903), 359; C. J. Ryder, circular letter, to Gladden, September 3, 1903, Alfred Lawless, Jr., to Gladden, January 30, February 1, 3, 1904, Gladden Papers. Though lynchings declined after a peak in 1892, Gladden was aware of the racial hatred reflected in their persistence and frequency after the turn of the century. Just before the sessions of the association in 1903 he preached on their legal and sociological causes. Gladden, "Murder as an Epidemic," Sermon, September 27, 1903, Gladden Papers.

rate schools and churches as the best training ground for Negroes. "We stand," he declared, "for no unnatural fusion of races, for no impracticable notions of social intercourse; but we do stand for perfect equality for the Negro before the law, and behind the law. . . . "[80] Apparently, he did not see any conflict between racial equality and segregation.

In 1904 Gladden laid down the presidency of the association because of his election as moderator of the National Council of the Congregational Churches. Quoting sympathetic southern educators, he urged greater vigor in promoting higher education. He introduced DuBois, who commended the association as the first organization to stand unwaveringly for comprehensive education for Negroes, and charged every member of the audience to read *The Souls of Black Folk*.[81] Though after 1904 Gladden was not involved in the administrative work of the association, he continued to be active in its annual meetings and to promote its activities. In addition, he spoke on several Negro platforms—Wilberforce University in Ohio in 1915, Atlanta University in 1917, a Negro "law and order" meeting in Columbus in 1907, and, on Emancipation Day in 1915, for the Columbus branch of the National Association for the Advancement of Colored People.[82]

Addressing the association in 1906 at the urgent request of its officers, who sensed mounting opposition to the Negro in the North, Gladden outlined two courses the nation could take in its dealings with the Negro: elevation to full citizenship or reduction to serfdom. Both movements were under way. Serfdom, the repression demanded by Vardaman of Mississippi and "Pitchfork" Ben Tillman of South Carolina, could result only in complete geographical segre-

[80] Washington Gladden, *The Negro's Southern Neighbors and His Northern Friends* (New York: Congregational Rooms, [1903]).

[81] Gladden, Address, [October 20, 1904,] Gladden Papers; *Congregationalist*, LXXXIX (October 29, 1904), 620.

[82] W. S. Scarborough to Gladden, January 19, 27, 1915, Thomas J. Brown to Gladden, April 12, 1917, Gladden Papers; *Ohio State Journal*, November 2, 1907, September 18, 1915.

gation of the races. Their program sprang from an unwarranted fear
of racial mingling—unwarranted because in all the activities of the
American Missionary Association there had been neither rape of
white teachers nor a tendency toward miscegenation—and from simple racial hatred. The movement toward serfdom blotted the North's
record, too, particularly in widespread efforts to keep Negroes out
of the trades. But confident that the attitude of progressive southerners would prevail, Gladden told his audience that a pervasive
movement was under way in the South to prepare Negroes for citizenship. The logic of the Christian doctrine of brotherhood was on
the side of this latter movement, and its success was therefore certain. Shortly after Gladden made this address to the association, a
mass meeting of Negroes at the Shiloh Baptist Church in Columbus
passed a resolution of gratitude for his public statements on behalf
of their race.[83]

Gladden prepared the address for publication, and Ida M. Tarbell
and John S. Phillips printed it in the *American Magazine* just before
they began to run Ray Stannard Baker's articles, "Following the
Color Line," which were published as a book in 1908. According to
Gladden, his article created quite a stir in the South. The letters
he received were mostly "bitter and violent, and sadly lacking in
logic," and they convinced him that "the Negroes of the South have
never, since the proclamation of emancipation, been exposed to more
serious perils than those which now environ them."[84]

This conviction reflected a realism that Gladden had come only
gradually to accept. Disposed to take long views of human history,
he had considered the progress of Negroes after the Civil War satisfactorily rapid and diversified. Though the North tended to forget

[83] Ryder to Gladden, September 28, 1906, Gladden Papers; *Ohio State
Journal,* October 26, 27, 1906; *Congregationalist,* XCI (November 3, 1906),
479. Gladden repeated substantially the same ideas in *Recollections,* "The Negro
Problem," pp. 369–76, written at about the same time as this address.

[84] John S. Phillips to Gladden, October 31, 1906, Gladden Papers; Washing-
ton Gladden, "The Negro Crisis: Is the Separation of the Two Races to Become
Necessary?", *American Magazine,* LXIII (January, 1907), 296–301; Gladden,
Sermon, February 13, 1907, Gladden Papers.

the Negroes whom it had freed, Gladden maintained a high level of interest in their improvement and worked through the American Missionary Association to meet their educational and religious needs. Reaction in the South against Negroes during and after the 1890's threatened to undo the gains of nearly forty years and to reduce them to what Gladden considered serfdom. It was this turn of events that shook Gladden's optimistic assessment of racial progress and made him realize the deep roots of racial hatred.

His views became increasingly realistic in a second important way. Until the early years of the twentieth century he tended to emphasize the duties of Negroes rather than their rights. Economic and educational improvement must precede, he thought, political and social equality. After reading DuBois' *The Souls of Black Folk,* he saw more clearly than before that political and social equality did not automatically follow economic and educational improvement, and that the denial of the former strongly impeded the achievement of the latter. Still, he tacitly assented to segregation as the best way in which Negroes could develop and ultimately make a great contribution to American life. His acceptance of segregation was not based on racism but on his assumption that Negroes could not exercise social equality fully until they achieved the standards of the white majority. Nevertheless, he might have neglected the plight of American Negroes altogether, as did most Americans in the progressive era. He was a busy pastor with more immediate social problems to preoccupy him. His interest testifies to the breadth of his humanitarianism.

Eleven

The Salvation of the City

The Social Gospel was essentially an urban movement. Its exponents were men—often, like Gladden, the products of rural communities—who saw that urbanization posed new problems for the churches. Many of them, like Gladden and Josiah Strong, proclaimed that a struggle for civilization was occurring in the cities. Strong implied this in *Our Country* (1885) and stated it explicitly in *The Challenge of the City* (1907).[1] Gladden lamented that American cities, which ought to be the "flower of civilization," were often instead the "smut of civilization." "Our cities," he maintained, "are the battle ground of Christian civilization; they are destined to become, more and more, the arena upon which our greatest conflicts for liberty and order and morality are to be waged."[2]

The city challenged the churches in several ways. It forced many of them to experiment with types of religious work oriented to urban conditions, such as Gladden's Bethel Sunday School and West Side Social Center. Others declined the challenge and followed their prosperous parishioners to the suburbs. Furthermore, the major

[1] Strong spoke on this theme under Gladden's auspices, and Gladden based a series of midweek services on *The Challenge of the City*. Strong to Gladden, April 20, May 4, November 27, December 10, 1908, Gladden Papers.

[2] Gladden, Sermons, "The Weapons of Our Warfare," February, 1888; February 21, 1892, Gladden Papers.

issues with which social gospelers dealt—industrialism, poverty, and immigration—were primarily, if not exclusively, urban problems. Finally, the rapid growth of cities paralyzed urban government and threatened civic integrity and public order. This chapter deals with the last challenge.

Regarding the city as a natural expression of man's social proclivities, Gladden insisted that of all political spheres it had the greatest effect on the individual. As the primary unit through which citizens could promote their common welfare, and existing to increase "the convenience, the comfort, the safety, the happiness, the welfare of the whole people," municipal government should expand its functions into areas closed to the national government. Gladden envisioned a marked extension of socialism on the urban level, as people discovered many things that they could do better co-operatively than individually. He particularly cherished the idea of the city providing art and music, which he especially enjoyed himself, and recreation for its residents.[3]

Like the Hebrew prophets, Gladden considered the city a religious entity. Ideally, city and church would share the work of salvation, a social as well as personal work. The Kingdom of God, Gladden asserted,

> is going to take hold of the world in a way that will tell immediately and directly on the interests that are central and vital. It is going to register itself at the police court, at the city prison, at the work house, in the Council Chamber.

He told his congregation that if God's "active presence is more clearly revealed in one place than in another, it is probably in the City Hall over there, for that is the vital center of this city."[4] In an original story in 1896, "A Christmas Eve at the End of the Twenty-

---

[3] Gladden, *Social Facts and Forces*, pp. 163–65, 174–78; Gladden, Sermons, "The Social Significance of Pictures," February 24, 1901, "The Social Significance of Music," March 3, 1901, Gladden Papers.

[4] Gladden, Sermons, December 4, 1898, "The City as a Savior," July 18, 1909, Gladden Papers; *Ohio State Journal*, January 19, 1914.

fourth Century," he portrayed the ideal city, Iramopolis, which had
no slums or saloons, and the center of which was a cathedral, the
seat of a united church. On another occasion he described the ideal
city as an institute of rights, the custodian of pure morality, a great
educational institution, and the promoter of welfare and happiness.
Until Americans caught the ideal of the city as "a great social organism, bound together by bonds that are not wholly economic," good
municipal government would be illusive.[5]

The contrast between this ideal and American cities in the nineteenth century dispirited Gladden. He saw many reasons for misrule:
corrupt alliances among politicians and between politicians and
public-service corporations; the intellectual and moral debasement
of the urban population by immigration from rural areas and abroad,
indiscriminate charity, and the exodus of the churches and the established classes; manipulation by state legislatures; partisanship and
the orientation of urban to national parties; and "the disease of local-
ism" fostered by ward politics.[6] Gladden averred that three groups
profited from the weakness of municipal governments: political
spoilsmen, public-service corporations, and the "vicious classes,"
saloonkeepers, gamblers, and their allies. Each had a vested interest
in perpetuating that weakness.[7] Against each Gladden proved a
zealous foe.

But for one episode, Gladden had little opportunity to work for
urban reform until he settled in Columbus. North Adams and Springfield were small, well-managed communities with strong traditions
of good citizenship. New York, on the other hand, was a burgeoning
metropolis where all of the forces threatening urban order were
intensified. When Gladden joined the staff of the *Independent* and

[5] *Ohio State Journal*, December 28, 1896; Gladden, Sermons, "The City That
Ought to Be," April 4, 1897, "Good Citizen," June 27, 1909, "Civic Religion,"
April 23, 1911, Gladden Papers.

[6] Gladden, *Social Facts and Forces*, pp.183–88; Gladden, *Social Salvation*,
pp. 206 f.

[7] Gladden, "What Can We Do for Our City Government?", Sermon, November 19, 1899, Gladden Papers.

settled in Brooklyn, the *New York Times* and *Harper's Weekly* were just beginning their exposures of the Tweed Ring. In April, 1871, the *Independent* denounced the ring as "a corrupt, self-constituted and practically a self-elected oligarchy," and by August, Gladden recalled, "the exposure had been so complete that no vestige of doubt was left in anybody's mind as to the guilt of the confederates."[8]

During William Hayes Ward's vacation in August, Gladden had complete charge of the paper. He faced, as he later put it, "one of the times of my life when I have come across something that needed to be hit and have had a chance to strike hard." Declaring that "the gates of the Tombs have never opened to receive criminals of deeper dye," criminals who conspired "not only against property, but against life and public virtue as well," he barraged the public with the facts uncovered by the *Times* and *Harper's.*[9] To Tweed's defiant reply, "What are you going to do about it?" he answered:

> We are going to turn you and all your creatures out of your offices. . . . We are going to get back as much as we can of the booty you have stolen. . . . We are going to use our best endeavors to send you to your own place, the penitentiary. At any rate, we are going to make the city and whole country too hot for you. . . . You have perverted our laws. You have corrupted our young men. You have done what in you lay to destroy our Government. There are some sins that a nation may never forgive, and yours is among them. . . . God may have mercy on you; but, as for us, we promise you that your ill-gotten booty shall be but a poor compensation for the inheritance of shame which shall be yours forever.[10]

The public fulfilled Gladden's declaration. Mass meetings in Cooper Institute led to effective prosecution by a citizens' committee, and the public obloquy to which Gladden contributed through the influential religious journal sealed the ring's fate. The *Independent* followed the case during the fall of 1871; and when Tweed died in

[8] *Independent*, XXIII (April 13, 1871); Gladden, *Recollections*, p. 204.

[9] Gladden, *Recollections*, p. 205; Rudolph, "Washington Gladden," pp. 77–79; *Independent*, XXIII (August 24, 1871).

[10] *Independent*, XXIII (August 31, 1871), 4.

1878, Gladden pronounced a final censure upon him in *Sunday Afternoon*.[11] This episode contributed to Gladden's lifelong interest in movements for reform in New York.

Columbus had all of the problems, except perhaps immigration, of modern cities. It was the capital of Ohio, and partisanship was more intense than anywhere Gladden had previously resided. It contained most of the state's charitable institutions, which were often political footballs. But it was more than a political center. Though conservative, economic growth was rapid and diversified. Columbus became an important railroad and manufacturing center, noted especially for its production of machinery and carriages. A diversified and prosperous agricultural region surrounded the city, and nearby were extensive resources of coal, gas, and limestone.[12] Population grew rapidly after the Civil War. In 1860 it stood at 18,554, in 1870 it had reached 31,274, and by 1880, three years before Gladden's arrival, it was 51,674. From 1880 to 1890, when it had 90,398 residents, Columbus grew faster than any other city in Ohio: while the state's population increased not quite 15 per cent, Columbus grew 75, Akron 67, Cleveland 63, and Toledo 62 per cent. By 1900 its population was over 125,000, and by 1910 it exceeded 180,000.[13] It was hard to keep up with such expansion. Gladden recalled that when he arrived in December, 1882, it was a "holely city," with paving on only Town and High streets, and those in bad condition.[14]

The city's administration in 1882 was as bad as its streets. Gladden remembered that public officials

> were often drunk in their offices. We had shooting affrays in the public places which were treated as jokes by the magistrates. We had news-

[11] Gladden, *Recollections*, p. 206; *Independent*, XXIII (September 7, 1871), 6, (November 16, 1871), 4; *Sunday Afternoon*, I (June, 1878), 565–66.

[12] Studer, *Columbus, Ohio*, p. 99; Roderick Peattie, ed., *Columbus, Ohio: An Analysis of a City's Development* (Columbus: Published by the Industrial Bureau of Columbus, Chamber of Commerce, 1930), pp. 18–19, 24–27, 32–33.

[13] Peattie, *Columbus, Ohio*, p. 3; *Ohio State Journal*, September 13, 1890.

[14] *Ohio State Journal*, December 19, 1912.

papers of large circulation which were supported by blackmail, which
were mainly devoted to the vilification and assassination of the character
of private persons. . . . The gambling houses were as wide open and as
well known as the restaurants, the big gamblers were conspicuous person-
ages on the public streets . . . and the newspapers occasionaly [*sic*]
reported the amounts won in gaming.[15]

The first and one of the most persistent dilemmas that confronted
Gladden was this breakdown in public order. During his first year
in Columbus he urged his own and other congregations, besides
awakening the public to the dangers of intemperance, to demand
the enforcement of existing laws against gambling and selling liquor
to minors and on Sundays, and he called for an ordinance closing
saloons by midnight. Calling attention to open violation of the gambling and liquor laws several months later, he urged participation
in party primaries to secure candidates who would enforce them.
Though hoping that the Republican primary the next Wednesday
evening would be over in time for people to attend prayer meeting,
he stressed the greater importance of the primary: "A man who
will neglect the primaries of his party to go to prayer-meeting is a
mighty poor Christian."[16]

In 1884 the Sunday revelers grew increasingly bold. Saloons were
crowded and disorderly, drunken men and women careened through
the streets at breakneck speed, and noise from the baseball park
echoed downtown. Gladden censured law-breaking from the pulpit
and met with several of his parishioners and other indignant citizens
to initiate prosecution and plan a protest meeting at the city hall.
After pointing out that a Sunday law re-enacted by both Republican and Democratic legislatures in 1882, 1883, and 1884 could
scarcely be considered archaic, he got the mass meeting to demand
its enforcement.[17]

[15] Gladden, Sermon, February 26, 1911, Gladden Papers.

[16] Gladden, "After the Elections," Sermon, October 14, 1883, Gladden Papers;
Washington Gladden, *The Consecration of the People: A Thanksgiving Sermon*
(Columbus, Ohio: Press of Nitschke Bros., 1883), pp. 14–19; *Ohio State Journal,*
March 17, 1884.

[17] *Ohio State Journal,* May 19, 24, June 23, July 17–18, 1884.

Like most similar efforts in Columbus during the 1880's, this attempt to secure law enforcement was unsuccessful. In 1885 Gladden again excoriated the lack of public spirit that could be seen in the city's failure to erect orphanages, hospitals, libraries, and art galleries and the weakness of public conscience that resulted in Columbus being "undoubtedly the worst governed of the cities of Ohio." Officials had allowed a prize fight in city hall, despite a state law against prize fighting, and rowdies from Cincinnati and Cleveland, where the authorities enforced the law, had come to Columbus to satisfy their lust for violence.[18]

Endeavoring to prick the public conscience, Gladden returned to the question year after year. In 1886 after studying the state's liquor laws, he called for stronger legislation against selling to minors and, since intemperance produced more crime and distress on Sundays than on other days, against selling on Sundays.[19] Doubting the wisdom of prohibition without overwhelming public support, he endorsed local option, which he had seen working effectively in Massachusetts. He emphasized that, though Neal Dow, the father of prohibition in Maine, considered him a vassal of the liquor dealers, he still thought of the "rum power" as "a vast, towering, overwhelming curse, against which all honest citizens ought to be in solid array."[20] In 1887 he announced the circulation of ominous

[18] Gladden, "What Will Become of Columbus?", Sermon, March 15, 1885, Gladden Papers.

[19] Gladden's argument for laws regulating conduct on Sundays was not based on religious grounds. In an address in 1889 to the Ohio Sabbath Association, which he had helped organize in 1888, he justified a statutory day of rest as essential to the public welfare. *Ohio State Journal*, December 12, 1888, February 22–23, 1889; Gladden, "The Civil Sabbath—Its Authority," [February 23, 1889,] Gladden Papers.

[20] Gladden, Sermons, "The State and Temperance," February 14, 1886; "Good Morals in Columbus," March 21, 1886, Gladden Papers. In Springfield, Gladden had worked actively to induce the aldermen to grant fewer licenses each year and spearheaded a Society for the Prevention of Crime, which prosecuted violators of the liquor laws and attempted to deny them licenses. The number of licenses declined from at least 144 in 1875 to 67 in 1881. Openly breaking with the prohibitionists, who in turn denounced him, he criticized their doctrinaire devotion to a single remedy for intemperance, their reliance on legal rather than moral means, and the failure of prohibition to prohibit. *Springfield*

threats "that the pastor of this church has to stop talking on this subject; that if he does not something serious will happen to him." The laws were moderate, even lenient, he observed, and obstinate disobedience spelled anarchy. "If you say nothing," he warned his congregation,

> if you do nothing, you rank yourselves with the anarchists. They have made the issue. They have said that the law shall not be enforced. Silence and inaction on your part consents to their decree, and puts the government of the city under their feet.

For the first time since he came to Columbus, the city council was considering a midnight-closing ordinance to supplement the state's laws against selling to minors and on Sundays. Gladden supported this ordinance but also called for enforcement of existing laws.[21]

Gladden spent part of his vacation in 1887 gathering information about law enforcement in eleven cities comparable to Columbus. At his invitation the mayor, several councilmen, and many prominent citizens attended the First Church and heard him report that these other cities allowed no open gambling and either wholly or partially enforced Sunday-closing laws. Driven out of other cities, he asserted, gamblers "found a shelter and safe refuge in Columbus," which was getting a reputation as "the snug harbor of the gambling fraternity." The community could not accept present conditions:

Republican, May 1, 17, September 18, 1875, April 14, 16, 22, May 13, 1879, April 13, 26, May 1, September 16, 20, October 19, November 8, 10, 18, 23, 1880, January 15, April 4, 8, 11, 20, 26, May 5, June 1, September 13, October 19, November 28, December 5, 1881; *Sunday Afternoon,* I (February, 1878), 181, (April, 1878), 377–78; *Good Company,* IV (1879), 185–86, V (1880), 90–91, 190–91; John R. Henly to Gladden, April 11, 1881, Gladden Papers. Gladden's fight with the prohibitionists continued in Columbus. Led by Dow, who resented Gladden's analysis of the defects of prohibition in Maine, they castigated him in the press, intimating that he was, if not the conscious, at least the unwitting, ally of the saloonists. *Ohio State Journal,* February 20, March 24, April 13, 28, May 1, 1883; Neal Dow to Gladden, March 16, 1883, William H. Fenn to Gladden, March 26, 1883, F. E. Clark to Gladden, April 5, 1883, Joshua L. Chamberlain to Gladden, April 7, 1883, Anson Phelps Tinker to Gladden, April 18, 1883, Gladden Papers.

[21] Gladden, "Good Order—Morals in Columbus," Sermon, [May 5, 1887,] Gladden Papers.

. . . the brawl of the all-night gin-mill, or the Sunday devoted to guz-
zling and carousing, or the troops of gamblers lying in wait at the doors
of their dens, or the droves of prostitutes filling High street so full at
night that decent women can not walk them unattended.[22]

The next year brought decided improvement. Gladden and the
Roman Catholic bishop of Columbus, John A. Watterson, endorsed
a citizens' league organized in December, 1887, to work mainly for
enforcement of the Sunday-closing law.[23] In the municipal election
in April, 1888, the reformers tasted victory. When the city council
rejected the midnight-closing ordinance, a wave of independent voting swept into office a new council that enacted the ordinance at its
first meeting. Under pressure from Gladden and the citizens' league,
it also passed an ordinance requiring the mayor and police board
to comply with the state's Sunday-closing law. Gladden heralded
this action in a sermon, "There Was Great Joy in That City," portraying families reunited for the first Sunday in many years.[24]

But his jubilation was short-lived. In September, 1888, noting an
organized rebellion against liquor and gambling laws, he expressed
his willingness to call out the militia. And in 1890 he circulated a
petition among the churches asking Mayor Philip Bruck to enforce
the laws.[25] Bruck enforced the midnight-closing law and broke up
the gambling dens, for which Gladden commended him, but the
saloons continued open Sundays. In January, 1891, Gladden urged
a citizens' league formed to work for enforcement of the Sunday-
closing law to "Agitate, agitate! Turn on the light!" He maintained,
however, that only municipal reorganization would assure permanent reform. Control of the police force rested with a board of five
commissioners, including the mayor, who also served as police judge.
Each commissioner could deny his responsibility for non-enforce-

[22] *Ohio State Journal*, September 3, 5, 1887.

[23] *Ibid.*, December 31, 1887, January 7, 17, 1888.

[24] Gladden, Sermons, "After the Verdict," April 8, 1888, "There Was Great
Joy in That City," May 13, 1888, Gladden Papers; *Ohio State Journal*, April 24,
26, May 5, 7–9, 14, 1888.

[25] *Ohio State Journal*, September 24, 1888, September 29, 1890.

ment of the laws. Gladden advised the league to work for municipal reorganization that would "give a single executive entire control of the police department and ample power to enforce its laws."[26]

Gladden's interest in strengthening the executive arm of municipal government was not new. Impressed by the reorganization of Brooklyn under Seth Low, he had appeared in 1885 before the newly formed Columbus Board of Trade to advocate Brooklyn's system, popularly known as the federal plan because it provided for a single executive, the mayor, and a legislative council. He called the five-member police board, with one member elected each year for a four-year term, a "hydra-headed monster" and a refuge of "rascality." The board of trade referred the question to its committee on legislation, and after about a year the committee reported in favor of the federal plan. In 1887 Gladden arranged for Low, whom he had met earlier that year in Washington at a convention of the Evangelical Alliance, to address a meeting in the First Church under the auspices of the University Club.[27]

Following Gladden's advice, the Citizens' League decided on March 5, 1891, to petition the legislature for a new charter on the federal plan. On March 12 Gladden stressed the necessity of abolishing the "present rickety, slipshod, imbecile, patched-up and insulting form of city government" and urged the Citizens' League to put pressure on the legislature then in session.[28] A delegation consisting of Mayor Bruck, the city solicitor, two police commissioners, and several citizens presented a federal-plan bill to one of the senators representing Columbus, but, despite his efforts, and largely because

[26] Gladden, "Victories in Columbus," Sermon, 1890, Gladden Papers; *Ohio State Journal,* January 6, 10, 1891.

[27] *Ohio State Journal,* December 2, 1885, December 8, 1886, December 30, 1887; Gladden to Gilder, May 17, 1888, *Century* Collection; Gladden, *Recollections,* p. 329. Gladden closely followed and endorsed Low's unsuccessful independent campaign for the mayoralty of New York City in 1897 and his successful campaign in 1901. Gladden, Sermons, "The Fight for Civilization Now Going on in New York," October 17, 1897; "Roosevelt and Low," December 8, 1901, Gladden Papers.

[28] *Ohio State Journal,* January 23, 30, February 6, 11, 21, 28, March 6, 13, 1891.

one of the representatives from Columbus vigorously opposed it, the bill failed to pass.[29] Gladden addressed a mass meeting of about eight hundred citizens on behalf of the bill, defended it against General John Beatty's allegation that it gave autocratic power to the executive, preached in its favor, and at the time of the crucial vote lobbied for it.[30]

After two more years of agitation Columbus finally got a federal-plan charter. Gladden opened the campaign in 1892 with two sermons on municipal politics. Raising the question "Have we any longer a republican form of government?", he decried legislative interference with municipal charters for the purpose of giving one party dominance. In the second sermon, "Who Ought to Govern Columbus?", he called for a constitutional amendment granting municipal home rule under the federal plan and criticized the Daugherty bill, a Republican "ripper" bill designed to oust the Democrats, who in 1890 had passed their own "ripper" bill for Columbus.[31] The *Ohio State Journal*, a Republican paper favoring the Daugherty bill, criticized Gladden's "Utopian idea of federalism," while the *Columbus Dispatch*, also a Republican paper, staunchly supported the federal plan.[32]

In November, 1892, Gladden again urged the Columbus Board of Trade to work for municipal home rule and the federal plan, which he considered "simply the American plan of administration." The board sent copies of his address, "The Government of Cities," to members of the legislature, with a letter from its president, William F. Burdell, commending Gladden's views as "worthy of the candid consideration of all men." The board then initiated primaries in each

[29] *Ibid.*, March 13–14, 16, 20–21, 25–26, 1891.

[30] *Ibid.*, March 17, 24–25, 1891; Gladden, "Our City and Its Government," Sermon, March 22, 1891, Gladden Papers.

[31] Gladden, "Have We Any Longer a Republican Form of Government?", Sermon, January 10, 1892, Gladden Papers; *Ohio State Journal*, January 16, February 22, 1892. Gladden had denounced an unsuccessful Democratic "ripper" bill in 1885, as well as the bill that did pass in 1890. *Ohio State Journal*, March 9, 14, 26, 1885, April 8, 1890.

[32] *Ohio State Journal*, March 17, April 8, 19, 1892.

ward to select delegates to a charter convention. The delegates divided into two distinct groups: a large majority of thirty-four Republicans supported the Daugherty bill, while a minority of four Democrats and seven Republicans wanted a straightforward federal plan. When the convention met in December, 1892, it elected Judge George K. Nash chairman and appointed a committee of seven under Henry C. Taylor to prepare a charter bill. Taylor had been chairman of the board of trade's committee on legislation that had studied Gladden's proposal in 1885. The committee recommended and the convention approved a bill on the federal plan. Though the *Ohio State Journal* thought it would "make a local monarch out of the next man elected," it saw deliverance from Democratic rule in any reorganization and pleaded for unity on the bill. By the end of February the bill had passed both houses, and it went into effect in the municipal election in April, 1893.[33]

This civic awakening did not occur in a vacuum. The federal plan enjoyed considerable vogue in the 1890's, and many cities turned to it as a device for improving administrative efficiency and law enforcement. In addition, numerous civic organizations and municipal leagues appeared in the early 1890's to study urban problems and encourage scientific government. Gladden contributed to this movement in several ways. He wrote "The Cosmopolis City Club," a serial novel about a fictional group of men who investigated urban conditions, exposed abuses, and successfully reorganized their city on the federal plan. It first appeared in the *Century* and then as a small volume in 1893. Gladden later claimed that five such leagues were born in 1892, nine in 1893, and twenty-six in 1894. He participated directly in the organization of the City Club of New York, which, at the suggestion of Professor E. R. A. Seligman, elected him a member in 1904; and, according to his testimony, his story had some influence in the formation in 1894 of the Civic Federation of Chicago, which he addressed that same year. He also endorsed the federal plan in 1894 before the Congregational Club of Chicago,

[33] *Ibid.*, November 2, 16, 20, 25, December 2, 7, 24, 1892, January 8–9, February 24, March 1, 1893.

many of whose members were active in civic affairs.[34] He participated in the National Conference for Good Government, held in
Philadelphia in January, 1894, out of which grew the National Municipal League. Writing to Richard W. Gilder about the forthcoming
conference, at which he, Edwin D. Mead of Boston, W. S. Rainsford, Charles A. Bonaparte, and Theodore Roosevelt were to speak,
Gladden observed that "The Cosmopolis City Club" "got in its work
in good season, didn't it?" He attended meetings of the National
Municipal League in subsequent years and addressed it on several
occasions.[35]

Although Gladden increasingly turned his attention to the structure of municipal government, he continued to demand the enforcement of liquor and gambling laws. Just before the first election
under the federal plan, he reviled the liquor dealers for opposing
reasonable restrictions: "I don't know but their lawless habit will
by and by become so inveterate that we shall be able to get what
we want by enacting ordinances requiring the saloons to be kept
open all night and all day Sunday." He commended the Anti-Saloon
League for its gradualism and urged the election of a mayor who
would enforce the laws.[36] Many Republicans who had backed the

[34] Washington Gladden, "The Cosmopolis City Club," *Century*, XLV (January–March, 1893), 395–406, 566–76, 780–92; Gladden, *Recollections*, pp.
329–30; Oswald Garrison Villard to Gladden, October 25, 1904, Lawrence
Veiller to Gladden, November 22, 1904, Gladden Papers; *Ohio State Journal*,
April 26, 1894; *Congregationalist*, LXXIX (May 3, 1894), 627. In 1895 Gladden
told the Congregational Association of Ohio that victories for reform in several
cities and the passing of popular apathy were signs of a new era in municipal
government. *Congregationalist*, LXXX (May 16, 1895), 771.

[35] Gladden to Gilder, December 22, 1893, *Century* Collection; *Ohio State
Journal*, January 27, 1894, April 24, May 27, 1895, May 5, 1897, February 8,
1899. In 1897 Gladden participated in the formation of a similar organization,
the League of American Municipalities, which limited its membership to
municipal officials, and at its first convention he presented a paper on "The
Federal Plan of Municipal Government." *Ohio State Journal*, September 8,
17, 25, October 1–2, 1897, April 18, 1900.

[36] Gladden, Sermon, March 19, 1893, Gladden Papers. Formally organized
in 1893, the Anti-Saloon League grew out of the efforts of Gladden and other
reformers in Ohio to secure a local option law. Officials of the league considered Gladden one of the most co-operative pastors. His church made contri-

new charter in the hope of gaining control were sadly disappointed when George Karb, a Democrat who, according to the *Ohio State Journal*, represented the "liberal element," won by a narrow margin. After the Ohio Supreme Court decided in a test case initiated by Karb that the new charter was constitutional, however, Karb quickly enforced the Sunday-closing law. Gladden told a large, reform-minded audience in Minneapolis that Columbus had "never enjoyed so excellent an administration." He attributed the improvement to the federal plan, which gave the mayor effective control through his appointment of the directors of the city's four departments.[37]

The Columbus Board of Trade was a constant and leading force for civic improvement. Gladden had close ties with its members, many of whom were his parishioners, and he served on its committee for municipal affairs for many years and as the committee's chairman for several terms.[38] He endorsed the board's temporarily unsuccessful attempt in 1894 to improve the quality of the city council by reducing it from thirty-eight to nineteen members.[39]

In 1894 the board also initiated the Taxpayers' League of Franklin

---

butions to the league, and he welcomed its first director, Howard H. Russell, and other speakers to his pulpit. He supported the league's successful campaigns for residential-district and county option in Ohio and served as a vice-president of the national Anti-Saloon League from as early as 1908 to 1913, when it took up the cause of national prohibition. *Ohio State Journal*, May 22, 1886, June 20, 29, 1887, February 21, 1888, April 14, 19, December 8, 1894, January 20, 1896, February 1, 1897, March 17, November 29, December 4, 1902, November 29, 1903, March 13, April 13, 1904, November 16, 1907, January 20, September 14, 1908, December 10, 1909, May 25, November 11, 13–15, 1913; *Congregationalist*, LXXIX (December 20, 1894), 917; Ernest H. Cherrington, compiler, *The Anti-Saloon League Year Book* (Columbus, Ohio: The Anti-Saloon League of America, 1908–9; Westerville, Ohio: 1910–18); Norman H. Dohn, "The History of the Anti-Saloon League" (unpublished Ph.D. dissertation, Ohio State University, 1959), pp. 21–23, 91–92, 141, 188–90.

[37] *Ohio State Journal*, April 4, 23, June 7, 12, 19, 26, 1893, January 20, 1894. In an article on "Fighting Intrenched Evil at Columbus," the *Congregationalist* reported in February, 1894, that Columbus no longer had a reputation as "the widest open city in America," but that the gamblers had fled to the suburbs. *Congregationalist*, LXXIX (February 22, 1894), 277.

[38] *Ohio State Journal*, February 7, 1894, February 6, 1895, February 5, 1896, February 2, 1898, February 8, 1899, February 16, 1901.

[39] *Ibid.*, February 7–8, March 18, 1894.

County, an organization to promote independence in municipal politics. Once again the board followed Gladden's lead, which in this case was a pre-election sermon underscoring "the absurdity of following party lines in municipal elections."[40] Gladden was on the committee that framed the new organization's statement of principles, and assumed the office of second vice-president. The league plunged into the work of surveillance with zest. It petitioned the city council against renewing and extending streetcar franchises for periods of twenty-five and fifty years without obtaining adequate recompense for the city.[41] Its committee on the board of education, consisting of Gladden and George W. Lattimer, a member of the First Church, charged the board with incompetence. When the board resentfully rejected the report of its own investigating committee, the league's committee, of which George W. Knight, another member of the First Church, had become chairman, attempted in 1896 to defeat unqualified candidates for the board.[42]

More significantly, in 1895 the Taxpayers' League introduced an independent candidate, David E. Williams, into the contest for the mayoralty. The Republicans, who had captured several offices in 1894, nominated Oliver M. Evans on a platform pledging law enforcement, while the Democratic candidate, Cotton H. Allen,

[40] Gladden, "The City Election and Its Issues," Sermon, April 1, 1894, Gladden Papers.

[41] *Ohio State Journal*, October 9, 28, November 10, 13, December 28, 1894, January 8, 24, February 5, May 28, 1895.

[42] *Ibid.*, February 15, December 11, 25, 1895, January 17, February 19, April 1, 1896. One member of the school board claimed that Gladden was "not the emulative gentleman which he poses before the public eye." This was just one of several disputes that Gladden had with the board of education. In 1899, in an attempt to gain control of all appointments, the board fired Abram Brown, a member of Gladden's church who had been in the school system for twenty-five years and principal of the Central High School for fifteen years. All the teachers at the school protested, including Alice Gladden, who resigned. Gladden publicly criticized the board, asserting in an article in the *Independent* that members of school boards were, "as a rule, decidedly less intelligent and less reputable than the persons whom they employ and direct." *Ohio State Journal*, June 15, 17, 23, 28, August 21, September, 9, 1899. In 1900 Gladden supported an unsuccessful attempt by the board of trade to reorganize the school board. *Ohio State Journal*, March 11, 13, 29, April 5, 1900.

refused to commit himself. The issue of streetcar franchises, on which Williams took a stronger stand than the other candidates, was secondary but important. Though nominally Republican, the *Dispatch* again chose independence and reform, while the *Ohio State Journal* declaimed that Williams would split the Republican vote and throw the election to Allen. Such Republicans as Edward Pagels, a former police chief, Burdell, the president of the Taxpayers' League, and General Beatty endorsed Williams. Though unable to attend one meeting of independents, Gladden sent a letter endorsing Williams and gave the final address at another such meeting. According to the *Ohio State Journal,* however, he was almost the only clergyman who risked the defeat of Evans to support Williams. Whether or not the *Journal* was right about this, its prediction that Williams would take enough votes away from Evans to give Allen the victory was evidently correct. Despite a resolution from the city council and a public protest from Gladden, Allen allowed the saloons to reopen on Sundays.[43]

After the election the Taxpayers' League became lost to view. It was replaced in December, 1895, by the Columbus Civic Federation, a reforming organization that grew out of evangelistic services conducted by B. Fay Mills, an aggressive social gospeler. Gladden was active in Mills's meetings and was in the forefront of the new organization. On December 3–4 the participating churches held a "Christian Convention" to discuss "The Sins of the City" and "The Redemption of the City." The consideration of politics fell to Gladden and Howard Russell, the founder of the Ohio Anti-Saloon League. On December 10 a committee under Gladden's chairmanship met to project a federation like the Civic Federation of Chicago, and two days later Gladden reported its plans to an assembly that included Bishop Watterson, Rabbi Weiss, James Kilbourne, a manufacturer and prominent Democratic politician, Joseph A. Jeffrey, the industrialist, and Ralph Lazarus, scion of the city's leading mercantile family. Deciding to hold public meetings only yearly, the Civic

---

[43] *Ohio State Journal,* March 26–27, 31, April 1, May 8, 1895; *Columbus Dispatch,* April 2, 1895.

Federation appointed a council of thirty, which included Gladden and several of his parishioners, to keep watch over the city. At the federation's request the clergy devoted their sermons on December 29 to law enforcement. Refuting Allen's excuses for laxity, Gladden pointed to Karb's successful administration. Several months later, Theodore Roosevelt visited Columbus at Gladden's request to recount his role as police commissioner in reforms in New York City.[44]

Despite its auspicious genesis, the Civic Federation was soon moribund. Samuel L. Black, who became mayor in 1897, partially enforced the liquor and gambling laws, but Gladden disliked his policy of choosing which laws to enforce.[45] When in 1899 the Republican Amity elected a candidate for the mayoralty, Judge Samuel J. Swartz, they prided themselves on having "turned the gang out of power." But scandal soon riddled Swartz's administration. Before the year was over, the city council impeached Joseph W. Dusenbury, the director of public safety, for graft, and a new and indignant Christian Citizens' League mounted a crusade to close saloons and theaters on Sundays. In 1900 another director of public safety resigned following the sensational revelation that he had turned over the regulation of gambling to a local liquor dealer.[46] Though conditions were generally better in 1900 than in 1883, law enforcement still concerned Gladden, and the precariousness of public order required perpetual vigilance on the part of the reformers. Unfortunately, public interest cooled almost as quickly as it became inflamed.

Gladden's service as a city councilman from 1900 to 1902, his most

[44] William G. McLoughlin, Jr., *Modern Revivalism: Charles Grandison Finney to Billy Graham* (New York: Ronald Press Co., 1959), pp. 341–42; *Ohio State Journal*, December 4–5, 11, 13, 24, 30–31, 1895, April 24, 1896; Theodore Roosevelt to Gladden, April 20, 1896, Gladden Papers. It is unclear when Gladden first met Roosevelt. According to *Recollections*, p. 330, Roosevelt began the acquaintance by writing to Gladden. During his vacation several months after Roosevelt's address in Columbus, Gladden visited him in New York to observe conditions under his administration as police commissioner. Gladden, Sermon, [September, 1896,] Gladden Papers.

[45] *Ohio State Journal*, April 6, July 18, September 6, 1897.

[46] *Ibid.*, April 15, July 10, 15, 18, 29, October 7, 1899, October 25, 1900.

direct participation in urban government, deepened his understanding of the complex problems facing the cities in their management of public utilities and their dealings with public-service corporations. Having long preached the duty of "men of substance and standing" to take part in municipal government, as did their peers in the well-governed cities of England and Germany, he felt some obligation to practice what he preached. However, his direct motivation for volunteering his candidacy was a rumor that a ring of councilmen had conspired to insure their own re-election and to make a corrupt alliance with several public-service corporations whose franchises were due to expire. Charles E. Miles, the alderman from his own ward, the seventh, was supposedly in the plot.[47]

Gladden announced through the newspapers on February 13, 1900, that he was willing to represent his ward, but that he would "make no canvass, pay no assessments, ask for no votes," a policy that many regarded as a bit of idealistic folly.[48] Though his church resolved not to discuss his candidacy or take any part in the campaign, many of his parishioners in the seventh ward actively supported him. Reformers were enthusiastic over his decision. Samuel M. Jones, the reforming mayor of Toledo, wrote to encourage him and sent to William Cowell, a former aide, a complete list of his friends and supporters in Columbus whom Cowell might enlist in Gladden's behalf.[49] Among those who congratulated Gladden on

[47] Ibid., March 28, 1901; Gladden, Recollections, pp. 336–37.

[48] According to the Ohio State Journal, he had held "several conferences with his friends," but Gladden claimed that he had consulted no one before announcing his candidacy. Ohio State Journal, February 14, 1900.

[49] Ibid., February 15–16, 1900; William Cowell to Gladden, February 13, 1900, Samuel M. Jones to Gladden, February 19, April 5, 1900, Gladden Papers; Gladden to Jones, February 20, 1900, Samuel M. Jones Papers, courtesy of Samuel M. Jones, III. Gladden and Jones had been friends since at least 1897, when Jones became mayor of Toledo. Jones had wired Gladden, "I am elected in spite of six hundred saloons, the street car company and the devil." Gladden subsequently lectured in Toledo for Jones's Society of Applied Christianity, and Jones spoke at the First Church. After Jones's re-election in 1899 Gladden entertained him in Columbus and commended his practical Christianity in the Outlook. He congratulated Jones on his re-election in 1903 and after his death in 1904 told the First Church that Jones had been the "most thorough-going

either his candidacy or his election were Seth Low, Clinton R.
Woodruff, secretary of the National Municipal League, Edward W.
Bemis, a staff member of the Bureau of Economic Research, Edwin
C. Dinwiddie, an officer of the Anti-Saloon League, S. S. McClure,
Lyman Abbott, and John R. Commons.[50]

Although Gladden refused to campaign personally, a city-wide
citizens' league and a committee of the seventh ward's residents
rallied behind him. The Republicans were certain to renominate
Miles, but the Democrats, hopelessly outnumbered in the wealthy
seventh ward, entertained the idea of putting Gladden on their
ticket. Howard Galbreath, a member of Gladden's committee, tried
to get the Democratic central committee to enter Gladden in their
primary; but, evidently realizing that Democrats would probably
vote for him anyway and that Gladden would have a better chance
as an independent, the committee refused. The *Ohio State Journal*
accused the Democratic planners of attempting to split the Republican vote in the seventh and two other normally Republican wards
by surreptitiously supporting independents. Though not an entry in
the Democratic primary, Gladden received more votes than either
regular candidate for the nomination, and consequently the Democrats did not nominate anyone in the seventh ward. After the primaries Gladden certified that he had spent no money to secure an
independent nomination, but that Galbreath had spent fifty cents
for petitions.[51]

The campaign centered on four issues: the renewal of streetcar

democrat" he had ever known. Hoyt Landon Warner, *Progressivism in Ohio,
1897–1917* (Columbus, Ohio: Ohio State University Press, 1964), pp. 26, 29;
Ohio State Journal, December 18, 1897, June 2, 1899; Gladden to Jones, April
4, 1899, Jones Papers; Washington Gladden, "Mayor Jones of Toledo," *Outlook*,
LXII (May 6, 1899), 17–21; Jones to Gladden, April 23, 1903, Gladden Papers;
Ohio State Journal, July 18, 1904.

[50] Seth Low to Gladden, March 19, 1900; Clinton R. Woodruff to Gladden,
April 10, 1900; Edward W. Bemis to Gladden, April 12, 1900; Edwin C. Dinwiddie to Gladden, April 13, 1900; McClure to Gladden, April 16, 1900; Abbott
to Gladden, April 19, 1900; John R. Commons to Gladden, May 2, 1900,
Gladden Papers.

[51] *Ohio State Journal*, February 16, 23–24, 27, March 3, 13, 1900.

franchises; the granting of franchises to interurban railroads that wanted to enter Columbus; the prices to be set in new contracts with the gas company; and the construction of a new dam for the waterworks. Candidates split into two groups, though not on partisan lines, one group, to which Gladden belonged, promising to secure concessions from the public-service corporations, the other group avoiding any specific commitment. Printing a cartoon of Christopher Columbus demanding on behalf of the people that the candidates state their views, the *Ohio State Journal* solicited comments from the candidates on each issue. Interestingly, Miles stood with the reformers for concessions.[52]

The race in the seventh ward captured the greatest public interest. Commending Miles's record, the *Ohio State Journal* charged that Joseph W. Dusenbury was working to defeat Miles, who had taken part in his impeachment a year earlier. The paper was sure that these tactics were unknown to Gladden, but it quoted a member of his committee as saying, "If Joe Dusenbury does his part we have Miles licked." Gladden's committee worked feverishly the weekend before the election, and he won by a majority of 908 to 832. Attributing his victory to "a remarkable uprising of the people of the Seventh ward," Gladden maintained:

> I have had absolutely nothing to do with it. It has not taken half an hour of my time. My advice has not been asked; I have known of the work only as from time to time I have accidentally heard of it.[53]

The new council consisted of ten Republicans, seven Democrats, and two independents, Gladden and Richard Reynolds, a councilman for twenty-three years who, having lost the Republican nomination, ran as an independent. Perhaps to show him the complexity of the campaign's issues, the Republican majority appointed Gladden chairman of its important committee on gas and electricity and a member of the committees on waterworks, the fire department,

52 *Ibid.*, March 18, 23, 1900.
53 *Ibid.*, April 1, 3, 1900.

railroads and viaducts, and sewers and drainage.[54] Few councilmen were competent to deal with the technical aspects of these problems. Three were lawyers, several owned small businesses, five or six were bookkeepers, one was a physician, and two or three ran saloons.[55] Though at first skeptical of Gladden, they gradually realized that he was not in the council to make speeches, and his relations with them were generally cordial.

Gladden helped forge policies advantageous to the city on three major issues—the streetcar franchises, the gas franchise, and municipal lighting. The public won its clearest victory in the settlement of the streetcar franchises, which in the past the city had granted indiscriminately, for long or indefinite periods of time and with little recompense to the city. The Columbus Street Railway Company, which had absorbed several small companies, claimed that its franchises ran in perpetuity, but the city's director of law, Ira Crum, insisted that several of the most important ones had lapsed. Even before his election Gladden was interested in the problem. In December, 1899, he warned the council against extending the franchises without securing adequate compensation, and in January, 1900, Mayor Swartz invited him to confer with municipal officials and the company's president regarding the rates to be set in a new ordinance.[56]

In February, 1900, the company offered to pay $50,000 in ten years for a twenty-five year extension on High Street, the backbone of its lines. The board of public works, which had joint jurisdiction with the city council, immediately rejected the offer, and Mayor Swartz announced that his administration opposed further piecemeal agreements.[57] On the recommendation of its committee on railroads and viaducts, of which Gladden was a member, the council

[54] *Ibid.,* April 9, 17, 1900.

[55] Gladden, *Recollections,* p. 338.

[56] *Ohio State Journal,* November 9, December 7, 1899, January 11, 25, February 7, 25, 1900; Samuel J. Swartz to Gladden, January 13, 1900, Gladden Papers.

[57] *Ohio State Journal,* February 27, March 3, 1900.

began in April to grant franchises to several interurban roads, which the Columbus Street Railway Company had tried to keep out of the city. Whereas the streetcar company charged five-cent cash fares and twenty-five cents for six tickets, the interurbans agreed to carry passengers within the city for five-cent cash fares and twenty-five cents for seven tickets and, in addition, to pay the city 2 per cent of their gross receipts within the city. In May Gladden opposed attempts by the company to get tacit recognition of the validity of its doubtful franchises, asserting that it had been a "fatal mistake" to allow "the ways and means of communication to be separate from the corporate life of the community."[58]

In June the board of public works declared franchises on thirteen streets forfeited and ordered the company to remove its tracks. But though its committee on railroads and viaducts agreed, the council refused to concur, giving rise to a suspicion of bribery.[59] Taking the initiative again, the company issued a report showing that it was impossible to reduce rates. Gladden refuted these calculations and charged that the company wanted the city to insure dividends on watered stock.[60] When the company then increased its annuity offer from $5,000 to $7,500, the board of public works rejected the new proposal and demanded instead a reduction in fares. Recommending the standard set by the interurbans, Gladden argued that the company had better streets and would reap greater profits than the interurbans. If it was dealing with another business corporation, he insisted, it would never make such an "extortionate demand."[61]

In September the company offered an annuity of $10,000 for ten years and an unspecified percentage of gross receipts, with an alternative plan for twenty-eight tickets for one dollar but no cash pay-

[58] *Ibid.*, April 17, 24, 28, May 1, 15, June 4, 1900.

[59] *Ibid.*, June 19, 26, 28–29, 1900.

[60] *Ibid.*, August 2–3, 1900. In 1905 Gladden generalized that "public service companies, street car lines, gas and electric lighting companies, and all such, are capitalized as a rule for from two to four times the cost of their plants." Gladden, *Christianity and Socialism*, p. 205.

[61] *Ohio State Journal*, July 27–28, September 9, 11, 1900.

ments to the city. Mayor Swartz, Gladden, and Crum opposed the offer, and the board of public works rejected it.[62] While this offer was under review, Gladden addressed the National Municipal League on "The Influence of Public Service Corporations on City Government." To combat overcapitalization and bribery, he recommended state laws enforcing publicity of accounts, limiting capitalization to the cost of physical plants and making stock-watering a penal offense, providing referenda for all public-service franchises, and creating strong regulatory boards. But his own conviction was "that nothing will reach the case except the public ownership and control of public service monopolies." Though public ownership was no panacea, he felt that cities were weaker in dealing with corporations than they would be in managing public services themselves.[63] In October he urged the Ohio Bankers' Association to improve the financial practices of public-service corporations.[64] In both addresses he held that such corporations posed a greater threat to municipal government than any other force.

On December 14 Gladden attacked the company's proposal to reduce fares only on purchases of a dollar's worth of tickets. The commuters who needed the reduction most could not afford twenty-eight tickets at a time. A cartoon in the *Ohio State Journal* the next day portrayed Gladden and Christopher Columbus holding a blanket with the inscriptions "blanket franchise" and "There's millions in it." Columbus said to Gladden, "A pretty valuable blanket, Doctor?" and Gladden replied, "It's worth about four millions." The *Journal* praised Gladden for his stand and speculated that the people might "rise en masse" and elect him mayor.[65]

At the close of the year Mayor Swartz and Crum got the board of public works to pass a blanket franchise on all streets for twenty-five

[62] *Ibid.*, September 12, 15, 27, October 2, 1900.

[63] Woodruff to Gladden, June 1, 1900, Gladden Papers; Gladden, "The Influence of Public Service Corporations on City Government," September 21, 1900, Gladden Papers.

[64] Gladden, "The Banker and the City," October 25, 1900, Gladden Papers.

[65] *Ohio State Journal*, December 14–16, 1900.

years, providing for five-cent fares, six tickets for twenty-five cents,
twenty-eight tickets for one dollar, transfers on cash fares only, an
annuity of ten thousand dollars for ten years, and a graduated percentage of gross receipts over one million dollars. The *Journal*
branded it "Mayor Swartz's Franchise Surrender," and Gladden
criticized its failure to meet the standard of seven tickets for twenty-
five cents set by the interurbans. When it appeared that the administration would ram the franchise through the council, ten of whose
members the company allegedly controlled, irate citizens held protest meetings in each ward. Gladden presided over a central meeting of more than twenty-five hundred, which demanded eight tickets
for twenty-five cents with universal transfers.[66] At the request of a
citizens' organization Gladden and several other councilmen invited
Tom L. Johnson, who later that year became mayor of Cleveland,
to address the council, which was considering the ordinance as a
committee of the whole. Himself a streetcar magnate, Johnson
wanted to buy the streetcar system and institute three-cent fares.
The council, however, refused to adjourn to the city hall so citizens
might hear Johnson, whom Gladden introduced, and Gladden himself rejected the three-cent fare as impracticable.[67]

Under public pressure, the council hurriedly abandoned Swartz's
ordinance, to the wild cheers of a crowd assembled outside its chamber. It passed a new ordinance that incorporated substantially what
Gladden had wanted, five-cent cash fares, seven tickets for twenty-
five cents, to increase to eight when gross receipts reached one and
three-quarter million dollars, and universal transfers. Unhappy with
the council's haste and with several amendments, however, Gladden
voted against it. But his role in fostering the climate of opinion that
led to this franchise, considered by the *Ohio State Journal* to be
one of the best ever obtained by an American city, was decisive.[68]

While a councilman, Gladden also promoted municipal ownership
of an electric lighting plant. Roused by the Civic Federation, the

[66] *Ibid.*, December 29–30, 1900, January 4, 11, 1901.
[67] *Ibid.*, January 22, 26–27, 1901.
[68] *Ibid.*, January 27, February 5, 1901.

voters had approved in 1896 a bond issue of $300,000 to construct a municipal plant to furnish electricity for street lighting. In 1897 the council issued $68,000 of the total for an experimental plant, which might be expanded in 1901 when the city's contracts with a private electric company expired.[69] Operating unsuccessfully on a small scale, the plant did not, in Gladden's opinion, provide a fair test of municipal ownership. In March, 1900, a resolution to furnish all of the city's street lighting with an enlarged plant died in council.[70] The new council, however, unanimously passed a resolution introduced by Gladden's committee on gas and electricity instructing Linus B. Kaufmann, the director of public improvements, to estimate the cost of enlargement.[71]

Because the previous council had failed to appropriate operational funds, Kaufmann had to close the plant during the summer of 1900. Asserting that he preferred debt to darkness, Gladden tried to prevent the shutdown by an unsuccessful resolution waiving the director's financial liability. In addition, conflicting laws placed responsibility for operating the plant with both the director and the council. To locate responsibility before the crucial question of expansion became more pressing, the council had the director of law sue Kaufmann for failure to continue its operation, a course that Gladden endorsed.[72] Meanwhile, Gladden and Kaufmann, investigating street lighting in other cities, visited Springfield and Dayton, Ohio, and Detroit, and Gladden's committee began to prepare an estimate of the cost of expanding the plant. Gladden and two other councilmen urged the judge who had heard the suit against Kaufmann to make an early decision, and in March, 1901, the judge established the director's responsibility.[73]

[69] Ibid., February 19, March 3, April 7, August 11, 1896, September 28, November 20, 1897, October 26, 1898.

[70] Ibid., March 27, 1900.

[71] Ibid., May 15, 1900.

[72] Ibid., June 6, 13, 16, 26, July 7, 10–11, 24, September 15, 1900.

[73] Ibid., November 24, 1900, January 12, February 12, 16, March 15, 1901; T. B. Many to Gladden, January 25, 1901, Gladden Papers.

In the middle of March Gladden demonstrated that the municipal plant could furnish light at a lower rate than private companies would offer and introduced an ordinance authorizing the issuance of $132,000 in bonds. However, his motion for a second reading under suspension of the rules failed to pass.[74] Meanwhile, convinced that the city's plant was a failure, Kaufmann began to advertise for bids for contract lighting, but the bids were exorbitant relative to the cost per lamp of the municipal plant and of the municipal plants that Gladden had studied. Moreover, Edmund B. Ellicott, the director of Chicago's municipal plant, whom the council had employed at Gladden's request, estimated that the cost per lamp with a complete municipal plant would be less than half the cost according to some of the private bids.[75] Within a week after Ellicott's report one of the private companies, though questioning Ellicott's accuracy, reduced its bid and offered to rent the small municipal plant. In a defense of Ellicott, Gladden asked how the company could now reduce substantially its original offer. The reply, that renting the municipal plant would reduce the cost of constructing a private plant, was not convincing.[76]

In July, 1901, the council finally passed Gladden's ordinance to erect a complete plant. Legal difficulties, however, retarded progress for another year. An injunction based on the alleged illegality of the original bond issue in 1896 prevented the council from issuing bonds to begin construction. As a precaution against an adverse decision, Gladden introduced a resolution calling for a special election on August 3 to authorize $200,000 in bonds. The council passed it unanimously, and Mayor John N. Hinkle, a crusader for municipal ownership of utilities, campaigned to win popular support. But an apathetic public failed to endorse the bonds. Discouraged by this result of a referendum, a political device that he supported ener-

[74] *Ohio State Journal,* March 15, 19, 1901.

[75] *Ibid.,* March 16, April 6, 11–12, 20, 1901.

[76] *Ibid.,* April 23, 27, 30, 1901.

getically, Gladden recommended maximum use of the existing plant and a reduction in contract lighting.[77]

The court finally lifted its injunction and left the city free to operate and improve its plant. Because of further legal difficulties, however, the council submitted a new bond issue of $175,000 to the voters in April, 1902. The electorate this time heartily endorsed the projected plant, and expansion began immediately. In 1905 a subcommittee of the council reported that, though political manipulation had augmented the final cost of enlargement, the cost per lamp with the municipal plant was considerably less than the previous contract price.[78]

Shortly after Gladden introduced his ordinance authorizing completion of the municipal lighting plant, his committee on gas and electricity had to begin negotiations with the Central Ohio Natural Gas and Fuel Company, whose franchise was due to expire on March 30, 1901. On March 19 a member of Gladden's committee, Samuel Bradford, introduced a resolution fixing the rates at the current price, twenty cents per thousand cubic feet. The company, which supplied fuel to the majority of Columbus' householders, claimed that it could temporarily supply gas at the current rate but would have to raise prices eventually. Gladden and Bradford tried to reach an understanding with J. O. Johnson, the company's general manager, but he insisted that the company could not accept the new franchise because its supply of natural gas was rapidly diminishing, and that if the council passed Bradford's ordinance, it would have to pull out of Columbus. The questions of whether the supply of natural gas was actually running out and whether the company would leave Columbus baffled Gladden's committee and the council.[79]

[77] *Ibid.*, July 6, 9–10, 16, August 4, 1901.

[78] *Ibid.*, March 4, 18, April 8, May 27, 1902, September 6, 1905. In *Recollections*, p. 345, Gladden affirmed that the municipal plant cost less than "any contract lighting that has ever been offered to the city."

[79] *Ohio State Journal*, March 19, 23, 26, 30, April 7, 1901; Gladden, *Recollections*, p. 343.

Although the franchise expired, the company continued to supply gas. On May 21 Gladden introduced a company-inspired ordinance continuing the current rate for two years but raising it to twenty-five cents for the third and fourth and to thirty cents for the last six of the ten years covered. The *Ohio State Journal* condemned the proposed increases, and Gladden, though conciliatory toward the company, publicly opposed the ordinance, maintaining that the company was in partnership with the city, had received important advantages from it, and must consider its welfare. Moreover, he felt that the company had earned sizable profits at the twenty-cent rate.[80] James J. Thomas, president of the city council, reinforced Gladden's contention and suggested that, if the company pulled out, the city might have the right to confiscate its gas mains.[81]

Unwilling either to jeopardize the city's gas supply by pressing for concessions or to accept rates that he considered unjust, Gladden held a referendum in his ward. Several other councilmen followed his example. Only about seventy-five of over twenty-five hundred voters attended the meeting in Gladden's ward, and they urged him to make the decision. In frustration he appealed to the residents of his ward again, this time asking them to mail their opinions to him. In the four other wards where meetings occurred large majorities opposed the ordinance, as did the citizens who appeared before Gladden's committee. But the verdict of the four hundred opinions that Gladden received from his ward and of the Bryden Road Improvement Association, an organization in his ward, favored its passage. The seventh was one of the wealthiest wards in Columbus, and its residents did not care to haggle over a small increase in gas rates.[82]

On June 25 the company notified its customers that it would terminate service on July 1, and "consternation abounded." A simultaneous rise in the price of the company's stock convinced many that its local owners were selling out to a syndicate that would have no

[80] *Ohio State Journal,* May 21–22, 27, 30, 1901.

[81] *Ibid.,* June 4, 11, 1901.

[82] *Ibid.,* June 18–19, 21–22, 28, 1901.

interest in keeping natural gas in Columbus, a possibility that Johnson had raised in May. It also became clear that the company could
market its gas elsewhere without any difficulty.[83] Panicky citizens
began to besiege the council with pleas to pass the ordinance.

On July 1 a new ordinance of which Gladden's committee had
had no knowledge enabled the council to test the company's real
intentions. Pledged to follow his constituents' advice but preferring
the new ordinance, which did not raise rates, Gladden was in
an uncomfortable predicament. He spoke for the new ordinance,
though voting against it. As the councilmen cast their votes, a militant crowd in the lobby hissed those voting against the more favorable ordinance. When they hissed Gladden, the council's president
ordered the sergeant-at-arms to eject the next hisser. The company
accepted the ordinance without further equivocation.[84] To avoid
misrepresentation, Gladden explained his dilemma through the press.

> My mistake was in submitting the matter to the vote of the people. I
> have come to the conclusion that the referendum is a very doubtful de-
> vice—partly because it is very difficult to get any adequate expression from
> the people; and partly because, in the case of a representative, he had
> better be free to follow his own judgment than be bound by any pledge to
> vote as the people direct.[85]

Gladden's role in settling the three major issues before the city
council from 1900 to 1902 was distinct and aggressive. He stood with
and often led the progressives in the administration, the council, and
in the public at large. In each case he tried to deal justly though
firmly in the public interest—in the cases of the streetcar and gas
franchises, against the encroachments of strong public-service corporations, and in the case of the lighting plant, against the opponents
of public ownership. Convinced that public-service corporations
threatened the integrity and efficiency of local government, he val-

---

[83] *Ibid.*, May 25, June 25, 30, 1901.

[84] *Ibid.*, July 2, 27, 1901.

[85] *Ibid.*, July 3, 1901. While not criticizing the referendum, which he continued to endorse, Gladden repeated the same criticism of his course in *Recollections*, p. 344.

ued highly his part in bringing two of them under control and in promoting public ownership.[86]

Gladden declined to run for another term. For two years he had been almost constantly in Columbus, cutting short his vacations and at times hurrying back from speaking engagements to attend council meetings on Monday nights and committee meetings on Friday nights. In addition, he had devoted considerable time to study of the issues at stake and to unofficial public conferences and meetings. He had returned his salary to the city. He did not encourage suggestions that he seek the mayoralty, and by February, 1901, the citizens' organization that had supported his campaign felt that his strength had declined, though it had earlier considered him a logical independent candidate for the mayoralty. In 1902 popular apathy discouraged the citizens' organizations from making independent nominations. Returning to its staunch Republicanism, Gladden's ward elected the regular candidate by a vote of 923 to 305.[87]

Gladden's experience as a minister-in-politics gave him a new flurry of popularity in reforming circles. His election without personal exertion seemed almost miraculous. Edward Steiner wanted him to address a non-partisan movement that was just beginning in Sandusky, and ministers in Zanesville, Ohio, and Lowell, Massachusetts, sought his aid for local campaigns for reform. He was invited to address the Municipal Lecture Association of Chicago, the St. Louis Exposition, the Minneapolis Civic and Commerce Association, the Cleveland Chamber of Commerce, and good government clubs in Marietta, Ohio, and at the University of Michigan. In 1906 the secretary of the Detroit Municipal League wrote for information on the terms of the gas franchise for use in a similar case in Detroit.[88] His experience added a practical note to his popularization

[86] Gladden, *Recollections*, pp. 345–49.

[87] *New York Times*, August 16, 1900; *Ohio State Journal*, February 27, 1901, March 14, April 8, 1902.

[88] Steiner to Gladden, March 21, 1900; J. Addison Seibert to Gladden, March 20, 1900; C. W. Huntington to Gladden, October 15, 1900; George R. Peck to Gladden, January 14, 1903; John R. Butler to Gladden, February 28, 1904; A. R. Rogers to Gladden, September 21, 1912; Otto W. Davis to Gladden,

of the civic ideal and enhanced the authority of his views on municipal government. Significantly, one historian of reform in Ohio places Gladden alongside Samuel M. Jones and Tom L. Johnson as a leader of the civic revival that commenced the progressive movement in Ohio.[89]

The federal-plan charter that Columbus acquired in 1893 did not usher in sweeping political reform. Political spoilsmen, corporate interests, and opponents of the laws regulating the sale of liquor and prohibiting gambling continued to undermine efficient municipal government. Moreover, the city's dependence on the state legislature for extensions of power and its vulnerability to legislative interference obstructed the progress of reform. Gladden had wanted the federal plan and home rule. He had gotten only the federal plan. Despite the Ohio Constitution's tacit protection of the cities from legislative juggling, the General Assembly had been able, with the acquiescence of the Ohio Supreme Court, to write special charters for individual cities through an intricate system of classification.[90] From time to time during the 1890's Gladden had specified additional reforms that he thought would raise the level of politics and extend the principle of home rule. In 1898, for example, he suggested that reformers work for the referendum, particularly on public-service franchises, the abolition of the ward system, and a rigorous corrupt-practices act to curtail the use of money in elections.[91]

Within a few months after his term in the city council expired, Gladden became involved in a movement to draft a coherent municipal code for all cities in Ohio. The Supreme Court, which during the late 1890's had been revising its position, appeared to be on the verge of invalidating the maze of special municipal charters, and

October 16, 1914; Howard Strong to Gladden, March 31, May 13, 24, 1916; Warren S. Hayden to Gladden, July 7, 16, 1913; J. R. Nichols to Gladden, October 7, 1901; Earl B. Hawks to Gladden, April 27, 1901; Delos F. Wilcox to Gladden, October 17, 1906, Gladden Papers.

[89] Warner, *Progressivism in Ohio,* Preface, pp. 41–46.

[90] *Ibid.,* p. 107.

[91] Gladden, "A Short Talk with Reformers about Some Possible Reforms," Sermon, November 27, 1898, Gladden Papers.

the state realized that it must undertake comprehensive reorganization. In 1898 Governor Asa Bushnell had appointed Judge David F.
Pugh of Columbus and Edward Kibler of Newark to draft a new
municipal code. When late in 1899 Pugh and Kibler published their
plan, which provided for the abolition of classification, municipal
reorganization on the federal plan, non-partisan elections, the merit
system, the referendum for franchises and bond issues, and municipal ownership of streetcars and telephones, Gladden heartily
endorsed it. He told his congregation:

> I know of nothing within our power, as citizens of Ohio, which would
> do more to hasten the coming of the kingdom of God than the adoption
> by our legislature of the main features of the municipal code.

He repeated his endorsement in January, 1900, asserting that such
a code was necessary to the survival of republican government.[92]

Senator Warren G. Harding introduced the code as an administra-
tration measure in 1900, but, partly because of opposition from representatives of the large cities, it failed to pass then and again in
1902. When the Supreme Court finally made action imperative,
Governor George K. Nash called for a special legislative session to
begin on August 25, 1902, to draft an acceptable code. Nash, who
had helped Columbus get its federal-plan charter in 1893, consulted
Gladden on desirable provisions. During the summer several plans
emerged. The State Board of Commerce presented a code granting
the cities broad, unspecified powers and authorizing conventions in
which each city could draft a charter based on the federal plan. Governor Nash's bill specifically defined municipal powers and provided
for a single form of organization, with a mayor and council, as
under the federal plan, but with elective commissions of public
works and public safety. Another plan, introduced by Representative
W. E. Guerin, Jr., enumerated the cities' powers but replaced the
commissions with single executives.[93]

[92] Warner, *Progressivism in Ohio*, pp. 107–8; Gladden, "What Can We Do
for Our City Government?", Sermon, November 19, 1899, Gladden Papers; *Ohio
State Journal*, January 8, 1900.

[93] *Ohio State Journal*, July 2, 1902; George K. Nash to Gladden, August 2,
1902, Gladden Papers; Warner, *Progressivism in Ohio*, pp. 109–10.

From August 27 to September 10 a special committee of the lower house conducted public hearings on the proposed codes. In a sermon on September 7 Gladden stressed the urgency of municipal reorganization and called for complete home rule. And in a public statement on September 9, though commending its enumeration of municipal powers, he severely criticized Nash's code for imposing one organic law on all cities, regardless of size. Moreover, he held that experience had shown government by commission to be "the feeblest of all administrative devices," as well as a scheme for dividing patronage. In the case of the proposed board of public service, the delegation of both executive and legislative powers, the lack of a provision for civil service, and the exclusion of the mayor from its crucial functions threatened to deliver the entire municipal administration into the hands of three men. Testifying at the legislative hearing, Gladden reiterated these criticisms and urged a specific authorization of municipal ownership of streetcar lines.[94]

During September Gladden participated in several futile attempts to deter passage of Nash's code without major modifications and publicly endorsed the State Board of Commerce's proposal for local charter conventions, the maximum of home rule. By October 20, however, both houses passed the unreformed bill.[95] In his sermon on Thanksgiving Day Gladden denounced the new code as an "ill-contrived, awkward, bungling piece of machinery" that would make municipal government more difficult than ever. Other students of municipal government reinforced his judgment, and even Republican papers lamented the failure of the Republican legislature to enact a progressive code.[96]

In the municipal elections in April, 1903, Gladden turned his

[94] Gladden, "Foundation Principles of Municipal Organization," Sermon, September 7, 1902, Gladden Papers; *Ohio State Journal*, September 9, 12, 1902. In *Social Salvation* (1902), pp. 206–35, Gladden repeated his endorsement of home rule and centralization and also called for abolition of the ward system, civil service in all municipal departments, and extension of the franchise to non-residents who rented property in the city.

[95] *Ohio State Journal*, September 13, 19, October 22, 1902.

[96] Gladden, "Present Needs of Our City," Sermon, November 27, 1902, Gladden Papers; Warner, *Progressivism in Ohio*, pp. 114–15.

energies to the election of competent officials. Early in the year, the
Columbus Board of Trade urged voters to demand good candidates
from their parties. A small group of men, deciding to organize the
independent voters into a solid bloc, organized the Non-partisan
Municipal Union. After agreeing to vote for the party candidates
selected by a committee of twenty, they began secretly to enlist their
trusted friends and had over a thousand members before any paper
learned of their activities. With about twenty-three hundred members at the time of the primaries, the Non-partisan Municipal Union
claimed an initial victory in the marked improvement in party nominations. A member of the committee of twenty, Gladden recalled
that, although there was no attempt to divide the recommendations
between the parties, the committee selected ten candidates from
one party and eleven from the other. Since there were thirty-four
candidates for seventeen offices, the committee made dual recommendations in several contests. Just before the election, the union
flooded the city with its recommendations.

The union supported Robert Jeffrey, the Republican candidate
for mayor, who campaigned for municipal ownership of the waterworks, expansion of the municipal lighting plant, and law enforcement. He was the natural choice for the committee of twenty, which
included several of Gladden's parishioners. Jeffrey won by a majority
of 3,135 votes, the largest in the city's history, and the voters elected
every candidate recommended by the union but one candidate for
constable. Though Jeffrey's victory was due partly to his great popularity among businessmen, the union undoubtedly augmented his
margin and was instrumental in electing other candidates. The
staunchly Republican *Ohio State Journal* blamed it for saddling the
city with bipartisan government.[97]

Jeffrey's administration was progressive and honest. Appropriately, he chose Gladden, his family's pastor and neighbor, to offer
prayer at his inauguration. Jeffrey immediately curbed gambling,

---

[97] *Ohio State Journal*, January 25, February 28, March 15, 27, April 7–8, 12,
1903; Washington Gladden, "An Experiment in Practical Politics," *Congregationalist*, LXXXVIII (May 2, 1903), 620.

but, apparently, he did not strictly enforce the Sunday-closing law. A newly formed Civic Union arraigned the administration for indifference to lawlessness, but, probably impatient with the organization's narrow concentration on the saloons and its failure to appreciate gradual progress, Gladden remained confident that Jeffrey was handling the problem as best he could.[98]

The Non-partisan Municipal Union was ready to function again in 1904, but, because of an attempt to subvert municipal elections to partisan ends by making them simultaneous with state and national campaigns, there was no election that year. Alarmed by an increase in independent voting, the Republican legislature in March, 1904, passed the Chapman bill, which, ostensibly to eliminate the cost of separate elections in the same year, moved municipal elections from spring to fall.[99] As soon as the bill came to the public's attention, Gladden branded it "the most mischievous measure which has been introduced into the general assembly since I have lived in Ohio." "The parties, in city politics," he declared, "stand for nothing but the spoils of office; not a vestige of a principle ever appears in them. . . . " Gladden saw that the bill would undermine the local independent organizations that were trying to hold the balance of power between the parties.[100]

---

[98] *Ohio State Journal*, April 21, May 6, 9, 17, September 21, October 29, December 16, 1903; Jeffrey to Gladden, August 12, 1904, Gladden Papers.

[99] Interestingly, in 1884 Gladden had begun single-handedly a movement to secure a constitutional amendment changing state elections from October to November. Previously occurring a month before presidential elections, state elections, considered pivotal, had invited outside interference and created political turmoil for much of each election year. Beginning quietly, Gladden secured the signatures of the governor, all the ex-governors but Rutherford B. Hayes, all the justices of the Ohio Supreme Court, both United States senators, and other leading men. As the cause gained momentum, thousands of people signed copies of the petition he had framed. The legislature submitted the question to the voters, who in 1885 approved the change. Gladden to General James M. Comly, November 18, 1884, James (Gen.) M. Comly Papers (Ohio Historical Society, Columbus); *Ohio State Journal*, November 13, 19, 28, 1884, January 6, 1885; Gladden, *Recollections*, pp. 317–18.

[100] *Ohio State Journal*, February 6, 24, 1904; Warner, *Progressivism in Ohio*, p. 146. Gladden also enlisted friends in other parts of Ohio to oppose the bill. Henry C. King to Gladden, February 25, 1904; Charles H. Small to Gladden, February 26, 1904; L. L. Faris to Gladden, February 29, 1904, Gladden Papers.

Governor Myron T. Herrick, a Republican, proposed a compromise: the enactment, after passage of the bill, of a constitutional amendment fixing municipal and state elections in alternate
years. The *Ohio State Journal,* a dubious friend of independence,
commended his suggestion, and a senator from Franklin County
promptly introduced a resolution authorizing a referendum on such
an amendment. After an address by Gladden, in which he charged
that the Chapman bill's purpose was to get rid of Mayors Jones and
Johnson, the Columbus Board of Trade took its stand against it.[101]
The senate passed the bill, including at Herrick's insistence the provision for a referendum. Though the lower house was reluctant and
held public hearings, at which Gladden urged that the bill be passed
only after the amendment was in the Ohio Constitution, it finally
concurred in the senate's action. In 1905 the amendment received
popular sanction, and thereafter state and county elections occurred
in November in even-numbered years and municipal elections in
November in odd-numbered years.[102]

By November, 1905, when the next municipal election occurred,
the Non-partisan Municipal Union was apparently defunct. A Democratic landslide, part of a statewide reaction against the Republican
bosses, swept Judge DeWitt C. Badger and most of his fellow candidates into office.[103] Though Badger was friendly to reform, a scandal
in the board of public service during the second year of his administration substantiated Gladden's criticisms of the new municipal code.
After the disclosure of wholesale bribery in paving contracts, one
board member resigned, another was dismissed, and the third disappeared. Gladden observed, "This devil of graft must be the one
who described himself in the Scripture: 'My name is Legion, for we
are many.' " The greatest danger to American liberty, he declared,
arose "from the selfish and sinister purposes of great combinations
of wealth, whose gains can only be secured by the destruction of
the integrity of the men who are charged with the administration

[101] *Ohio State Journal,* February 24–26, 28, 1904.

[102] *Ibid.,* March 4, 8–9, 11, 1904, November 11, 1905.

[103] *Ibid.,* November 8, 1905; Warner, *Progressivism in Ohio,* p. 165.

of our laws."[104] Several months after the exposure, he called for the extension of civil service rules to the board of public service, and the Columbus Board of Trade printed his address in its publication and mailed copies to every member of the legislature and to each commercial organization in Ohio.[105]

In 1907 the major issue in the election in Columbus was temperance. Before the primaries Gladden worked with a committee, including President Thompson of the Ohio State University, Joseph A. Jeffrey, and several businessmen, to secure the Republican nomination for E. L. McCune, who also had the backing of the Anti-Saloon League. Gladden warned Republicans against wasting their votes in the primary on other temperance candidates who would not possibly defeat Charles A. Bond, the candidate of the Liberal League and the Republican machine.[106] But when Bond won the nomination, with the help of not a few Democrats, Gladden threw his support to the Democratic candidate, Judge Thomas J. Duncan, who pledged strict law enforcement. Two Republican papers, the *Dispatch* and the *Ohio State Journal,* and such Republicans as Judge David F. Pugh, Alexis Cope, a former state treasurer, and David K. Watson, a former state attorney-general, did likewise. Gladden stated that he had not found a Republican who was not planning to vote for Duncan, and Duncan announced that Gladden and other prominent Republicans had persuaded him to accept the Democratic nomination.[107] In addition, the People's Independent League, a labor organization, endorsed Duncan. Revealing that breweries controlled over half the saloons in the city, the *Ohio State Journal* maintained that the real issue was brewery control of the city's government. In a sermon on "The City That Ought to Be" Gladden lauded the new surge of independence and, without naming Duncan, made it clear that his parishioners should vote for law enforcement. At a

---

[104] *Ohio State Journal,* November 19, 1906, February 18–20, March 11, April 3, 1907; Gladden, Sermon, October 11, 1908, Gladden Papers.

[105] *Ohio State Journal,* November 22, December 8, 1907.

[106] *Ibid.,* August 29, September 5, 9–10, 12, 1907.

[107] *Ibid.,* September 13–14, 26, 29, October 6, 11, 15, 26, 1907.

midweek prayer meeting he castigated the bigotry of "liberals" who defied the wishes of an overwhelming majority of the citizenry.[108]

The climax of Duncan's campaign was a mass rally the Saturday before the election. Over five thousand crowded the Memorial Hall to hear Governor J. Frank Hanly of Indiana, a Republican, whom Gladden escorted to the platform, and Governor Joseph W. Folk of Missouri, a Democrat, whom Duncan accompanied. But the reformers' strength was illusive. Bond won by a plurality of over five thousand votes, the largest ever given a Republican candidate for mayor. To everyone's surprise Bond promptly announced, "The saloons will observe the law under my administration." And he was as good as his word.[109] Gladden's interpretation of Bond's policy was probably correct:

> . . . The whole question was so lifted into the light by the great debate that those who nominated Mr. Bond find it inexpedient to carry out the policy with which they entered this campaign, and they have been constrained to adopt the policy against which they fought.[110]

In 1909 the reformers had a more direct success. They won the Republican nomination for George S. Marshall, who as city solicitor had exposed the scandals involving the board of public service. He campaigned successfully against Frank R. Vance, a conservative Democrat, on a platform calling for tax increases on public-service corporations, a reduction of streetcar fares, and law enforcement. After the election Gladden offered the victory of "a man better equipped for his task than we have ever had in the City Hall" as a special cause for Thanksgiving Day that year. At a mass meeting sponsored by the YMCA Gladden envisaged the "new Columbus" coming down gradually from heaven, and Marshall responded by pledging to follow righteous principles.[111]

[108] *Ibid.*, October 27, 30–31, 1907; Gladden, "The City That Ought to Be," Sermon, October 27, 1907, Gladden Papers.

[109] *Ohio State Journal*, November 3, 6, 1907, January 10, 27, 1908.

[110] *Ibid.*, November 8, 1907.

[111] Warner, *Progressivism in Ohio*, p. 251; *Ohio State Journal*, September 8, November 3, 1909; Gladden, Sermon, Thanksgiving, 1909, Gladden Papers; *Ohio State Journal*, January 3, 1910.

Unfortunately, Marshall was too righteous for some people. For one thing, he enforced the Sunday-closing laws too energetically for many of the Germans, who preferred a "continental" Sabbath. Perhaps more significantly, his attempt to deal impartially with the streetcar strike in 1910 alienated both workingmen, who resented his use of the National Guard to establish order, and businessmen, who blamed him for failing to suppress violence. It seemed likely that George Karb, the Democratic nominee in 1911, would make concessions to the "liberals," despite his promises to enforce the liquor laws. The Socialist candidate, Alvah Eby, captured a great part of the working-class vote.

Gladden supported Marshall's unsuccessful campaign in 1911. He contributed ten dollars to the campaign fund. And he became a vice-president of the Civic Betterment League, formed to work for Marshall's re-election and to demand law enforcement if he lost.[112] The league organized a corps of thirty-five speakers who addressed nightly meetings in private homes. On November 3 Marshall's supporters held a mass meeting at which Gladden spoke. But it hardly compared with a Socialist rally the next night, to which five or six thousand came to hear William D. Haywood and Ella Reeve Bloor. On election day the voters cast 18,861 votes for Karb, 12,761 for Marshall, and 10,648 for Eby. Marshall lost a second race against Karb in 1913, a race in which Gladden apparently had no part.[113] Thereafter, perhaps because of his advancing age and the distractions of World War I, Gladden took little part in municipal elections.

But Gladden did make one more contribution to the improvement of municipal government and, at the same time, to progressivism in Ohio. He supported the advance guard of reform in the revision of the Ohio Constitution in 1912, and after the achievement of municipal home rule by constitutional amendment he worked to modernize the government of Columbus. When the call for a constitutional convention went out in 1911, groups interested in special reforms organized campaigns to elect delegates favorable to their

[112] *Ohio State Journal*, September 6, 16, 1911, January 23, 1912.
[113] *Ibid.*, October 18, November 4–5, 8, 1911, November 6, 1913.

causes. Gladden participated in the formation of the United Constitution Committee of Franklin County, which included representatives of over a hundred labor, agricultural, civic, and professional organizations. The United Constitution Committee, which, according to the historian of progressivism in Ohio, was "the best organized of all the pre-convention movements in the cities," held public meetings for discussion of the most pressing constitutional issues and nominated three candidates, one each selected by the representatives of labor, agriculture, and business and the professions. The business and professional groups chose Professor George W. Knight, a member of Gladden's congregation, whom Gladden, though himself in the running, supported. The United Constitution Committee's candidates, pledged to support direct legislation, municipal home rule, and judicial reform, were all elected.[114]

Progressives controlled the convention, and the forty-two amendments that emerged from its sessions in the early months of 1912 bore their imprint. The convention's platform became a pulpit for many of the nation's leading preachers of the progressive creed, including Theodore Roosevelt, Governor Hiram Johnson of California, and William Jennings Bryan. At Roosevelt's suggestion Gladden entertained him during his visit, and, when Roosevelt appeared at the convention to make his first public declaration for the popular review of state judicial decisions, he sat between Gladden and the convention's president, Herbert S. Bigelow.[115]

Gladden followed all of the convention's proceedings, but his greatest interest was in municipal reorganization. Like other urban reformers, he had seen the crippling effects of the municipal code of 1902, which had deterred the advent of home rule. At the call of the Municipal Association of Cleveland the mayors and representatives of fifty-three cities assembled in Columbus on January 23 to formu-

[114] *Ibid.*, September 12, 1911; Warner, *Progressivism in Ohio*, pp. 298–99.

[115] Roosevelt to Gladden, February 7, 1912, Gladden Papers; *Ohio State Journal*, February 14, 22, 1912; George E. Mowry, *Theodore Roosevelt and the Progressive Movement* (New York: Hill and Wang, 1946), pp. 212–14. One humorous aspect of Roosevelt's visit was a rumor that he became intoxicated at Gladden's house. William A. Ernst to Gladden, July 11, 1912, Gladden Papers.

late a home-rule amendment to present to the convention. The conference elected Mayor Newton D. Baker of Cleveland chairman, drafted an amendment, and organized itself as the Ohio Municipal League.[116] Before adjourning, the league heard an address by Gladden, who was to become its president in 1914, on "The Government of Cities." After censuring American municipal government, and particularly the code of 1902, Gladden made a strong plea for home rule; he also recommended extension of the franchise to non-residents who occupied premises or did business within city limits and to women who paid city taxes, legal provision for the cities to elect or employ non-resident experts, the short ballot, the initiative and referendum, the divorce of urban and national politics, and civil service in all municipal departments. He repeated these suggestions to the Civic Betterment League of Columbus in February.[117] The Ohio Municipal League's home-rule amendment, which provided for a variety of charters, the extension to the cities of all the powers not specifically denied them, and municipal ownership of public utilities, received the approval of the constitutional convention.[118]

Gladden endorsed most of the other important amendments proposed by the convention. In a front-page interview for the *Ohio State Journal* he endorsed the initiative and referendum and claimed to have written the plank on the initiative and referendum on which the delegates from Franklin County had campaigned. These devices, he said, were "the completion and fulfillment of our democracy." He also endorsed amendments providing for licensing the sale of liquor, judicial reform, the abolition of capital punishment, woman suffrage, and the direct primary. Though doubting at first that

[116] Warner, *Progressivism in Ohio*, pp. 330–31.

[117] Washington Gladden, *The Government of Cities: Address at the Conference of Ohio Cities, Columbus, January 25, 1912* (Cleveland: Issued by the Ohio Municipal League, 1912); *Ohio State Journal*, January 26, February 16, 1912, January 22–23, 1914; Francis W. Coker to Gladden, January 30, 1914, Gladden Papers. Gladden's address circulated widely in 1912 and for several years thereafter. Mayo Fesler to Gladden, February 6, 1914; Claude H. Anderson to Gladden, January 23, 1917, Gladden Papers.

[118] Warner, *Progressivism in Ohio*, p. 332.

women really wanted to vote, he supported woman suffrage when he sensed its popularity and even appeared at a suffragist rally in Columbus.[119]

As the referendum on the convention's forty-two amendments drew closer, Gladden reaffirmed his conviction that the convention had been "quite the best representative assembly" he had ever seen in Columbus. And when opponents of the amendments argued that, when in doubt, voters should vote "no," he suggested that, since the convention had given such careful attention to its work, voters, when in doubt, should say "yes." The United Constitution Committee of Franklin County issued an open letter by Gladden and President Thompson bearing this same advice. In the election on September 3 thirty-four of the amendments passed, and of those that Gladden had specifically endorsed only woman suffrage and the abolition of capital punishment failed. In a sermon after the election Gladden emphasized the significance of the amendments that gave greater power to the people. In all such measures, he said, "the great Ruler of the universe has a deep interest." "Nineteen centuries of history have been marching steadily in this direction—to the enfranchisement and enthronement of the common people." He urged those in his congregation who deprecated the common people to recognize their capacity for self-government.[120]

Home rule was, to his mind, the most significant extension of democracy, enabling the cities to frame new charters and to experiment without legislative interference. Following Cleveland, the first city to use its opportunity, the city council of Columbus voted in February, 1913, to hold a referendum on the question of a charter on May 6. An organization that wanted to present a commission

[119] *Ohio State Journal,* March 18, August 26, 28, 1912.

[120] Warner, *Progressivism in Ohio,* pp. 340, 342, 351; Gladden, Sermons, "Next Tuesday," September 1, 1912, "A Talk with the Neighbors about the New Laws," September 15, 1912, Gladden Papers. Joseph A. Jeffrey, Gladden's parishioner, had publicly opposed most of the amendments, particularly one establishing workmen's compensation. He wrote: " . . . If in doubt, vote no on all of said amendments. We have all prospered under the old constitution, and let us hold on to that." *Ohio State Journal,* September 2, 1912.

plan of government directly to the voters, the Commission Government League, met opposition from a group, including Gladden and Knight, that preferred to have a convention representing all points of view work out a proposal that would receive overwhelming popular approval. On February 28 about five hundred representatives of 103 civic, labor, professional, and religious organizations met and, with Gladden presiding, organized as the Municipal Charter League. The league adopted the principles of non-partisan elections, the short ballot, and the centralization of municipal authority and elected President Thompson to its presidency and Gladden to its executive committee. Its chief purpose was to nominate fifteen candidates for the charter commission that would, if the voters approved reorganization, frame a new organic law.[121]

The league rapidly gained new members. By March 13, when it held its third meeting, 470 organizations had appointed 2,350 delegates. It was necessary to hold subsequent meetings in the Memorial Hall. The meetings were almost unmanageable, as was the slate of 162 names proposed for nomination to the charter commission. The *Ohio State Journal* observed that these nominees represented every position from "radical progressive" to "reactionary standpat." Gladden declined to accept nomination and worked with a committee to induce the weaker candidates to withdraw. This committee selected fifteen candidates to push as a progressive ticket, but only eight of these men won nomination by the Municipal Charter League. Among the defeated reformers was George W. Knight. The league's candidates had opposition from only two other candidates, although it had been expected that there would be other tickets, and fourteen of them were elected to the commission.[122]

The charter commission, which began its work in the fall, was rent by disagreement over the form of government to recommend. It was almost equally divided between the advocates of a federal plan, with a mayor and council, and the proponents of the commis-

[121] *Ohio State Journal*, February 22, March 1, 1913; Warner, *Progressivism in Ohio*, p. 443.

[122] *Ohio State Journal*, March 7, 14, 21–22, 24, April 2, 6, May 7, 1913.

sion form. Disenchanted with the federal plan, which he had favored during the late 1880's and 1890's, Gladden had been growing increasingly favorable to experiments with commissions.[123] Galveston and Des Moines had pioneered in this new form, and by 1913 about two hundred cities had adopted it. Consequently, he appeared before the charter commission to urge its adoption. The major defects of the federal plan were, in his opinion, its division between the executive and legislative branches, which resulted in frequent deadlocks between the mayor and council, its susceptibility to partisanship, and its failure to allow for the accumulation of skill and experience. Though he recognized defects in the commission plan, he preferred its centralization of executive and legislative authority in a single, small body. He proposed several modifications in the usual features of commissions: enlargement of the commission from five to between eleven and fifteen members; nomination on a general ticket, with some form of proportional representation, for three- or four-year terms without remuneration; and selection by the commission of a business manager, who would appoint departmental heads and be responsible for their performance.[124]

The supporters of the commission plan attempted to bring public pressure to bear on the charter commission to accept either Gladden's proposal or a straight commission plan. After an address by L. D. Upson of Dayton, an expert on municipal government, a mass meeting called by Gladden and other clergymen, businessmen, and labor leaders endorsed the commission-manager scheme. Organized labor was almost solidly on the side of government by commission. But, though the charter commission at first voted down the federal plan, Gladden and supporters of the commission plan faced ultimate defeat. In November the charter commission tentatively approved a proposal mixing features of both plans. It provided for

[123] Gladden, Sermons, "Where Are We in Democracy?", February 25, 1906 Thanksgiving, 1909, Gladden Papers; Woodruff to Gladden, September 6, 11 1909, Gladden Papers.

[124] Gladden, "The City Charter," [October 7, 1913,] Gladden Papers; *Ohio State Journal,* October 8, 1913.

both a mayor and business manager and for four commissioners elected by districts. Gladden joined those who denounced this "mongrel" scheme, but he was willing to accept it with several changes, particularly abolition of election by districts.[125]

Stung by criticism, the charter commission rescinded its approval and finally adopted the principal features of the federal plan. When it completed its work in March, 1914, much of the public was hostile to its proposed charter. Split by the issue, the Municipal Charter League did not campaign for the charter, which carried on May 5 by a small margin. Never doctrinaire, Gladden announced his willingness to accept the charter and to make the best of its advantages, which included the short ballot, longer terms of service, abolition of the ward system in the election of seven councilmen at large, and, above all, home rule. If it failed to pass, he noted, Columbus would still be "a creature of the legislature . . . a big municipal baby, tied to the apron strings of the general assembly."[126]

In the thirty years since Gladden had come to Columbus, he had helped to effect many changes in its administration. A constant foe of lawbreakers, spoilsmen, and greedy public-service corporations, he had taken a hand in chastening and restricting all of them. His ideal was to transform the city from a bastion of corruption into the City of God. His method was to awaken citizens to the ideal and to their responsibility for the public welfare. In a democracy public opinion was the lever of reform, and the mass meetings, published letters, and committees were all devices to metamorphose public opinion into concerted action. And here again is the key to his distrust of purely political methods of reform. The best form of government in the hands of corrupt men would be more destructive than an inefficient form, while good men, supported by an alert and responsible citizenry, could promote well-being and order despite organizational disadvantages.[127] He wanted both: men who would

[125] *Ohio State Journal,* October 9, 12, 15, 17, November 20, 25, 1913.

[126] *Ibid.,* December 5, 1913, May 2, 1914.

[127] Gladden, *Christianity and Socialism,* pp. 227–28.

ward off the grafters and plunderers, and a form of government that would stiffen their resistance and reduce temptation. Many people have called Gladden the "first citizen" of Columbus. The description seems apt, for his range and constancy of interest in civic betterment are still without par in the history of his adopted city.

Twelve

Varieties of Protestant Unity

The modern ecumenical movement in Protestantism is not the child of the mid–twentieth century alone, even though its contemporary dimensions give it greater public recognition and promise than it has had in the past hundred years. Progressive churchmen in the late nineteenth century made determined attempts to reunite the churches in spirit and in organization on virtually every level of religious activity. Liberal theology seemed to offer not only a reduction in the number of doctrinal issues dividing Protestants but also a new consensus of belief, broad, pragmatic, and flexible, in which they could find a basis at least for co-operation and, hopefully, for reunion. And the Social Gospel, by focusing the churches' attention on the influence of Christianity on human affairs, minimized the importance of creedal distinctions and made abundantly clear the need for concerted Christian social action. The existing state of denominationalism, these churchmen argued, was not only unnecessary and a hindrance to the effective Christianization of society; it was also a violation of Christ's teaching of the primacy of love and, thus, a sin. Moreover, as they attempted to discern human progress, they sometimes saw co-operation in economic, political, and international affairs replacing an individualistic, competitive, and often harmful spirit of laissez faire. It was easy to view religious co-operation as an integral part of the same transformation. Gladden's ministry provides an excellent example of the varied nature of this early ecumenical movement. Not only did his concern for Christian unity span almost his entire mature career, but it also found expression in support for the complete spectrum of ecumenical efforts, ranging from simple interdenominational co-operation, through consolidation of rival local congregations, to full organic union among similar denominations.

Gladden's experience as religious editor of the *Independent*, involving as it did a continuous, comprehensive survey of religious events, undoubtedly contributed to his ecumenicity and wide-ranging interest in attempts at federation and union among the Protestant churches. In fact, while Gladden worked in this capacity, the *Independent* strongly endorsed ecumenical ventures. It gave frequent notice to the international meeting in New York in 1873 of the Evangelical Alliance, a federation created in London in 1846, with an American branch founded in 1867. Anxious to have the Alliance pursue as inclusive a policy as possible, the *Independent* cautioned it against adopting a doctrinal basis for co-operation and argued for the admission of Universalist representatives. Following the meeting in New York, the paper commended the Alliance for getting Protestants to talk over their common problems and aims.[1] Similarly, the *Independent* looked favorably upon overtures to reunion made by representatives of several Presbyterian bodies, expressed hope that Unitarians and Congregationalists might at least accord each other fraternal recognition, and decried sectarian rivalries on foreign mission fields. Confident that "the centrifugal forces" of Protestantism were "nearly spent," it predicted "a strong tendency toward the reunion and consolidation of the shattered and scattered sects."[2]

[1] "The Evangelical Alliance," *Independent,* XXV (April 17, 1873), 496; "The Baptists and the Alliance," (June 5, 1873), 721; "A Word to the Evangelical Alliance," (September 18, 1873), 1168; "Knocking at the Door," (October 2, 1873), 1233; "The Evangelical Alliance," (October 9, 1873), 1264; "The Fruits of the Alliance," (October 16, 1873), 1298.

[2] "Presbyterian Union," *Independent,* XXV (May 29, 1873), 688; "Fellowship With Unitarians," XXVI (December 17, 1874), 14, "A Strange Chapter in the History of Missions," (April 16, 1874), 16.

After Gladden went to Springfield, he began to chafe under the effects of denominational competition in small towns and rural areas, a prominent phenomenon in western Massachusetts, and to call for ecclesiastical co-operation in such communities. In *Sunday Afternoon* he placed much of the blame on the "denominational boss" who put "the interests of his own sect above the interests of Christ's kingdom." Intense sectarianism led to the planting of more churches than were needed, especially in sparsely populated areas; it would be better, Gladden observed, to have "one church which stands on its own feet, instead of two which must go on crutches."³ He emphasized this theme in sermons to his own congregation. Concluding that sectarianism was one of the chief factors contributing to the unattractiveness of village life, he suggested that all the churches in each county create a commission to plan and execute consolidation.⁴ It is apparent that this problem was much on his mind, for he repeated his suggestion for county-wide interdenominational planning at the tenth anniversary of the Memorial Church of Springfield, a non-denominational evangelical church, and through the *Independent*.⁵

Gladden's greatest contribution to ecumenicity during the early stages of his ministry was a fictional story, "The Christian League of Connecticut," published serially in the *Century* in 1882–83 and then issued in book form. The initial suggestion came from Roswell Smith, but the story itself was Gladden's own creation. Set in the hypothetical town of New Albion in the late 1870's, the plot was an account of how co-operation first transformed religious and social conditions in one typical community and then began to spread. Beginning with the desire of a prominent layman and a Congregational minister to find some form of co-operation midway between simple fellowship and organic denominational union, ecumenicity quickly led to the organization of the Christian League of New

³ "Sects and Schisms," *Sunday Afternoon*, III (January, 1879), 88–89; "One Worth More Than Two," *Good Company*, IV (1879), 91–92.

⁴ Gladden, "Problems of Evangelization, II, The Country Towns," Sermon, May 15, 1881, Gladden Papers.

⁵ *Springfield Republican*, October 14, November 6, 1875.

Albion, which was designed to bring the churches together, not on a doctrinal basis, but simply in Christian work. At first, the league conducted a comprehensive canvass of New Albion, assigning to each church a district in which its ministry would be recognized as pre-eminent. Then the co-operating churches pooled their resources to plant a new, non-denominational church in an unchurched working-class neighborhood. But the league soon found that it could unite the churches to deal with local social problems: to promote temperance, without settling on any single approach to strong drink, it began a campaign for the enforcement of existing liquor laws; to consolidate and improve the scattered efforts of local charities, it established a central organization, patterned, interestingly, after the Union Relief Association of Springfield; and to meet the needs of young workingmen, it opened the Young Men's Union Club, complete with coffee room, smoking room, game and reading room, and gymnasium. It soon became clear that there was, in fact, only one church in New Albion, albeit with several different congregations. The league ultimately reached beyond New Albion to deal with the overchurching of the neighboring village of Monroeville and established the Christian League of Bradford County, which would work toward the consolidation of feeble churches like those found there. Ultimately, the spirit of co-operation took hold elsewhere, resulting in the Christian League of Connecticut and other similar bodies in the United States and England.[6]

This story, Gladden's most successful literary work to that time, made a significant contribution to Protestant co-operation. Co-operative church planning, known in the late nineteenth century as "comity," actually began on foreign mission fields. The basic principles of this early form of ecumenism were the recognition by each denomination that it alone could not evangelize the entire world, the assignment of geographical spheres of influence to the denomina-

[6] Washington Gladden, "Roswell Smith," Century, XLIV (June, 1892), 310–13; Washington Gladden, "The Christian League of Connecticut," Century, XXV (November, 1882), 50–60, (December, 1882), 181–91, (January, 1883), 339–49, XXVI (May, 1883), 65–79; Washington Gladden, The Christian League of Connecticut (New York: Century Co., 1883).

tions participating in comity agreements, and the acceptance by each denomination of the work and standards of the others. Gladden's idealistic but vivid portrayal of co-operation in New Albion was one of the principal influences sparking the idea that similar comity arrangements might be reached in home missions. With the breakdown of theological differences that occurred in the nineteenth century, it was possible for many Protestants to accept Gladden's contention that denominational labels meant relatively little when viewed in the perspective of the immense challenges to religion in America. The idea spread, and in 1890–91 a group of denominational officials held a series of meetings in Maine to establish a comity arrangement for New England. Many later agreements on comity followed the pattern set in Maine, and this type of co-operation became widespread, especially in New England and the North Central states. Gladden himself, following the progress of comity, concluded that he had played an important and constructive role in the birth of the movement.[7]

Co-operative church planning was only one reflection of a growing dissatisfaction with sectarian competition in the late nineteenth century. The ecumenical spirit also took the form of attempts at denominational merger, particularly through the reunion of groups that had once been united or the union of those with relatively insignificant differences. Gladden had a minor part, but one reflecting his continued interest in eliminating denominational competition, in two series of discussions between Congregationalists and other churches. When the Congregational council met in Chicago in 1886, it took its first step toward merger with another denomination by appointing a special committee, which included Gladden, to make overtures to the Free Baptists. The Free Baptists had originally

[7] Lyle E. Schaller, *Planning for Protestantism in Urban America* (New York and Nashville: Abingdon Press, 1965), pp. 96–99; Charles S. Macfarland, *Christian Unity in Practice and Prophecy* (New York: Macmillan Co., 1933), pp. 129 f.; Gladden, *Recollections,* p. 275. Ray Stannard Baker, the muckraking journalist, informed Gladden in 1907 that he remembered reading "The Christian League" as a teen-ager and that it had stirred him deeply. Baker to Gladden, October 7, 1907, Gladden Papers.

separated from Congregationalism during the Great Awakening of
the eighteenth century, and the only important difference between
the two groups was over infant baptism. But although the Congregationalists continued to entertain the possibility of such a merger,
the Free Baptists found their fellowship with other Baptist groups
growing stronger, and this attempt came to nothing.[8]

In 1892 and 1895 the Congregational council's committee on
church union made further attempts to promote ecumenical discussions among evangelical churches. The most promising possibility of
merger seemed to be with the Christian Connection, known more
formally as the General Convention of the Christian Church, one of
several denominations stemming from the "Christian," or Camp-
bellite movement of the early nineteenth century. Gladden was
active in support of such a merger, and he was largely responsible
for a successful conference at Piqua, Ohio, in 1896, called by a joint
committee of the Ohio Christian Conference and the Central Ohio
Congregational Conference. But this effort met hostile reaction in
some sections of the Christian Connection, particularly fear on the
part of the more orthodox of "selling out" to the Congregationalists;
and by 1898 it was clear that there would be no immediate merger.
The two groups united in 1931 as the Congregational Christian
churches, but there was no lineal connection between the two
episodes.[9]

A far more important series of negotiations for church merger,
and one in which Gladden participated more actively, occurred
from 1902 to 1908 between the National Council of Congregational
Churches, the Church of the United Brethren in Christ, and the
Methodist Protestant church. During these negotiations, which
appeared frequently to be certain of success, Gladden strongly

    [8] Congregationalist, LXXI (October 28, 1886), 359, LXXX (October 17, 1895),
577–78; Atkins and Fagley, American Congregationalism, pp. 345–47.
    [9] Congregationalist, LXXX (November 7, 1895), 681, LXXXI (April 30, 1896),
715, LXXXII (March 25, 1897), 403, LXXXIII (January 6, 1898), 24; Atkins and
Fagley, American Congregationalism, pp. 350–53; Hudson, Religion in America,
pp. 124, 416.

urged ultimate organic union but, frankly recognizing the obstacles to this ideal, counseled gradualism. He became one of the chief spokesmen for the proposed merger, interpreting and defending it to the constituencies of all three denominations.

The movement originated with the United Brethren. In 1901 their General Conference appointed a Commission on Church Union to explore the possibilities of union with similar denominations, but this body made no overtures to comparable commissions of other churches. The next year a group of twenty-two laymen and ministers from Dayton, Ohio, the national headquarters of the United Brethren, circulated an appeal to their bishops to initiate discussions leading to organic union with denominations similar in polity and doctrine, specifically the Methodist Protestant church, the Evangelical Association, the United Evangelical church, and the Cumberland Presbyterian church. Shortly thereafter, W. M. Weekley, church extension secretary for the United Brethren, brought this proposal to the attention of William Hayes Ward, editor of the *Independent* and chairman of the Congregational National Council's Commission on Unity With Other Denominations. Ward requested that the Congregationalists be included in any discussions. Of the other denominations approached by the United Brethren, only the Methodist Protestants expressed interest. There had been overtures between the Methodist Protestants and the Congregationalists since at least 1898, when the Congregational National Council at Portland, Oregon, had singled out the Methodist Protestant church as a possible body with which to unite. In 1899 the Central West Association of Congregational Churches in Illinois had begun local negotiations with the Methodist Protestants in that area, and by 1902 the Congregational Commission on Unity was making concrete proposals for national discussions to the president of the Methodist Protestant General Conference, Chancellor D. S. Stephens of Kansas City University. Because of these negotiations, and also because of Ward's request, the United Brethren formally extended their invitation to the Congregationalists. And since the

Christian Connection had also been discussing merger with the Congregationalists, they were also welcomed.[10]

The first major step toward union was a meeting of representatives of the four denominations at the headquarters of the Methodist Protestant church in Pittsburgh on April 22–23, 1903. A member of the Congregational Commission on Unity, Gladden attended the meeting and served as presiding officer. The United Brethren delegates introduced a basis for union that the other groups could not fully accept; it included an evangelical confession of faith, a system of superintendence over local churches by bishop-like officers, ownership by the new denomination of all institutions and property belonging to the combining bodies, and a new name. When the United Brethren and Methodist Protestants insisted that the combining churches recognize their various confessions of faith as substantially alike and reaffirm them, the Christian Connection, a church unalterably opposed to all doctrinal statements but the Bible, withdrew from the discussions. The three remaining groups still found substantial differences of polity that would impede easy organic union. Although they had broken away from the Methodist Episcopal church in 1830 in order to create a more democratic polity with lay representation, the Methodist Protestants had officials with considerable power over individual churches; the United Brethren had bishops and presiding elders; the Congregationalists had no hierarchy and were organized only in loose state and local associations, to which they refused to grant any legislative or judicial powers. The representatives at Pittsburgh finally agreed to unite in a national federation in anticipation of ultimate organic union and appointed a subcommittee to work out the details of union on the following lines: reaffirmation of existing doctrinal statements as "essentially the same"; temporary union through a General Council, represent-

---

[10] *Religious Telescope*, LXVIII (October 8, 1902), 1286; Kenneth James Stein, "Church Unity Movements in the Church of the United Brethren in Christ until 1946" (unpublished Th.D. dissertation, Union Theological Seminary, 1965), pp. 113–14; H. K. Painter, "Methodist Protestants and Congregationalists," *Congregationalist*, LXXXVII (November 1, 1902), 621.

ing the three denominations in proportion to membership, which would have only advisory functions; and retention of denominational autonomy and separate names, but with the addition "in affiliation with the General Council of the United Churches."[11]

The subcommittee appointed at Pittsburgh consisted of fifteen members, five from each denomination. Ward, who became its chairman, and Gladden were influential participants and gave the most determined support to the movement for union of any of the negotiators. Meeting in Washington on May 27, 1903, this subcommittee produced two documents of major significance for the proposed merger: a *Church Union Syllabus*, addressed to the national bodies of the three denominations, summarizing the progress of union to date, affirming their general doctrinal agreement, and providing for an advisory General Council, with one representative for every five thousand members, to pave the way for organic union; and a *Letter to the Churches*, designed to explain the more formal pronouncement and to promote fraternity and mutual knowledge among the three denominations. Gladden and W. M. Weekley were designated to present the *Syllabus* to the national bodies.[12]

Following this speedy and unanimous action by the subcommittee, there was a tremendous wave of enthusiasm in each of the three combining churches. Gladden urged caution and deliberation but also shared in the general optimism. In an article for the *Congregationalist* he discounted the importance of creedal differences and predicted that problems of polity would be most serious: "The critical question will be, how to adjust our freer customs to their

[11] Ward to Gladden, March 16, 1903, Gladden Papers; *Ohio State Journal,* April 25, 1903; Gladden, Sermon, April 26, 1903, Gladden Papers; Douglas R. Chandler, "The Formation of the Methodist Protestant Church," in Emory S. Bucke, ed., *The History of American Methodism* (3 vols.; New York and Nashville: Abingdon Press, 1964), I, 662–63; Stein, "Church Unity Movements," pp. 115–16; "Four Denominations Consider Union," *Congregationalist,* LXXXVIII (May 2, 1903), 624–25.

[12] *Congregationalist,* LXXXVIII (May 2, 1903), 624–25, (June 6, 1903), 789, (July 11, 1903), 45; "Proposals for Union with Methodist Protestants and United Brethren," *ibid.,* LXXXVIII (July 11, 1903), 66.

stronger forms of government." But even polity seemed less difficult an issue to Gladden after the meetings at Pittsburgh and Washington than it had appeared before. Congregationalists were finding their excessive independence a disadvantage, he averred, while the other groups were moving toward more democratic systems of government. He urged immediate co-operation in educational and missionary enterprises preliminary to full organic union.[13]

There were few dissenters from the enthusiastic approval of the plans for merger at this stage. With Gladden's co-operation, Charles C. Creegan of the American Board of Commissioners for Foreign Missions launched a missionary campaign in Ohio that included representatives of the United Brethren and Methodist Protestant churches. The capstone of this effort was a rally, over which Gladden presided, in the First Congregational Church of Columbus.[14] A Congregational assembly in Michigan, with leaders from twelve states present, gave unanimous approval to the proposals. Methodist Protestants and United Brethren were invited to participate in the Central Ohio Congregational Conference in April, 1904, and to discuss what each church could contribute to the others. And the Congregational Club of St. Louis heard addresses by Weekley, a United Brethren, and Chancellor Stephens, a Methodist Protestant, on the topic of union.[15] Gladden spoke at the Southeast Ohio Conference of the United Brethren, held at Otterbein College in Westerville in October, 1903, and gave a series of addresses at the United Brethren seminary in Dayton in November.[16] In addition, each of the denomi-

[13] Washington Gladden, "The Proposed Tripartite Union," *Congregationalist*, LXXXVIII (August 1, 1903), 152–53.

[14] Creegan to Gladden, August 19, 1903, Gladden Papers; *Ohio State Journal*, October 3, 1903; *Congregationalist*, LXXXVIII (November 14, 1903), 708. This endeavor was so successful that Creegan later tried it elsewhere in the country. Creegan to Gladden, December 12, 1904, February 8, 1905, Gladden Papers.

[15] "A Church Union Approved," *Congregationalist*, LXXXVIII (August 29, 1903), 283, "The Three Denominations in Ohio," LXXXIX (May 7, 1904), 634; *Congregationalist*, LXXXVIII (December 19, 1903), 942.

[16] *Ohio State Journal*, October 16, 1903; G. A. Funkhauser to Gladden, July 6, November 3, 7, 1903, Gladden Papers.

national papers carried descriptive articles on the other groups by leaders in those groups.[17]

The first official action on the subcommittee's proposals by one of the national bodies came when the Methodist Protestant General Conference met in Washington in May, 1904, and gave unqualified approval. Gladden presented the committee's reports, and, according to a Methodist Protestant editor, his "strong and gracious presentation of the syllabus" aided its passage. Gladden was encouraged by this approval, but the speed with which the Methodist Protestants wanted to move alarmed him. Once again, he was willing to discount the importance of doctrinal differences, and, though noting that Congregationalists tended to be strongest in urban areas, while the United Brethren and Methodist Protestants were largely rural, he was even prepared to minimize social and educational differences. But he preferred a slower procedure that would allow "our creed and our polity [to] grow out of our common life." The United Brethren, he noted, had an episcopal form of government, the Methodist Protestants, a modified presbyterian form, and the Congregationalists, a congregational form. It would be best, he argued, for the denominations to co-operate in missionary and educational enterprises, while these political differences were resolved.[18]

After this action by the Methodist Protestant General Conference, the National Council of Congregational Churches and the United Brethren General Conference quickly followed suit. The Congregationalists, meeting in Des Moines in October, 1904, received unanimously the report of their Commission on Church Union and empowered another committee, on which Gladden also sat, to select

[17] Bishop J. S. Mills, "The United Brethren in Christ," *Congregationalist*, LXXXVIII (September 19, 1903), 394–96, *United Brethren Review*, XV (May-June, 1904), 129–34; John F. Cowan, "The Methodist Protestants—Who? What? Where?", *Congregationalist*, LXXXVIII (September 26, 1903), 427–29, *United Brethren Review*, XV (May-June, 1904), 134–40; A. T. Perry, "The Congregationalists," *United Brethren Review*, XV (May-June, 1904), 140–46.

[18] John F. Cowan, "The Methodist Protestants on Union," *Congregationalist*, LXXXIX (June 4, 1904), 780; Gladden, "Church Mergers," Sermon, June 5, 1904, Gladden Papers; Washington Gladden, "A Proposal for Church Union," *Congregationalist*, LXXXIX (June 11, 1904), 819–20.

their delegates to the General Council of the United Churches.[19] Just before the United Brethren General Conference met in Topeka in May, 1905, the uniting denominations held joint missionary rallies in three areas where they were all fairly strong, Baltimore, Dayton, and Pittsburgh. Gladden addressed the rally in Pittsburgh on April 11. The desire for organic union was expressed repeatedly.[20] The United Brethren Conference opened auspiciously on May 11 with the Bishops' Quadrennial Address, in which the bishops asked, "Is not the handwriting of the coming of the kingdom seen upon the wall in this syllabus of a federated union?" On May 15 the delegates turned to the report on union, greeting Gladden's presentation of the *Church Union Syllabus* with resounding applause. The only significant opposition came from a minister from eastern Pennsylvania who called the proposal a "scheme" by the "highest officials of the Church" and openly criticized Gladden's views of the Bible. The General Conference approved the report by a vote of 251–5.[21]

With formal approval thus acquired from the highest bodies of the three denominations, the provisional General Council held its first meeting in Dayton in February, 1906. Enthusiasm was still strong as preparations for this meeting went ahead. The *Religious Telescope* of the United Brethren declared that "in doctrine, in missionary, educational, and evangelistic zeal, and in devout spirituality," the three groups were "already virtually one." Both Methodist Protestants and Congregationalists, the latter scheduling a special train to carry their most distinguished men to Dayton from the East, shared in this buoyant optimism.[22] But the delegates had scarcely arrived in Dayton when ambiguity of purpose became apparent.

[19] *Congregationalist*, LXXXIX (October 22, 1904), 573, (October 29, 1904), 604–7, (November 12, 1904), 677.

[20] *Ibid.*, XC (April 8, 1905), 457, (May 6, 1905), 635, (May 13, 1905), 647.

[21] *Official Report of the Proceedings and Debates of the Twenty-fourth General Conference of the United Brethren in Christ, Held in Topeka, Kansas, May 11–22, 1905* (Dayton, Ohio: United Brethren Publishing House, 1905), pp. 26–29, 278–81, 283–93, 494–505, 515, 533; *Congregationalist*, XC (May 27, 1905), 711, 715; Gladden, "Flying Scout," Sermon, May 21, 1905, Gladden Papers.

[22] *Religious Telescope*, LXXII (January 10, 1906), 36, (January 24, 1906), 100.

In preliminary meetings of each delegation on February 6 the lack of specific plans led to some confusion. Although the Congregationalists passed unanimously a resolution endorsing organic union and the Methodist Protestants seemed to echo this sentiment, there was still uncertainty as to whether the General Council should be content with federation or push on to a complete, organic merger.[23]

When the first session of the General Council opened on February 7, Gladden presided as temporary chairman and spoke on the history of the movement. Still an advocate of gradualism, he urged the General Council to deal first with the consolidation of educational and missionary programs before undertaking the more difficult questions of organic union.[24] Indeed, in a "whirlwind of enthusiasm," the council created a committee of forty-five, fifteen members from each denomination, to work out a plan of organic union. This committee divided into three subcommittees, on church property and vested interests, doctrine, and polity. These subcommittees set to work at once and on February 8 produced their respective reports. The committee on doctrine, headed by President W. Douglas Mackenzie of the Hartford Theological Seminary (Congregational), drafted a satisfactory statement that would serve, not as a doctrinal test, but as a confession of common beliefs. At its presentation, this confession was met by applause and the spontaneous singing of the Doxology. The committee on church property and vested interests reported that, although there were no insuperable obstacles to union, it needed more time to work out concrete proposals. The committee on polity encountered the greatest difficulty but won approval for a report providing that the local congregation would be the basic unit of the new denomination and that the national governing body would be representative and democratic. To allow the committees on church property and polity time to work out necessary

[23] *Ibid.*, LXXII (February 14, 1906), 196–97.

[24] W. R. Funk to Gladden, August 4, 1905, Gladden Papers; *Congregationalist*, XC (August 12, 1905), 208; *Religious Telescope*, LXXII (February 7, 1906), 161, 164, (February 14, 1906), 196–97.

details, the General Council agreed to meet again a year later.[25]

The problems that would eventually wreck this tripartite union were already apparent. Revealingly, the *Religious Telescope* could note both the bewildering speed of the proceedings and the delegates' conviction that "they were on holy ground, in the divine presence."[26] Denominational organs and church officials continued to take a bright view of the movement's prospects, and there was another round of descriptive articles dealing with the meeting at Dayton and with each of the co-operating denominations.[27] But the problem that Gladden had predicted would be most serious, polity, began to stir up an opposition that grew increasingly militant. Some Congregationalists saw in the existing agreements a surrender of the local church to "bishops disguised as superintendents." One United Brethren bishop felt compelled to defend his church's system of clerical itinerancy and supervision for small rural churches, and for months after the meeting at Dayton the *Religious Telescope* carried statements from laymen and pastors who feared the loss of their denominational distinctives and absorption by liberal Congregationalists.[28] Gladden soon had a demonstration of the difficulty involved even in the limited initial federation that he desired. At the annual meeting of the American Board of Commissioners for Foreign Missions in October, 1906, he introduced a resolution calling for co-operation with the foreign mission societies of the United Brethren and Methodist Protestant churches. The American Board

[25] Stein, "Church Unity Movements," pp. 118–21.

[26] *Religious Telescope*, LXXII (February 14, 1906), 196–97, 205.

[27] *Congregationalist*, XCI (February 17, 1906), 217, 224–26; C. E. Wilbur, "Methodist Protestants and the Dayton Council," *ibid.*, XCI (March 3, 1906), 314, Bishop W. M. Weekley, "The United Brethren View of the Union Movement," *ibid.*, (March 10, 1906), 356; D. S. Stephens, "The Objects of This Council," *United Brethren Review*, XVII (March-April, 1906), 65–79, Bishop J. S. Mills, "Co-ordination in Church Work," *ibid.*, (March-April, 1906), 79–84; George P. Morris, "Methodist Protestants at Close Range," *Congregationalist*, XCI (April 28, 1906), 608, "United Brethren at Close Range," *ibid.*, (May 5, 1906), 649, "Tri-Union—Its Probable Effect on Congregationalism," *ibid.*, (May 12, 1906), 682.

[28] Dwight H. Platt to Gladden, February 17, 1906, Gladden Papers; *Religious Telescope*, LXXII (April 11, 1906), 454.

accepted the proposal, appointing Gladden chairman of a committee to approach the other denominations' societies. But Gladden's committee got nowhere, despite the fact that Methodist Protestant and United Brethren representatives had been at the American Board's sessions. The executive committee of the United Brethren Foreign Mission Society claimed that it had no authority to act and that, at the current stage of the movement toward union, public knowledge that such consolidation was under way would actually do more harm than good.[29]

As the date for the second meeting of the General Council drew close, there were other indications that the movement was bogging down. The subcommittees on polity and church property met in Pittsburgh on November 21–22, 1906, and, though the polity committee drafted a statement safeguarding the autonomy of the local church, both committees admitted serious problems. Then Bishop J. S. Mills of the Eastern Conference of the United Brethren reversed himself and publicly stated that he favored federation, not organic union. The *Religious Telescope* also began to lose its enthusiasm for organic union, probably because the Congregationalists were successfully advancing their position on the autonomy of the local congregation.[30]

The meeting of the General Council in Chicago in March, 1907, further illustrated that support for organic union was lagging in some sections of each denomination. Called to order by Gladden, the General Council accepted an *Act of Union* that included the confession of faith adopted at Dayton and eight articles of agreement. This *Act of Union* anticipated a voluntary, gradual union, particularly on the local level. Congregational associations and United Brethren and Methodist Protestant annual conferences would continue to have jurisdiction over their respective constituencies; there

[29] *Ohio State Journal,* October 12, 1906; *Congregationalist,* XCI (October 20, 1906), 498–503; S. S. Hough to Gladden, November 7, 1906, Gladden Papers.

[30] *Congregationalist,* XCI (December 1, 1906), 728, 744–45; *Religious Telescope,* LXXII (December 26, 1906), 1638; William J. Zuck to Gladden, March 5, 1906, Gladden Papers.

would be no boundary changes or local mergers without the consent of those congregations affected. Organic union would occur first at the national level. A permanent General Council, consisting of representatives elected proportionally by regional conferences and associations, would meet quadrennially and might either create new agencies for missionary, educational, and benevolent purposes or utilize existing societies. But, apparently at the insistence of the United Brethren delegates, the *Act of Union* did not include the specific protection of local congregational autonomy so carefully provided by previous reports of the committee on polity. Bishop Mills was satisfied. In a letter to members and ministers of the United Brethren church, he joined the other bishops in declaring that nothing vital had been surrendered and that all legal difficulties had now been removed.[31]

The next major step in consummating the tripartite union was to secure the official approval of the national bodies of the three denominations to the *Act of Union*. The members of the General Council had hardly left Chicago, however, before resistance developed. While Gladden prepared an explanatory paper on the *Act of Union* and sent it to all Congregational pastors and state and local associations, the *Congregationalist* began to attack the omission of any protection of Congregational principles, especially local autonomy.[32] The first national body to consider the *Act of Union* was the Congregational council, scheduled to hold its triennial session in Cleveland in October, 1907. Between the meeting of the General Council of the uniting churches in March of that year and the beginning of the Congregational sessions, Congregational churches and associations from one end of the country to the other took public stands for or against this final plan for organic union. Within Ohio there was a typical cleavage, with the preponderance of opinion

[31] Stein, "Church Unity Movements," pp. 121–23; *Religious Telescope*, LXXIII (March 27, 1907), 10.

[32] Asher Anderson to Gladden, March 27, 1907, W. Douglas Mackenzie to Gladden, March 28, 1907, Gladden Papers; *Congregationalist*, XCII (March 30, 1907), 412, 418–19, (April 6, 1907), 459.

supporting merger. In April Gladden led a discussion on union at the Central Ohio Congregational Conference and won a favorable decision. But within the Cleveland association there was strong sentiment against it, led by Dan Freeman Bradley, an outspoken theological liberal who feared the loss of congregational autonomy. Although the majority at the annual meeting of the Congregational Association of Ohio in May favored the *Act of Union,* for which Gladden spoke fervently, dissension prevented the association from instructing its delegation to the national council.[33] Elsewhere, there were also hostile reactions. In May the *Congregationalist* estimated that there had so far been more favorable than negative actions by churches and associations. But the opposition of influential men like Bradley and of prominent churches like the Broadway Tabernacle in New York City and the First Congregational Church of Terre Haute were discouraging omens, so much so that Asher Anderson, secretary of the National Council of Congregational Churches and a supporter of organic union, suggested that Gladden might as well anticipate that a majority of delegates to the council at Cleveland would be instructed to vote against the *Act of Union.*[34]

This division of Congregationalists over the proposal went so far that Gladden felt constrained to interject a word of counsel through the *Congregationalist.* Taking positions was legitimate, he admitted, if the churches involved were informed; but, even so, it would be fairer to wait for the meeting of the national council before becoming intransigent. In submitting the proposal to the churches, Gladden noted, he and his associates had hoped for discussion, not precipitate action. Moreover, autonomy was a sacred principle that neither he nor any other Congregational participants contemplated sacrificing. Those who feared its loss had not studied the *Act of Union,* which provided for only federation locally and organic union

[33] *Ohio State Journal,* April 18, May 16, 1907; William E. Cadmus to Gladden, April 19, 1907, Gladden Papers; Dan Freeman Bradley, "Tri-Church Union and the Congregational Program," *Congregationalist,* XCII (April 20, 1907), 528.

[34] *Congregationalist,* XCII (May 4, 1907), 614, (May 11, 1907), 641; Anderson to Gladden, May 3, 1907, Gladden Papers.

only nationally. Finally, Gladden contended, "the one thing that we must not have and will not have is a quarrel about the promotion of Christian union. I trust that most of us have a sense of humor sufficiently strong to see that that would not do."[35] This line of reasoning was not enough for the intractable opponents of the merger. One of their main spokesmen, William E. Barton of Illinois, predicted denominational suicide under the *Act of Union* and suggested organic union only between the Congregationalists and the Methodist Protestants and perhaps federation between them and the United Brethren.[36]

When the Congregational National Council met in October, it delivered a serious but not necessarily fatal blow to tripartite union. The issue was referred to a special committee of twenty-eight, which included Gladden and Barton and others of all shades of opinion, and this commitee held a series of open sessions at which speeches and resolutions both pro and con were read. Sharing Gladden's opinion that ecumenicity ought not fragment a denomination in the process of merging with other denominations, the committee worked hard to produce a compromise that would not lead to open friction on the floor of the council. Finally, the committee adopted a report giving general approval to the proposal for merger but inviting the Methodist Protestants and United Brethren to join with Congregationalists in referring the *Act of Union* back to the General Council for further revision, especially along lines preserving the autonomy of the local church.[37] Gladden, Mackenzie, and Ward were appointed to present this action to the other two denominations. Like many Congregationalists, Gladden did not consider this decision a permanent blow to tripartite union; though he

[35] Washington Gladden, "The Debate over Tri-Union," *Congregationalist*, XCII (May 18, 1907), 661–62.

[36] William E. Barton, "The Proposed Suicide of a Denomination," *Congregationalist*, XCII (June 29, 1907), 863, "Union That Unites," (August 31, 1907), 275.

[37] *Congregationalist*, XCII (October 19, 1907), 533–34, 545; *Ohio State Journal*, October 10, 12, 17, 1907; Atkins and Fagley, *American Congregationalism*, p. 354.

did not think delay necessary, he predicted the ultimate achievement of union.[38]

But Gladden's confidence was ill founded. Mackenzie and Ward were deeply discouraged. And with good reason! When they appeared before the Methodist Protestant General Conference in May, 1908, they found that denomination convinced that the Congregationalists had rejected union unilaterally and finally. No amount of explaining could convince them otherwise, and the Methodist Protestants refused to send the *Act of Union* back to the General Council for revision.[39] However, the action of the Congregational National Council was not entirely to blame for the Methodist Protestants' action. The Methodist Episcopal Church, from which the Methodist Protestants had separated in 1830, had begun to make overtures, and the Methodist Protestants found the prospect of being grafted back on the main trunk of Methodism more appealing than the tripartite merger. In addition, the United Brethren, who also interpreted the Congregationalists' action as a final repudiation of union, worked assiduously to woo the Methodist Protestants into a bilateral merger. Consequently, the Methodist Protestant General Conference appointed a new committee to negotiate with the United Brethren and other Methodist groups.[40] Ultimately, in 1939, the two Methodist groups consummated their reunion.

The United Brethren also did their share to bury the tripartite merger. Their bishops reported at the United Brethren General Conference in 1909 what other denominational spokesmen and journals had been saying since the Congregational action in 1907: the movement was dead, principally because of the Congregationalists'

[38] "The Present Status of Tri-Union," *Congregationalist*, XCII (October 26, 1907), 560, 566–67; Bishop J. S. Mills to Gladden, October 21, 1907, Gladden Papers.

[39] Mackenzie to Gladden, February 24, March 6, 1908, Ward to Gladden, February 28, April 14, 1908, Gladden Papers; Stein, "Church Unity Movements," p. 125.

[40] Mackenzie to Gladden, May 23, 1905, Gladden Papers; Frederick E. Maser, "The Story of Unification, 1874–1939," in *American Methodism*, III, 416–17, 444; *Religious Telescope*, LXXIII (October 23, 1907), 4, LXXIV (May 27, 1908), 10, (June 10, 1908), 2.

unwillingness to move ahead without further compromises. Accepting this conclusion, the General Conference took no action on the *Act of Union*.[41]

There were numerous reasons for the failure of this promising movement besides the incidental desire for haste on the part of Methodist Protestants and United Brethren. Despite Gladden's tendency to minimize theological differences, there were substantial and disruptive doctrinal factors. After accepting a confession of faith at Dayton, the negotiators themselves did not raise theological issues. Nevertheless, each denomination had vocal critics of the theological implications of the union. Since none of the denominations was really confessional or rooted in a strong creedal tradition, there were natural suspicions of the intentions of the negotiators in drafting a common statement of faith. Moreover, Congregationalism seemed to some United Brethren and Methodist Protestants to be too susceptible to liberalism, or even to Unitarianism and Universalism. Polity was probably the most important disruptive factor. Gladden's analysis was basically correct. The problems of amalgamating episcopal, presbyterian, and congregational features into an acceptable compromise were overwhelming. The United Brethren were particularly suspicious of congregational autonomy, the Congregationalists of centralized authority in the form of episcopal superintendency. In addition, there were undoubtedly secondary disruptive factors. The geographical distribution of the three denominations was uneven, with the Congregationalists most widespread, the United Brethren concentrated chiefly in Pennsylvania, Ohio, Indiana, and Illinois, and the Methodist Protestants centered in Maryland, Delaware, Washington, D. C., and West Virginia. Although this distribution meant that there was relatively little overlapping and that local mergers would probably have been infrequent, it actually prevented the three groups from knowing each

---

[41] *Official Report of the Proceedings and Debates of the Twenty-fifth General Conference of the United Brethren in Christ, Held in Canton, Ohio, May 13–24, 1909* (Dayton, Ohio: United Brethren Publishing House, Otterbein Press, 1909), pp. 26–27; Stein, "Church Unity Movements," p. 126.

other intimately, except in special circumstances, such as those exploited by Gladden in central Ohio. Gladden chose to minimize differences in social and educational status, but these too contributed to the breakdown in negotiations. The very fact that Gladden had to defend the intellectual and social stature of the United Brethren and Methodist Protestants testifies to the ingrained prejudices of sophisticated Congregationalists. And the United Brethren and Methodist Protestants had their own hesitation about adjusting to Congregational standards.[42] Finally, the negotiators' eagerness and enthusiasm in the early stages of discussion, when many basic and difficult questions remained to be settled, created expectations that were impossible to satisfy and a psychological climate that could not be maintained through the terminal stages, when compromise and hardheaded realism were prime necessities. Gladden's caution, had it prevailed on all sides, might well have saved an endeavor that initially had seemed providential.

At the same time that he was deeply involved in pressing plans for this tripartite merger, Gladden participated in an incidental way in a series of events that culminated in the greatest ecumenical achievement of his generation, the creation of the Federal Council of the Churches of Christ in America. Beginning in 1894 under the energetic leadership of Elias B. Sanford, the roots of the Federal Council were planted in the formation (in which Gladden participated) of the Open and Institutional Church League. This organization was important to the movement for federation because it brought not only individual Christians but also churches together, because it set a pattern for the Federal Council of federation for social service, and because its leadership, especially Sanford's, was instrumental in the creation of the Federal Council.[43] In the early 1900's federative activities began to pr' liferate. Federations of

---

[42] Stein, "Church Unity Movements," pp. 126–40.

[43] Charles S. Macfarland, *Christian Unity in the Making: The First Twenty-five Years of the Federal Council of the Churches of Christ in America, 1905–1930* (New York: Federal Council of the Churches of Christ in America, 1948), p. 124; Hopkins, *Rise of the Social Gospel*, pp. 154, 303–4.

churches appeared in several important cities and states. Gladden lent his support to the organization of the Ohio Federation of Churches, one of the first state federations, serving on a committee appointed by the Congregational Association of Ohio to explore federation with other denominations, hosting the first annual meeting of the Ohio Federation in Columbus, and addressing its first and second annual meetings.[44]

As state and local federation progressed, a movement for a national federation broader in scope than the Open and Institutional Church League also made rapid strides forward. In 1901 Sanford helped to organize the National Federation of Churches and Christian Workers, in some respects the lineal continuation of the Open and Institutional Church League and the direct forerunner of the Federal Council of Churches. In 1903 the federation began to arrange for an Inter-Church Conference on Federation at Carnegie Hall in New York City in November, 1905. An official Congregational delegate and moderator of the National Council of Congregational Churches, Gladden presided over the Inter-Church Conference on November 16, 1905, its second day of sessions. In informal remarks, he suggested that the churches, in addition to singing and praying together, might co-operate in dealing with social problems, such as the care of the poor, and in making public statements (such as a memorial on persecution of Russian Jews by the czarist regime that he introduced to the conference) carrying the combined weight of the participating denominations.[45] It was

[44] Elias B. Sanford, *Origin and History of the Federal Council of the Churches of Christ in America* (Hartford: S. S. Scranton Co., 1916), pp. 181, 185–86; Charles H. Small to Gladden, February 11, 1901, D. R. Miller to Gladden, September 11, 1903, Gladden Papers; *Religious Telescope,* LXIX (December 9, 1903), 1538, (December 16, 1903), 1570.

[45] Elias B. Sanford, ed., *Federal Council of the Churches of Christ in America: Report of the First Meeting of the Federal Council, Philadelphia, 1908* (New York: Revell Press, 1909), p. iii; Sanford, *Origin and History of the Federal Council,* p. 208; Elias B. Sanford, ed., *Church Federation: Inter-Church Conference on Federation, New York, November 15–21, 1905* (New York: Fleming H. Revell Co., 1906), pp. 51–53; Sanford to Gladden, October 29, 1905, Gladden Papers; *Congregationalist,* XC (October 21, 1905), 561–62, (November 25, 1905), 752–53.

a Plan of Federation recommended to the participating denominations by this Inter-Church Conference that became the constitution
of the Federal Council, organized in 1908 with thirty denominations
representing about seventeen million communicants.[46]

The Federal Council's orientation to social problems and social
service, symbolized by its "Social Creed of the Churches" adopted in
1908 and revised in 1912, gave the Social Gospel the official recognition and support of the most representative body in Protestantism.
Appropriately, Gladden's special activities in the Federal Council
were precisely along the lines of Christian involvement in social
affairs that he had done so much to advance. In 1908, the year of
the Federal Council's birth, he served on the Commission on International Relations. Thereafter, his activities were in conjunction with
the Federal Council's far-reaching social service program. In 1912
he shared the platform with Walter Rauschenbusch at a social service meeting during the Federal Council's annual convention. And
in 1913 he was appointed to its official Commission on the Church
and Social Service. Beginning in 1910 with an inquiry into a steel
strike in South Bethlehem, Pennsylvania, this commission investigated a series of industrial disputes, usually, as in the case of the
steel strike, concluding impartially but decisively that greater justice
lay on the side of labor than on the side of management. During
Gladden's service on this commission it studied and reported on the
savage mining strike in Colorado in 1913–14, an appropriate coinci-
dence in view of Gladden's personal investigation of a strike there
in 1904.[47]

After the organization of the Federal Council in 1908, Gladden's
ecumenical interests centered on the problems of rural religion.
This concern was not new for him, as his criticisms of rural sectarianism in the 1870's and 1880's bear witness. But it received new

---

[46] Sanford, *Federal Council: Report of the First Meeting*, p. iii.

[47] Hopkins, *Rise of the Social Gospel*, pp. 306–17; Sanford to Gladden, April
27, 1908, Rauschenbusch to Gladden, November 11, 1912, Strong to Gladden,
March 27, 1913, Macfarland to Gladden, March 27, 1913, May 2, 1914,
Atkinson to Gladden, April 18, May 2, 1914, Gladden Papers.

impetus from the Federal Council itself and from the progressive movement, which devoted significant but neglected attention to the general deterioration of rural life. The first great impetus to the movement to save rural life came from Theodore Roosevelt's appointment in 1908 of a Commission on Country Life under his Chief Forester, Gifford Pinchot. Following this commission's first report in 1909, in which it urged the creation of varied organizations to give stability and vitality to rural life, a variety of local organizations and studies were launched. Ohio, for example, was the subject of a Rural Life Survey in 1909. This survey brought to light the decay of religion in the country, indicating that only 5 per cent of Ohio's rural churches had ministers who did not have more than one congregation to serve and that many congregations had no minister at all.[48]

Alarmed by such revelations, churchmen took steps to resuscitate rural religion and, indirectly, social life generally. There were numerous attempts to meet the challenge by experiments with larger parishes, served by ministers with more than one charge, or with community churches and united churches. Gladden preferred the community church or united church, which usually had a resident minister and was affiliated with one or several denominations. In most cases, this solution was more satisfactory than the stop-gap circuit system of larger parishes.[49]

Gladden took an instrumental part in the organization of two union churches, one in his native town of Owego, the other in the village of Dublin, a suburb of Columbus. Both events occurred in 1912. During his summer vacation in Owego in 1912, he assisted in reuniting the Congregational church, which he had joined as a boy, with the Presbyterian church from which it had seceded over the issue of slavery. The new organization became the First Presbyterian Union Church of Owego; it utilized the old Congregational building

<hr>

[48] Harlow Lindley, *Ohio in the Twentieth Century* (*The History of the State of Ohio*, ed. Carl Wittke [6 vols.; Columbus, Ohio: Ohio State Archaeological and Historical Society, 1941–44]), VI, 380.

[49] Hudson, *Religion in America*, pp. 412–13.

for social purposes and the Presbyterian edifice for regular services. Gladden returned to preach at the first service in November, 1912.[50]

The organization of the Dublin Community Church was more spectacular. A quiet farming village of three hundred inhabitants, with a total population of about one thousand within a radius of two or three miles, Dublin had three churches, Methodist, Presbyterian, and Christian, and there were three more outside of the village but still within that radius. The Christian church, temporarily without a minister, had not held regular services for several years; the Methodist church, served by a minister with four other charges, held services only every other week; the Presbyterian church, with a minister who also served a church in Worthington, held regular weekly services. Following a series of union revival services in 1909–10, there had been talk of consolidation, but this came to nothing. Suddenly, on June 16, 1912, a cyclone hit Dublin, wrecking the Methodist and Presbyterian buildings but leaving the Christian church, the largest of the edifices, untouched. This seemingly providential catastrophe inspired new discussions of union. A delegation approached Gladden for advice, and on June 20 he went out to counsel and preach to the temporarily united congregations in the Christian church.

The rural church was a dying institution, Gladden concluded; it might seem to have the breath of life, but only because it was pumped in "by a vigorous working of the denominational bellows." Sectarianism was bad anywhere, but in the country it was particularly wasteful and divisive. Even where several churches of different denominations were justifiable, they ought to think of themselves as related units of a single "municipal church." In short, Christians must recognize that their obligation to co-operate for the salvation of the community superseded their obligation to co-operate with other congregations in distant places for sectarian purposes. In a community like Dublin, Gladden maintained, the problem was very

[50] Arnold W. Bloomfield to Gladden, August 20, September 17, 30, October 7, 13, 1912, April 23, 1914, Lawrence R. Howard to Gladden, April 20, 1914, Gladden Papers; Gladden, Sermon, November 3, 1912, Gladden Papers.

simple. There should be but a single congregation. Such a congregation could support one ample building and one competent minister
and could serve as a rural social center, the "radiating point of your
intelligence, your public spirit, your movements for better moral
and material conditions." Returning to Dublin on July 14, Gladden
bore down on this theme again: the only thing that could save
Christianity in rural areas was "the wiping out of existence of thousands of churches."

With Gladden's encouragement, the church people of Dublin
moved forward toward union. Finding it easier to reorganize on an
entirely new basis than on the foundation of one of the existing
churches, they formed the Congregational Church of Dublin (later
called the Dublin Community Church), which received all the
property and members of the dissolving churches. Byron R. Long,
a former pastor of the Mayflower Congregational Church of Columbus who was then serving as director of the Associated Charities of
Columbus, became acting minister at Gladden's recommendation,
and during the early months of Long's ministry the new church
acquired a membership nearly twice that of the previous three
churches together. On March 4, 1913, the church was recognized
and received by an ecclesiastical council of the Central Ohio Congregational Conference. Gladden presided as moderator of the
council and preached the council sermon.[51]

In Gladden's thinking, the establishment of the Dublin Community Church was a model of what ought to occur throughout rural
America. After 1912 he threw his energies into the concerted efforts
of Protestant leaders to make Ohio an experimental station for solutions to the problems of rural life. In 1914 he became aware of a
pioneer survey of religious conditions in Ohio by Warren H. Wilson,
a Presbyterian minister first associated with the Department of
Church and Labor of the Board of Home Missions of his denomina-

[51] *Ohio State Journal*, June 29, 1912; "Historical Sketch," *Dublin Community
Church: Fiftieth Anniversary, March 4, 1913–March 3, 1963* (n.p., 1963); Glad-
den, Sermons, June 30, July 14, 1912, Gladden Papers; Washington Gladden,
"The Story of Dublin," *Congregationalist*, XCVIII (April 24, 1913), 567.

tion and then superintendent of a separate Department of Church and Country Life of the same board. Gladden supported Wilson's efforts to persuade the Federal Council of Churches, which had its own Commission on the Church and Rural Life under Gifford Pinchot and Charles O. Gill, another minister, to use Ohio as a laboratory for the reconstruction of rural religion. The Federal Council was responsive to Wilson's appeal, and in August, 1914, Gill established his base of operations just a few blocks from Gladden's home in Columbus. He contacted, and became executive secretary of, the Ohio Rural Life Association, like Roosevelt's Commission on Country Life an organization concerned with general rural conditions, and began a fuller investigation than Wilson's preliminary survey.[52]

Meanwhile, denominational officials in Ohio began their own movement to meet the same challenge. But they quickly co-ordinated their efforts with those of the Federal Council. In February, 1915, the Ohio Home Missions Council, composed of denominational secretaries or superintendents of home mission work, held a Country Life Institute at Chillicothe and decided to organize a commission representing the denominations in Ohio for co-operation. Denominational representatives then established a permanent Commission on Interchurch Co-operation at a subsequent meeting at Columbus in March. As chairman of a committee on federation of the Congregational Association of Ohio, Gladden was drawn into the planning officially at this stage, although he had taken an informal interest in the movement earlier. The Commission on Interchurch Co-operation commended Gill's preparation of a rural-church map of Ohio, urged the formation of an interdenominational commission in each county to study conditions and co-ordinate religious activities on the basis of "denominational reciprocity," and held meetings looking to more solid federation in the state. Gladden spoke enthusiastically for these efforts at the conference of the Congregational Association of Ohio in May, 1915, and at meetings of other denominations later that

[52] Hopkins, *Rise of the Social Gospel*, p. 283; Warren H. Wilson to Gladden, April 21, 1914, Gladden Papers; Gladden, Address, [May, 1915,] Gladden Papers.

year.[53] The zenith of this movement for the rehabilitation of rural religion occurred in December, 1915, when the Federal Council held its national convention in Columbus and officially recognized Ohio as its field of experimentation. As a representative of the Federal Council, Gladden served on the reception committee for President Wilson, the convention's featured speaker, and opened the meetings with a strong appeal for an end to sectarian rivalry.[54]

During 1916 and 1917 Gladden continued to participate in and support the rural-life movement. He helped to arrange a conference on the church and rural life in conjunction with the Extension Department of the Ohio State University during Farmers' Week in the winter of 1916–17, and he addressed the Interdenominational Conference of the Ohio Rural Life Association in August, 1917.[55] Of greater importance, he gave the movement national publicity through articles demonstrating the seriousness of rural problems and interpreting the efforts that were being made to solve them. In "What Ails the Church?", published in January, 1916, in the *Congregationalist,* he summarized the results of Wilson's and Gill's surveys, indicating that one-fourth of Ohio's townships had no resident minister, although each was sure to have from three to seven churches, and concluded that the "good old Gospel" and an "outpouring of the Spirit" were not enough. What is meant by an "outpouring of the Spirit" in a town of five or six hundred with four or five churches, he contended, is "four or five hysterical revivals all going at once, then a lively scrap for the converts, and then a relapse into deeper stagnation, leaving the last state of that town worse than the first." The only solution that he could see was the elimination of many churches.[56] And in "Empty Pews in the Country Church—Why?",

[53] Charles O. Gill to Gladden, February 19, 1915, Gladden Papers; Gladden, Address, [May, 1915,] Sermon, July 2, 1915, Gladden Papers.

[54] *Ohio State Journal,* November 21, December 5, 9–10, 1915; *Congregationalist,* C (December 23, 1915), 923–24.

[55] Gill to Gladden, September 8, 1916, Gladden Papers; *Ohio State Journal,* August 5, 1917.

[56] Washington Gladden, "What Ails the Church?", *Congregationalist,* CI (January 13, 1916), 74.

published in May, 1916, in *Everybody's Magazine,* he offered the general rule, based on surveys in Ohio and Indiana, that the more churches there were in a rural community, the fewer church members there would be. "The church ought to be in every community the unifying, harmonizing influence," he argued; but the plain truth was that "in hundreds and thousands of rural neighborhoods the church is one of the chief obstacles to the unity and co-operation on which the economic and moral welfare of the community depend."[57] Gladden saw the rural-life movement as the remedy for a malady of which he had been aware for several decades. His diagnosis—that overchurching and sectarian rivalry were not only symptoms of, but also causes of, rural decay remained unchanged. But now, in the 1910's, he found the churches more willing than before to act in concert, and he did as much as his old age would allow to insure the success of rural co-operation.

[57] Washington Gladden, "Empty Pews in the Country Church—Why?", *Everybody's Magazine*, XXXIV (May, 1916), 615.

Thirteen

Progressive Religion in the Balance

By the beginning of the twentieth century the liberal theology of which Gladden was a leading spokesman had largely supplanted the orthodoxy that had prevailed in the American Protestant churches before the Civil War. This theology, including an optimistic view of man, a broadened base of religious authority in which reason and conscience were tests of and checks on biblical authority, an evolutionary doctrine of progress, and a moralistic standard of Christian experience, had become the consensus of many seminaries and of the better educated clergymen of the major denominations.[1]

At first a revolt against the restraints of tradition, liberalism itself became a tradition, subject to new revolts. Despite their predominance in ecclesiastical circles, the liberals had never dented the theological conservatism of large sections of the Protestant public. During the late nineteenth century the liberals and conservatives— even granting the heresy trials of the period—had worked together in relative peace. The threats of materialistic science and social upheaval had required at least superficial unity. Moreover, in their early deviations from traditional theological norms, the liberals had been cautious. But, for a variety of reasons, some of them obscure, the full flowering of liberalism and the Social Gospel after the turn of the century shattered this accord and precipitated first psycho-

---

[1] Cauthen, *American Religious Liberalism,* pp. 3–5.

logical, then ecclesiastical, schisms in Protestant ranks. Although the name "Fundamentalists" was not coined until 1920, when Curtis Lee Laws, the editor of the Baptist *Watchman-Examiner*, used it with reference to those intent on defending the essentials of orthodoxy, a variety of leaders and organizations of the fundamentalist persuasion appeared after 1900 to challenge the dominance of liberalism. Bible institutes, leagues to protect the Bible from destructive criticism, and conservative books and pamphlets (the most famous of which was a series published in 1910 under the general title *The Fundamentals*) took up the orthodox cause, making the infallibility of the Bible the principal line of defense against theological innovation.[2]

The most famous conflicts between the fundamentalists and liberals, or modernists, as they came to be called, occurred after 1920— the Scopes "monkey trial" at Dayton, Tennessee, and the battles over denominational societies and seminaries. For more than a decade before Gladden's death, however, fundamentalism was crystallizing as a potent force in American religion. Seeing it as a threat to the humane, socially conscious faith that he had been trying to foster, Gladden opposed it adamantly. Although it is an injustice to the best side of fundamentalism to accept Billy Sunday, the famous "baseball evangelist," as a spokesman for the movement, one can glimpse significant aspects of the increasingly fractious struggle within Protestantism in a dramatic confrontation between Gladden and Sunday that began in 1911. Public reactions to this protracted episode illustrate the breadth of the cleavage that divided those at opposite ends of the theological spectrum.

Gladden, it is important to recognize, was not opposed to evangelism or even to the work of professional evangelists (as distinct from the evangelistic work of men in the pastoral ministry). Throughout his career he rather consistently supported such evangelists, or

---

[2] Hudson, *Religion in America*, pp. 363–71; Norman F. Furniss, *The Fundamentalist Controversy, 1918–1931* (New Haven: Yale University Press, 1954), pp. 9–13; William Hordern, *A Layman's Guide to Protestant Theology* (New York: Macmillan Co., 1955), pp. 57–58.

revivalists. In 1878 he participated actively in a revival conducted by Dwight L. Moody in Springfield. Before the revival began, he introduced to the North Church the new hymns popularized by Moody's songster, Ira Sankey; he served on the committee that planned the meetings; he led one of a series of prayer meetings preparatory to Moody's arrival; and he counseled converts after every one of Moody's services. During the revival his own church received fifty-one new members, most of them, apparently, converted by Moody.[3] Although he could not agree with all of Moody's statements, particularly his literal interpretations of the Bible, he admired Moody's candor and gentleness and his central theme of the love of God. Moody's seriousness, epitomized when on one occasion he reprimanded his audience for applauding his entrance into the building, appealed to Gladden.[4]

Similarly, though sometimes to a lesser degree, Gladden supported most of the evangelists who came to Columbus before Billy Sunday. Enthusiastically participating in a very unusual revival under B. Fay Mills in 1895–96, he presided over a meeting of ministers that arranged Mills's campaign, sat on the platform when Mills preached, opened the First Church for midday services, and wrote the introduction for a memorial book on the revival. Converted to the Social Gospel by George D. Herron in 1893, Mills was, according to the foremost historian of modern revivalism, "one of the first and perhaps the only professional revivalist ever to break with the emphasis upon individual reform and to preach primarily a doctrine of social responsibility and social action." The social orientation of Mills's sermons, which precipitated not only numerous conversions but also a wave of civic reform, undoubtedly accounted for

[3] *Springfield Republican*, September 11, October 11, 1875, October 30, 1877, January 19, February 21, April 22, 1878; Gladden, Sermons, "The Good Part," [1878,] "The Salvation I Need," March 23, 1885, Gladden Papers; Washington Gladden, "Clear-Headed, Broad-Minded, Great-Hearted," *Congregationalist*, XCIX (November 12, 1914), 634.

[4] *Springfield Republican*, February 14, 19, March 9, 1878; *Sunday Afternoon*, I (April, 1878), 375–76, III (September, 1879), 858–59.

Gladden's wholehearted involvement.[5] In 1905 Gladden invited Lyman Abbott to preach for a week in the First Church on topics that would involve, in Abbott's words, "an appeal to the will, a definite acceptance of Christ, and a definite choice of the Christian life," but that would be in the context of the Social Gospel and liberal theology.[6] That same year, as moderator of the Congregational national council, Gladden endorsed William J. Dawson, an English clergyman who was conducting evangelistic services in the United States.[7] And in 1910 Gladden publicly supported J. Wilbur Chapman, Billy Sunday's mentor. Informing Gladden that he wanted to consult him on the problems confronting the churches and to adjust his work to those problems, Chapman declared, "I believe that this is the day for the Social note to be sounded, and while men may not agree on all theological points, I cannot see why we should not . . . get together in this great work about which you speak in your sermons." Perhaps misled by Chapman, who, despite this avowal of the Social Gospel, was quite conservative in his social philosophy, Gladden spoke at one of Chapman's services in Dayton in March and defended the subsequent revival in Columbus in a sermon in the First Church.[8]

Despite this record of support, Gladden always had reservations about revivalism. Certainly, he could never accept much of the theology of orthodox evangelists like Moody and Chapman, who preached biblical infallibility and the substitutionary theory of the atonement

[5] *Ohio State Journal*, May 24, 28, November 1, 20, 23, December 12, 17, 21, 1895; *Congregationalist*, LXXX (November 28, 1895), 853; McLoughlin, *Modern Revivalism*, pp. 336–37. Noting Mills's emphasis on the social aspects of Christianity, Gladden called him "a new type of evangelist." Henry Stauffer (ed.), *The Great Awakening in Columbus, Ohio, under the Labors of Rev. B. Fay Mills and His Associates* (Columbus, Ohio: W. L. Lemon, 1896), pp. 5, 12.

[6] Abbott to Gladden, January 16, February 9, 1905, Gladden Papers; *Ohio State Journal*, April 19, 1905.

[7] *Congregationalist*, XC (January 14, 1905), 44, (February 11, 1905), 173, 184.

[8] J. Wilbur Chapman to Gladden, February 20, 24, 1910, Gladden Papers; McLoughlin, *Modern Revivalism*, p. 383; *Dayton Daily News*, March 4, 1910; *Ohio State Journal*, March 21, 1910; Converse Diaries, March 23, 1910, Gladden Papers.

and often opposed evolution and biblical criticism. He supported them in spite of some of their views. In view of this fact, his experiment with Abbott in 1905 had great significance as an attempt to preserve the evangelical appeal for decision within a liberal theological framework. Moreover, Gladden always felt that the popular fascination with revivals led to the neglect of other means of evangelism. In *The Christian Pastor* (1898) Gladden, clearly reflecting the influence of Bushnell's *Christian Nurture*, contended that revivalism had a disastrous effect on more gradualistic, and what should be more normal, methods of winning and nurturing souls. The sustained influence of church and home, he wrote, would produce more durable results than the temporary excitement of the evangelistic meeting—and without any unfortunate psychological aftereffects. Finally, Gladden did not believe that revivalism was the answer to the slow progress that the churches were making relative to the growth of population. He argued, even in his remarks at Chapman's revival in Dayton, that this form of evangelism made only a slight impression on the unchurched masses and that only re-establishment of the churches' social role would bring them the influence they were seeking.[9]

By 1908, after Billy Sunday had begun to achieve repute in the towns and small cities of the Midwest, Gladden was even more impatient with revivalism. This impatience was not peculiar to Gladden; rather, it was part of the most important opposition to revivalism in the evangelical churches since the days of Finney. Some of his statements seemed to carry oblique references to Sunday's style. In *The Church and Modern Life* he called for a new evangelism that would "find its motive not in self-love," the usual consideration behind appeals for conversion, but "in love that identifies the self with the neighbor." This new evangelism would seek to reconcile races, bring peace to industry, ethicize business, uproot social vice, cleanse politics, and simplify life.[10] Preaching on the financial panic

[9] Gladden, *Christian Pastor*, pp. 384–98; *Dayton Daily News*, March 4, 1910.

[10] McLoughlin, *Modern Revivalism*, pp. 347–48; Gladden, *The Church and Modern Life*, pp. 182–90.

of 1907, Gladden underscored the need for a religious awakening but added that he would regret any attempt to create it by "some great, spectacular, evangelistic meetings," especially of the type based on "auctioneer methods" that repelled reasonable people. The Men and Religion Forward Movement, which began in 1911 and linked religion and social service, seemed to Gladden to be more compatible with the advances of the last fifty years within Protestantism.[11]

By 1911 an organized movement began in Columbus to secure Sunday for an evangelistic campaign. There was opposition to these early negotiations, but it was mostly the predictable hostility of churches without strong revivalistic traditions, such as the Episcopal, Lutheran, and Universalist. But, significantly, from the very outset Gladden assumed the leadership of the opposition to Sunday. Joined by the ministers of the Eastwood, Plymouth, Grandview, and South Congregational churches, he signed a remonstrance sent by nineteen ministers to the Columbus Ministerial Association, which had appointed a committee to approach Sunday; eighteen Lutheran ministers signed their own protest. However, a majority of sixty-three ministers, including the pastor of the Mayflower Congregational Church, voted to call Sunday to Columbus after hearing the committee's report.[12]

To Gladden, Sunday exaggerated all of the worst features of previous revivalists. During the various stages of the controversy, Gladden elaborated four principal objections to Sunday's work: Sunday's theology was a crude form of "medievalism"; Sunday's financial methods were characterized by an insatiable desire for personal profit; Sunday's personal conduct and speech were violent and vulgar; and, largely because of these three features, Sunday's appearances had deleterious effects on the communities where he

[11] Gladden, Sermons, January 5, 1908; "Men and Religion," September 24, 1911; November 19, 1911; March 28, 1912, Gladden Papers.

[12] *Ohio State Journal,* January 21, 31, March 17, 19–20, 22, 1911; Alfred E. Isaacs to Gladden, March 23, 1911, Carl S. Patton to Gladden, March 27, 1911, Gladden Papers.

preached. Explaining his part in circulating the remonstrance to the ministerial association, Gladden wrote: " . . . It is quite impossible for me to approve of a type of evangelism which is distinguished by irreverence and greed, even though it may result in the temporary reduction of the number of saloons." Moreover, Gladden wrote in the *Ohio State Journal*, Sunday was "a man whose greed for gain is his most distinguishing trait," a man "full of intolerance and bitterness," a man who profaned the sacred name by mixing it with vulgarity.[13] In March, 1912, he circulated a pamphlet written by Dr. Hugh T. Morrison, a physician in Springfield, Illinois, which analyzed the results of Sunday's revival there two years after its conclusion. This analysis, published several months earlier by the *Christian Century*, described Springfield after Sunday's revival as a "burnt-out district" and denounced Sunday's "extreme sensationalism and blood-curdling irreverence."[14] And in May, 1912, Gladden published in the *Independent* an article, "Samples of Modern Evangelism," listing scurrilous and vulgar statements made by a prominent evangelist. He did not attribute these quotations to Sunday, but that they came from Sunday was an implicit conclusion.[15]

Gladden's efforts were not enough to stem the enthusiasm for Sunday, which, like a steam roller, crushed all obstacles in its path. Three of the Congregational churches, Mayflower, North, and Plymouth, joined in the preparations during 1912 for Sunday's arrival. The pastor of the Plymouth Church, who had signed Gladden's remonstrance in 1911, publicly repudiated his original stand, impugning the evidence on which he had based his opposition, and threw himself with vigor into the campaign.[16] As in other large cities, the churches, which were not gaining members in proportion to the

[13] *Ohio State Journal*, April 2, 1911, February 1, 1912.

[14] *Ibid.*, March 21, 1912; *Congregationalist*, XCVII (April 6, 1912), 470.

[15] Washington Gladden, "Samples of Modern Evangelism," *Independent*, LXXII (May 23, 1912), 1101–3.

[16] *Ohio State Journal*, April 23, 1912, February 13, 1913, January 3, 1914; *Congregationalist*, XCVII (December 26, 1912), 970, XCVIII (April 10, 1913), 509, C (April 1, 1915), 417.

growth of population, turned to Sunday in confused desperation. Examining the astonishing change from suspicion or hostility to acceptance and co-operation on the part of many clergymen, Sunday's biographer attributes it to a growing anxiety and a new willingness to wink at sensationalism in the pulpit. Sunday got results. To those in this confused state of mind, this was a convincing answer to criticisms of Sunday. However, this was not Sunday's only appeal. His simple solutions to complex problems were attractive to many middle-class citizens who had never felt comfortable with the liberal Social Gospel. Satisfied with the progress of conservative reform, distracted by the growing intensity of the prohibition movement, and still basically susceptible to the simplistic fundamentalism that Sunday preached, these people contributed to a mounting reaction against the Social Gospel, a reaction on which Sunday capitalized and to which he gave popular leadership.[17]

Both Gladden and Sunday realized the importance to Sunday of a successful revival in Columbus. The evangelist was then in a transitional stage of his career. He had proven his ability to arouse the religious fervor of the towns and small cities of the Midwest but had only recently begun to test his appeal in major metropolitan centers. Spokane, which he visited in 1909, was the first city with a population exceeding 100,000 in which he preached. Toledo, his field of battle for the Lord in 1911 when Columbus opened negotiations with him, numbered about 168,000 and was his largest city before 1912. Columbus, with over 180,000, would set new records and might well determine his future course.[18] Their recognition of this fact helps to explain both Gladden's intransigent opposition to the revival and Sunday's eagerness, despite the disheartening hostility of a large bloc of ministers, to accept the invitation. Although Sunday threatened that if the opposition in Columbus did not subside he

[17] William G. McLoughlin, Jr., *Billy Sunday Was His Real Name* (Chicago: University of Chicago Press, 1955), pp. 190–93, 195–96; McLoughlin, *Modern Revivalism*, pp. 397–402.

[18] McLoughlin, *Billy Sunday*, pp. 46–47; Donald E. Pitzer, "The Ohio Campaigns of Billy Sunday with Special Emphasis upon the 1913 Columbus Revival" (unpublished M.A. thesis, Ohio State University, 1962), p. 35.

would accept invitations from the two or three hundred cities that he estimated were clamoring for his services, he finally concluded that the fruits of a revival there were worth the risks.[19]

Sunday's revival in Columbus far surpassed all predictions. This was due partly to the solid groundwork of Sunday's supporters and partly to his own talent at swaying crowds. The Columbus Evangelistic Association, organized to handle the promotional and financial aspects of the revival, issued a pamphlet, *Some Truths Concerning the Billy Sunday Campaign,* containing accounts of his earlier meetings designed to counter criticisms, particularly Gladden's. It divided the city into 230 districts and organized cottage prayer meetings in each district, arranged for the 60 co-operating pastors, representing 14 denominations, to exchange pulpits in a show of unity, and held a large prerevival rally at the Southern Theater.[20] And about a month before Sunday's arrival his advance agent came on the scene to stir up enthusiasm, denounce the critics as "dirty dogs" and allies of liquor dealers, thieves, and liars, and announce that Sunday would "spring new sensations in Columbus."[21]

The revival began with the formal dedication of Sunday's tabernacle on December 26, 1912. An audience of roughly four thousand heard the minister of the prominent Washington Street Congregational Church of Toledo, Ernest Bourner Allen, a friend of Gladden's and a colleague in many denominational affairs, tell how his own attitude had changed from suspicion to wholehearted support of Sunday. Daniel Poling, who was then secretary of the Ohio Society of Christian Endeavor, delivered the dedicatory prayer.[22] During the revival itself Sunday and his supporters kept popular enthusi-

[19] *Ohio State Journal*, April 2, November 24, 1912.

[20] *Ibid.*, September 18, December 5, 19, 1912; Pitzer, "Ohio Campaigns of Billy Sunday," pp. 91–92.

[21] Pitzer, "Ohio Campaigns of Billy Sunday," pp. 90–91; *Ohio State Journal*, December 5, 1912.

[22] *Ohio State Journal*, December 27, 1912. A few months later, Allen wrote an article for the *Congregationalist*, praising Sunday's achievements in Toledo. Ernest Bourner Allen, "Toledo Two Years After," *Congregationalist*, XCVIII (April 24, 1913), 564–66.

asm at white heat. On January 11, 1913, when Sunday issued the first call for sinners to hit the "sawdust trail," about four hundred responded, a new record for the first invitation that led some ministers to anticipate thirty thousand converts. The newspapers lauded Sunday and usually gave the revival from six to ten columns on the first and second pages. When an anonymous letter-writer, "Billy Monday," satirized the revival and suggested that Sunday would reach an unbeatable climax by converting Gladden and the Reverend Christian Schaer, the pastor of St. John's Independent Protestant Church, who also refused to co-operate, the *Ohio State Journal* denounced such attacks on Sunday as "without good judgment."[23]

As if to indicate that he was too big a man to answer personal criticisms, Sunday declared before coming to Columbus that he would not wage a war of words with Gladden. Yet, he recognized Gladden as his most formidable foe from the beginning and, giving the lie to his pacific protestations, singled out Gladden for special abuse. Visiting Columbus in April, 1912, to select a site for his tabernacle, he told reporters: "I have no animus against anyone, no ill will. I have no quarrel with Dr. Gladden. I am no Unitarian. . . . I am willing to abide by the numbers that I bring into the church by my methods." This single comment contained both his disclaimer of personal belligerence and the telling insinuation that Gladden was a Unitarian. Mrs. Sunday, known affectionately to admirers as "Ma," had already indicated in March, 1911, which of these contradictory tendencies would prevail: "We will roll right over Dr. Gladden."[24] And a widespread rumor had it that, in a moment of irritation, Sunday himself called Gladden a "bald-headed old mutt."[25]

The revival had hardly begun when Sunday began to punctuate his sermons with biting condemnations of liberal theology and the Social Gospel. Thus, on December 29, 1912, in his first address, he declared: "This universal fatherhood of God and brotherhood of

---

[23] *Ohio State Journal,* January 11, 23–24, 1913.

[24] *Ibid.,* March 31, 1911, February 2, 1912.

[25] Atkins, *Religion in Our Times,* p. 53.

man is all rot." On January 1, 1913, he denounced "bastard evolution" and biblical criticism: "If there ever was evolution, why don't
we evolute now?" On January 5 he added two other scapegoats, the
Parliament of Religions of 1893, "one of the biggest curses that ever
came to America," and the liberal ministers who "are giving a book
review and tacking a verse of Scripture to the end of it and calling
it a sermon." On January 26 he flayed the Social Gospel—"the church
is talking social service—social rot"—and, once again, biblical criticism—"When the latest scholarship says one thing and the Word of
God another, the latest scholarship can go plumb to hell." On
February 7 he came closer to naming Gladden, and in so doing
gave credence to the rumor that he called Gladden a "bald-headed
old mutt."

> The trouble with a lot of you people in Columbus is you have had a lot
> of mutts here, professing to be preachers, who have been preaching a
> lot of tommy rot, and it's no wonder you have lost your idea of what is
> truth.

At one time or another Sunday ridiculed virtually every one of the
causes and ideas with which Gladden was identified.[26] In addition,
he vindictively arraigned the ministers of the non-co-operating
churches, represented in the popular mind by Gladden. "I don't
see," he said, "how a minister can lift his voice against a brother
minister who is trying to do God's work in a different way. That's
something that even a saloon-keeper wouldn't do."[27]

Deeply troubled by the fact that he had not been able to prevent
Sunday from coming to Columbus, Gladden became comparatively
silent on the issue for the duration of the revival. Although he did
not hesitate to state his own views forthrightly, he kept his hostility
out of his pulpit. Anxious to present an alternative to Sunday's theology, he began during the second week in January, 1913, a series
of midweek lectures on "The Foundations of Faith." "It may be the
last opportunity I will ever have to give you the substance of my

[26] *Ohio State Journal,* December 30, 1912, January 2, 6, 27, February 8, 1913.
[27] *Ibid.,* January 1, 1913.

teachings for the last thirty years," he told his parishioners, "but it will be the best legacy I could leave with you."[28] This series of lectures, which ran until Easter, was exactly what Gladden intended it to be, a summary of the theology that he had been developing since the 1870's. Covering such topics as "God and Man," "Nature and the Supernatural," "Sin and Salvation," "The Atonement," "Heaven and Hell," and "The Incarnation," he explained simply and succinctly the reasons for and the nature of his mature liberalism.[29] Published in 1913 as *Present Day Theology*, these lectures constituted his last comprehensive theological work. *Present Day Theology* received the warm commendation of such distinguished Protestant figures as Theodore Irving Reese, Episcopal bishop coadjutor of southern Ohio, Charles R. Brown, dean of the Yale Divinity School, William J. Tucker, president of Dartmouth College, and Douglas Clyde Macintosh, professor of systematic theology at Yale.[30] But to Sunday's supporters it was just a final proof of Gladden's infidelity.

Gladden refrained from any statements or actions that would mar the dignity of his position. For example, in a sermon entitled "Walking in Integrity," he observed, with obvious reference to Sunday's techniques, that a crowd is usually less rational than the individuals composing it, but he carefully avoided applying this generalization to Sunday's revivals.[31] Likewise, he did not attempt to fan the smoldering opposition to the revival that still existed. When a member of another church, one that was supporting Sunday, proposed transferring his membership to the First Congregational Church, Gladden

[28] *Ibid.*, January 9, 1913.

[29] Interestingly, Gladden gave his lecture on "Heaven and Hell" the same day that Sunday, preaching his famous sermon on "Hell," denounced as liars those who denied the existence of a literal hell. *Ibid.*, February 12, 1913.

[30] Gladden, *Present Day Theology*, p. 18; Theodore Irving Reese to Gladden, August 9, 1913, Charles R. Brown to Gladden, September 16, November 26, 1913, Tucker to Gladden, October 15, 1913, Douglas Clyde Macintosh to Gladden, n.d., Gladden Papers.

[31] *Ohio State Journal*, February 3, 1913.

arranged for the man to be received inconspicuously at a midweek prayer meeting.[32]

Gladden came closest to public criticism of the revival during its course in an episode involving his "municipal church," the General Council of the Churches and Religious Societies of Columbus, organized in 1910. At the meeting of the council on February 17, 1913, the committee on amusements, composed of the ministers of the First Universalist and Mayflower Congregational churches, reported that dancing and attendance at theaters had risen during the revival and predicted further increase following the revival. The committee explained that the increase during the revival had occurred because many who came, often from out of town, to attend the meetings had been turned away from the tabernacle and that the additional post-revival increase would result from the need, induced by the revival, for sustained psychological stimulus. The ministers of the churches supporting Sunday met immediately to discuss the report and to vent their hostility toward this apparent attack on Sunday. As president of the council, Gladden explained that the report merely represented the views of the committee, not any official position of the council, and challenged the hostile ministers to become active in the council. For his own part, he insisted, he had not known about the committee's report until the meeting of the council at which it was submitted.[33] More than a year later Gladden did openly subscribe to the committee's thesis, but at the time of the revival he attempted only to defend the committee's right to express its opinion.[34]

After the revival ended on February 16, 1913, the *Ohio State Journal* proclaimed "Sunday's Campaign Eclipses Every Known Revival Record." For Sunday, who characteristically staked his reputation on statistics, the facts were simple and clear. During seven

[32] W. E. Henderson, "The Inescapable Christ," *First Church News,* VI (February, 1936), 11.

[33] *Ohio State Journal,* February 18, 20–21, 23, 1913.

[34] *Ibid.,* April 7, 1914.

weeks of preaching he had made 18,149 converts.[35] Apparently, his techniques were improving. In small midwestern towns he had converted about 20 per cent of the population, but in Spokane and Toledo, his first big cities, he had roused only 5 and 4 per cent, respectively, to the point of spiritual decision. It had seemed that, for both physical and cultural reasons, the metropolis would be relatively harder to revive than the small, homogeneous community. But his converts in Columbus totaled approximately 10 per cent of the population. The first Sunday after his departure the churches of Columbus took in over five thousand new members and the second Sunday almost three thousand more. The revival's managers even referred some converts—certainly at the converts' quittstion—Gladden. Convinced that he was successfully meeting the challenge of the metropolis, Sunday turned after 1913 to even larger cities, particularly in the East.[36] According to the historian of Sunday's revivals in Ohio, the campaign in Columbus was the first of his twenty most successful revivals and marked the beginning of his most spectacular decade.[37]

For those unimpressed by numbers, there were other reasons for rejoicing. Opponents of the saloon claimed that the revival hurt the liquor business and led to the actual closing of some saloons. And if voluntary abstention by a revived citizenry was not enough, Sunday's most publicized convert, Chief of Police Charles E. Carter, was ready to enforce the liquor laws with unprecedented vigor. Moreover, Sunday's supporters contended that the revival improved the business life of the city. Following the lead of one member of the Columbus Evangelistic Association, downtown merchants began to close their stores on Saturday evenings in order to encourage church attendance among their employees, and some of these merchants maintained this practice as late as November, 1913. In addition, some businessmen allegedly increased their employees' wages after

[35] *Ibid.*, February 17, 1913.

[36] McLoughlin, *Billy Sunday*, pp. 46–47; Pitzer, "Ohio Campaigns of Billy Sunday," pp. 136–37; *Ohio State Journal*, March 3, February 19, 1913.

[37] Pitzer, "Ohio Campaigns of Billy Sunday," pp. 41, 35.

Sunday made pointed remarks favoring a living wage.[38]

The original dispute over inviting Sunday to Columbus was only a minor skirmish compared to the furor that arose after Sunday left Columbus. An article by Gladden in the *Congregationalist,* "The Trouble with Mr. Sunday," in May, 1913, precipitated a bitter controversy between Gladden and many of his fellow clergymen. Noting that inquiries concerning the revival in Columbus had been filling his mailbox for months, Gladden explained that he was breaking his silence only because of a rumor that his attitude had changed. He then elaborated his four principal objections to Sunday's brand of evangelism in the most incisive criticism of Sunday yet written. The revival in Columbus furnished much new ammunition for his arsenal. First, he could not accept "the intolerance and violence which are the native breath of Mr. Sunday." This intolerance was symbolized by a statement that Sunday repeated in substance throughout the revival: "The Fatherhood of God and the Brotherhood of Man is the worst rot that ever was dug out of hell, and every minister who preaches it is a liar." Sunday regularly consigns evolutionists, higher critics, social gospelers, and Unitarians to hell, Gladden wrote, and "the enraptured audience yells its applause. . . . The scene at a Spanish bull fight is really, when you think of it, less horrible." To illustrate the most extreme extent of Sunday's intolerance, Gladden cited the case of one of Sunday's ministerial supporters in Toledo, George R. Wallace of the First Congregational Church. After hearing Sunday's sermon on evolution, Wallace privately remonstrated with him. "The next day on the platform," Gladden continued,

> Mr. Sunday turned to the protesting minister, shook his fist in his face and yelled: "Stand up there, you bastard evolutionist! Stand up with the atheists and the infidels and the whoremongers and the adulterers and go to hell!" I have these words from Dr. Wallace himself. . . .

[38] *Ibid.,* pp. 124–25, 138–41; Theodore T. Frankenberg, *Spectacular Career of Rev. Billy Sunday, Famous Baseball Evangelist* (Columbus, Ohio: McClelland & Co., 1913), p. 170. Frankenberg, the main source for these social results of the revival, admittedly wrote in defense of Sunday and, while agreeing that Sunday was controversial, discounted criticisms of his methods.

Grimly Gladden added: "Statistics—of a sort—were kept of the number of 'conversions'; but of the number of those sent to hell, by name, no record, I believe was made. It is a great omission; for that is a large part of the business."[39]

Second, Gladden objected to Sunday's commercialism. At a conference on evangelism in 1912 "one of the leading evangelists" had told a younger man, "I've got all those other fellows skinned a mile in the free-will offering." The name of this prominent evangelist was not known to him, Gladden admitted, but "only one man could have truthfully said it." The twenty-one thousand dollars that Sunday took out of Columbus as a free-will offering, Gladden continued, was enough to pay the average Congregational minister's salary for twenty years. The very phrase "free-will offering" was a misnomer, in view of the prearranging of contributions, the pressuring of large donors, and the manipulating of rivalry between cities carried on by Sunday's lieutenants.

Third, Gladden objected to Sunday's theology as "the most hopeless form of mediaeval substitutionism." "Salvation is a matter of contract; hell is a literal pit of fire and brimstone; the Bible is verbally infallible; every man who teaches the Higher Criticism is a liar."

Finally, Gladden discounted the positive results of Sunday's revivals. Although reports were conflicting, he was certain that the vaunted moral revolution that came in Sunday's wake was a fallacy. Springfield, Illinois, went wet in the midst of a revival and in spite of Sunday's personal crusade against saloons. Portsmouth and Springfield, Ohio, had both been dry before Sunday's revivals but went wet a few months later. Moreover, Sunday's vulgarity appreciably lowered public reverence, stimulated censoriousness, and commercialized popular attitudes toward Christian service. In addition, even if many of Sunday's converts became active church members, there would certainly be thousands who, after professing conversion, looked back with chagrin at their actions and completely

[39] Washington Gladden, "The Trouble with Mr. Sunday," *Congregationalist,* XCVIII (May 29, 1913), 728 f.

turned their backs on the churches. These would be harder than ever to reach with the Gospel.[40]

The response to Gladden's article was immediate and sharp. In Columbus, where Gladden had preached for over three decades and where, by all reasonable standards, he was highly respected, the clergy rose almost en masse to Sunday's defense. The Reverend Dr. T. H. Campbell, pastor of the influential King Avenue Methodist Church, openly attacked Gladden on totally unrelated issues. Gladden had raised a great hue and cry over "tainted money," Campbell asserted, "yet within the last year he has advocated the giving of licenses to saloons for money. That's what I call 'tainted money!' " Sunday's theology, by implication unlike Gladden's, was "that of the New Testament, without any Universalism or Unitarianism thrown in."[41] At the monthly meeting of Columbus ministers in June, the Reverend Dr. John W. Day of the First Presbyterian Church, head of the Columbus Evangelistic Association, introduced a resolution deprecating the published attack on Sunday by "a local pastor who bitterly opposed his coming to our city and was not present at a single service during the campaign." Of the ministers who had co-operated with Sunday, twenty-three voted for Day's resolution and only five against it. In a reply printed in the *Columbus Dispatch* Gladden charged his critics with inconsistency:

> Mr. Sunday can send men to hell by platoons, right and left, day after day, and these good brethren can listen and applaud; it is only when I question his right and his power to do it that they rise in their wrath. The liberty of speech and the right of private judgment seems to be confined, just at present, to Mr. Sunday.[42]

The *Ohio State Journal* announced that it did not print any letters about Gladden's article because most of those it received were "unchristian and abusive."[43]

[40] *Ibid.*, 728–29.

[41] *Ohio State Journal*, June 2, 1913.

[42] *Ibid.*, June 3, 1913; "Billy Sunday and the Christian Public," *Congregationalist*, XCVIII (June 12, 1913), 792.

[43] *Ohio State Journal*, June 6, 1913.

While only a handful of ministers rose to Gladden's defense, the protest against his criticism of Sunday was loud and sustained. The minister of the Broad Street Methodist Church referred glowingly to Gladden's influence on his own career. But this did not bespeak the popular mood. More characteristic was the reaction of the Reverend W. C. Stevenson of the Russell Street Baptist Church, who organized a mass meeting to rebuke Gladden. On June 8, 1913, Stevenson preached on "The Real Trouble with Dr. Gladden" and brought in eight of Sunday's converts to testify. A sign in front of Stevenson's church asked, "Billy Sunday or Dr. Gladden, Which?" Studiously avoiding Gladden's name in his sermon, Stevenson questioned his sincerity and charged him with opposing virtually every evangelist who had visited Columbus in the past twenty years. Stevenson and Sunday's converts accused Gladden of failing to support foreign missions, trying to "make himself popular with the crowd by preaching damnable heresies" instead of the Bible, and sending "hell and damnation into the lives of others" by voting for liquor licenses in Ohio.[44]

In the flurry of excitement over Sunday, Gladden's theology became a more important public issue than it had been since the heresy trials of the 1870's. Gladden's critics assailed his liberalism on two levels. On a secondary level they voiced a number of criticisms involving irrelevant issues, such as his endorsement of a state system of liquor licensing. These criticisms were in the nature of fault-finding for the purpose of justifying their opposition to him, as if to demonstrate that one who departed from the fundamentals of the faith would inevitably go wrong on all kinds of issues. But on their principal level of criticism his opponents assailed his theology on pragmatic grounds. Liberalism, they charged, led straight to spiritual deadness; it dried up the sources of support for evangelism and foreign missions; it consisted of a refined but effete, emasculated message; it contributed to infidelity and secularism. On neither

44 *Ibid.*, June 11, 5, 9, 1913.

level did his critics examine his theology on systematic intellectual, historical, or even biblical grounds.

The most determined attack came from John B. Koehne, a Congregationalist of New London, New Hampshire, whom the conservative ministers of Columbus brought to the city twice, once for a single address at the First Presbyterian Church in December, 1913, and then for a series of nine lectures on "Fundamentals of Christianity" at the same church in March, 1914. Koehne's announced purpose in speaking in Columbus was to disprove Gladden's liberal doctrines.[45] He published these lectures in 1914 as a small pamphlet, *Future Punishment: An Examination of Dr. Washington Gladden's "Present Day Theology" Theory of Hell.* Actually, Koehne's argument was not a reasoned theological critique, but a scurrilous and unrefined rejection of liberalism and all its works. Setting out to repudiate Gladden's *Present Day Theology*, Koehne concentrated on the question of future punishment, interestingly enough, the same issue that had involved Gladden in controversy in the 1870's.

A fair sample of Koehne's style appeared in his preface, in which he impugned Gladden's intentions in writing *Present Day Theology:*

> Then [Gladden] dreams: "Since the theology of Jesus is full of hard sayings that have never been thoroughly understood, why not think out and publish a theology of my own. If I write it, and omit any hard sayings perhaps at least I can understand parts of it!" This he did, and here it is.

Again, with reference to the origins of Gladden's views on future punishment, Koehne wrote:

> . . . He has rummaged into an ancient heap of scrap iron. There he found pieces of theological armor, worn centuries ago by that Goliath of Unitarianism, ARIUS. To Dr. Gladden, even the fragments looked priestly as well as gigantic in intellectual majesty.
>
> He carted them to his study. He scraped off the rust. He patched, oiled and polished each separate doctrine. Then he beeswaxed them together with poetry. As it lay upon the floor, vast, gloomy, mysterious, he was sure he could wear it over the robes of his evangelical faith, and that nobody would know the difference. Putting a Bible in his pocket, he

[45] *Ibid.*, December 6, 1913, March 14, 1914.

foolishly crawled inside. Once within, he was utterly lost in its sepulchral darkness. He has never since been able to find his way out.[46]

Koehne also cited Gladden's views on the fatherhood of God and on the atonement, in each case linking Gladden with Unitarianism and infidelity, which Koehne considered synonymous, and accusing Gladden of elevating "social consciousness" and such sources as Howells' *A Boy's Town* and Tennyson's poems above the words of the Bible. That many of Gladden's statements were excessively optimistic and sentimental is not in question, as the criticisms of liberal theology by the neo-orthodox theologians of the postwar era have demonstrated. But Koehne failed in his purpose of invalidating *Present Day Theology.* The work was extreme and in activity rather than reasoned. He was denunciatory and unfair rather than objective. And he utilized caricature, twisted Gladden's statements out of context, and relied on *ad hominem* arguments rather than constructing a systematic critique of Gladden's ideas themselves. For example, he ridiculed the "milk-cheeked, rose-lipped" "dilettantes" in the seminaries who saw themselves "mincing daintily and coquettishly" into "flower-strewn" pulpits "to fascinate and thrill to tears, sweet girlish intellects" by "blowing soap-bubble sermonettes."[47]

Future Punishment contained a supplement, entitled "A Criticism of Dr. Washington Gladden's Arraignment of 'Billy' Sunday," which, according to Koehne, the *Congregationalist* refused to publish. Gladden's judgment was unsafe, Koehne contended, because it was based on hearsay, because scores of ministers and laymen who had worked with Sunday rejected it, and because, after Gladden had labored for thirty years in Columbus, his own colleagues had united against him to invite Sunday. Then Koehne criticized Gladden on the same grounds that Gladden had used against Sunday. Gladden was intolerant: to wit, his attack on Sunday. He was motivated by a

[46] John B. Koehne, *Future Punishment: An Examination of Dr. Washington Gladden's "Present Day Theology" Theory of Hell* (Chicago: The Platform, 1914), Preface.

[47] *Ibid.*, pp. 3, 7, 12–16, 28–29, 30–33.

commercial spirit, drawing a salary—Koehne estimated between five and six thousand dollars—that would support six average ministers. Gladden's theology was unscriptural. And, finally, Gladden failed to win substantial numbers of converts and to accomplish any permanent moral revolution. During the previous year Gladden had taken twenty-four members into his church on profession of faith, Koehne reported, and most of these had probably come from his Sunday school. At this rate it would take Gladden 850 years—actually, using Koehne's assumptions, it would take 750 years—to win as many converts as Sunday had won in Columbus in seven weeks. Estimating the First Church's annual expenses as $7,000 for the salary of Gladden and his associate and $14,000 to run the church, Koehne calculated that this process would cost the First Church $17,900,000. According to one historian, Sunday had converted that many at a cost, including the free-will offering and offerings for charity, of only $43,684.91, and Sunday frequently boasted of dispensing salvation at a cost of roughly $2.00 per soul.[48] The conclusion was explicit: the churches, particularly the liberal churches, were not doing their job. Moreover, Koehne argued, Gladden had been in Columbus more than thirty years without producing a moral revolution. How could he justifiably criticize Sunday for a lack of moral improvement, when Sunday had been on the scene only seven weeks?[49]

Following Koehne's efforts, the controversy over Billy Sunday became anticlimactic in Columbus. In an attempt to keep the fires of revival burning and to disseminate pure doctrine, the clergy organized a Bible conference under the auspices of the Winona Bible Conference at Winona Lake, Indiana, where Sunday's headquarters were located. The roster of speakers included G. Campbell Morgan, an English evangelist of fundamentalist leanings who was popular in the United States, C. I. Scofield, the chief editor of the Scofield Reference Bible, which became the favored edition of fundamentalism, and Billy Sunday. But there was nothing like the for-

[48] Pitzer, "Ohio Campaigns of Billy Sunday," pp. 127, 132.

[49] Koehne, *Future Punishment*, Supplement.

mer unanimity among the evangelical churches that had participated in Sunday's revival. Because of strong objections to the theology of the speakers, the Congregational ministers decided unanimously against formal participation, and the Methodist clergy left the question of participation up to the individual churches. And, while in the midst of planning the Bible conference, the ministerial association passed a resolution commending Gladden's thirty-one-year ministry in Columbus. Two Congregational ministers, those of the North and Plymouth churches, did support the conference. But otherwise, as the minister of the Mayflower Church explained in the press, Congregationalists remained aloof from the conference and its "sixteenth century type" of theology.[50] Perhaps significantly when Sunday arrived in Columbus the conference in a grand climax, he drew only two thousand persons, far less than the Memorial Hall would hold and the smallest crowd to which he had ever preached in Columbus.[51] The Winona Bible Conference held another series of meetings in Columbus in December, 1914, featuring James M. Gray, the president of the Moody Bible Institute in Chicago and an editor of the Scofield Reference Bible; but apparently, this conference had even less clerical support than the first.[52] It seems plausible to assume that some clergymen—perhaps many—who had grasped at Billy Sunday because he got results were not prepared to embrace organized fundamentalism, with its tenets of biblical infallibility, the substitutionary atonement, and premillennialism and its rejection of evolution, biblical criticism, and social Christianity.

Whatever the exact state of clerical opinion during 1914 and 1915, Gladden was disturbed by the growing militancy of the fundamentalists. He even entertained the idea of holding a Bible conference in Columbus that would furnish a platform for liberal, socially-oriented evangelicals.[53] And in an article in the *Biblical World*,

[50] *Ohio State Journal*, January 13, 21, 31, February 2, 4, 1914.

[51] *Ibid.*, February 17, 1914.

[52] *Ibid.*, December 5, 1914.

[53] Hugh Black to Gladden, September 23, 1914; George B. Stewart to Gladden, November 4, 1915, Gladden Papers.

"A Dangerous Crusade," he revealed his alarm at a rising opposition to biblical criticism. Analyzing this opposition in the context of fundamentalism, he pointed out that it had the backing of wealthy social conservatives, that popular evangelists were not only identifying themselves with it but also supplying much of its leadership, that it capitalized on popular ignorance, and that it intimidated many clergymen who feared accusations of heresy.[54] Although dealing primarily with the fate of biblical studies, Gladden clearly linked his own experience with Billy Sunday and the threat to liberalism of the fundamentalist movement.

Gladden had good reasons for alarm, at both the increasing popularity of Billy Sunday and the progress of fundamentalism. Despite minor eddies of opposition, after 1913 Sunday won overwhelming acceptance in the evangelical churches. Gladden continued to provide information to those who wanted to keep Sunday out of their cities: Henry Preserved Smith of the Union Theological Seminary in New York; Congregational, Episcopal, and Unitarian churchmen in Boston; and a Presbyterian layman in Rochester.[55] But Sunday's organization rolled on. Even within Congregationalism, which had been relatively responsive to liberal theology, Gladden's point of view temporarily lost ground. In the same issue of the *Congregationalist* in which Gladden's article, "The Trouble with Mr. Sunday," appeared, the editors observed that Gladden's criticisms would "convince many that [Sunday] is a man whose methods and spirit disqualify him for effective Christian service."[56] By March, 1914, though admitting the validity of criticisms of Sunday's vulgarity and intolerance, they declared their unwillingness to discount his posi-

[54] Washington Gladden, "A Dangerous Crusade," *Biblical World*, XLIV (July, 1914), 6–7.

[55] Henry Preserved Smith to Gladden, February 8, 1914; George H. Parkinson to Gladden, February 17, 1914; Alexander Mann to Gladden, January 25, 1915; George W. Owen to Gladden, February 19, 1915; Charles W. Wendte to Gladden, April 2, 1915; Herbert W. Gates to Gladden, March 9, 1915, Gladden Papers.

[56] *Congregationalist*, XCVIII (May 29, 1913), 717–18.

tive evangelistic achievements.[57] Thereafter, they gave increasing attention to Sunday's revivals, most of it favorable, and by 1915 they were prepared to judge the permanent effects of Sunday's campaigns "overwhelmingly in their favor."[58] By the end of 1916 the editors were promoting their paper by offering, free with subscriptions for the rest of 1916 and all of 1917, either of "Two Spicy Biographies" of Sunday and were running each week "a live and stirring story" by an observer of Sunday's meetings.[59] And, irony of ironies, in March, 1917, the *Congregationalist* printed a statement in which Irving Maurer, who later that year became Gladden's successor in Columbus, admitted his antagonism to professional evangelism but stated that he had "been compelled to recognize the immodest opportunities for good which this movement exhibits."[60]

This episode was, in terms of its immediate results, a decided defeat for Gladden. It marked the low point of his influence and prestige, not only in Columbus but also in evangelical circles across the United States. He was simply outvoted by the overwhelming majority of American Protestants. It was also a setback for his religious progressivism, demonstrating that the Social Gospel and liberal theology had permeated the thought of the average church-goer to a far lesser extent than he had realized. Characteristically, Gladden did not admit defeat or even the possibility of the permanent eclipse of liberalism, though he did occasionally lament the successes of Sunday and other fundamentalists. In the long run, Gladden's confidence was well placed. After the hiatus of war and "normalcy," the formative influence of liberal thought in the prewar era furnished the starting point for theological reconstruction and the adaptation of the churches' social message, now refined as by fire, to the new problems of the mid-twentieth century.

[57] "One More Word about Billy Sunday," *ibid.*, XCIX (March 12, 1914), 353.

[58] *Congregationalist*, XCIX (May 21, 1914), 693–94, C (January 28, 1915), 103–4, (March 4, 1915), 269.

[59] *Ibid.*, CI (November 23, 1916), 665.

[60] *Ibid.*, CII (March 1, 1917), 270.

Fourteen

The Golden Rule and the Nations

Gladden's faith in the universal applicability of the Gospel was unbounded. The doctrine of human brotherhood was the norm, and the ethic of love was the stimulus of domestic, religious, political, and economic justice. Likewise, he had unwavering faith in the complete efficacy of the Gospel. More than an ideal, the Golden Rule alone could redeem earthly society. While Gladden's attempt to delineate the implications of the Gospel for America's pressing social problems never diminished, America's rapid rise to world power during the 1890's greatly expanded his horizon. Seeing no difference between spheres of human relations that would impair the relevance of the Golden Rule, he applied the same ethic to individuals, classes, and nations. The conviction that nations could and must act morally became both logically and chronologically the final article of his faith.

Like most Americans of his day, Gladden awakened only gradually to America's potential importance in international politics. The country concentrated after the Civil War on economic growth and domestic problems. But the strengthening of cultural ties with the Old World, the increasingly apparent need for foreign markets, and growing American self-confidence brought about a gradual breakdown of indifference to international affairs. A man of wide-ranging interests, Gladden shared in this quickening of world-consciousness.

With the increasing chauvinism that accompanied it, however, he had no sympathy. Of English ancestry and strongly influenced by English letters and religion, he disliked the Anglophobia that had persisted throughout the century. He agreed with Josiah Strong, who bluntly declared: "The Anglo-Saxon is the representative of two great ideas, which are closely related. One of them is that of civil liberty. . . . The other . . . is that of a pure spiritual Christianity."[1]

Trips to England in 1888, 1891, 1894, and 1898 reinforced Gladden's belief that England and America were essentially during Mrs Gladden accompanied him on the last visit, during which he attended the International Missionary Conference in London. Though the trip was to include western Europe, Gladden's greatest interest was in England. Writing to Richard W. Gilder for introductions to Englishmen who might facilitate his study of social problems, he remarked: "It is the English people in particular that I want to know."[2]

The Gladdens spent at least six weeks in England and Scotland, and only about a month altogether in Belgium, Holland, France, Switzerland, and Germany. After landing at Liverpool they made their way to London via Chester, Wolverhampton, Birmingham, and Stratford. The visit to Chester, where Gladden saw the cathedral that Charles Kingsley had served and heard deeply moving stories about him, was something of a pilgrimage. In Wolverhampton and Birmingham Gladden visited Congregational clergymen whom he knew by reputation. He spent a Sunday in Birmingham and was impressed by its quietness and order.

Once in London, the Gladdens had little interest in the mission-

[1] Strong, *Our Country,* p. 160.

[2] Smith to Gladden, March 22, 1883, Gladden to children, May 28, 1888, Gladden Papers; Gladden to Gilder, April 29, 1888, *Century* Collection. About threescore letters from the Gladdens to their children, almost the only extant family correspondence, reveal their reactions to European conditions.

ary conference. From the Arundel Hotel on the Strand they wandered out, often separately, through slums and boulevards, to see churches, museums, and palaces. Gladden became enthusiastic about the government's provision of cheap or free popular amusements, particularly museums and galleries. To economize rather than to get a realistic view of England, they traveled by trams and busses, took second-class and third-class accomodations, and ate in restaurants that Gladden was sure his son Fred would consider "joints." Gladden investigated the Peabody "model tenements," Toynbee Hall, and one of Octavia Hill's slum gardens, interviewing Warden Samuel Barnett of Toynbee Hall and Miss Hill, England's leading female reformer. In addition, he attended meetings of Anglican and Congregational clergymen. His friendship with Dean Fremantle, who was then the Canon of Canterbury, began at one of these meetings. He also attended a session of Parliament, and he had several contacts with English editors. The English publisher of the *Century* entertained him at the National Liberal Club.[3]

Gladden found England less different from America than New York City was from New Orleans. When asked if he was a foreign delegate to the missionary convention, he automatically replied, "No, I am an American." The English were law-abiding, religious, loyal, and in many ways more progressive than their American cousins. He was sure that the current struggles between "privilege and tradition on the one side and the claims of struggling humanity on the other" would end in complete democracy.[4]

On the other hand, Continental Europe was truly foreign. There were differences of manners, dress, and speech (though Gladden spoke some German and a little French). Moreover, the Gladdens felt like spiritual strangers. Admiring their cathedrals, he yet

[3] Mrs. Gladden to Alice Gladden, June 7, 1888; Gladden to congregation of the First Church, June 10, 1888; Mrs. Gladden to children, June 14, 18, July 1, 4, 1888; Gladden to children, June 8, 17, 26, 28, July 7, 1888; Mrs. Gladden to Frederick Gladden, June 21, 1888, Gladden Papers.

[4] Gladden, *Recollections*, p. 354; Gladden to congregation of the First Church, July 16, 1888, Gladden Papers.

doubted that "the good Catholics of Antwerp" worshiped more than beauty. He tried to be charitable but thought that

> . . . these processions, and these genuflexions, and these incantations, and all this pomp and gorgeousness of altar and vestment and ceremonial, are a hideous caricature of the religion that was taught and exemplified by Jesus Christ of Nazareth.

In Protestant Holland he also felt estranged. The austere Reformed churches had gone, in his opinion, to the opposite extreme from Roman Catholicism. And after experiencing a "continental" Sabbath, even in sober Amsterdam, he wrote to his parishioners, "I do not like the way they keep it." He admired the cathedral of Cologne but stood aghast at a display of its relics: It was all very wonderful, very wonderful; the wonder was that this kind of nonsense could claim the credence of intelligent human beings. . . . " Crowds of Genevans boating on the Sabbath surprised Mrs. Gladden, and Gladden speculated that Rousseau had influenced Geneva more profoundly than had Calvin. The noise and bustle of Paris wearied them, and the "mumeries [*sic*] of the gorgeously arrayed priests" at a high mass in Paris deepened their dislike of European Catholicism.[5]

In 1891 Gladden returned to England, possibly accompanied by his daughter Alice, for the International Congregational Council. He briefly surveyed political and economic conditions in Switzerland, but then, and again in 1894, his primary interest was in England. After each trip he condensed his impressions in sermons stressing the bonds between England and America.[6] He sympathetically reviewed current English issues, such as Irish home rule and disestablishment of the Anglican church, and he tried to allay antago-

[5] Gladden to congregation of the First Church, July 16, 22, 1888; Gladden to children, July 18, 24, 1888; Mrs. Gladden to children, July 29, August 8, 13, 19, 1888, Gladden Papers.

[6] Gladden to congregation of the First Church, August 23, 1891, Gladden Papers; *Ohio State Journal*, September 29, October 6, 13, 20, 1888, May 10, September 19, 26, October 3, 10, 17, 1891, June 5, 1894, March 2, 1895.

nism to English aristocracy and monarchy.[7] He reminded his•
congregation

> . . . that the men who founded this nation were English men; that the
> ideas which lie at the basis of our national life are English ideas; that our
> institutions, religious, social, political, are largely shaped from English
> models; that it was English brains, English pluck, and English faith that
> gave us the country of which we are so justly proud.

When he arrived in England, he felt like he was "only coming
home, from the west, to see the old folks."[8] Citing an article in the
Century by Henry Cabot Lodge, he observed in 1891 that 86 per
cent of those listed in Appleton's *Cyclopedia of American Biography*
came from British and 74 per cent from English stock. The American Revolution was no cause for permanent animosity: "We had
some little family trouble when we set up housekeeping for ourselves," he concluded, "but that was a long time ago. . . . "[9] Like
Josiah Strong, Gladden insisted that England and America would
"stand together, in the coming days, for the defense and extension
of Christian civilization."[10]

Before Gladden made his fourth and final trip to England, which
was itself an attempt to promote Anglo-American understanding,
the two countries came dangerously close to war. In July, 1895, Secretary of State Richard Olney charged Britain, embroiled with Venezuela over the boundary between Venezuela and British Guiana,
with violating the Monroe Doctrine. When Lord Salisbury rejected
Olney's "twenty-inch-gun" blast, President Cleveland, riding a crest
of jingoism, obtained a congressional appropriation for a commission to investigate and fix the boundary, which, if necessary, the
United States would fight to maintain.

[7] Gladden, Sermons, [September, 1888]; [January, 1889]; "Is England a
Democracy?", [1891]; October 18, 1891; October 7, 1894, Gladden Papers.

[8] Gladden, Sermon, [September, 1888,] Gladden Papers.

[9] Gladden, "Impressions of a Great Council," Sermon, September 27, 1891,
Gladden Papers.

[10] Gladden, "The Future of the Aristocracy," Sermon, October 11, 1891,
Gladden Papers.

In his Christmas sermon a few days after Cleveland's inflammatory action, Gladden arraigned both Cleveland and Salisbury for approaching war with apparent relish. His evening congregation unanimously passed a resolution, introduced by President James Canfield of the Ohio State University, denouncing the war mania and sent it to a representative and both senators from Ohio, President Cleveland, and the British embassy.[11] Two weeks later, Gladden again preached on the issue. Agreeing that some iniquities "must be scourged with war," he considered it, nevertheless, "a sarcasm upon all that we hold highest and dearest and divinest" for "the most enlightened, the most Christian nations on earth" to fight with any difference at all. He found "splendid proof" of the supremacy of Christ" in Britain's agreement to co-operate with Cleveland's commission, a decision based, however, as much upon strategic considerations as upon public opinion.[12]

Gladden was even more delighted with the Olney-Pauncefote treaty for general arbitration between Britain and the United States, which grew out of the controversy over the Venezuelan boundary.[13] When the Senate killed the treaty, he announced that it was

> a melancholy and discouraging fact that so many as twenty-six men can be elected to the Senate . . . who are unwilling to submit the differences arising between civilized and Christian states to the peaceful methods of arbitration.[14]

Gladden's enthusiasm for Anglo-American solidarity and for international arbitration was common to many Protestant clergymen of his day. Lyman Abbott, for example, popularized the same themes from his pulpit in Plymouth Church and through the *Outlook*.

[11] *Ohio State Journal*, December 23, 1895.

[12] Gladden, "Peace at Any Price or War for Nothing," Sermon, January 12, 1896, Gladden Papers.

[13] Washington Gladden, "Anglo-American Comity," *Congregationalist*, LXXXI (June 25, 1896), 1002–3; Gladden, "The Ways of Peace," Sermon, November 26, 1896, Gladden Papers.

[14] Gladden, Sermon, January 2, 1898, Gladden Papers.

Gladden's interest in arbitration was strengthened by Walter A. Mahony, a staunch supporter of the annual conferences on international arbitration that began in 1895 at Lake Mohonk, New York. For several years Gladden was a member of the Columbus Board of Trade's committee on arbitration.[15]

The loophole in Gladden's condemnation of war was his distinction between wars among civilized Christian nations, which would be ostensibly unnecessary, and wars by civilized nations to repress or punish barbarism. By this distinction he justified the Spanish-American War. Reports of Spanish butchery against the Cuban rebellion that began in 1895 horrified Americans. In a sermon more than a year before the United States declared war on Spain, Gladden pondered the alternatives facing the United States. Though Americans sympathized with the Cubans, there was no effective revolutionary government that the United States could justifiably recognize. He hoped that diplomacy might induce Spain to reform her colonial administration. If there was no other recourse, however, he was willing to sanction a war against barbarism. But war would necessarily entail American administration or annexation. "People as ignorant, superstitious, brutal and degraded as those who inhabit Cuba," he asserted, "are not capable of self-government." The United States could intervene, but only with the motives "of a large humanity, of a pure philanthropy."[16]

Nevertheless, Gladden accepted the war reluctantly. Fearing that the yellow journals and jingo politicians would stampede the country into precipitate conflict after the explosion of the *Maine*, he reminded his congregation of the horrors of war, horrors that he had seen during the Civil War. The loss of manpower and the accumulation of debt, he warned, were realities to which "your jingo Congressman and your shriek journalist, and your thrifty speculator are utterly oblivious." The burden would fall on the common people:

---

[15] Brown, *Abbott*, pp. 162–64; *Ohio State Journal*, May 30, October 4. November 22, 1908.

[16] *Ohio State Journal*, January 5, 1897.

The people—always the people, the poor people! . . . It is their bodies, mangled by the deadly engines of war, that will be heaped on every battle field; it is they who must work, in the long dull years that follow to draw from the soil and beat from the forges, and fashion in the looms, the interest on these war debts that perhaps never will be paid! God save the people![17]

A week before President McKinley sent his war message to Congress, Gladden discounted all but humanitarian motives for the impending conflict. Those who urged war did not speak for the American people, who, he was sure, were pained by the threat of conflict. If war was necessary, it must be "the holiest war that was ever waged on the face of the earth—a war into which lust of conquest and bloodthirsty passion must be permitted to enter."[18]

After the declaration of war Gladden continued to insist that the nation must maintain pure motives if it was to be ennobled, not degraded, by its involvement. The Sunday following McKinley's war message he reasserted that the war would be justified only if the United States assumed responsibility for Cuba. This theme stood out in the sermons he preached for several weeks thereafter.[19]

Gladden placed high value on English friendship during the war. In a letter to the *Ohio State Journal* he quoted an article by an English Congregational clergyman whom he knew approving America's holy crusade.[20] In June he announced that he would lecture in England during the summer, at his own expense, on "Causes and Issues of the Present War" and "Reasons for Friendship between England and America." He summarized his thoughts on the war in a departing sermon on "American Duty and American Destiny," a condensation of which appeared in the *Outlook* in July. The United States

[17] Gladden, "God Save the People," Sermon, February 27, 1898, Gladden Papers.

[18] Gladden, "War Impending," Sermon, April 3, 1898, Gladden Papers.

[19] *Ohio State Journal,* April 18, 25, May 9, 1898; Washington Gladden, *Our Nation and Her Neighbors* (Columbus, Ohio: Quinius & Ridenour, 1898); Gladden, "The Dependence of Individual Morality upon National Morality," Sermon, May 1, 1898, Gladden Papers.

[20] *Ohio State Journal,* May 12, 1898.

had felt a divine call to free Cuba. The pressing question was what
to do with Cuba after the war. The answers of both imperialists and
anti-imperialists were unacceptable. Both groups assumed that
purely selfish motives must govern American policy. The imperialists' talk about manifest destiny seemed "no better than piracy" to
Gladden. He warned:

> We are not going to be dragged into any war for purposes of conquest
> —neither for the acquisition of territory nor for the extension of trade.
> . . . And those who are preaching this jingoism to-day should be warned
> that the Nation has a conscience that can speak and make itself heard,
> and that will paralyze its arm whenever it is lifted to do injustice to any
> weaker people.

The anti-imperialists, he presumed, did not want to accept the burden of civilizing Cuba. Between "the wolf who goes marauding"
and "the pig who wallows in his own fat" Gladden could see little
difference. Both followed the rule of self-interest. Though he cautioned against any "Quixotic crusade for the righting of all human
wrongs," Gladden insisted that if at the end of the war the Cubans
had no stable republican government, the United States would have
"to lift them up and lead them on into larger liberty and more
abundant life."[21]

Gladden filled at least a score of major engagements in England,
mainly in and around London, Liverpool, Yorkshire, and Wolverhampton. He spoke in churches, lecture halls, and municipal buildings, and often the mayor or a Member of Parliament introduced
him. Dean Fremantle welcomed him to Ripon, where he spoke to
a small but influential audience. At Derby over twelve hundred
people crowded a temperance hall, and after the address they
clapped, according to Gladden, "till I should think their hands must
have smarted well; and then they all got on their feet and gave
three cheers." Every meeting deepened Gladden's belief in Anglo-

---

[21] *Ibid.*, June 12, 27, 1898; Washington Gladden, "The Issues of the War,"
Outlook, LIX (July 16, 1898), 673–75. Abbott, the editor of the *Outlook*, supported the war on basically the same grounds as did Gladden. Brown, *Abbott*,
pp. 167–68.

American solidarity.[22] His English publisher, James Clarke, issued the two addresses as a small pamphlet, for which Dean Fremantle wrote an introduction.

Gladden assured his English audiences that Americans were "not actuated at this time by the greed of new territory." Instead, the report of Senator Redfield Proctor of Vermont on Cuban conditions had convinced Gladden and his countrymen that "the horrors of Armenia had been outdone" at their very doors. To be sure, some Americans were always willing to fight, but they were not in control; rather, "the enlightened conscience of the nation" held "the casting vote in all its greater affairs." The Teller Amendment, disclaiming any intention to annex Cuba, Gladden explained, must lo set aside. There was simply no republic to recognize. The United States would have to assume the administration of both Cuba and the Philippines: "To help them overthrow the Government of Spain, and then go away and let them set up savagery in the place of tyranny would be a disreputable proceeding." His nation was realizing, he averred, that it was "a moral organism, and that, as such, the supreme law of its conduct must be the law of love. . . . " In his second address he enumerated reasons for Anglo-American friendship and envisioned co-operation in civilizing the rest of the world.[23]

After his return from England, Gladden repeated his address on "Reasons for Friendship between England and America" and preached and wrote on English education, religion, and society.[24] The war had ended during the summer, sooner than anyone had expected, and the disposition of the former Spanish colonies occu-

[22] *Ohio State Journal*, June 25, 1898; Gladden to family, July 26, August 9, 13, 17, 1898, Gladden Papers; Gladden, *Recollections*, pp. 357–58.

[23] Washington Gladden, *England and America: Addresses Delivered in England during the Summer of 1898* (London: James Clarke & Co., 1898), pp. 12, 17, 21, 24–25, 38–45, 50–52.

[24] *Ohio State Journal*, September 10, 12, November 11, 1898; Gladden, Sermons, "What Will Become of the English Church?", September 25, 1898, "Social Progress of the English People," [October 2, 1898,] Gladden Papers; Washington Gladden, "Social Progress of the English People," *Outlook*, LX (December 24, 1898), 1002–4.

pied the nation's attention. Gladden opposed adherence to the Teller Amendment and maintained that the English people expected the United States to assume their administration. He denied that annexation would violate fundamental American principles, a cardinal contention of the anti-imperialists, arguing that "semi-civilized races" could practice democracy only after lengthy preparation. Though a democracy, England was providing such tutelage "with great benefit to herself as well as to the peoples under her care." If governed by "high moral qualities," America could "give justice and order and security to the hapless peoples now upon its hands." "With all our country's faults," he declared,

> I believe that there burns at her heart the sacred fire of love for humanity, and I believe that the day is coming when many nations shall rise up to call her blessed, and to own in her the champion of the down-trodden and the deliverer of the oppressed.[25]

On December 18, a week after Spain ceded the Philippines, Puerto Rico, and Guam to the United States and relinquished sovereignty over Cuba, Gladden returned to the question of America's colonial obligations. Setting the former Spanish possessions free was to him "a morally unthinkable proposition." He found it

> . . . simply amazing that grown men, with the pages of history open before their eyes, should go on applying the maxims of our Declaration of Independence to populations like those of the Philippines.

"Degraded races" did not "work their way up to civilization"; stronger races lifted them up to it. Thus, enlightened nations could justly claim for civilization vast areas that were "occupied and rendered worthless and malarious and pestilent by barbarism." They could remake the world in the mold of Western culture through education, industrial development, civil and religious freedom, and missionary work.[26] In February, 1899, when the Senate ratified the

---

[25] Gladden, Sermon, September 18, 1898, Gladden Papers; *Ohio State Journal,* November 25, 1898.

[26] Gladden, "The Signing of the Treaty," Sermon, December 18, 1898, Gladden Papers.

treaty that embodied Spain's concessions, Gladden reminded his
congregation of the churches' responsibility to promote humanitarian
ventures in these new fields.[27]

Gladden remained optimistic about humanitarian imperialism
during the jarring years following the Spanish-American War. When
the Philippine insurrection under Aguinaldo broke out in 1899, he
counseled vigorous restoration of order. The burden of administration might be irksome, but there could be no shirking of duty. Gladden thought it curious that many who had been "most fierce" for
war were not so eager to assume the obligations of victory. The
anti-imperialists condemned the suppression of Aguinaldo's forces
as the crushing of a Philippine republic. But Gladden could see no
republic worthy of the name: "It has no capital, no constitution, no
civil institutions, no seat except in the saddle of Aguinaldo." Spanish
rule had been severe and cruel, but the worst government was preferable to anarchy. And under an independent Philippine government
there would be only anarchy. Republicanism in the hands of semi-
civilized peoples was, as in the Latin American states, a shadow that
covered corruption and chaos. In common with many American
thinkers of his day, Gladden assumed that "the habit of self-government, the instinct of self-government [were] bred in the very bone
of the Anglo-Saxon peoples. . . . " The strong, he declared, must
help the weak: "The solidarity of the race makes it impossible that
any be left behind."[28] In 1905 he wrote to Edward W. Ordway, secretary of the Philippine Independence Committee, that American
administration in the Philippines under William Howard Taft had
been generally beneficent and that allegations of oppression were
unjust. Likewise, he felt that, despite unfortunate incidents, America's role in Cuba had been statesmanlike. Disappointed by the
prospect of American withdrawal in 1902, he maintained that care-

[27] Gladden, "Who Is My Neighbor?", Sermon, February 26, 1899, Gladden
Papers.

[28] Gladden, Sermons, "The Problem of the Philippines," September 3, 1899;
"The People of the Philippines," September 10, 1899, Gladden Papers.

ful tutelage for "a good many years" would have been better.[29]

Gladden's comments on international affairs during the 1890's and 1900's were equally buoyant. The expansion of American influence, particularly in the Far East, the growing popularity of international arbitration, evidenced by numerous treaties of arbitration and by the organization of conferences at The Hague, and the apparent awakening of Japan, China, and Russia to the modern world encouraged him to think that the realization of human brotherhood was not far off.

He expected that the major powers, though uniting at times to crush barbarism, would recognize the fatuity of general wars among themselves. Moreover, he believed that the spread of Western civilization, especially by England and the United States, would universalize arbitration and make even minor, punitive wars unnecessary. During the war between Greece and Turkey over Crete in 1897 he denounced the major European powers for not uniting to

> . . . sink that horrible Ottoman Empire to the bottom of the Black Sea; to give little Greece the territory inhabited by her people; and then to arrange for the wise government of all that territory so long cursed by the oppression of the Turk.

Paralyzed by fear that it might not get the lion's share of the Turkish spoils, each power stood by while Greece confronted "the colossal diabolism" that had been "wasting Europe."[30] When in 1900 the major powers intervened to quell the Boxer Rebellion in China, Gladden suggested that such co-operation, "moved by one impulse of chivalry and humanity," presaged universal peace. "I will not predict that there will be no more war," he declared:

> I know not with what dying spasms the ape and the tiger in our humanity may yet turn and rend us; but this I know that there never was a day

---

[29] Gladden to Edward W. Ordway, March 4, 1905, Edward W. Ordway Papers (Manuscript Division, New York Public Library), on microfilm in Gladden Papers; Gladden, "Good News from the Wide World," Sermon, September 22, 1901, Gladden Papers.

[30] Gladden, "The War in the East," Sermon, April 25, 1897, Gladden Papers.

when the rulers of the earth so dreaded war, or the peoples so hated it, as they do today . . . that never until today was it clearly seen that it is possible, by reason, to compose the strife of nations and to guide the destinies of mankind.[31]

Gladden interpreted events in the Far East with extraordinary optimism. He hoped that Japanese victory in the Sino-Japanese War of 1894–95 would open the door for "the entrance of civilizing and Christianizing influences into the vast mongolian population." Following Japan's example, the rest of Asia would end its long cultural stagnation.[32] During the Boxer Rebellion he observed that the old Confucian civilization, doomed because it looked backward, was dying, and that a new civilization was "waiting to make up the information." As old barriers disintegrated, the ideas and customs of different societies would experience healthy competition, and the fittest would survive. The universal mingling of peoples, a prerequisite of complete brotherhood, was inevitable. The role of the United States in establishing the "open door" in China stimulated Gladden's national pride. Maintenance of the territorial integrity of China would be "the greatest triumph yet recorded in history." The opening of China to Western influences and the democratic revolution under Sun Yat-Sen he considered a national conversion.[33] Like most Americans, he sympathized with Japan's ostensible defense of the "open door" in the Russo-Japanese War in 1904–5. In addition, he hoped that the war would strengthen the sentiment for peace and thus prove doubly beneficial.[34]

[31] Gladden, "The Prospects of Universal Peace," Sermon, September 23, 1900, Gladden Papers.

[32] Gladden, Sermon, [January, 1895,] Gladden Papers.

[33] Gladden, Sermons, "The Chinese Tragedy," June 8, 1900; "The Chinese People," September 2, 1900; "The Chinese Mind," September 9, 1900; "China and the Powers," September 16, 1900; "Good News from the Wide World," September 22, 1901; December 27, 1908; February 18, 1912, Gladden Papers.

[34] Gladden, Sermons, "The Japanese Mind," February 28, 1904; September 11, 1904, Gladden Papers. Gladden quite naturally rejoiced when the war resulted in the moderate Russian revolution of 1905. Overwhelmed by the "metamorphosis of an absolute despotism into a liberal monarchy," he called it "the most momentous event of modern history." Gladden, Sermon, November 5, 1905, Gladden Papers.

Gladden believed that war was becoming increasingly unlikely. He was intrigued by Jean de Bloch's *The Future of War,* the work that had prompted the czar of Russia to propose the First International Peace Conference at The Hague in 1899. Bloch argued that science had so perfected the machinery of destruction that any war between two great powers would mean the virtual annihilation of one and the economic ruin of the other. "Here in the house of God," Gladden asserted after reviewing Bloch's thesis, "before the altars where the pitiful Christ is worshipped, is the place to consider well what war means, in the first years of the twentieth century." He granted, however, that one more great war might occur, a war that would fully verify Bloch's contention. This idea reinforced other hopeful signs—lengthening periods of peace, the multiplication of treaties of arbitration, and the fact that the Christian nations were accepting the "White Man's Burden" and "simply taking possession of the earth." Even the accelerating European armaments race, by increasing the devastation that any major war would bring, strengthened the nations' disposition to settle differences by peaceful means.[35]

The outbreak of World War I in the summer of 1914 stunned Gladden but did not destroy his faith in the imminent end of war. For the last four years of his life his thoughts centered on preparedness, American involvement, and the outcome of the war. Despite the war, and despite recurring illness, his final years were serene and productive. In a sermon at the end of 1913 he admitted that he had been too sanguine. The Balkan wars, political reaction in China, and the Mexican revolution constituted "a series of moral disasters" that demonstrated "that the ape and tiger were not yet extirpated from the breasts of those rude peoples." They were the "works of the lawless one" whom St. Paul had prophesied would arise "at the latter day" to contest the progress of the Kingdom of God. But as

[35] Gladden, Sermons, November 2, 1902; December 28, 1902; September 3, 1905; April 9, 1911; September 3, 1911, Gladden Papers.

such, they signified that the final triumph of the Kingdom was near.[36]

Though Gladden also attributed the European war to "the inheritance of the ape and tiger," he could hardly dismiss England, France, and Germany as "rude peoples." Assuming, however, that self-interest must govern their policies, these nations had failed to see the need for altruism in international affairs. In Gladden's opinion, the "fundamental reason for the war" was their determination "to seek their own national aggrandizement with no regard for the welfare of the rest." Though none of them would gain enough to offset the negative effects of war, their conflict might illustrate the futility of force and produce a "mighty revulsion against war." It seemed to Gladden as if God,

> . . . after long patience with this crippling infidelity, had determined to gather up into one colossal object lesson, the natural consequences of it and let the world and the church see precisely what is involved in this purblind policy.

He was certain that a modern war could not last long. The disruption of international trade would bring widespread starvation, and starvation would put an end to it.[37]

Gladden's opportunities to preach were limited. He retired in January, 1914, and Carl S. Patton, his associate since 1911, took complete charge of the First Church. When Gladden did preach, however, he usually dealt with the war. Beginning in December, 1914, he gave five midweek lectures on "War and the Bible," including "How the Bible Has Been Used in Support of War," "What the Bible Has Done to Promote Peace," and "The Church and the Peace

[36] Gladden, "Christmas and Antichrist," Sermon, December 21, 1913, Gladden Papers.

[37] Gladden, "What the War Must Bring," in Washington Gladden and Carl S. Patton, *War and Peace: Two Sermons Preached in First Congregational Church, August 9 and 16, 1914* (Columbus, Ohio: Privately printed, 1914), pp. 17–34; Washington Gladden, "What the War Must Bring," *Congregationalist,* XCIX (September 17, 1914), 347; Washington Gladden, *The Futility of Force: Sermon Preached in First Congregational Church, August 23, 1914* (Columbus, Ohio: Privately printed, 1914).

Movement." Some of his sermons were studies of novels on the war or of books on war in general.[38]

At times Gladden preached as if the war would actually accelerate human progress. At the end of 1914 he thought that it might result in "a commonwealth of man—in a federation of nations." A few months later he observed that "theological mediaevalists and reactionaries, who are required by their theories to believe that everything is going to the bad," found confirmation for their pessimism in the war. But he was certain that the world had taken greater strides toward universal peace in the previous six months than in the past millennium. Horrified by this war, the nations were ready to make future wars impossible, to remove "the last and the deadliest obstacle in the path of human progress."[39]

Gladden denounced the idea that war was an essential training ground for courage. War might produce self-sacrifice and heroism, he told the First Congregational Church of Detroit, whose pastor was his good friend Gaius Glenn Atkins, but negative qualities more than offset these virtues. "Can it be," he asked, "that men can only be persuaded to devote themselves to high ideals, to noble services, by giving them the privilege of killing somebody whom they do not know and who has never done them any harm?" Moreover, though war might quicken religious enthusiasm, this enthusiasm would invariably give way to reaction and religious paralysis.[40]

He also rejected the argument that wars always had existed and always would exist. Less than a century earlier, men had said the same thing about slavery. Human progress had transformed many spheres of life, and, though it had made little headway in interna-

[38] Gladden, Sermons, "Bible Stories of War," "The Attitude of the Bible toward War," "How the Bible Has Been Used in Support of War," "What the Bible Has Done to Promote Peace," "The Church and the Peace Movement," [December, 1914–January, 1915,] "Mr. Britling Sees It Through," November 10, 1916, Gladden Papers; Ohio State Journal, December 3, 1914, March 6, 1915, July 1, 1916.

[39] Gladden, Sermons, December 27, 1914; March 14, 1915, Gladden Papers.

[40] Washington Gladden, Is War a Moral Necessity? Sermon before First Congregational Church of Detroit, April 18, 1915 (Detroit: Privately printed, 1915).

tional relations, it would ultimately eliminate war as well. An international league of peace that would bind men into a visible brotherhood must displace national sovereignty, "the one stupendous anomaly of civilization."[41] Declaring again and again that the war would convince mankind of the folly of self-interest and result in permanent peace, he asserted:

> It is hardly possible for me to believe that the world can go through such a furnace as that through which it is now passing and come out at the end of it the same old world. I think that we are going to see tremendous mental changes. . . . [42]

Gladden's absorbing concern was the establishment of peace. Ready to embrace any attempt to end the war and create enduring peace, he identified himself with movements whose ideologies ranged from doctrinaire pacifism to cautious military preparedness. Peace was his main goal, and the means by which he would achieve it were nebulously inchoate. He considered himself a pacifist, but, though one aggressive advocate of preparedness classified him with Tolstoy as an extreme pacifist, he never accepted the principle of absolute non-resistance.[43] Moreover, whatever his private opinions, he did not publicly discuss questions of international law or specific American actions. He viewed the war in moralistic terms, and his utterances were generalizations rather than concrete, precise analyses.

In 1915 Gladden circulated a pamphlet on *The Great War* consisting of six sermons that he had preached in 1914. He assumed that American entry was neither desirable nor likely, and he advocated unequivocally an immediate end to hostilities. Lyman Abbott, an early advocate of American preparedness and participation, commended the six sermons but emphasized that peace without justice—

[41] Gladden, "Human Nature Unchangeable," Sermon, May 30, 1915, Gladden Papers.

[42] Gladden, "The Peace to Pray for," Sermon, June 17, 1915, Gladden Papers; *Ohio State Journal*, June 28, 1915.

[43] *Ohio State Journal*, February 1, 1916.

that is, peace without an Allied victory—would not be acceptable. In addition, Gladden began early in 1915 to oppose preparedness in addresses in various parts of the country, and he tried unsuccessfully to publish an antipreparedness article, "Militaristic Theology."[44]

Gladden lent his support to the peace movement in a variety of ways, some of which are impossible to trace. He became president of the "Ministers' Union," an organization composed mainly of clergymen in New England, which, according to one of its founders, tried to rouse public opinion to demand that the fighting stop. In a letter to the *Ohio State Journal* he ridiculed Lloyd George's assertion that in the event of German victory, unpreparedness would imperil the United States. In the first place, Germany would not win; secondly, if she did win, she would be so weak that she could not invade the United States for decades.[45] Gladden incorporated this theme in a lengthy doggerel for the *Independent:*

> Some folks is layin' awake o' nights,
>   Harkin' fer noises of furrin invaders,
> Conj'rin' up all sorts o' frights,
>   Wond'rin' when we shall see the raiders;
> Nuthin's doin' yit, es fur's I know,
>   But while their common sense is dozin',
> Some on 'em's lettin' their guess-crop grow,
>   An' workin' their wits on jest supposin'.

> .   .   .   .

> S'posin' some nation, bleedin' 'n' pale,
>   Sore with her waounds 'n' faint from fightin',—
> Bendin' under a burden o' bale
>   That toilin' years won't greatly lighten,

---

[44] Rockwell H. Potter to Gladden, January 12, 25, 1915; Hamilton Holt to Gladden, January 26, 1915; Ernest H. Abbott to Gladden, January 26, February 19, 1915; Lyman Abbott to Gladden, January 30, 1915; Sydney Strong to Gladden, February 5, 1915; Editors, *Atlantic Monthly,* to Gladden, April 21, 1915, Gladden Papers.

[45] William J. Batt to Gladden, April 27, 1915, Gladden Papers; Batt to Maurer, January 31, 1928, First Church archives; *Ohio State Journal,* March 2, 1915.

> Sh'd stagger aout o' her pool o' blood,
> To run amuck, when she knew she couldn't,
> An' strike at aour land! Yas! S'posin' she should;
> An' then, agin, *supposin' she shouldn't!*
>
> . . . .
>
> We *kin* hev' war, ef we want it so;
> Hev it we shall, ef we keep on s'posin' it;
> The camel gits inter the tent, you know,
> By dent o' pokin' his pesky nose in it;
> But ef we keep on, ez aour fathers begun,
> Bound to be friends with every nation,
> There's nothin' onlikelier, under the sun,
> Than war, for another generation

The poem went on to suggest that an unarmed and amicable United States could lead the nations into permanent peace.[46]

During 1915 and 1916 Gladden worked hard to stem the mounting desire for preparedness. He endorsed the organization of a branch of the American Peace Society in Columbus. After a German submarine sank the *Falaba* in March, 1915, killing one American, he urged President Wilson to request a congressional appropriation of twenty millions for the Red Cross to divide equally between both sides, and to call a peace conference of the neutral nations, which would meet at The Hague for the duration of the war, "offering mediation and awaiting overtures from any or all of the belligerents." Repeating this proposal to his congregation, he expressed his hesitation to use force "or even the threat of force" to end the war.[47]

Throughout most of the war Gladden had close ties with the Church Peace Union, founded in February, 1914, by Andrew Carnegie, with the co-operation of a prominent group of Protestants, Roman Catholics, and Jews. The outbreak of war disrupted the

[46] Washington Gladden, "S'posin'," *Independent,* LXXXIV (October 25, 1915), 129.

[47] *Ohio State Journal,* March 20, 1915; Gladden to Woodrow Wilson, March 31, 1915, First Church archives; Gladden, "The Call to Our Country," Sermon, April 11, 1915, Gladden Papers.

organization's first project, an international peace conference at
Constance, but the conference continued to function as the World
Alliance for International Friendship through the Churches. Though
invited to the conference in Constance, Gladden was unable to
attend. He did co-operate with the American branch of the alliance,
which received strong support from the Federal Council of the
Churches of Christ in America, and in 1916 he became its president.[48] Gladden also served on the Church Peace Union's prize committee, which, beginning in 1915, made annual awards for essays on
peace. The first year Gaius Glenn Atkins and Reinhold Niebuhr
won, respectively, the prizes for the best essays by a minister and by
a theological student. In addition, Gladden made addresses for the
Church Peace Union and supplied Frederick Lynch, its secretary
and editor of the *Christian Work*, with articles, editorials, and sermons to be used in the peace movement.[49]

Gladden had somewhat looser ties with the League to Enforce
Peace, organized in Philadelphia in June, 1915, after a series of
informal meetings sponsored by the New York Peace Society. Hamilton Holt, the editor of the *Independent* and a close friend of Gladden's, was one of its prime movers, and William Howard Taft
became its president. Though Gladden lent his name to the call for
the organizational meeting in Philadelphia, it is not clear whether
he attended himself. Since it included both pacifists and militarists,
he may have hesitated to support it energetically. The League to
Enforce Peace was the principal organization supporting creation
of a league of nations during the war, and, probably for that reason,
Gladden did co-operate with its leaders. Its justification of force

[48] E. Ellsworth Shumaker to Gladden, July 27, 1915, World Alliance for
Promoting International Friendship through the Churches to Gladden, [April,]
1916, Sidney Gulick to Gladden, March 28, April 10, 1916, Gladden Papers;
Charles S. Macfarland, *Pioneers for Peace through Religion: Based on the
Records of the Church Peace Union (Founded by Andrew Carnegie), 1914–1945*
(New York: Fleming H. Revell Co., 1946), p. 46.

[49] Frederick Lynch to Gladden, May 19, August 28, 1914, January 9, April
24, 30, 1915, January 21, 24, September 19, 1916, July 30, 1917, Robert U.
Johnson to Gladden, April 15, 22–23, 1915, Atkins to Gladden, April 27, 1915,
Gladden Papers; Macfarland, *Pioneers for Peace*, pp. 17–21, 40–41, 46, 54.

as a means of establishing peace helped many pacifists—and perhaps Gladden—to accept eventual American entry into the war.[50]

The controversy over preparedness penetrated the churches, many of which had traditionally supported the peace societies of the nineteenth century. Congregationalism had a particularly vocal group of pacifists, including Gladden, Frederick Lynch, Charles E. Jefferson of the Broadway Tabernacle in New York, and Howard A. Bridgman, editor of the *Congregationalist*. When the national council met in New Haven in 1915, preparedness quickly became a central issue. Jefferson introduced a resolution criticizing "the organized and desperate efforts to stampede the nation . . . with wild and extravagant expenditures for ships and guns," urging the United States to avoid a policy of preparedness, and calling for a league of nations. Gladden at once endorsed it, arguing that "there has not been a day since Cornwallis surrendered in which there is so little danger of an invasion as today," and that preparedness would diminish American influence for peace. A committee under Gladden worked out a compromise resolution opposing any increase in armaments "not necessitated by grave considerations of national defense." Early in 1916, Gladden signed a petition against preparedness that was circulated by the Church Peace Union. Similar to Jefferson's original resolution, it had been altered slightly to avoid recognition.[51]

As the movement for preparedness gained strength, Gladden became adamantly pacifistic. Through the *New Republic* he declared that war could be nothing but a curse. The losses suffered by all the powers involved, including the victors, would be greater than any gains. To die for one's country might be heroic, Gladden admitted,

[50] *Ohio State Journal*, May 31, June 18, 1915; William H. Short to Gladden, May 10, September 2, 1915, January 13, March 1, 1916, F. H. Rike to Gladden, February 26, 1916, Gladden Papers; Ruhl J. Bartlett, *The League to Enforce Peace* (Chapel Hill: University of North Carolina Press, 1944), Preface, pp. 31–39, 217; Ray H. Abrams, *Preachers Present Arms* (New York: Round Table Press, 1933), pp. 164–65.

[51] *Ohio State Journal*, October 26–27, 1915; *Congregationalist*, C (November 4, 1915), 668; Lynch to Gladden, January 10, February 4, 1916, Gladden Papers; Abrams, *Preachers Present Arms*, p. 37.

but there was nothing "sweet" or "beautiful" in killing for one's country.[52] In his sermon on Thanksgiving Day he asserted that, since she had no traditional international policy, the United States must decide between pacifism and militarism. While a pacifistic policy would contribute to the continuance of peace, militarism would weaken American influence and lead, probably within a generation, to another major conflagration. And in his Christmas sermon he decried the growing probability of war with the Germans, a people with whom Americans had "no legitimate quarrel." Suspicion, fear, and misunderstanding had led the nations to increase their armaments and, consequently, to wage a war that they all claimed was defensive. The United States must set a new example of trust and brotherhood by judging other nations by her own motives.[53]

In November, 1915, Henry Ford invited Gladden to join other well-known Americans on his peace ship, *Oscar II*, which was to go to Europe to rally the proponents of peace. Gladden declined because of illness, but he defended Ford's venture against ridicule and criticism. "It is a shame to our humanity," he said, "that this nation and all the neutral nations sit dumb in the presence of such a spectacle." There was no prejudice against the American munitions-makers who got "millions of money out of this butchery," only against those who protested the holocaust. It was time, he asserted, for neutrals to use every peaceful influence to separate the belligerents, all of whom, though allegedly fighting in self-defense, would settle for nothing but decisive victory. England and France were bent on conquering Germany, even though they had entered the war to prevent German conquest. "A drawn battle," he felt, would furnish "the only promising basis for permanent peace."[54]

After Wilson abandoned his opposition to preparedness and, in December, 1915, introduced a program for strengthening Ameri-

[52] Washington Gladden, "A Pacifist's Apology," *New Republic*, V (November 20, 1915), 75–76; Herbert Croly to Gladden, November 12, 1915, Gladden Papers.

[53] *Ohio State Journal*, November 26, 1915; Gladden, Sermon, December 26, 1915, Gladden Papers.

[54] *Ohio State Journal*, November 26, 30, December 16, 1915.

can defenses, the antipreparedness organizations redoubled their activities. Wilson defended his program in Columbus on December 10. Gladden, who sat at Wilson's table and gave the invocation at a dinner in his honor, apparently objected to the new policy in a letter to Wilson, accompanied by one of his printed sermons on the war. Replying on December 14, Wilson admitted that he doubted his own judgment when men like Gladden differed with him and expressed his desire to square his conduct with Gladden's ideals.[55] In occasional addresses Gladden continued to criticize the administration's program for preparedness. He maintained that the munitions-makers and the Army League and Navy League were the chief proponents of preparedness and that, as "people to whom war is a trade," they were not reliable guides for the nation. Furthermore, he considered the campaign for preparedness absurd because its advocates did not even agree on which belligerent might attack the United States. The United States would not enter the war, and she would be in no danger when it was over. If she insisted on "trailing in the wake of the militaristic nations," she would "share in their bloody retributions."[56]

In the early months of 1916 the foes of preparedness launched a major attack on Wilson's program. The Anti-Preparedness Committee, which included such reformers as Lillian D. Wald, Paul U. Kellogg, Jane Addams, John Haynes Holmes, and Florence Kelley, protested at public hearings held on February 8–9 by the Military Affairs Committees of the House and Senate, and it appears that Gladden joined its delegation. With funds from the Church Peace Union, the Anti-Preparedness Committee began a "Truth about Preparedness Campaign." For several weeks in April, Gladden, Rabbi Stephen Wise, and Adolph A. Berle, a Congregational minister, supplemented by a corps of secondary speakers, toured major cities to arouse public opinion. After making several addresses in

---

[55] *Ibid.*, December 11, 1915; Wilson to Gladden, December 14, 1915, Gladden Papers.

[56] *Ohio State Journal*, February 14, 23, 1916; Gladden, "Getting Ready for War," Sermon, [1916,] Gladden Papers.

the East, Gladden had to shorten his schedule because of illness.[57] Gladden also helped to bring to Columbus William Jennings Bryan, who had resigned from the cabinet in protest against Wilson's strong note to Germany after the sinking of the *Lusitania*. Bryan appeared in March, 1916, under the auspices of the local branch of the Ohio Anti-Militarist League, of which Gladden was president, and assailed preparedness, as well as Wilson's refusal to warn Americans against traveling on armed Allied merchant ships.[58] Whatever the influence of the antipreparedness crusaders, the measures for defense that Congress finally passed in May and June, 1916, were considerably weaker than those recommended by Wilson.[59]

The Forks of the Road, a book that Gladden had tried unsuccessfully to get published in 1915, appeared just as Congress was enacting its first legislation for preparedness. Besides timely relevance, it had considerable prestige as the Church Peace Union's prize essay for 1916.[60] Ever a propagandist, Gladden sent a thoughtfully inscribed copy to Wilson. Gaius Glenn Atkins, who had won the prize in 1915, commended its strong, constructive message, while other pacifists took renewed courage from its eloquent words to preach against preparedness. William Jennings Bryan requested a copy of Gladden's original essay to print in the *Commoner*.[61]

[57] Lillian D. Wald, Paul Kellogg, Hollingsworth Wood, Crystal Eastman, and Charles Hallinan to Gladden, February 5, 1916; Lynch to Gladden, February 21, 24, April 12, 1916; Eastman to Gladden, February 26, March 4, 9, 14, 1916; Charles R. Brown to Gladden, April 14, 1916, Gladden Papers.

[58] *Ohio State Journal,* March 6–8, 1916; Thomas M. Sherman to Gladden, March 9, 1916, Gladden Papers.

[59] Arthur S. Link, *Woodrow Wilson and the Progressive Era, 1910–1917* (New York: Harper & Row, Publishers, 1954), pp. 187–88.

[60] Lynch to Gladden, June 5, 1915, March 14, May 4, 1916, Edward C. Marsh to Gladden, October 6, 29, 1915, January 4, 1916, Gladden Papers; "The Peace-Prize Essay," *Literary Digest,* LII (June 24, 1916), 1848. In early 1916 Gladden considered having the book published at his own expense. H. P. Ward to Gladden, March 13, 18, 1916, Gladden Papers.

[61] Wilson to Gladden, May 12, 1916; Atkins to Gladden, May 15, 1916; William Burnet Wright to Gladden, May 15, 1916; George D. Black to Gladden, May 31, 1916; Ward to Gladden, June 5, 1916; Paul Moore Strayer to Gladden, June 24, 1916; Ross W. Sanderson to Gladden, June 27, 1916; William Jennings Bryan to Gladden, July 2, [1916,] Gladden Papers.

In *The Forks of the Road* Gladden condemned not only the churches' failure to prevent war, but also their willingness to condone or sanctify it. Their theology had, if anything, strengthened human animosities: "What is the use," he asked, "of telling men to love their enemies when they know that God is going to plunge all his enemies into a fiery pit and watch them burning there eternally?" Moreover, he charged that they had not provided the world with a coherent social philosophy. They had cultivated the spirit of individualism rather than that of brotherhood. The inevitable consequences of this heresy were the ill will and distrust that led to the multiplication of armaments and ultimately to war. Faintly grasping the idea of brotherhood, the churches had made some inroads on evil; but industry, politics, and especially international relations were still largely in the grip of Antichrist. Gladden found the principle of preparedness to be both a source of conflict and a reflection of a deeper evil in the affairs of nations. Every instrument of war revealed the belief that force was more reliable than good will.[62]

The churches and the nations stood, in Gladden's words, at "the forks of the road." For the churches the choice was between nationalistic tribal gods and the universal Father of mankind. For the warring nations it was between the old policies of self-interest and militancy and the new mandate of permanent peace and co-operation through an international league. The United States and the other neutrals, which should have pressed for mediation from the beginning, must determine which alternative would lead most quickly to a final settlement. To approach the conference table heavily armed and then try to stand for peace and good will would not only be hypocrisy but would also be an obstacle to their professed goals.[63]

Gladden's occasional sermons and articles throughout 1916 bore these same themes. He saw an international league as a moral and

[62] Washington Gladden, *The Forks of the Road* (New York: Macmillan Co., 1916), pp. 19, 23–25, 34–35, 40, 44, 51.

[63] *Ibid.*, pp. 71, 99–105, 112, 119–20, 129.

spiritual as well as practical necessity.[64] When the United States continued to accelerate her program of preparedness, he predicted a gruesome outcome. Sowing distrust, America would reap havoc. In a brief article on "The Unescapable Law" in the *Independent,* he admitted his bewilderment that "the people of the United States, after watching this retribution for two years, are now making haste to set it [the law of love] at defiance! It's a mad world, my masters!"[65] In earlier days men had all carried arms for self-defense. Mutual trust, "the replacing of the ape and tiger psychology of human relations by the human psychology of good-will," had made private arms unnecessary. Nations could also go without arms, if they would only trust each other. Though the United States could set the example, she appeared ready to plunge into the "Gehenna of militarism" herself and in so doing to inflict great injury on the world. "God grant that I may not live to see it!" Gladden cried.[66]

During the presidential campaign in 1916 Gladden, a lifelong Republican who had voted the Progressive ticket in 1912, endorsed Wilson—as did practically all reformers—largely because of Wilson's progressive policies. He admired Charles Evans Hughes, the Republican candidate, but regretted his decision to leave the Supreme Court for a partisan campaign. Preparedness was a secondary but important factor in Gladden's decision. Though he disapproved of Wilson's capitulation on preparedness, he felt that the Republicans were more to blame for the agitation for preparedness than the Democrats and that Wilson might withstand militaristic pressure more successfully than Hughes.[67]

When on December 18, 1916, the President sent a note to the

[64] *Ohio State Journal,* July 17, December 1, 1916; Gladden, "The New Internationalism," Sermon, September 10, 1916, Gladden Papers; Washington Gladden, "The Pilgrim Church and Vital Americanism," *Congregationalist,* CI (December 28, 1916), 878–79; Gladden, *The Interpreter,* p. 96.

[65] Washington Gladden, "The Unescapable Law," *Independent,* LXXXVIII (November 13, 1916), 279.

[66] Washington Gladden, "A Plea for Pacifism," *Nation,* CIII (August 3, 1916), Supplement 2.

[67] *Ohio State Journal,* October 17, 1916; *New York Times,* October 22, 1916; Wilson to Gladden, October 24, December 5, 1916, Gladden Papers.

belligerents asking them to state their war aims, Gladden found reason to believe that he had made the right choice. Earlier in the year, he had joined the American Neutral Conference Committee, an organization closely allied with the Church Peace Union. It appears that he had co-operated with the committee in urging Wilson to call a conference of the neutral powers to offer mediation to the belligerents and formulate a program for peace. In co-operation with the Women's Peace Party and other pacifist organizations, the committee held a demonstration on New Year's Eve in New York's Washington Square. Gladden addressed the mass meeting, apparently praising Wilson's note as a step toward peace. On his return to Columbus he conferred with Wilson and found him undisturbed by his meager success in promoting peace.[68] Wilson spoke for the whole neutral world, Gladden asserted. That the belligerents were not really fighting to end war was evident from their unwillingness to accept "peace without victory." If the war resulted in the temporary subjugation of either side, Gladden thought, the settlement would be only a truce, and it would be virtually impossible to establish permanent peace for a long time to come.[69]

Wilson's overture to the belligerents was unsuccessful, however, and a rapid succession of incidents led the United States into the war. Like Lynch, Jefferson, and most other opponents of preparedness, Gladden reluctantly but loyally submitted to the course of events. After Wilson severed diplomatic relations with Germany in February, 1917, the editor of the *Ohio State Journal* reported that Gladden agreed with him that Americans should support Wilson's policies: "Yes, there is no other way," Gladden said.[70] Gladden was reluctant at this stage, however, to sanction American participation.

[68] Lynch to Gladden, August 2, December 19, 1916, Rebecca Shelly to Gladden, August 24, 26, November 29, 1916, Holt to Gladden, August 28, September 12, 1916, Lella Faye Secor to Gladden, January 6, 1917, Gladden Papers; Gladden to Stanton C. Kelton, December 25, 1916, First Church archives; *Ohio State Journal,* January 4–5, 1917.

[69] Gladden, "The President as Peacemaker," Sermon, January 7, 1917, Gladden Papers; *Ohio State Journal,* January 8, 1917.

[70] *Ohio State Journal,* February 26, 1917; Abrams, *Preachers Present Arms,* pp. 54–55.

In a brief manuscript on the war he recoiled at the loss of life it would inflict. "The right to live is central," he concluded, "and in the perfected civilization it will not be questioned, even in the interests of social justice. The recognition of it makes war unthinkable." The title of this work, which he was unable to get published, "Killing Wrong-Doers as a Cure for Wrong-Doing," amused Walter Rauschenbusch, whose experience during the war was tragic because of his pacifism and his German ancestry. Agreeing with Gladden's thesis, Rauschenbusch predicted that without a successful democratic settlement, which Wilson would find virtually impossible to obtain, the war would have no justification.[71]

On February 19 Gladden left Columbus to preach for two months at the First Congregational Church of Los Angeles. Since his retirement in 1914 he had served as interim pastor for several Congregational churches. In the fall of 1914 he had toured California with his son George, visiting old friends and preaching for churches, colleges, and Congregational associations. Several pastors in southern California urged him to counteract the growing influence of fundamentalism by spreading the Social Gospel and liberal theology.[72] Early in 1916 he had made a three-week tour of the East. And in the fall of 1916 he had agreed to preach for two months in the United Congregational Church of Bridgeport, Connecticut. While there he encouraged the church to call William Horace Day, pastor of the First Congregational Church of Los Angeles. Day's removal to

[71] It is difficult to fix accurately the date of this manuscript. The fact that its tone suggests composition before American entry kept Harper and Brothers from publishing it without revisions, which Gladden refused to make. Though Gladden spoke of the United States having broken "from the moorings of comparative pacifism" and launched into the maelstrom, he may have had Wilson's program of preparedness in mind. On the other hand, he submitted it for publication and circulated it among friends after the United States had entered the war. Gladden, "Killing Wrong-Doers as a Cure for Wrong-Doing," [1917,] Gladden Papers; Ripley Hitchcock to Gladden, March 27, May 1, 8, 1917, Lynch to Gladden, April 4, 1917, Walter Rauschenbusch to Gladden, November 17, 1917, Gladden Papers.

[72] Henry K. Booth to Gladden, January 18, 1914; Henry M. Streeter to Gladden, January 22, May 7, 20, July 31, November 20, 1914; Morris H. Turk to Gladden, May 15, June 10, 23, September 8, 17–18, 1914; Horace Porter to Gladden, May 16, August 18, 1914; Charles S. Nash to Gladden, July 8, 28, August 25, 28, September 29, 1914, Gladden Papers.

Bridgeport opened the door for Gladden to fill the interim engagement in Los Angeles in 1917. His schedule in California was so strenuous—he spoke thirty-three times in forty-four days—that he had a physical breakdown after his return to Columbus. The church in Bridgeport invited him to return during Day's vacation in the summer of 1917, but because of illness he was unable to accept.[73]

By the time he returned to Columbus in April, Gladden had become a convert to the cause of the war. "Making the World Safe for Democracy," the title of his first sermon in the First Church, replaced "peace without victory" in his utterances on the war. He believed that Wilson had exhausted all avenues to peace and finally had had to recognize German aggression against the United States. Wilson had lifted the issue to a height at which a few things seem clear." This was no national quarrel. Submarine warfare was, as Wilson said, "a warfare against mankind." America would fight, Gladden maintained, not for herself but "for the supreme good of freedom, which shall be shared with all the nations, the least and the greatest." The appeal of Wilson's war aims was irresistible. Suddenly forgetting his earlier conviction that war was nothing but a curse, Gladden proclaimed: "This war needn't be a curse; it may be the greatest blessing that has ever befallen this land." He foresaw dangers to American democracy—a lowering of the nation's moral tone, corruption, and the retardation of social reform. But he was sure that they were not as great as the possibilities for "heroic and splendid service." His optimism was amazing. Asked by Frederic Almy if, after fifty years of ministry, he saw any cause for pessimism, he replied, "Not one."[74]

---

[73] *Ohio State Journal*, March 23, 1916; Frederick B. Curtis to Gladden, September 6, 1916, April 25, 1917, W. E. Hatheway to Gladden, September 25, 1916, Day to Gladden, January 13, March 16, April 13, 1917, James A. Blaisdell to Gladden, March 2, 12, 1917, William P. Kimball to Gladden, March 13, 1917, Patton to Gladden, March 17, July 5, 1917, Charles H. Parkhurst to Gladden, June 6, 1917, Gladden Papers; Gladden to Mrs. Jeffrey, April 5, 1917, First Church archives.

[74] *Ohio State Journal*, January 19, February 10, 1917; Gladden, "Making the World Safe for Democracy," Sermon, April 29, 1917, Gladden Papers; Frederic Almy, "The Conquest of Poverty," *Proceedings of the National Conference of Social Work, 1917* (Chicago: Rogers & Hall Co., Printers, 1917), pp. 3–4.

During his last year Gladden retained a keen interest in the war and the changes that it was likely to produce. In commerce and industry it was demonstrating the appalling extent of American wastefulness, the rapacity of "sharpers of the world of trade," and the need for, and possibility of, greater governmental restriction of individual freedom.[75] Religion would have to change radically: "The church must cease to sanction those principles of militaristic and atheistic nationalism by which the rulers of the earth have so long kept the world at war." The war, he hoped, would hasten the emergence of a religion of social service and accelerate the ecumenical movement.[76] Similarly, he sensed new challenges and envisioned new advances in postwar education and domestic life.[77] The war even disarmed his opposition to prohibition, which the voters of Ohio rejected by only a small margin in November, 1917. Anticipating a resounding victory at the next election, he asserted that the war had "made some things appear practicable which we thought not long ago impossible. Prohibition is one of them."[78]

Gladden saw the war as a great test of America's faith and character. He warned against unworthy motives and an unhealthy "super-patriotism." The last article to come from his pen, printed posthumously, suggested that those who prayed for God to damn the Kaiser had learned their prayers "from the Kaiser."[79] But he never doubted that the United States was fighting for democracy.

[75] Gladden, "The School of War and Its Lessons," Sermon, July 1, 1917, Gladden Papers; *Ohio State Journal*, September 13, 1917. When the national Congregational council met in Columbus in October, 1917, Gladden presided at its sessions on "Industry and Fraternity" and spoke on industrial reconstruction after the war. *Ohio State Journal*, October 15, 1917.

[76] Gladden, quoted in Buckham, *Progressive Religious Thought*, p. 247; *Ohio State Journal*, May 12, October 4, 1917; Gladden, "Religion After the War," Sermon, September 2, 1917, Gladden Papers.

[77] Gladden, Sermons, "Education after the War," September 19, 1917; "The Family after the War," September 26, 1917, Gladden Papers.

[78] *Ohio State Journal*, November 12, 1917.

[79] *Ibid.*, May 20, 1918; Washington Gladden, "Do We Believe in God?", *Independent*, VC (July 20, 1918), 87. The *Congregationalist* rejected an article censuring "Super-Patriotism" because of public sensitivity to criticisms of the American war effort. Bridgman to Gladden, May 31, 1918, Gladden Papers.

It was a reaction against democracy by the antiquated autocracies of Europe that had started the war. "The central army is fighting," he said, "to make war perpetual, while the western army is fighting to make war impossible." In a letter to a patriotic rally held by the religious organizations of Columbus, he distinguished between nationalism grounded in "justice and righteousness" and "the nationalism whose basis is force and whose purpose is the subjugation of mankind." The two, he asserted, "cannot live together on this planet." If the democracies won, they would treat Germany fairly and admit her, presumably reformed, to the postwar "commonwealth of man, the federation of the world."[80] An interpreter of God's acts in human history, Gladden was committed to a spiritual and moral interpretation of political events. He often said that one could learn what God was doing in the world from the newspapers. Furthermore, as an optimist, he overestimated men's devotion to ideals that he identified, perhaps too closely, with the message of Christianity.

Gladden was relatively active until November, 1917. In June he spoke at commencements at Ohio University and the University of Akron. In September he traveled to Chicago to perform the second marriage of Governor James M. Cox of Ohio. And in October he participated in the national Congregational council, which met in Columbus. When he rose to speak on "The Range of the Social Demand of the Gospel," his fellow Congregationalists stood to honor him. He also continued to send letters and sermons to Wilson.[81] At the end of October Carl S. Patton left Columbus to accept a call to the First Congregational Church of Los Angeles. Gladden had hoped to preach regularly until the church could find another pastor, but his health was too precarious for the church to rely on him. A month after Patton left, Irving Maurer, who had been in Columbus for the Congregational council, agreed to leave his church

[80] Gladden, "The High Calling of America," Sermon, September 23, 1917, Gladden Papers; *Ohio State Journal*, March 29, June 24, 1918.

[81] Gladden to Alice Kelton, June 22, 1917, First Church archives; *Ohio State Journal*, June 21, September 16, October 14, 1917; Joseph P. Tumulty to Gladden, January 11, September 22, 27, 1917, Gladden Papers.

in Northampton, Massachusetts, for the prestigious post in Columbus. Since Gladden had suffered a stroke of paralysis during the last week of November, the church had to engage visiting speakers until Maurer arrived in January.[82]

Gladden struggled to regain his strength. In January a visitor from the *Ohio State Journal* found him working in an armchair on the second floor of his house, with a table and materials in front of him. His right arm paralyzed, he learned to write with his left hand and experimented with a typewriter. He had his telephone connected with the church so he could hear the services on Sundays. By February he was walking around his room. Alice read with him and he went through several biographies and autobiographies, enjoying especially Hamlin Garland's *A Son of the Middle Border*.[83] For the first time in years his friends were unable to have a joint birthday celebration for him and Dr. James F. Baldwin, an intimate friend and a member of the First Church. Instead, Maurer had the congregation deluge him with cards and letters.[84] By Easter he was able to attend church.

During his last months Gladden wrote a few letters to the *Ohio State Journal* dealing with various aspects of the war.[85] In addition, beginning in January he composed a poem each week for the calendar of the First Church. The war furnished themes for many of them. In the "Peace Hymn of the Republic," which appeared in the calendar on February 24, he summarized his reprehension of war and his hopes for peace:

> Our eyes have seen the splendor of the coming of
> the king;
> Watched the Greater Glory dawning and the morning
> brightening;

[82] *Ohio State Journal*, July 24, 26, November 17, 19, 29, December 2, 1917.

[83] *Ibid.*, January 13, 1918; Gladden to Alice Kelton, January 28, 1918, First Church archives; *Congregationalist*, CIII (February 21, 1918), 234.

[84] *Ohio State Journal*, February 11, 1918.

[85] *Ibid.*, January 23, February 14, March 20, 29, 1918.

Hailed the advent of the peoples, which the better
　　day shall bring,
　　　　For God is marching on.

Gone that ancient curse of bondage; for God smote
　　it, and it fell;
Darker curse for our undoing still o'ercame us like
　　a spell;
War, the spawn of demons, lingered—blackest spirit
　　out of hell,
　　　　But God is marching on.

He hath sworn, he will perform it; lo! the day of
　　wrath is here;
For the nations now are hurrying to make his
　　judgment clear;
And all the earth is waiting for the glad day to
　　appear,
　　　　When God is marching on.

　．　　．　　．　　．　　．　　．　　．　　．　　．　　．　　．

Thus the Greater Glory shineth on through ancient
　　forms of strife,
In the hearts of men abounding now when better
　　deeds are rife;
As they died by dealing death to men, we live by
　　sharing life;
　　　　For Love is marching on.[86]

He wrote a "War Hymn of the First Congregational Church" especially for servicemen from the First Church.[87] His vision was bright in "America and Her Allies," written the previous autumn and included in a collection of these *Calendar Verses:*

O Land of lands, my Fatherland,
　　The beautiful, the free,

[86] Washington Gladden, *Calendar Verses* (Columbus, Ohio: McClelland & Co., 1918), p. 21.

[87] *Ibid.*, p. 41.

All lands and shores to freedom dear
   Are ever dear to thee;
All sons of Freedom hail thy name
   And wait thy word of might,
While round the world the lists are joined
   For liberty and light.

Hail sons of France, old comrades dear!
   Hail Britons brave and true!
Hail Belgian martyrs ringed with flame!
   Slavs fired with visions new!
Italian lovers mailed with light!
   Dark brothers from Japan!
From East to West all lands are kin
   Who live for God and man.

Here endeth war! Our bands are sworn!
   New dawns the better hour
When lust of blood shall cease to rule,
   When Peace shall come with power;
We front the fiend that rends our race
   And fills our homes with gloom;
We break his scepter, spurn his crown,
   And nail him in his tomb!

Now, hands all round, our troth we plight
   To rid the world of lies,
To fill all hearts with truth and trust
   And willing sacrifice;
To free all lands from hate and spite
   And fear from strand to strand;
To make all nations neighbors
   And the world one Fatherland![88]

On July 1 headlines in the *Ohio State Journal* announced: "Rev. Dr. Washington Gladden Dying." A second stroke, occurring on June 29, had left him unconscious, though without pain. The previous night he had gone riding with John Preston, his Negro coachman, in an electric automobile that the church had given him in

---

[88] *Ibid.*, p. 43.

1915. His sons Frederick and George came from the East to be at his bedside. He never regained consciousness, and on July 2 he died. Editorial tributes, letters, and sketches and photographs in papers across the country testified to his national stature. Rabbi Stephen Wise spoke glowingly of his service to humanity, and President Wilson wrote to Gladden's family, "His death has impoverished us." For two hours on the day of his funeral a steady stream of admirers, representing all classes and religions, filed silently past his coffin in the church. One bouquet of roses bore the inscription, "A Token of Catholic Gratitude." Local clergymen formed an escort of honor. The chimes of Trinity Church (Episcopal), the only other church on Capitol Square, pealed out Gladden's favorite hymn and the assembled mourners sang, "O Master, Let Me Walk with Thee."[89]

[89] *Ohio State Journal,* May 5, 1915, July 1–4, 7–8, 1918; Wilson to Frederick C. Gladden, July 3, 1918, First Church archives.

Fifteen

Prophet of the Social Gospel

When Gladden entered semiretirement in 1914, the *Outlook,* in one of its numerous tributes to his career, concluded that his preaching had been prophetic in two senses: he had declared the will of God as he had seen it; and he had forecast with surprising accuracy the direction of events in American religious, social, and political life. At first "the utterances of a prophet speaking to a generation very few of whom read the signs of the times," his statements had become "records of fulfillment." Moreover, the *Outlook* maintained, he had done as much as any man to change the attitudes of thoughtful Americans toward social and economic conditions.[1] This theme—that his ministry had been prophetic—ran through many contemporary estimates of his career. One influential Congregational minister, who as a seminarian had heard him lecture and had subsequently read all of his books, felt that Gladden had ennobled the ministry for many young clergymen and linked them with "the great line of prophets." George P. Morris, an associate editor of the *Congregationalist,* called Gladden a "Prophet of Social Christianity" and asked: "Who has been as versatile and still carried so much weight? Who has spoken so often and so sensibly as a rule?" Morris doubted that the message of any other contemporary American clergyman had "found its way so generally into the libraries of progressive

[1] "Washington Gladden," *Outlook,* CVI (January 24, 1914), 160–61.

English-speaking people" as had Gladden's.[2]

Though it is impossible to measure precisely the extent of Gladden's influence, it is abundantly clear that, as one of the earliest and most prolific exponents of liberal theology and the Social Gospel, he broke the path that many younger men were to follow. The gradual triumph of his views among American Protestants during the last quarter of the nineteenth century can be seen in the transformation of his own reputation. In the 1870's the *Congregationalist* had considered him a dangerous radical in theology, but in 1915 it acclaimed him the "Grand old man of Congregationalism"; and after his death it observed that, while Congregationalists "[called] no man master save Jesus Christ," if diꞯꞯꞯꞯ il "ꞯꞯꞯꞯ ꞯꞯꞯꞯ ꞯꞯꞯ ꞯꞯ ꞯꞯꞯꞯ ꞯꞯꞯꞯ ꞯꞯ ꞯ ꞯꞯꞯꞯꞯꞯ position," they would have chosen Gladden.[3] After the turn of the century Congregational churchmen in such diverse places as Springfield, Massachusetts, York, Nebraska, Minneapolis, and Long Beach organized "Washington Gladden Clubs" to study and spread social Christianity.[4] Lyman Abbott felt that no man in the country had been "more identified . . . with the advance movement of thought in the Church of Christ, both theologically and socially," or had "represented that advance with greater clearness, courage and level-headedness" than Gladden. And John W. Buckham thought that it would be hard to find any man who had done more to spread progressive religious and social ideas. "Washington Gladden," he declared, "was an apostle—may we not say *the* apostle in this country?—of Applied Christianity."[5]

Gladden influenced the thought of his age in several ways. Per-

[2] Harry N. Dascomb to Gladden, February 14, 1906, January 12, 1914, Gladden Papers; George P. Morris, "Washington Gladden—A Prophet of Social Christianity," *Congregationalist*, LXXXIV (November 1, 1902), 617.

[3] *Congregationalist*, C (November 4, 1915), 672; "The Passing of Washington Gladden," *Congregationalist*, CIII (July 11, 1918), 38.

[4] Charles D. Reid to Gladden, October 17, 1905; E. Merle Adams to Gladden, January 13, 1917; Clarence R. Chaney to Gladden, November 26, 1906; Samuel Baumann to Gladden, March 19, 1916, Gladden Papers.

[5] Abbott to Gladden, October 28, 1908, Gladden Papers; Buckham, *Progressive Religious Thought*, pp. 217, 220.

haps most importantly, his example in the last quarter of the nineteenth century had a formative impact on several younger men who
became in their own right apostles of social Christianity. Walter
Rauschenbusch, whom many consider the most incisive thinker
among the social gospelers, wrote to Gladden:

> You are one of the veterans who made it easier for us of the next genera-
> tion to see our way and to get a hearing. You have done a noble day's
> work and have lived to see the reapers going out to the harvest which you
> helped to sow.

And in *Christianizing the Social Order* (1912) he singled out Gladden, Josiah Strong, and Richard T. Ely as pioneers of Christian
social thought twenty-five years earlier. "These men," he remarked,
"had matured their thought when the rest of us were young men,
and they had a spirit in them which kindled and compelled us."[6]
Shailer Mathews, like Rauschenbusch a prominent Baptist edu-
cator, credited the same three men with awakening his interest in
the social message of Christianity.[7] Ely himself acknowledged a
personal debt to Gladden, especially for Gladden's early articles on
socialism, which struck what Ely considered a "safe balance."[8]
Graham Taylor, who had been a young pastor in Hartford when
Gladden was in Springfield, testified to Gladden:

> When at Hartford I was impelled to be outward bound on the unknown
> social deep, your signals at Springfield helped me point my course in the
> right direction. Ever since I have always looked at least to see which
> way you were going.

And Mrs. Sleppey of the West Side Social Center claimed that
Taylor had told approximately a thousand social workers at a convention in Chicago that, of all the great people he had ever known,

[6] Rauschenbusch to Gladden, December 2, 1908, Gladden Papers; Walter
Rauschenbusch, *Christianizing the Social Order* (New York: Macmillan Co.,
1912), p. 9.

[7] Shailer Mathews, *New Faith for Old: An Autobiography* (New York: Macmillan Co., 1936), p. 48.

[8] *Congregationalist*, CI (February 10, 1916), 202–4.

Gladden had exercised the greatest influence on him and had been the guiding star of his life.[9]

Gladden popularized his liberal and social Christianity through innumerable writings and addresses. Several of his books were translated into French and German, and all of his publications with Houghton, Mifflin and Company were issued simultaneously in England. A professor of sociology at Washburn College in Kansas told Gladden that his books were "household" with his students. The Commission on the Church and Social Service of the Federal Council of Churches included several of them in its bibliographies and reading lists for pastors and churches, which were issued by the thousands. One man who had read all of Gladden's books observed that they were well worn and in continued demand in libraries around Los Angeles. And Gaius Glenn Atkins, who doubted that the work of any contemporary minister had been more influential or more pregnant, found all of Gladden's books in the Detroit Public Library "worn with reading and pencil marked in a way to pain the Librarian."[10]

In addition to speaking in churches, for religious gatherings, before civic groups, and at Chautauqua, Gladden was popular as a speaker for college commencements and chapel services. He appeared at Wellesley, Mount Holyoke, Smith, and many other eastern colleges, as well as at such public institutions as the University of Michigan, the Ohio State University, and Miami University (Ohio).[11] Though responsibilities to his own congregation always limited his freedom to travel, his correspondence reveals that he

[9] Taylor to Gladden, November 13, 1913; Dora T. Sleppey to Gladden, May 31, 1917, Gladden Papers.

[10] *Ohio State Journal*, September 25, 1904; D. M. Fisk to Gladden, January 1, 1907, Charles S. Macfarland to Gladden, August 17, 1912, Nathan Dana Dodge to Gladden, May 12, 1913, Gladden Papers; Atkins, *Religion in Our Times*, p. 53.

[11] Caroline Hazard to Gladden, January 13, June 29, 1900; Mary E. Woolley to Gladden, October 9, 1906; Jean T. Johnson to Gladden, May 24, June 1, 1911; James B. Angell to Gladden, June 12, 1902; William Oxley Thompson to Gladden, November 15, 19, 1910; Guy Potter Benton to Gladden, August 27, 1910, Gladden Papers.

spoke in all types of schools and in all parts of the country. On a single trip to the West in 1912 he delivered twenty-seven addresses, eight of them at universities.[12] His relations with Ohio State University were especially close. One professor who as a student had frequently heard him there doubted if any man "ever exerted a greater or more far-reaching influence upon our student body than did Dr. Gladden in his day."[13] Gaius Glenn Atkins first met Gladden in the mid-1880's while a student at the Ohio State University. He maintained that Gladden made his own ministry possible:

> He resolved my doubts; he gave a quality and direction to my thinking which I cannot and do not seek to escape. His noble preaching was the supreme spiritual force in my college life. His books taught and guided me in the beginning of my work.[14]

Similarly, Dan Freeman Bradley, another prominent Congregationalist, testified that he began to be deeply influenced by Gladden during his days at Oberlin College.[15] Many outside of Congregationalism also felt the appeal of Gladden's message. Bishop William Scarlett of the Protestant Episcopal church, a man noted for the social orientation of his ministry, recalls how his personal acquaintance with Gladden in Columbus and Gladden's continued interest in him during his days in college and seminary and in his early pastoral work helped him to see the relevance of Christianity and to stay in the ministry.[16]

Besides occasional lectures, Gladden gave several important series of addresses at educational institutions. He was one of only four men invited to give more than one course under the Lyman Beecher Foundation at Yale Seminary. In 1893 he gave the lectures later pub-

---

[12] Gladden, "Round about Zion," Sermon, December 8, 1912, Gladden Papers.

[13] William McPherson, "An Appreciation of Dr. Washington Gladden," *First Church News,* VI (February, 1936), 7.

[14] Gaius Glenn Atkins, "Washington Gladden—and After," *Religion in Life,* V (Autumn, 1936), 597; *Congregationalist,* CI (February 10, 1916), 202–4.

[15] *Congregationalist,* CI (February 10, 1916), 202–4.

[16] William Scarlett to Gladden, March 8, 1918, Gladden Papers; Scarlett to author, November 26, 1964.

lished as *Tools and the Man*, the first discussion under the Beecher Foundation of industrial problems, and in 1902 he returned to give the series that appeared as *Social Salvation*.[17] Between 1893 and 1903 he served three terms on the staff of preachers at Harvard University. Under the guidance of Professor Francis G. Peabody, another social gospeler, six preachers were selected each year, partly on the basis of their ability to attract students to Harvard's experimental voluntary chapel services, to conduct chapel and vespers, and to counsel students. Each preacher spent about six weeks of the academic year at Harvard, usually divided into two terms, one before and one after Christmas; he resided in Wadsworth House in the College Yard, where students might come on weekdays for religious guidance and advice on personal problems. Most of Gladden's visitors sought vocational advice, but many came with questions about science and religion or with moral and spiritual problems. Charles R. Brown, a Congregational minister who became dean of the School of Religion at Yale, was a student at Harvard when Gladden preached there in 1893. Though Gladden surprised the students by entering the chapel dressed like an ordinary banker or businessman, Brown recalled, he spoke with power and by his simplicity encouraged students to come to him for counsel. Gladden received an invitation to serve a fourth term, but, though his congregation had always encouraged him to accept on previous occasions, he declined because he felt that such lengthy absences were detrimental to his pastoral work.[18]

Gladden also gave at least three series of lectures at the Bangor

[17] Edgar DeWitt Jones, *The Royalty of the Pulpit: A Survey and Appreciation of the Lyman Beecher Lectures on Preaching Founded at Yale Divinity School, 1871, and Given Annually (with Four Exceptions) since 1872* (New York: Harper & Bros., Publishers, 1951), pp. 151–55.

[18] Gladden, *Recollections*, pp. 324–27; Hugh Hawkins, "Charles W. Eliot, University Reform, and Religious Faith in America, 1869–1909," *Journal of American History*, LI (September, 1964), 211; Francis G. Peabody to Gladden, March 18, April 3, June 5, 1902, March 12, 25, 1903, Charles W. Eliot to Gladden, March 28, 1900, May 29, June 11, 1902, Gladden Papers; Charles Reynolds Brown, *They Were Giants* (New York: Macmillan Co., 1934), pp. 213–14.

Theological Seminary, reaching not only the seminarians but also many ministers from Maine who attended the seminary's convocations. In 1908 he gave the Enoch Pond Lectures on Applied Christianity, in 1911 the George Shepard Lectures on Preaching, and in 1914 the Samuel Harris Lectures on Literature and Life.[19] He delivered his lectures on "The Vocation of the Preacher" at a number of schools, including the Chicago Theological Seminary and Vanderbilt University.[20] He worked diligently to enlist young men in the ministry. Irving Maurer heard him while a student at Beloit College in 1904. Gladden's description of the ministry as "the unequalled profession" partly influenced Maurer, who had intended to enter the legal profession, to choose instead the ministry.[21] Undoubtedly, Gladden's stature and public influence exemplified for many seminarians and young clergymen what the parish ministry might ideally be.[22]

By the beginning of the twentieth century, when he began to receive eulogistic tributes from private correspondents, civic and religious organizations, and the press, Gladden had come to symbolize a Protestantism radically different from that of the mid-nineteenth century. A host of admirers followed the leadership that he shared with Strong, Abbott, and Rauschenbusch in adjusting the Christian faith to modern intellectual currents and in making it relevant to the conditions of an urban, industrial society. Some recognized a purely personal debt to him: he had shown them how to be both intelligent moderns and sincere Christians. Others considered

[19] David N. Beach to Gladden, November 10, 21, 1906, July 13, 23, 1907, February 23, 1911, December 12, 16, 1913; Eugene W. Lyman to Gladden, February 25, 1911; Calvin M. Clark to Gladden, February 12, 1914, Gladden Papers.

[20] Gladden, Lectures on "The Vocation of the Preacher," "The Teacher," "The Evangelist," "The Apostle," "The Prophet," "The Friend," n.d., Gladden Papers; Gladden to Taylor, March 23, 1914, Taylor Papers; Taylor to Gladden, March 25, June 2, 1914, Gladden Papers; Congregationalist, XCVIII (July 10, 1913), 55.

[21] Maurer, "Glimpses of Washington Gladden," First Church archives.

[22] Bruce Barton popularized Gladden's success in the ministry in one of several articles on the clerical profession. Bruce Barton, "Four Who Answered," Congregationalist, XCIX (May 28, 1914), 711.

his contributions to good citizenship primary. At the dedication of
the Columbus Athletic Club's new building in 1916 the toastmaster
had only to mention "the first citizen of Columbus," and the members shouted "Gladden, Gladden."[23] But those who understood the
basic relationship between his thought and activities agreed with
Lyman Abbott that Gladden was not "a preacher of the Gospel *and*
a moral reformer" but "a preacher of a Gospel that is a moral
reform."[24] For Gladden religion and reform were inseparable.

By his own definition and by the judgment of his contemporaries,
Gladden was an interpreter and mediator. His special distinction,
George P. Morris wrote, was

that men within highly organized American clergymen, during this period
of disintegration of old beliefs and reconstruction of new, he has kept his
eyes open to the new knowledge of scientists, Biblical scholars, and soci-
ologists, and has interpreted this new truth for the spiritual, ethical, and
political guidance of his fellow-men, not only in this country, but to some
degree throughout the English-speaking world.[25]

He interpreted theology and biblical criticism to laymen, the values
of Christianity to social reformers, the needs of humanity to the
churches, and Americans to themselves. He sought, moreover, to
interpret individuals, classes, and nations to each other. His attempts
at mediation were not always successful. He and his fellow liberals
did not convince all Protestants that biblical criticism and evolution
were not only safe but also positive bulwarks of a rational faith, as
the increasing strength of fundamentalism in the twentieth century
demonstrates. In addition, war and reaction began even before his
death to overshadow the optimism that had illuminated his faith.
Nor did economic classes always find his efforts at impartiality grati-
fying or accept the spirit of good will that he consistently preached.
But his good sense and ability to grasp the common interests of

[23] *Ohio State Journal,* January 23, 1916.

[24] "Washington Gladden," *Outlook,* LXXXII (January 27, 1906), 155.

[25] George P. Morris, "A Preacher and Patriot," *Century,* LXXI (March, 1906),
815–16.

divergent groups generally enabled him, according to friendly observers, to gain a broad hearing on theological and social questions.[26]

The Christian prophet, Gladden declared, was not primarily a
censor of society. To awaken "ever so little of the element of genuine good will" in men he considered a nobler function than to convince them merely of "righteousness and judgment." In his last book,
The Interpreter, he contrasted the method of John the Baptist,
which was "banning" or denouncing evil, with that of Jesus, which
was "blessing" or "cherishing the good." In his own life, he remi-
nisced, he had done some fighting against evil. But if he had it to
live over, he was sure that he would do a great deal less "banning"
and much more "blessing."[27] He was, after all, an optimist who
believed

> . . . that the humblest and most prosaic life, is filled, crowded, with
> the most beautiful, the most glorious opportunities; that even the seamy
> side of it is jeweled with splendid chances of manhood and womanhood;
> that every day and every hour the good angels of our destiny are whisper-
> ing, singing, shouting their invitations in our ears to take from the open
> hand of time treasures of immortal worth.[28]

The two major themes that Gladden attempted most frequently
to interpret to his age have been captured in the "Gladden Window"
of the First Congregational Church of Columbus. Two large central
figures represent Charity and Justice, the two themes. A lancet to
the left of Charity consists of three medallions illustrating corporate
acts of mercy: visiting the needy, ministering to the sick, and feeding the hungry. To the right of Justice are medallions illustrating the
co-operation of capital and labor, arbitration of industrial disputes,
and citizenship. Four medallions at the base of the window are

[26] "Washington Gladden," *Outlook*, XCIII (December 4, 1909), 766–67;
"Washington Gladden," *Outlook*, CVI (January 24, 1914), 160–61; "Washington
Gladden," *Outlook*, CXIX (July 17, 1918), 442; "Yet Speaketh," *Independent*,
XCVIII (May 17, 1919), 237.

[27] Gladden, Sermon, 1911, Gladden Papers; Gladden, *The Interpreter*, p. 244.

[28] Washington Gladden, *The School of Life* (Boston: Pilgrim Press, 1911),
p. 31.

personally commemorative of Gladden: the pulpit he used for many years in the First Church, his study in the tower, the hills back of Williams College, and a symbol of his great hymn, "O Master, Let Me Walk with Thee."[29]

[29]"The Gladden Window," *First Church News*, VI (February, 1936), 3.

Bibliography

PRIMARY SOURCES

Manuscript Collections

Century Collection. Manuscript Division, New York Public Library.

James (Gen.) M. Comly Papers. Ohio Historical Society, Columbus.

Richard T. Ely Papers. State Historical Society of Wisconsin, Madison.

George Junior Republic Records, 1859–1958. Collection of Regional History and University Archives, Cornell University, Ithaca, New York.

George Gladden Papers. Ohio Historical Society, Columbus.

Washington Gladden Papers. Ohio Historical Society, Columbus.

Miscellaneous Papers, Washington Gladden Folder. Manuscript Division, New York Public Library.

Washington Gladden Papers and Church Records. The First Congregational Church archives, Columbus, Ohio.

Samuel M. Jones Papers. Courtesy of Samuel M. Jones, III.

Henry D. Lloyd Papers. State Historical Society of Wisconsin, Madison.

Edward W. Ordway Papers. Manuscript Division, New York Public Library.

Jacob G. Schurman Papers. Collection of Regional History and University Archives, Cornell University, Ithaca, New York.

Graham Taylor Papers. Newberry Library, Chicago.

Record Group 3/e, Office of the President, William Oxley Thompson (1899–1926). Ohio State University Archives, Columbus.

Books and Pamphlets by Gladden
(In Chronological Order)

Songs of Williams, ed. S. W. GLADDEN. New York: Baker & Godwin, 1859.

Amusements: Their Uses and Their Abuses. North Adams, Mass.: James T. Robinson & Co., 1866.

Plain Thoughts on the Art of Living. Boston: Ticknor & Fields, 1868.

From the Hub to the Hudson: With Sketches of Nature, History and Industry in North-Western Massachusetts. Boston: New England News Company, 1869.

Salt without Savor. North Adams, Mass.: James T. Robinson & Co., 1870.

Being a Christian: What It Means and How to Begin. Boston: Congregational Publishing Society, 1876.

The Christian Way: Whither It Leads and How to Go On. New York: Dodd, Mead & Co., 1877.

Constitution and By-Laws of the Union Relief Association, also Report on Organization. (Gladden *et al.*) Springfield, Mass.: Atwood & Noyes, Printers, 1877.

Was Bronson Alcott's School a Type of God's Moral Government? A Review of Joseph Cook's Theory of the Atonement. Boston: Lockwood, Brooks & Co., 1877.

The Lord's Prayer: Seven Homilies. Boston: Houghton, Mifflin & Co., 1880.

The Christian League of Connecticut. New York: Century Co., 1883.

The Consecration of the People: A Thanksgiving Sermon. Columbus, Ohio: Press of Nitschke Bros., 1883.

Myrrh and Cassia: Two Discourses to Young Men and Women. Columbus, Ohio: A. H. Smythe, 1883.

Things New and Old in Discourses of Christian Truth and Life. Columbus, Ohio: A. H. Smythe, 1883.

A Life Worth Living: A Discourse in Memory of John Thomas Short. Columbus, Ohio: A. H. Smythe, 1884.

Applied Christianity: Moral Aspects of Social Questions, Boston: Houghton, Mifflin & Co., 1886.

Parish Problems: Hints and Helps for the People of the Churches, ed. WASHINGTON GLADDEN. New York: Century Co., 1887.

Burning Questions of the Life That Now Is and of That Which Is to Come. New York: Century Co., 1890.

Santa Claus on a Lark and Other Christmas Stories. New York: Century Co., 1890.

Who Wrote the Bible? A Book for the People. Boston: Houghton, Mifflin & Co., 1891.

The Cosmopolis City Club. New York: Century Co., 1893.

The Great Commoner of Ohio: Discourse in Memory of Rutherford Birchard Hayes. Columbus, Ohio: Press of Nitschke Bros., 1893.

Tools and the Man: Property and Industry under the Christian Law. Boston: Houghton, Mifflin & Co., 1893.

The Church and the Kingdom. New York: Fleming H. Revell Co., 1894.

Working People and Their Employers. New York: Funk & Wagnalls Co., 1894.

Moral Gains and Losses of the Temperance Reformation. Charlottesville, Va.: Progress Print, 1895.

॥ ⅲ ⅲⅲ॥ ⅲⅲⅲⅲⅲ ⅲⅲ ⅲ॥. ॥ⅲⅲⅲⅲⅲ Age. ⅈⅈⅈⅈⅈⅈ: Houghton, Mifflin & Co., 1895.

Seven Puzzling Bible Books: A Supplement to "Who Wrote the Bible?" Boston: Houghton, Mifflin & Co., 1897.

Social Facts and Forces. New York: G. P. Putnam's Sons, 1897.

The Christian Pastor and the Working Church. Edinburgh: T. & T. Clark, 1898.

England and America: Addresses Delivered in England during the Summer of 1898. London: James Clarke & Co., 1898.

Our Nation and Her Neighbors. Columbus, Ohio: Quinius & Ridenour, 1898.

How Much Is Left of the Old Doctrines? A Book for the People. Boston: Houghton, Mifflin & Co., 1899.

Victoria. Columbus, Ohio: Chaucer Press, 1901.

Rights and Duties. Ann Arbor, Mich.: Published by the Board of Regents of the University of Michigan, 1902.

Social Salvation. Boston: Houghton, Mifflin & Co., 1902.

The Negro's Southern Neighbors and His Northern Friends. New York: Congregational Rooms, [1903].

The State University: What It Stands For. Columbus, Ohio: n.p., 1903.

Witnesses of the Light. Boston: Houghton, Mifflin & Co., 1903.

Where Does the Sky Begin? Boston: Houghton, Mifflin & Co., 1904.

Christianity and Socialism. New York: Eaton & Mains, 1905.

The New Idolatry. New York: McClure, Phillips & Co., 1905.

The Church and Modern Life. Boston: Houghton, Mifflin & Co., 1908.

The Practice of Immortality. Boston: Pilgrim Press, 1908.

The Nation and the Kingdom. Boston: Published by the American Board of Commissioners for Foreign Missions, 1909.

Recollections. Boston: Houghton Mifflin Co., 1909.

Fifty Years in the Ministry. Columbus, Ohio: Lawrence Press Co., 1910.

The Labor Question. Boston: Pilgrim Press, 1911.

The School of Life. Boston: Pilgrim Press, 1911.

The Government of Cities: Address at the Conference of Ohio Cities, Columbus, January 25, 1912. Cleveland: Issued by the Ohio Municipal League, 1912.

Present Day Theology. Columbus, Ohio: McClelland & Co., 1913.

Federation for Service. Philadelphia: American Baptist Publication Society, Social Service Series, 1914.

The Futility of Force: Sermon Preached in First Congregational Church, August 23, 1914. Columbus, Ohio: Privately printed, 1914.

Live and Learn. New York: Macmillan Co., 1914.

War and Peace: Two Sermons Preached in First Congregational Church, August 9 and 16, 1914 (with CARL S. PATTON). Columbus, Ohio: Privately printed, 1914.

Is War a Moral Necessity? Sermon before First Congregational Church of Detroit, April 18, 1915. Detroit: Privately printed, 1915.

Another War with Mexico? Columbus, Ohio: Champlin Press, 1916.

Commencement Days: A Book for Graduates. New York: Macmillan Co., 1916.

The Forks of the Road. New York: Macmillan Co., 1916.

The Life Unfailing. Columbus, Ohio: McClelland & Co., 1916.

Religion after the War. Columbus, Ohio: Privately printed, 1917.

Calendar Verses. Columbus, Ohio: McClelland & Co., 1918.

The Interpreter. Boston: Pilgrim Press, 1918.

The Followers of the Star. Columbus, Ohio: Champlin Press, n.d.

The Shepherd's Story. Columbus, Ohio: Champlin Press, n.d.

Our First Love: Have We Lost It? Boston: Pilgrim Press, n.d.

Articles by Gladden
(In Chronological Order)

"The Relations of Soil Culture to Soul Culture," *Annual Report of Proceedings of the Berkshire Agricultural Society*, XVI (1869), 5–17.

"The Hoosac Tunnel," *Scribner's Monthly,* I (December, 1870), 143–59.

"Edward Eggleston," *Scribner's Monthly,* VI (September, 1873), 561–64.

"Tom Noble's Christmas," *Sunday Afternoon,* I (January, 1878), 71–77.

"Superfluous Praying," *Sunday Afternoon,* II (August, 1878), 137–42.

"How to Use the Bible," *Sunday Afternoon,* II (November, 1878), 451–56.

"To Bolt or Not to Bolt," *Scribner's Monthly,* XX (October, 1880), 906–13.

"Protestantism in Italy," *Scribner's Monthly,* XXI (March, 1881), 681–88.

"Hail and Farewell," *Century,* XXIII (December, 1881), 307.

"The Increase of Divorce," *Century,* XXIII (January, 1882), 411–20.

"The Christian League of Connecticut," *Century,* XXV (November, 1882), 50–60, (December, 1882), 181–91, (January, 1883), 339–49; XXVI (May, 1883) 65–79.

"Christ͏͏͏ ͏͏͏͏ ͏͏͏͏͏͏ ͏͏͏͏͏͏͏͏," *Andover Review,* I (January-June, 1884), 13–24.

"The Use and Abuse of Parties," *Century,* XXVIII (June, 1884), 270–75.

"Three Dangers," *Century,* XXVIII (Midsummer, 1884), 620–27.

"Christianity and Wealth," *Century,* XXVIII (October, 1884), 903–11.

"The Bible in the Sunday-school," *Century,* XXIX (November, 1884), 146–48. Attributed to Gladden.

"Christianity and Popular Amusements," *Century,* XXIX (January, 1885), 384–92.

"The Strength and Weakness of Socialism," *Century,* XXXI (March, 1886), 737–49.

"The Labor Question," *Century,* XXXII (June, 1886), 326–28.

"Is It Peace or War?", *Century,* XXXII (August, 1886), 565–76.

"The Aberrations of Democracy," *Andover Review,* XII (July-December, 1889), 385–99.

"The Embattled Farmers," *Forum,* X (November, 1890), 315–22.

"Migrations and Their Lessons," *Ohio Archaeological and Historical Publications,* III (1891), 179–85.

"Roswell Smith," *Century,* XLIV (June, 1892), 310–13.

"The Municipal Idea of the Church," *Review of Reviews,* VI (October, 1892), 305–7.

"The Problem of Poverty," *Century,* XLV (December, 1892), 245–56.

"The Cosmopolis City Club," *Century,* XLV (January-March, 1893), 395–406, 566–76, 780–92.

"The Perfect Law of Charity," in ISABEL C. BARROWS, ed., *Proceedings of the National Conference of Charities and Correction, 1893.* Boston: Press of George H. Ellis, 1893.

"Relief Work—Its Principles and Methods," *Review of Reviews,* IX (January, 1894), 38–40.

"The New Bible," *Arena,* IX (February, 1894), 294–304.

"The Myth of Land-Bill Allen," *Century,* XLVII (February, 1894), 609–15.

"The Anti-Catholic Crusade," *Century,* XLVII (March, 1894), 789–95.

"Religion and Wealth," *Bibliotheca Sacra,* LII (January, 1895), 153–67.

"Samuel Galloway," *Ohio Archaeological and Historical Publications,* IV (1895), 263–78.

"Rutherford Birchard Hayes," *Ohio Archaeological and Historical Publications,* IV (1895), 338–61.

"Francis Charles Sessions," *Ohio Archaeological and Historical Publications,* IV (1895), 292–310.

"The Relation of Corporations to Public Morals," *Bibliotheca Sacra,* LII (October, 1895), 607–28.

"Tainted Money," *Outlook,* LII (November 30, 1895), 886–87.

"The Bible as Literature," *Outlook,* LIII (June 27, 1896), 1207–8.

"A Campaign of Cross-Purposes," *Outlook,* LIV (August 1, 1896), 208–9.

"The Junior Republic at Freeville," *Outlook,* LIV (October 31, 1896), 778–82.

"Protestants at Providence," *Outlook,* LVI (August 14, 1897), 937–39.

"The Social Problems of the Future," *Outlook,* LVII (December 11, 1897), 904–11.

"The Social Problems of the Future," in LYMAN ABBOTT, AMORY H. BRADFORD, CHARLES A. BERRY, GEORGE A. GORDON, WASHINGTON GLADDEN, and WILLIAM J. TUCKER, *The New Puritanism.* New York: Fords, Howard, and Hulbert, 1898.

"The Issues of the War," *Outlook,* LIX (July 16, 1898), 673–75.

"Social Progress of the English People," *Outlook,* LX (December 24, 1898), 1002–4.

"Mayor Jones of Toledo," *Outlook,* LXII (May 6, 1899), 17–21.

"The Spread of Socialism," *Outlook,* LXII (May 13, 1899), 116–22.

"Moral Tendencies of Existing Industrial Conditions," *Outlook,* LXIII (December 9, 1899), 871–77.

"What to Do with the Workless Man," in ISABEL C. BARROWS, ed., *Proceedings of the National Conference of Charities and Correction, 1899.* Boston: George H. Ellis, 1900.

"Public Service Companies and City Government," *Outlook,* LXVI (October 27, 1900), 502–8.

"Prof. Edward Orton," *Ohio Archaeological and Historical Publications,* VIII (1900), 409–32.

"The Church and Social Problems," *International Quarterly,* XI (April, 1905), 135–47.

"The Church and the Reward of Iniquity," *Independent,* LVIII (April 20, 1905), 867–70.

"Rockefeller and the American Board," *Outlook,* LXXIX (April 22, 1905), 984–87.

"Mr. Rockefeller as a Truth Teller," *Independent,* LVIII (June 8, 1905), 1290–91.

"The Relations of Moral Teachers to Predatory Wealth," *Addresses before the New York State Conference of Religion,* Series IV (April, 1906).

"The Negro Crisis: Is the Separation of the Two Races to Become Necessary?", *American Magazine,* LXIII (January, 1907), 296–301.

"Henry Churchill King," *Outlook,* LXXXV (January 26, 1907), 223–28.

"Tearing Down Prosperity," *Independent,* LXII (April 18, 1907), 881–84.

"The Social Function of the Family," *Social Education Quarterly,* I (January, 1908), 3–8.

"The Municipal Church: The Crying Need of It, and a Program of Its Possible Work," *Century,* LXXX (August, 1910), 493–99.

"The Case against the Labor Union," *Outlook,* XCVII (February 25, 1911), 465–71.

"Reasons for the Unions," *Outlook,* XCVII (March 4, 1911), 497–502.

"Industry and Democracy," *Outlook,* XCVII (March 18, 1911), 589–95.

"Cross-Lights and Counter-Claims," *Outlook,* XCVII (April 15, 1911), 827–32.

"The Church and the Labor Question," *Outlook,* XCVIII (May 6, 1911), 35–40.

"An Experience with Newspapers," *Outlook,* XCIX (October 14, 1911), 387–88.

"John Bascom," *Nation,* XCIII (November 23, 1911), 491.

"Marriage as Friendship," *Good Housekeeping,* LIV (April, 1912), 488–91.

"Samples of Modern Evangelism," *Independent,* LXXII (May 23, 1912), 1101–3.

"Bethlehem," *Woman's Home Companion,* XXXIX (December, 1912), 8.

"Easter Festival," *Woman's Home Companion*, XL (March, 1913), 8.

"Back to the Home," *Good Housekeeping*, LVI (May, 1913), 675–78.

"A Dangerous Crusade," *Biblical World*, XLIV (July, 1914), 3–14.

"The Anti-Papal Panic," *Harper's Weekly*, LIX (July 18, 1914), 55–56.

"Anti-Catholic Agitation," *Harper's Weekly*, LIX (September 12, 1914), 255–56.

"Laissez Faire in Religion," *Atlantic Monthly*, CXIV (October, 1914), 497–503.

"Tainted Newspapers, Good and Bad," *University of Kansas News-Bulletin*, XV (November 30, 1914).

"One Still Strong Man," *Outlook*, CIX (January 13, 1915), 95–99.

"Religion and the Schools," *Atlantic Monthly*, CXV (January, 1915), 57–68.

"Dr. Ward's Credo: A Review of 'What I Believe and Why?' ", *Independent*, LXXXIV (October 18, 1915), 105–6.

"S'posin'," *Independent*, LXXXIV (October 25, 1915), 129.

"A Pacifist's Apology," *New Republic*, V (November 20, 1915), 75–76.

"The Shepherd's Story," in Phebe A. Curtiss, comp., *Christmas Stories and Legends*. Indianapolis: Meigs Publishing Co., 1916, revised and enlarged, 1952.

"Empty Pews in the Country Church—Why?", *Everybody's Magazine*, XXXIV (May, 1916), 613–17.

"A Plea for Pacifism," *Nation*, CIII (August 3, 1916), Supplement 2.

"The Unescapable Law," *Independent*, LXXXVIII (November 13, 1916), 279.

"Back to Pentecost," *Biblical World*, L (October, 1917), 203–11.

"Do We Believe in God?", *Independent*, VC (July 20, 1918), 87.

"The Future of the Christian Church," *Review of Reviews*, LVIII (August, 1919), 202.

Contemporary Religious Writings

Abbott, Lyman. *Christianity and Social Problems*. Boston: Houghton, Mifflin & Co., 1896.

Bascom, John. *A Sermon on Temperance*. Boston: T. R. Marvin & Son, 1863.

Bushnell, Horace. *God in Christ: Three Discourses Delivered at New Haven, Cambridge, and Andover, with a Preliminary Dissertation on Language*. Hartford: Brown & Parsons, 1849.

_____. *Sermons on Living Subjects*. New York: Charles Scribner's Sons, 1890 ed.

FISKE, JOHN. *The Idea of God as Affected by Modern Knowledge*. Boston: Houghton, Mifflin & Co., 1885.

HERRON, GEORGE D. *Between Caesar and Jesus*. New York: Thomas Y. Crowell & Co., 1899.

_____. *The Call of the Cross*. New York: Fleming H. Revell Co., 1892.

_____. *The Christian Society*. New York: Fleming H. Revell Co., 1894.

KOEHNE, JOHN B. *Future Punishment: An Examination of Dr. Washington Gladden's "Present Day Theology" Theory of Hell*. Chicago: The Platform, 1914.

MATHEWS, SHAILER. *The Social Gospel*. Philadelphia: Griffith & Rowland Press, 1910.

STRONG, JOSIAH. *The New Era*. New York: Baker & Taylor Co., 1893.

_____. *Our Country*. New York: Baker & Taylor Co., 1885.

PEABODY, FRANCIS G. *Jesus Christ and the Social Question: An Examination of the Teaching of Jesus in Its Relation to Some of the Problems of Modern Social Life*. New York: Macmillan Co., 1915.

RAUSCHENBUSCH, WALTER. *Christianity and the Social Crisis*. Boston: Pilgrim Press, 1907.

_____. *Christianizing the Social Order*. New York: Macmillan Co., 1912.

_____. *A Theology for the Social Gospel*. New York: Macmillan Co., 1918.

Printed Diaries, Reminiscences, and Collections of Letters

ADDAMS, JANE. *Twenty Years at Hull-House*. New York: Macmillan Co., 1910.

ATKINS, GAIUS GLENN. *Religion in Our Times*. New York: Round Table Press, 1932.

AUSTEN, JESSICA TYLER (ed.). *Moses Coit Tyler, 1835–1900: Selections from His Letters and Diaries*. New York: Doubleday, Page & Co., 1911.

BASCOM, JOHN. *Things Learned by Living*. New York: G. P. Putnam's Sons, 1913.

BENJAMIN, S. G. W. *The Life and Adventures of a Free Lance*. Burlington, Vt.: Free Press Co., 1914.

CHENEY, MARY BUSHNELL (ed.). *Life and Letters of Horace Bushnell*. New York: Harper & Bros., 1880.

ELY, RICHARD T. *Ground under Our Feet: An Autobiography*. New York: Macmillan Co., 1938.

MATHEWS, SHAILER. *New Faith for Old: An Autobiography*. New York: Macmillan Co., 1936.

SCHLESINGER, ARTHUR M. *In Retrospect: The History of a Historian*. New York: Harcourt, Brace & World, Inc., 1963.

STEINER, EDWARD A. *From Alien to Citizen: The Story of My Life in America*. New York: Fleming H. Revell Co., 1914.

TARBELL, IDA M. *All in the Day's Work: An Autobiography*. New York: Macmillan Co., 1939.

WHITE, WILLIAM ALLEN. *The Autobiography of William Allen White*. New York: Macmillan Co., 1946.

WILLIAMS, CHARLES R. (ed.). *Diary and Letters of Rutherford Birchard Hayes: Nineteenth President of the United States*. 5 vols. Columbus: Ohio State Archaeological and Historical Society, 1922–26.

Newspapers

Columbus Dispatch. Columbus, Ohio, April 2, 1895.

Dayton Daily News. Dayton, Ohio, March 4, 1910.

New York Times. New York, August 16, 1900, October 22, 1916, October 25, 1964.

Ohio State Journal. Columbus, Ohio, November, 1882–July, 1918.

Springfield Republican. Springfield, Mass., January, 1875–May, 1882.

Periodicals

Congregationalist. Boston, Volumes LXVI, LXVIII–CIII, June, 1881–December, 1881; January, 1883–September, 1891; November, 1892–April, 1908; January, 1909–April, 1917; July 19, August 23, 30, November 22, 1917–December, 1918.

Independent. New York, Volumes XXIII–XXVII, 1871–January, 1875.

Religious Telescope. Dayton, Ohio, Volumes LXVIII–LXXIV, 1902–8.

Sunday Afternoon: A Magazine for the Household, renamed *Good Company* (1879). Springfield, Mass., Volumes I–VIII, 1878–81.

United Brethren Review. Dayton, Ohio, Volumes XIII–XIX, 1902–8.

Williams Quarterly. Williamstown, Mass., Volumes IV–VI, 1856–59.

Articles

ALMY, FREDERIC. "The Conquest of Poverty," in *Proceedings of the National Conference of Social Work, 1912, Chicago: Rogers & Hall Co. Printers 1912*

MURPHY, STARR J. "A Reply to Dr. Gladden," *Independent,* LVIII (May 18, 1905), 1097–99.

Reports, Yearbooks, and Proceedings

Addresses and Papers Presented at the Diamond Jubilee, 1827–1902, of First Congregational Church, North Adams. North Adams, Mass.: Advance Press, 1902.

BARROWS, ISABEL C. (ed.). *Proceedings of the National Conference of Charities and Correction, 1899.* Boston: George H. Ellis, 1900.

BRINKERHOFF, GENERAL R., Chairman. "Report of Committee on Prisons," Board of State Charities Circular No. 4. Norwalk, Ohio: Laning Printing Co., State Printers, 1893.

Catalogue of the Officers and Students of Williams College for the Academic Year, 1853–1854. Williamstown, Mass.: Published by the Students, 1853.

Charities of Columbus: Report of Committee on Charities and Corrections of the Chamber of Commerce. Columbus, Ohio: Privately printed, 1910.

CHERRINGTON, ERNEST H. (comp.). *The Anti-Saloon League Year Book.* Columbus, Ohio: Anti-Saloon League of America, 1908–9; Westerville, Ohio: 1910–18.

Clubana, A Collection of Essays Read before the Literary and Social Club of the First Congregational Church, Columbus. Columbus, Ohio: A. H. Smythe, 1885.

Confession of Faith, Form of Covenant, and Catalogue of Members, of the Independent Congregational Church of Owego. Owego, N. Y.: Printed at the Owego *Times* Office, 1857.

Directory of the First Congregational Church, Columbus, Ohio. Columbus, Ohio: Nitschke Press, 1895, 1904.

Dublin Community Church: Fiftieth Anniversary, March 4, 1913–March 3, 1963. n.p., 1963.

The Golden Jubilee of the First Congregational Church, Columbus, Ohio, 1852–1902. Columbus: Privately printed, 1902.

The International Congregational Council, London, 1891: Authorised Record of Proceedings. London: James Clarke & Co., 1891.

The National Council of the Congregational Churches of the United States: Addresses, Discussions, Minutes, Statements of Benevolent Societies, Constitution, etc. of the Twelfth Triennial Session, Des Moines, Iowa, October 13–30, 1904. Boston: Published by Order of the National Council, 1904.

The National Council of the Congregational Churches of the United States: Addresses, Reports, Statements of Benevolent Societies, Constitution, Minutes, Roll of Delegates, etc. of the Thirteenth Triennial Session, Cleveland, Ohio, October 8–17, 1907. Boston: Published by Order of the National Council, 1907.

Official Report of the Proceedings and Debates of the Twenty-fourth General Conference of the United Brethren in Christ, Held in Topeka, Kansas, May 11–22, 1905. Dayton, Ohio: United Brethren Publishing House, 1905.

Official Report of the Proceedings and Debates of the Twenty-fifth General Conference of the United Brethren in Christ, Held in Canton, Ohio, May 13–24, 1909. Dayton, Ohio: United Brethren Publishing House, Otterbein Press, 1909.

The Ohio Bulletin of Charities and Correction. Board of State Charities Circular No. 7. Columbus: Board of State Charities, 1896.

Proceedings of the Second International Congregational Council, Held in Tremont Temple, Boston, Massachusetts, September 20–29, 1899. Boston: Press of Samuel Usher, 1900.

Sanford, Elias B. (ed.). *Church Federation: Inter-Church Conference on Federation, New York, November 15–21, 1905.* New York: Fleming H. Revell Co., 1906.

_____. *Federal Council of the Churches of Christ in America: Report of the First Meeting of the Federal Council, Philadelphia, 1908.* New York: Revell Press, 1909.

Interviews and Correspondence

Interview with Carl H. Bogart, May 13, 1963.

Interview with Mrs. William Lloyd Evans, April 24, 1963.

Frederic W. Heimberger to author, December 28, 1964.

Mrs. Clyde B. Hightshoe to author, October 4, 1964.

Interview with Mrs. Stanton C. Kelton, May 21, 1966.

Interview with Walter Rumsey Marvin, Martha Kinney Cooper Ohioana Library (State Office Building, Columbus, Ohio), May 15, 1963.

Interview with Kenneth L. Sater, May 21, 1963.

Bishop William Scarlett to author, November 26, 1964.

ᴵⁿᵗᵉʳᵛⁱᵉʷ ᵂⁱˡˡⁱᵃᵐ ᴺ. ᴼˡⁱᵛᵉʳ ᵐᵘⁿᵈᵉⁿ ʲⁱⁱⁱⁱⁱ ⁱ ⁱ, ⁱⁱⁱⁱⁱⁱ

Interview with Mrs. Frederick Shedd, May 14, 1963.

Interview with Dr. and Mrs. Robert Sigafoos, May 6, 1963.

Interviews with Mrs. William Starin, April 25, May 8, 1963.

Richard M. Steiner to author, May 31, 1964.

Interview with Miss Celia Vandegriff, April 19, 1963.

David A. Warren, Cornell University, to author, September 29, 1966.

Public Documents

Washington Gladden Estate, #35501, Franklin County (Ohio) Probate Court, Document 23.

SECONDARY WORKS

Biographies, Obituaries, Book Reviews, and Studies of Gladden (In Chronological Order)

Review of *Who Wrote the Bible?* in *Nation*, LIII (September 17, 1891), 222.

"Dr. Gladden's Election," *Outlook*, LXIV (April 14, 1900), 855–56.

"Washington Gladden," *Outlook*, LXXXII (January 27, 1906), 154–55, 163.

"An Apostle of Applied Christianity," *McClure's Magazine*, XXVI (February, 1906), 448–50.

MORRIS, GEORGE P. "A Preacher and Patriot," *Century*, LXXI (March, 1906), 815–16.

"Washington Gladden," *Outlook*, XCIII (December 4, 1909), 766–67.

RHOADES, LEWIS A. "A Venerable American Preacher," *Dial*, XLVIII (January 16, 1910), 46–48.

"Dr. Washington Gladden's Plea for a Municipal Church," *Current Literature*, XLIX (October, 1910), 412–14.

MACFARLANE, PETER CLARK. "Washington Gladden: The First Citizen of Columbus," *Collier's Weekly*, XLIX (June 29, 1912), 20–21.

"Washington Gladden," *Outlook*, CVI (January 24, 1914), 160–61.

"The Peace-Prize Essay," *Literary Digest*, LII (June 24, 1916), 1848.

TAYLOR, GRAHAM. "Washington Gladden," *Survey*, XL (July 13, 1918), 422.

"Washington Gladden," *Outlook*, CXIX (July 17, 1918), 422.

"Yet Speaketh," *Independent*, XCVIII (May 17, 1919), 237.

"Washington Gladden," *The Congregational Year-Book: Statistics for 1918*. Boston: Pilgrim Press, 1919.

JONES, WILLIAM E. "Dr. Gladden and First Church," *First Church News*, II (February, 1929), 5–6.

HENDERSON, W. E. "The Inescapable Christ," *First Church News*, VI (February, 1936), 11.

MCPHERSON, WILLIAM. "An Appreciation of Dr. Washington Gladden," *First Church News*, VI (February, 1936), 7.

"Washington Gladden: One Hundred Years," *First Church News*, VI (February, 1936), 13–14.

SIEBERT, WILBUR A. "A Reminiscence," *First Church News*, VI (February, 1936), 10.

MILLER, MRS. O. A. "Mrs. Washington Gladden," *First Church News*, VI (February, 1936), 5.

"The Gladden Window," *First Church News*, VI (February, 1936), 3.

ATKINS, GAIUS GLENN. "Washington Gladden—and After," *Religion in Life*, V (Autumn, 1936), 593–604.

JAGSCH, ALMA. "Washington Gladden: A Prophet of Social Justice." Unpublished M.A. thesis, Ohio State University, 1938.

RUDOLPH, C. FREDERICK, JR. "Washington Gladden: Essays on Modern Man." Unpublished B.A. honors thesis, Williams College, 1942.

HILLMAN, JAMES DEVEE. "The Contribution of Washington Gladden to the Social Movement in American Protestantism." Unpublished Th.D. thesis, Southern Baptist Theological Seminary, 1951.

KELLER, CHARLES R. "Dr. Washington Gladden," *Our Church Chronicle* (North Adams, Mass.: Published annually in the interest of the North Adams Congregational Church, April, 1953), pp. 5–9.

SHOVER, JOHN L. "Washington Gladden and the Labor Question," *Ohio Historical Quarterly*, LXVIII (October, 1959), 335–52.

Dᴀ᙮᙮ⱡ᙮᙮ᴀ᙮ ᙮᙮᙮᙮ᴀ᙮᙮ ᙮᙮᙮ Wᴏ᙮᙮᙮᙮᙮᙮᙮ ᙮᙮᙮᙮᙮᙮᙮᙮᙮ ᙮᙮᙮᙮᙮᙮᙮ ᙮᙮᙮ ᙮᙮ ᙮᙮ " ᙮᙮᙮᙮᙮᙮ lished M.A. thesis, Ohio State University, 1960.

FRY, CHARLES GEORGE. "Washington Gladden As Preacher." Unpublished M.A. thesis, Ohio State University, 1961.

LATTIMER, DAVID W. "Washington Gladden," in WILLIAM COYLE (ed.), *Ohio Authors and Their Books: Biographical Data and Selective Bibliographies for Ohio Authors, Native and Resident, 1796–1950.* New York: World Publishing Co., 1962.

Other Biographies

ALBRIGHT, RAYMOND W. *Focus on Infinity: A Life of Phillips Brooks.* New York: Macmillan Co., 1961.

BACON, BENJAMIN WISNER. *Theodore Thornton Munger.* New Haven: Yale University Press, 1913.

BERMAN, MILTON. *John Fiske: The Evolution of a Popularizer.* Cambridge: Harvard University Press, 1961.

BRASTOW, LEWIS O. *Representative Modern Preachers.* New York: Macmillan Co., 1904.

BROWN, CHARLES REYNOLDS. *They Were Giants.* New York: Macmillan Co., 1934.

BROWN, IRA V. *Lyman Abbott: Christian Evolutionist.* Cambridge: Harvard University Press, 1953.

CROSS, BARBARA M. *Horace Bushnell: Minister to a Changing America.* Chicago: University of Chicago Press, 1958.

FRANKENBERG, THEODORE T. *Spectacular Career of Rev. Billy Sunday, Famous Baseball Evangelist.* Columbus, Ohio: McClelland & Co., 1913.

HIBBEN, PAXTON. *Henry Ward Beecher: An American Portrait.* New York: George H. Doran Co., 1927.

JONES, HOWARD MUMFORD. *The Life of Moses Coit Tyler: Based upon an Unpublished Dissertation from Original Sources by Thomas Edgar Casady.* Ann Arbor: University of Michigan Press, 1933.

McLOUGHLIN, WILLIAM G., JR. *Billy Sunday Was His Real Name.* Chicago: University of Chicago Press, 1955.

MERRIAM, GEORGE S. *The Life and Times of Samuel Bowles.* 2 vols. New York: Century Co., 1885.

MUNGER, THEODORE T. *Horace Bushnell: Preacher and Theologian.* Boston: Houghton Mifflin Co., 1899.

NEVINS, ALLAN. *Study in Power: John D. Rockefeller, Industrialist and Philanthropist.* 2 vols. New York: Charles Scribner's Sons, 1953.

SMITH, THEODORE CLARKE. *The Life and Letters of James Abram Garfield.* 2 vols. New Haven: Yale University Press, 1925.

WADE, LOUISE C. *Graham Taylor: Pioneer for Social Justice, 1851–1938.* Chicago: University of Chicago Press, 1964.

Articles

ARTER, BILL. "Tainted Money and PR," *Columbus Dispatch*, March 7, 1965.

BAYLEN, JOSEPH O. "A Victorian's 'Crusade' in Chicago, 1893–1894," *Journal of American History*, LI (December, 1964), 418–21.

HAWKINS, HUGH. "Charles W. Eliot, University Reform, and Religious Faith in America, 1869–1909," *Journal of American History*, LI (September, 1964), 191–213.

MANN, ARTHUR. "British Social Thought and American Reformers of the Progressive Era," *Mississippi Valley Historical Review*, XLII (March, 1956), 672–92.

MATHEWS, SHAILER. "The Development of Social Christianity in America during the Past Twenty-five Years," *Journal of Religion*, VII (July, 1927), 376–86.

PETERSON, WALTER F. "American Protestantism and the Higher Criticism, 1870–1910," *Transactions of the Wisconsin Academy of Sciences, Arts, and Letters*, L (February 26, 1962), 321–29.

ROBERTS, ROBERT R. "The Social Gospel and the Trust-Busters," *Church History,* XXV (1956), 239–57.

Rudolph, Frederick, "Chinamen in Yankeedom: Anti-Unionism in Massachusetts in 1870," *American Historical Review,* LIII (October, 1947), 1–29.

General Reference Works

Dictionary of Wisconsin Biography. Madison: State Historical Society of Wisconsin, 1960.

JOHNSON, ALLEN, DUMAS MALONE, and HARRIS E. STARR (eds.). *Dictionary of American Biography.* 21 vols. and Index. New York: Charles Scribner's Sons, 1928–44.

LEONARD, JOHN W. (ed.). *Woman's Who's Who of America, 1914–1915.* New York: American Commonwealth Co., 1914.

LOEW, JOHN ADAMS (ed.). *Williamsiana: A Bibliography of Pamphlets and Books Relating to the History of Williams College, 1793–1911.* Williamstown, Mass.: Published by the Trustees, 1911.

Who Was Who in America, I, 1897–1942: A Companion Volume to "Who's Who in America." Chicago: A. N. Marquis Co., 1942.

Monographs and General Histories

ABELL, AARON I. *The Urban Impact on American Protestantism, 1865–1900.* Cambridge: Harvard University Press, 1943.

ABRAMS, RAY H. *Preachers Present Arms.* New York: Round Table Press, 1933.

ATKINS, GAIUS GLENN, and FREDERICK L. FAGLEY. *History of American Congregationalism.* Boston: Pilgrim Press, 1942.

BARROWS, JOHN HENRY. *The World's Parliament of Religions.* 2 vols. Chicago: Parliament Publishing Co., 1893.

BARTLETT, RUHL J. *The League to Enforce Peace.* Chapel Hill: University of North Carolina Press, 1944.

BREMNER, ROBERT H. *American Philanthropy.* Chicago: University of Chicago Press, 1960.

————. *From the Depths: The Discovery of Poverty in the United States.* New York: New York University Press, 1956.

BUCKE, EMORY S. (ed.). *The History of American Methodism.* 3 vols. New York and Nashville: Abingdon Press, 1964.

BUCKHAM, JOHN WRIGHT. *Progressive Religious Thought in America: A Survey of the Enlarging Pilgrim Faith.* Boston: Houghton Mifflin Co., 1919.

CARTER, PAUL A. *The Decline and Revival of the Social Gospel: Social and Political Liberalism in American Protestant Churches, 1920–1940.* Ithaca, N . Y.: Cornell University Press, 1956.

CAUTHEN, KENNETH. *The Impact of American Religious Liberalism.* New York: Harper & Row, Publishers, 1962.

COLVIN, D. LEIGH. *Prohibition in the United States: A History of the Prohibition Party and of the Prohibition Movement.* New York: George H. Doran Co., 1926.

COPE, ALEXIS. *History of the Ohio State University, 1870–1910. (History of the Ohio State University,* ed. THOMAS C. MENDENHALL *et al.,* Vol. I.) Columbus: Ohio State University Press, 1920.

COPELAND, ALFRED MINOT (ed.). *A History of Hampden County.* 3 vols. Century Memorial Publishing Co., 1902.

CROSS, WHITNEY R. *The Burned-Over District: The Social and Intellectual History of Enthusiastic Religion in Western New York, 1825–1850.* Ithaca, N. Y.: Cornell University Press, 1950.

DOHN, NORMAN H. "The History of the Anti-Saloon League." Unpublished Ph.D. dissertation, Ohio State University, 1959.

DOMBROWSKI, JAMES. *The Early Days of Christian Socialism in America.* New York: Columbia University Press, 1936.

DOUGLASS, H. PAUL. *The Springfield Church Survey: A Study of Organized Religion with Its Social Background.* New York: George H. Doran Co., 1926.

DULLES, FOSTER RHEA. *Labor in America: A History.* 3d ed.; New York: Thomas Y. Crowell Co., 1966.

FURNISS, NORMAN F. *The Fundamentalist Controversy, 1918–1931.* New Haven: Yale University Press, 1954.

GOSSETT, THOMAS F. *Race: The History of an Idea in America.* Dallas: Southern Methodist University Press, 1963.

HAYS, SAMUEL P. *The Response to Industrialism, 1885–1914.* Chicago: University of Chicago Press, 1957.

HIGHAM, JOHN. *Strangers in the Land: Patterns of American Nativism, 1860–1925.* New Brunswick, N. J.: Rutgers University Press, 1955.

HOFSTADTER, RICHARD. *The Age of Reform: From Bryan to F. D. R.* New York: Alfred A. Knopf, Inc., 1955.

HOLBROOK, STEWART H. *The Golden Age of Quackery.* New York: Collier Books, 1962.

HOPKINS, CHARLES H. *The Rise of the Social Gospel in American Protestantism, 1865–1915.* New Haven: Yale University Press, 1940.

HORDERN, WILLIAM. *A Layman's Guide to Protestant Theology.* New York: Macmillan Co., 1955.

HUDSON, WINTHROP S. *Religion in America.* New York: Charles Scribner's Sons, 1965.

HUGHLEY, J. NEAL. *Trends in Protestant Social Idealism.* Morningside Heights, N. Y.: King's Crown Press, 1948.

JOHNSON, ROSS SEYMOUR. "The A.P.A. in Ohio." Unpublished M.A. thesis, Ohio State University, 1948.

JONES, EDGAR DEWITT. *The Royalty of the Pulpit: A Survey and Appreciation of the Lyman Beecher Lectures on Preaching Founded at Yale Divinity School, 1871, and Given Annually (with Four Exceptions) since 1872.* New York: Harper & Bros., Publishers, 1951.

KINGMAN, LEROY W. (ed.). *Owego Sketches by Owego Authors.* Owego, N. Y.: Gazette Press, 1904.

KINZER, DONALD L. *An Episode in Anti-Catholicism: The American Protective Association.* Seattle: University of Washington Press, 1964.

KROUT, JOHN A. *The Origins of Prohibition.* New York: Alfred A. Knopf, 1925.

LEE, ALFRED E. *History of the City of Columbus: Capital of Ohio.* 2 vols. New York: Munsell & Co., 1892.

LINDLEY, HARLOW. *Ohio in the Twentieth Century. (The History of the State of Ohio,* ed. CARL WITTKE, Vol. VI) Columbus: Ohio State Archaeological and Historical Society, 1944.

LINK, ARTHUR S. *Woodrow Wilson and the Progressive Era, 1910–1917.* New York: Harper & Row, Publishers, 1954.

LOETSCHER, LEFFERTS A. *The Broadening Church: A Study of Theological Issues in the Presbyterian Church since 1869.* Philadelphia: University of Pennsylvania Press, 1957.

LOZIER, JOHN W. "The Hocking Valley Coal Miners' Strike, 1884–1885." Unpublished M.A. thesis, Ohio State University, 1963.

MACFARLAND, CHARLES S. *Christian Unity in the Making: The First Twenty-five Years of the Federal Council of the Churches of Christ in America, 1905–1930.* New York: Federal Council of the Churches of Christ in America, 1948.

————. *Christian Unity in Practice and Prophecy.* New York: Macmillan Co., 1933.

————. *Pioneers for Peace through Religion: Based on the Records of the Church Peace Union (Founded by Andrew Carnegie), 1914–1945.* New York: Fleming H. Revell Co., 1946.

MARK, MARY LOUISE, and CARL H. BOGART. *Leisure in the Lives of Our Neighbors: Gladden Community House, Columbus, Ohio.* Columbus: Ohio State University School of Social Administration, 1941.

MATHEWS, LOIS KIMBALL. *The Expansion of New England: The Spread of New England Settlement and Institutions to the Mississippi River, 1620–1865.* Boston: Houghton Mifflin Co., 1909.

MAY, HENRY F. *Protestant Churches and Industrial America.* New York: Harper & Bros., Publishers, 1949.

McGIFFERT, ARTHUR CUSHMAN. *The Rise of Modern Religious Ideas.* New York: Macmillan Co., 1915.

McLOUGHLIN, WILLIAM G., JR. *Modern Revivalism: Charles Grandison Finney to Billy Graham.* New York: Ronald Press Co., 1959.

MOTT, FRANK LUTHER. *A History of American Magazines, 1741–1905.* 4 vols. Cambridge: Harvard University Press, 1938–57.

MOWRY, GEORGE E. *Theodore Roosevelt and the Progressive Movement.* New York: Hill & Wang, 1946.

PEATTIE, RODERICK (ed.). *Columbus, Ohio: An Analysis of a City's Development.* Columbus: Published by the Industrial Bureau of Columbus, Chamber of Commerce, 1930.

PETERSON, JOHN ALVAH. "The Origins and Development of a Social Settlement: A History of the Godman Guild Association, 1898–1958." Unpublished M.A. thesis, Ohio State University, 1959.

PITZER, DONALD E. "The Ohio Campaigns of Billy Sunday with Special Emphasis upon the 1913 Columbus Revival." Unpublished M.A. thesis, Ohio State University, 1962.

REIMERS, DAVID M. *White Protestantism and the Negro.* New York: Oxford University Press, 1965.

RUDOLPH, FREDERICK. *Mark Hopkins and the Log: Williams College, 1836–1872.* New Haven: Yale University Press, 1956.

SANFORD, ELIAS B. *Origin and History of the Federal Council of the Churches of Christ in America.* Hartford: S. S. Scranton Co., 1916.

SCHALLER, LYLE E. *Planning for Protestantism in Urban America.* New York and Nashville: Abingdon Press, 1965.

SHOVER, JOHN L. "The Attitude of American Intellectuals toward the Labor Movement, 1890–1900." Unpublished Ph.D. dissertation, Ohio State University, 1957.

SMITH, J. E. A. (ed.). *History of Berkshire County, Massachusetts, with Biographical Sketches of Its Prominent Men.* 2 vols. New York: J. B. Beer & Co., 1885.

SMITH, H. SHELTON. *Changing Conceptions of Original Sin: A Study in American Theology since 1750.* New York: Charles Scribner's Sons, 1955.

SPEAR, W. F. *History of North Adams, Massachusetts, 1749–1885.* North Adams, Mass.: Hoosac Valley News Printing House, 1886.

SPRING, LEVERETT W. *A History of Williams College.* Boston: Houghton Mifflin Co., 1917.

STAUFFER, HENRY (ed.). *The Great Awakening in Columbus, Ohio, under the Labors of Rev. B. Fay Mills and His Associates.* Columbus: W. L. Lemon, 1896.

STEIN, KENNETH JAMES. "Church Unity Movements in the Church of the United Brethren in Christ until 1910." Unpublished Th.D. dissertation, Union Theological Seminary, 1965.

STUDER, JACOB H. *Columbus, Ohio: Its History, Resources, and Progress.* Columbus: Privately printed, 1873.

SWEET, WILLIAM WARREN. *The Story of Religion in America.* 2d ed.; New York: Harper & Bros., Publishers, 1950.

WALKER, WILLISTON. *A History of the Congregational Churches in the United States.* New York: Christian Literature Co., 1894.

WARNER, AMOS G. *American Charities.* New York: Thomas Y. Crowell Co., Publishers, 1894.

WARNER, HOYT LANDON. *Progressivism in Ohio, 1897–1917.* Columbus, Ohio: Ohio State University Press, 1964.

WEISBERGER, BERNARD A. *They Gathered at the River: The Story of the Great Revivalists and Their Impact upon Religion in America.* Boston: Little, Brown & Co., 1958.

WEISENBURGER, FRANCIS P. *Ordeal of Faith: The Crisis of Church-going America, 1865–1900.* New York: Philosophical Library, 1959.

WISH, HARVEY. *Society and Thought in Modern America: A Social and Intellectual History of the American People from 1865.* 2d ed.; New York: David McKay Co., 1962.

WOODS, ROBERT A., and ALBERT J. KENNEDY (eds.). *Handbook of Settlements.* New York: Charities Publication Committee, 1911.

Index